BEING AND TIME

BEING AND TIME

MARTIN HEIDEGGER

Translated by
John Macquarrie & Edward Robinson

HARPER & ROW, PUBLISHERS
New York, Hagerstown, San Francisco, London

Dedicated to

EDMUND HUSSERL

in friendship and admiration

Todtnauberg in Baden, Black Forest
8 April 1926

CONTENTS

DIVISION TWO: DASEIN AND TEMPORALITY

TRANSLATORS' PREFACE

MORE than thirty years have passed since *Being and Time* first appeared, and it has now become perhaps the most celebrated philosophical work which Germany has produced in this century. It is a very difficult book, even for the German reader, and highly resistant to translation, so much so that it has often been called 'untranslatable'. We feel that this is an exaggeration.

Anyone who has struggled with a philosophical work in translation has constantly found himself asking how the author himself would have expressed the ideas which the translator has ascribed to him. In this respect the 'ideal' translation would perhaps be one so constructed that a reader with reasonable linguistic competence and a key to the translator's conventions should be able to retranslate the new version into the very words of the original. Everybody knows that this is altogether too much to demand; but the faithful translator must at least keep this ahead of him as a desirable though impracticable goal. The simplest compromise with the demands of his own language is to present the translation and the original text on opposite pages; he is then quite free to choose the most felicitous expressions he can think of, trusting that the reader who is shrewd enough to wonder what is really happening can look across and find out. Such a procedure would add enormously to the expense of a book as long as *Being and Time*, and is impracticable for other reasons. But on any page of Heidegger there is a great deal happening, and we have felt that we owe it to the reader to let him know what is going on. For the benefit of the man who already has a copy of the German text, we have indicated in our margins the pagination of the later German editions, which differs only slightly from that of the earlier ones. All citations marked with 'H' refer to this pagination. But for the reader who does not have the German text handy, we have had to use other devices.

As long as an author is using words in their ordinary ways, the translator should not have much trouble in showing what he is trying to say. But Heidegger is constantly using words in ways which are by no means ordinary, and a great part of his merit lies in the freshness and penetration which his very innovations reflect. He tends to discard much of the traditional philosophical terminology, substituting an elaborate vocabulary of his own. He occasionally coins new expressions from older roots, and he takes full advantage of the ease with which the German language lends itself to the formation of new compounds. He also uses familiar

expressions in new ways. Adverbs, prepositions, pronouns, conjunctions
are made to do service as nouns; words which have undergone a long
history of semantical change are used afresh in their older senses; specialized modern idioms are generalized far beyond the limits within which
they would ordinarily be applicable. Puns are by no means uncommon
and frequently a key-word may be used in several senses, successively or
even simultaneously. He is especially fond of ringing the changes on
words with a common stem or a common prefix. He tends on the whole
to avoid personal constructions, and often uses abstract nouns ('Dasein',
'Zeitlichkeit', 'Sorge', 'In-der-Welt-sein', and so forth) as subjects of
sentences where a personal subject would ordinarily be found. Like
Aristotle or Wittgenstein, he likes to talk about his words, and seldom
makes an innovation without explaining it; but sometimes he will have
used a word in a special sense many times before he gets round to the
explanation; and he may often use it in the ordinary senses as well. In
such cases the reader is surely entitled to know what word Heidegger is
actually talking about, as well as what he says about it; and he is also
entitled to know when and how he actually uses it.

We have tried in the main to keep our vocabulary under control,
providing a German-English glossary for the more important expressions, and a rather full analytical index which will also serve as an English-
German glossary. We have tried to use as few English terms as possible
to represent the more important German ones, and we have tried not to
to use these for other purposes than those we have specifically indicated.
Sometimes we have had to coin new terms to correspond to Heidegger's.
In a number of cases there are two German terms at the author's disposal
which he has chosen to differentiate, even though they may be synonyms
in ordinary German usage; if we have found only one suitable English
term to correspond to them, we have sometimes adopted the device of
capitalizing it when it represents the German word to which it is etymologically closer: thus 'auslegen' becomes 'interpret', but 'interpretieren'
becomes 'Interpret'; 'gliedern' becomes 'articulate', but 'artikulieren'
becomes 'Articulate'; 'Ding' becomes 'Thing', but 'thing' represents
'Sache' and a number of other expressions. In other cases we have coined
a new term. Thus while 'tatsächlich' becomes 'factual', we have introduced 'factical' to represent 'faktisch'. We have often inserted German
expressions in square brackets on the occasions of their first appearance
or on that of their official definition. But we have also used bracketed
expressions to call attention to departures from our usual conventions, or
to bring out etymological connections which might otherwise be overlooked.

In many cases bracketing is insufficient, and we have introduced footnotes of our own, discussing some of the more important terms on the occasion of their first appearance. We have not hesitated to quote German sentences at length when they have been ambiguous or obscure; while we have sometimes taken pains to show where the ambiguity lies, we have more often left this to the reader to puzzle out for himself. We have often quoted passages with verbal subtleties which would otherwise be lost in translation. We have also called attention to a number of significant differences between the earlier and later editions of Heidegger's work. The entire book was reset for the seventh edition; while revisions were by no means extensive, they went beyond the simple changes in punctuation and citation which Heidegger mentions in his preface. We have chosen the third edition (1931) as typical of the earlier editions, and the eighth (1957) as typical of the later ones. In general we have preferred the readings of the eighth edition, and our marginal numbering and cross-references follow its pagination. Heidegger's very valuable footnotes have been renumbered with roman numerals and placed at the end of the text where we trust they will be given the attention they deserve. Hoping that our own notes will be of immediate use to the reader, we have placed them at the bottoms of pages for easy reference, indicating them with arabic numerals.

In general we have tried to stick to the text as closely as we can without sacrificing intelligibility; but we have made numerous concessions to the reader at the expense of making Heidegger less Heideggerian. We have, for instance, frequently used personal constructions where Heidegger has avoided them. We have also tried to be reasonably flexible in dealing with hyphenated expressions. Heidegger does not seem to be especially consistent in his use of quotation marks, though in certain expressions (for instance, the word 'Welt') they are very deliberately employed. Except in a few footnote references and some of the quotations from Hegel and Count Yorck in the two concluding chapters, our single quotation marks represent Heidegger's double ones. But we have felt free to introduce double ones of our own wherever we feel that they may be helpful to the reader. We have followed a similar policy with regard to italicization. When Heidegger uses italics in the later editions (or spaced type in the earlier ones), we have generally used italics; but in the relatively few cases where we have felt that some emphasis of our own is needed, we have resorted to wide spacing. We have not followed Heidegger in the use of italics for proper names or for definite articles used demonstratively to introduce restrictive relative clauses. But we have followed the usual practice of italicizing words and phrases from languages other than English and German, and have italicized titles of books, regardless of Heidegger's procedure.

We have received help from several sources. Miss Marjorie Ward has collated the third and eighth editions, and made an extremely careful study of Heidegger's vocabulary and ours, which has saved us from innumerable inconsistencies and many downright mistakes; there is hardly a page which has not profited by her assistance. We are also indebted to several persons who have helped us in various ways: Z. Adamczewski, Hannah Arendt, J. A. Burzle, C. A. Campbell, G. M. George, Fritz Heider, Edith Kern, Norbert Raymond, Eva Schaper, Martin Scheerer, John Wild. If any serious errors remain, they are probably due to our failure to exploit the time and good nature of these friends and colleagues more unmercifully. We are particularly indebted to Professor R. Gregor Smith who brought us together in the first place, and who, perhaps more than anyone else, has made it possible for this translation to be presented to the public. We also wish to express our appreciation to our publishers and to Max Niemeyer Verlag, holders of the German copyright, who have shown extraordinary patience in putting up with the long delay in the preparation of our manuscript.

We are particularly grateful to the University of Kansas for generous research grants over a period of three years, and to the University of Kansas Endowment Association for enabling us to work together in Scotland.

AUTHOR'S PREFACE TO THE SEVENTH GERMAN
EDITION

THIS treatise first appeared in the spring of 1927 in the *Jahrbuch für Phänomenologie und phänomenologische Forschung* edited by Edmund Husserl, and was published simultaneously in a special printing.

The present reprint, which appears as the seventh edition, is unchanged in the text, but has been newly revised with regard to quotations and punctuation. The page-numbers of this reprint agree with those of the earlier editions except for minor deviations.[1]

While the previous editions have borne the designation 'First Half', this has now been deleted. After a quarter of a century, the second half could no longer be added unless the first were to be presented anew. Yet the road it has taken remains even today a necessary one, if our Dasein is to be stirred by the question of Being.

For the elucidation of this question the reader may refer to my *Einführung in die Metaphysik*, which is appearing simultaneously with this reprinting under the same publishers.[2] This work presents the text of a course of lectures delivered in the summer semester of 1935.

[1] See Translators' Preface, p. 15.
[2] Max Niemeyer Verlag, Tübingen, 1953. English translation by Ralph Manheim, Yale University Press and Oxford University Press, 1959.

... δῆλον γὰρ ὡς ὑμεῖς μὲν ταῦτα (τί ποτε βούλεσθε σημαίνειν ὁπόταν ὂν φθέγγησθε) πάλαι γιγνώσκετε, ἡμεῖς δὲ πρὸ τοῦ μὲν ᾠόμεθα, νῦν δ' ἠπορή-καμεν ...

'For manifestly you have long been aware of what you mean when you use the expression "*being*". We, however, who used to think we understood it, have now become perplexed.'[1]

Do we in our time have an answer to the question of what we really mean by the word 'being'?[1] Not at all. So it is fitting that we should raise anew *the question of the meaning*[2] *of Being*. But are we nowadays even perplexed at our inability to understand the expression 'Being'? Not at all. So first of all we must reawaken an understanding for the meaning of this question. Our aim in the following treatise is to work out the question of the meaning of *Being* and to do so concretely. Our provisional aim is the Interpretation[3] of *time* as the possible horizon for any understanding whatsoever of Being.[4]

But the reasons for making this our aim, the investigations which such a purpose requires, and the path to its achievement, call for some introductory remarks.

1 'seiend'. Heidegger translates Plato's present participle ὂν by this present participle of the verb 'sein' ('to be'). We accordingly translate 'seiend' here and in a number of later passages by the present participle 'being'; where such a translation is inconvenient we shall resort to other constructions, usually subjoining the German word in brackets or in a footnote. The participle 'seiend' must be distinguished from the infinitive 'sein', which we shall usually translate either by the infinitive 'to be' or by the gerund 'being'. It must also be distinguished from the important substantive 'Sein' (always capitalized), which we shall translate as 'Being' (capitalized), and from the equally important substantive 'Seiendes', which is directly derived from 'seiend', and which we shall usually translate as 'entity' or 'entities'. (See our note 1, H. 3 below.)

2 'Sinn.' In view of the importance of the distinction between 'Sinn' and 'Bedeutung' in German writers as diverse as Dilthey, Husserl, Frege and Schlick, we shall translate 'Sinn' by 'meaning' or 'sense', depending on the context, and keep 'signification' and 'signify' for 'Bedeutung' and 'bedeuten'. (The verb 'mean' will occasionally be used to translate such verbs as 'besagen', 'sagen', 'heissen' and 'meinen', but the noun 'meaning' will be reserved for 'Sinn'.) On 'Sinn', see H. 151, 324; on 'Bedeutung', etc., see H. 87, and our note 3, p. 120 below.

3 Heidegger uses two words which might well be translated as 'interpretation': 'Auslegung' and 'Interpretation'. Though in many cases these may be regarded as synonyms, their connotations are not quite the same. 'Auslegung' seems to be used in a broad sense to cover any activity in which we interpret something 'as' something, whereas 'Interpretation' seems to apply to interpretations which are more theoretical or systematic, as in the exegesis of a text. See especially H. 148 ff. and 199 f. We shall preserve this distinction by writing 'interpretation' for 'Auslegung', but 'Interpretation' for Heidegger's 'Interpretation', following similar conventions for the verbs 'auslegen' and 'interpretieren'.

4 '. . . als des möglichen Horizontes eines jeden Seinsverständnisses überhaupt . . .' Throughout this work the word 'horizon' is used with a connotation somewhat different from that to which the English-speaking reader is likely to be accustomed. We tend to think of a horizon as something which we may widen or extend or go beyond; Heidegger, however, seems to think of it rather as something which we can neither widen nor go beyond, but which provides the limits for certain intellectual activities performed 'within' it.

INTRODUCTION

EXPOSITION OF THE QUESTION OF THE MEANING OF BEING

I

THE NECESSITY, STRUCTURE, AND PRIORITY OF THE QUESTION OF BEING

¶ *1. The Necessity for Explicitly Restating the Question of Being*

THIS question has today been forgotten. Even though in our time we deem it progressive to give our approval to 'metaphysics' again, it is held that we have been exempted from the exertions of a newly rekindled γιγαντομαχία περὶ τῆς οὐσίας. Yet the question we are touching upon is not just any question. It is one which provided a stimulus for the researches of Plato and Aristotle, only to subside from then on *as a theme for actual investigation.*[1] What these two men achieved was to persist through many alterations and 'retouchings' down to the 'logic' of Hegel. And what they wrested with the utmost intellectual effort from the phenomena, fragmentary and incipient though it was, has long since become trivialized.

Not only that. On the basis of the Greeks' initial contributions towards an Interpretation of Being, a dogma has been developed which not only declares the question about the meaning of Being to be superfluous, but sanctions its complete neglect. It is said that 'Being' is the most universal and the emptiest of concepts. As such it resists every attempt at definition. Nor does this most universal and hence indefinable concept require any definition, for everyone uses it constantly and already understands what he means by it. In this way, that which the ancient philosophers found continually disturbing as something obscure and hidden has taken on a clarity and self-evidence such that if anyone continues to ask about it he is charged with an error of method.

At the beginning of our investigation it is not possible to give a detailed

---

[1] '. . . *als thematische Frage wirklicher Untersuchung*'. When Heidegger speaks of a question as 'thematisch', he thinks of it as one which is taken seriously and studied in a systematic manner. While we shall often translate this adjective by its cognate, 'thematic', we may sometimes find it convenient to choose more flexible expressions involving the word 'theme'. (Heidegger gives a fuller discussion on H. 363.)

account of the presuppositions and prejudices which are constantly reimplanting and fostering the belief that an inquiry into Being is unneces-
3 sary. They are rooted in ancient ontology itself, and it will not be possible to interpret that ontology adequately until the question of Being has been clarified and answered and taken as a clue—at least, if we are to have regard for the soil from which the basic ontological concepts developed, and if we are to see whether the categories have been demonstrated in a way that is appropriate and complete. We shall therefore carry the discussion of these presuppositions only to the point at which the necessity for restating the question about the meaning of Being becomes plain. There are three such presuppositions.

1. First, it has been maintained that 'Being' is the 'most universal' concept: τὸ ὄν ἐστι καθόλου μάλιστα πάντων.[1] *Illud quod primo cadit sub apprehensione est ens, cuius intellectus includitur in omnibus, quaecumque quis apprehendit.* 'An understanding of Being is already included in conceiving anything which one apprehends in entities.'[1,ⅱ] But the 'universality' of 'Being' is not that of a *class* or *genus*. The term 'Being' does not define that realm of entities which is uppermost when these are Articulated conceptually according to genus and species: οὔτε τὸ ὄν γένος.[ⅲ] The 'universality' of Being 'transcends' any universality of genus. In medieval ontology 'Being' is designated as a '*transcendens*'. Aristotle himself knew the unity of this transcendental 'universal' as a *unity of analogy* in contrast to the multiplicity of the highest generic concepts applicable to things. With this discovery, in spite of his dependence on the way in which the ontological question had been formulated by Plato, he put the problem of Being on what was, in principle, a new basis. To be sure, even Aristotle failed to clear away the darkness of these categorial interconnections. In medieval ontology this problem was widely discussed, especially in the Thomist and Scotist schools, without reaching clarity as to principles. And when Hegel at last defines 'Being' as the 'indeterminate immediate' and makes this definition basic for all the further categorial explications of his 'logic', he keeps looking in the same direction as ancient ontology,

---

[1] ' "... was einer am Seienden erfasst" '. The word 'Seiendes', which Heidegger uses in his paraphrase, is one of the most important words in the book. The substantive 'das Seiende' is derived from the participle 'seiend' (see note 1, p. 19), and means literally 'that which is'; 'ein Seiendes' means 'something which is'. There is much to be said for translating 'Seiendes' by the noun 'being' or 'beings' (for it is often used in a collective sense). We feel, however, that it is smoother and less confusing to write 'entity' or 'entities'. We are well aware that in recent British and American philosophy the term 'entity' has been used more generally to apply to almost anything whatsoever, no matter what its ontological status. In this translation, however, it will mean simply 'something which *is*'. An alternative translation of the Latin quotation is given by the English Dominican Fathers, *Summa Theologica*, Thomas Baker, London, 1915: 'For that which, before aught else, falls under apprehension, is *being*, the notion of which is included in all things whatsoever a man apprehends.'

except that he no longer pays heed to Aristotle's problem of the unity of Being as over against the multiplicity of 'categories' applicable to things. So if it is said that 'Being' is the most universal concept, this cannot mean that it is the one which is clearest or that it needs no further discussion. It is rather the darkest of all.

2. It has been maintained secondly that the concept of 'Being' is   **4** indefinable. This is deduced from its supreme universality,[iv] and rightly so, if *definitio fit per genus proximum et differentiam specificam*. 'Being' cannot indeed be conceived as an entity; *enti non additur aliqua natura*: nor can it acquire such a character as to have the term "entity" applied to it. "Being" cannot be derived from higher concepts by definition, nor can it be presented through lower ones. But does this imply that 'Being' no longer offers a problem? Not at all. We can infer only that 'Being' cannot have the character of an entity. Thus we cannot apply to Being the concept of 'definition' as presented in traditional logic, which itself has its foundations in ancient ontology and which, within certain limits, provides a justifiable way of characterizing "entities". The indefinability of Being does not eliminate the question of its meaning; it demands that we look that question in the face.

3. Thirdly, it is held that 'Being' is of all concepts the one that is self-evident. Whenever one cognizes anything or makes an assertion, whenever one comports oneself towards entities, even towards oneself,[1] some use is made of 'Being'; and this expression is held to be intelligible 'without further ado', just as everyone understands 'The sky *is* blue', 'I *am* merry', and the like. But here we have an average kind of intelligibility, which merely demonstrates that this is unintelligible. It makes manifest that in any way of comporting oneself towards entities as entities—even in any Being towards entities as entities—there lies *a priori* an enigma.[2] The very fact that we already live in an understanding of Being and that the meaning of Being is still veiled in darkness proves that it is necessary in principle to raise this question again.

Within the range of basic philosophical concepts—especially when we come to the concept of 'Being'—it is a dubious procedure to invoke self-evidence, if indeed the 'self-evident' (Kant's 'covert judgments of the common reason')[3]

---

[1] '. . . in jedem Verhalten zu Seiendem, in jedem Sich-zu-sich-selbst-verhalten . . .' The verb 'verhalten' can refer to any kind of behaviour or way of conducting oneself, even to the way in which one relates oneself to something else, or to the way one refrains or holds oneself back. We shall translate it in various ways.

[2] 'Sie macht offenbar, dass in jedem Verhalten und Sein zu Seiendem als Seiendem a priori ein Rätsel liegt.' The phrase 'Sein zu Seiendem' is typical of many similar expressions in which the substantive 'Sein' is followed by the preposition 'zu'. In such expressions we shall usually translate 'zu' as 'towards': for example, 'Being-towards-death', 'Being towards Others', 'Being towards entities within-the-world'.

[3] ' "die geheimen Urteile der gemeinen Vernunft" '.

is to become the sole explicit and abiding theme for one's analytic—'the business of philosophers'.

By considering these prejudices, however, we have made plain not only that the question of Being lacks an *answer*, but that the question itself is obscure and without direction. So if it is to be revived, this means that we must first work out an adequate way of *formulating* it.

5 ¶ 2. *The Formal Structure of the Question of Being*

The question of the meaning of Being must be *formulated*. If it is a fundamental question, or indeed *the* fundamental question, it must be made transparent, and in an appropriate way.[1] We must therefore explain briefly what belongs to any question whatsoever, so that from this standpoint the question of Being can be made visible as a *very special* one with its own distinctive character.

Every inquiry is a seeking [Suchen]. Every seeking gets guided before-hand by what is sought. Inquiry is a cognizant seeking for an entity both with regard to the fact t h a t it is and with regard to its Being a s it is.[2] This cognizant seeking can take the form of 'investigating' ["Untersuchen"], in which one lays bare that which the question is about and ascertains its character. Any inquiry, as an inquiry about something, has *that which is asked about* [sein *Gefragtes*]. But all inquiry about something is somehow a questioning of something [Anfragen bei . . .]. So in addition to what is asked about, an inquiry has *that which is interrogated* [ein *Befragtes*]. In investigative questions—that is, in questions which are specifically theo-retical—what is asked about is determined and conceptualized. Further-more, in what is asked about there lies also *that which is to be found out by the asking* [das *Erfragte*]; this is what is really intended:[3] with this the inquiry reaches its goal. Inquiry itself is the behaviour of a questioner, and therefore of an entity, and as such has its own character of Being. When one makes an inquiry one may do so 'just casually' or one may formulate the

---

[1] '. . . dann bedarf solches Fragen der angemessenen Durchsichtigkeit'. The adjective 'durchsichtig' is one of Heidegger's favourite expressions, and means simply 'transparent', 'perspicuous', something that one can 'see through'. We shall ordinarily translate it by 'transparent'. See H. 146 for further discussion.

[2] '. . . in seinem Dass- und Sosein'.

[3] '. . . das eigentlich Intendierte . . .' The adverb 'eigentlich' occurs very often in this work. It may be used informally where one might write 'really' or 'on its part', or in a much stronger sense, where something like 'genuinely' or 'authentically' would be more appropriate. It is not always possible to tell which meaning Heidegger has in mind. In the contexts which seem relatively informal we shall write 'really'; in the more technical passages we shall write 'authentically', reserving 'genuinely' for 'genuin' or 'echt'. The reader must not confuse this kind of 'authenticity' with the kind, which belongs to an 'authentic text' or an 'authentic account'. See H. 42 for further discussion. In the present passage, the verb 'intendieren' is presumably used in the medieval sense of 'intending', as adapted and modified by Brentano and Husserl.

question explicitly. The latter case is peculiar in that the inquiry does not become transparent to itself until all these constitutive factors of the question have themselves become transparent.

The question about the meaning of Being is to be *formulated*. We must therefore discuss it with an eye to these structural items.

Inquiry, as a kind of seeking, must be guided beforehand by what is sought. So the meaning of Being must already be available to us in some way. As we have intimated, we always conduct our activities in an understanding of Being. Out of this understanding arise both the explicit question of the meaning of Being and the tendency that leads us towards its conception. We do not *know* what 'Being' means. But even if we ask, 'What *is* "Being"?', we keep within an understanding of the 'is', though we are unable to fix conceptually what that 'is' signifies. We do not even know the horizon in terms of which that meaning is to be grasped and fixed. *But this vague average understanding of Being is still a Fact.*

However much this understanding of Being (an understanding which is already available to us) may fluctuate and grow dim, and border on mere acquaintance with a word, its very indefiniteness is itself a positive phenomenon which needs to be clarified. An investigation of the meaning of Being cannot be expected to give this clarification at the outset. If we are to obtain the clue we need for Interpreting this average understanding of Being, we must first develop the concept of Being. In the light of this concept and the ways in which it may be explicitly understood, we can make out what this obscured or still unillumined understanding of Being means, and what kinds of obscuration—or hindrance to an explicit illumination—of the meaning of Being are possible and even inevitable.

Further, this vague average understanding of Being may be so infiltrated with traditional theories and opinions about Being that these remain hidden as sources of the way in which it is prevalently understood. What we seek when we inquire into Being is not something entirely unfamiliar, even if at first[1] we cannot grasp it at all.

In the question which we are to work out, *what is asked about* is Being— that which determines entities as entities, that on the basis of which

---

[1] 'zunächst'. This word is of very frequent occurrence in Heidegger, and he will discuss his use of it on H. 370 below. In ordinary German usage the word may mean 'at first', 'to begin with', or 'in the first instance', and we shall often translate it in such ways. The word is, however, cognate with the adjective 'nah' and its superlative 'nächst', which we shall usually translate as 'close' and 'closest' respectively; and Heidegger often uses 'zunächst' in the sense of 'most closely', when he is describing the most 'natural' and 'obvious' experiences which we have at an uncritical and pre-philosophical level. We have ventured to translate this Heideggerian sense of 'zunächst' as 'proximally', but there are many border-line cases where it is not clear whether Heidegger has in mind this special sense or one of the more general usages, and in such cases we have chosen whatever expression seems stylistically preferable.

[woraufhin] entities are already understood, however we may discuss
them in detail. The Being of entities 'is' not itself an entity. If we are to
understand the problem of Being, our first philosophical step consists in
not μῦθόν τινα διηγεῖσθαι,ᵛ in not 'telling a story'—that is to say, in not
defining entities as entities by tracing them back in their origin to some
other entities, as if Being had the character of some possible entity. Hence
Being, as that which is asked about, must be exhibited in a way of its own,
essentially different from the way in which entities are discovered. Accordingly, *what is to be found out by the asking*—the meaning of Being—also
demands that it be conceived in a way of its own, essentially contrasting
with the concepts in which entities acquire their determinate signification.

In so far as Being constitutes what is asked about, and "Being" means
the Being of entities, then entities themselves turn out to be *what is interrogated*. These are, so to speak, questioned as regards their Being. But if
the characteristics of their Being can be yielded without falsification, then
these entities must, on their part, have become accessible as they are in
themselves. When we come to what is to be interrogated, the question of
Being requires that the right way of access to entities shall have been
obtained and secured in advance. But there are many things which we
designate as 'being' ["seiend"], and we do so in various senses. Everything
we talk about, everything we have in view, everything towards which we
comport ourselves in any way, is being; what we are is being, and so is
how we are. Being lies in the fact that something is, and in its Being as it is;
in Reality; in presence-at-hand; in subsistence; in validity; in Dasein;
in the 'there is'.[1] In *which* entities is the meaning of Being to be discerned?
From which entities is the disclosure of Being to take its departure? Is
the starting-point optional, or does some particular entity have priority
when we come to work out the question of Being? Which entity shall we
take for our example, and in what sense does it have priority?

If the question about Being is to be explicitly formulated and carried
through in such a manner as to be completely transparent to itself, then
any treatment of it in line with the elucidations we have given requires
us to explain how Being is to be looked at, how its meaning is to be understood and conceptually grasped; it requires us to prepare the way for
choosing the right entity for our example, and to work out the genuine
way of access to it. Looking at something, understanding and conceiving it,
choosing, access to it—all these ways of behaving are constitutive for our
inquiry, and therefore are modes of Being for those particular entities

---

[1] 'Sein liegt im Dass- und Sosein, in Realität, Vorhandenheit, Bestand, Geltung,
Dasein, im "es gibt".' On 'Vorhandenheit' ('presence-at-hand') see note 1, p. 48, H. 25.
On 'Dasein', see note 1, p. 27.

which we, the inquirers, are ourselves. Thus to work out the question of Being adequately, we must make an entity—the inquirer—transparent in his own Being. The very asking of this question is an entity's mode of *Being*; and as such it gets its essential character from what is inquired about—namely, Being. This entity which each of us is himself and which includes inquiring as one of the possibilities of its Being, we shall denote by the term *"Dasein"*.[1] If we are to formulate our question explicitly and transparently, we must first give a proper explication of an entity (Dasein), with regard to its Being.

Is there not, however, a manifest circularity in such an undertaking? If we must first define an entity *in its Being*, and if we want to formulate the question of Being only on this basis, what is this but going in a circle? In working out our question, have we not 'presupposed' something which only the answer can bring? Formal objections such as the argument about 'circular reasoning', which can easily be cited at any time in the study of first principles, are always sterile when one is considering concrete ways of investigating. When it comes to understanding the matter at hand, they carry no weight and keep us from penetrating into the field of study.

But factically[2] there is no circle at all in formulating our question as we have described. One can determine the nature of entities in their Being without necessarily having the explicit concept of the meaning of Being at one's disposal. Otherwise there could have been no ontological knowledge heretofore. One would hardly deny that factically there has been such knowledge.[3] Of course 'Being' has been presupposed in all ontology up till now, but not as a *concept* at one's disposal—not as the sort of thing we are seeking. This 'presupposing' of Being has rather the character of taking a look at it beforehand, so that in the light of it the entities presented to us get provisionally Articulated in their Being. This guiding

8

---

[1] The word 'Dasein' plays so important a role in this work and is already so familiar to the English-speaking reader who has read about Heidegger, that it seems simpler to leave it untranslated except in the relatively rare passages in which Heidegger himself breaks it up with a hyphen ('Da-sein') to show its etymological construction: literally 'Being-there'. Though in traditional German philosophy it may be used quite generally to stand for almost any kind of Being or 'existence' which we can say that something *has* (the 'existence' of God, for example), in everyday usage it tends to be used more narrowly to stand for the kind of Being that belongs to *persons*. Heidegger follows the everyday usage in this respect, but goes somewhat further in that he often uses it to stand for any *person* who has such Being, and who is thus an 'entity' himself. See H. 11 below.

[2] 'faktisch'. While this word can often be translated simply as 'in fact' or 'as a matter of fact', it is used both as an adjective and as an adverb and is so characteristic of Heidegger's style that we shall as a rule translate it either as 'factical' or as 'factically', thus preserving its connection with the important noun 'Faktizität' (facticity'), and keeping it distinct from 'tatsächlich' ('factual') and 'wirklich' ('actual'). See the discussion of 'Tatsächlichkeit' and 'Faktizität' in Sections 12 and 29 below (H. 56, 135).

[3] '. . . deren faktischen Bestand man wohl nicht leugnen wird'.

activity of taking a look at Being arises from the average understanding of Being in which we always operate and *which in the end belongs to the essential constitution*[1] *of Dasein itself.* Such 'presupposing' has nothing to do with laying down an axiom from which a sequence of propositions is deductively derived. It is quite impossible for there to be any 'circular argument' in formulating the question about the meaning of Being; for in answering this question, the issue is not one of grounding something by such a derivation; it is rather one of laying bare the grounds for it and exhibiting them.[2]

In the question of the meaning of Being there is no 'circular reasoning' but rather a remarkable 'relatedness backward or forward' which what we are asking about (Being) bears to the inquiry itself as a mode of Being of an entity. Here what is asked about has an essential pertinence to the inquiry itself, and this belongs to the ownmost meaning [eigensten Sinn] of the question of Being. This only means, however, that there is a way— perhaps even a very special one—in which entities with the character of Dasein are related to the question of Being. But have we not thus demonstrated that a certain kind of entity has a priority with regard to its Being? And have we not thus presented that entity which shall serve as the primary example to be *interrogated* in the question of Being? So far our discussion has n o t demonstrated Dasein's priority, nor has it shown decisively whether Dasein may possibly or even necessarily serve as the primary entity to be interrogated. But indeed something like a priority of Dasein has announced itself.

¶ *3. The Ontological Priority of the Question of Being*

When we pointed out the characteristics of the question of Being, taking as our clue the formal structure of the question as such, we made it

---

[1] 'Wesensverfassung'. 'Verfassung' is the standard word for the 'constitution' of a nation or any political organization, but it is also used for the 'condition' or 'state' in which a person may find himself. Heidegger seldom uses the word in either of these senses; but he does use it in ways which are somewhat analogous. In one sense Dasein's 'Verfassung' is its 'constitution', the way it is constituted, '*sa condition humaine*'. In another sense Dasein may have several 'Verfassungen' as constitutive 'states' or factors which enter into its 'constitution'. We shall, in general, translate 'Verfassung' as 'constitution' or 'constitutive state' according to the context; but in passages where 'constitutive state' would be cumbersome and there is little danger of ambiguity, we shall simply write 'state'. These states, however, must always be thought of as constitutive and essential, not as temporary or transitory stages like the 'state' of one's health or the 'state of the nation'. When Heidegger uses the word 'Konstitution', we shall usually indicate this by capitalizing 'Constitution'.

[2] '. . . weil es in der Beantwortung der Frage nicht um eine ableitende Begründung, sondern um aufweisende Grund-Freilegung geht.' Expressions of the form 'es geht . . . um . . .' appear very often in this work. We shall usually translate them by variants on '. . . is an issue for . . .'.

clear that this question is a peculiar one, in that a series of fundamental considerations is required for working it out, not to mention for solving it. But its distinctive features will come fully to light only when we have delimited it adequately with regard to its function, its aim, and its motives.

Hitherto our arguments for showing that the question must be restated have been motivated in part by its venerable origin but chiefly by the lack   9 of a definite answer and even by the absence of any satisfactory formulation of the question itself. One may, however, ask what purpose this question is supposed to serve. Does it simply remain—or *is* it at all—a mere matter for soaring speculation about the most general of generalities, *or is it rather, of all questions, both the most basic and the most concrete?*

Being is always the Being of an entity. The totality of entities can, in accordance with its various domains, become a field for laying bare and delimiting certain definite areas of subject-matter. These areas, on their part (for instance, history, Nature, space, life, Dasein, language, and the like), can serve as objects which corresponding scientific investigations may take as their respective themes. Scientific research accomplishes, roughly and naïvely, the demarcation and initial fixing of the areas of subject-matter. The basic structures of any such area have already been worked out after a fashion in our pre-scientific ways of experiencing and interpreting that domain of Being in which the area of subject-matter is itself confined. The 'basic concepts' which thus arise remain our proximal clues for disclosing this area concretely for the first time. And although research may always lean towards this positive approach, its real progress comes not so much from collecting results and storing them away in 'manuals' as from inquiring into the ways in which each particular area is basically constituted [Grundverfassungen]—an inquiry to which we have been driven mostly by reacting against just such an increase in information.

The real 'movement' of the sciences takes place when their basic concepts undergo a more or less radical revision which is transparent to itself. The level which a science has reached is determined by how far it is *capable* of a crisis in its basic concepts. In such immanent crises the very relationship between positively investigative inquiry and those things themselves that are under interrogation comes to a point where it begins to totter. Among the various disciplines everywhere today there are freshly awakened tendencies to put research on new foundations.

Mathematics, which is seemingly the most rigorous and most firmly constructed of the sciences, has reached a crisis in its 'foundations'. In the controversy between the formalists and the intuitionists, the issue is one of obtaining and securing the primary way of access to what are supposedly the objects of this science. The relativity theory of *physics* arises from the tendency to exhibit the interconnectedness of Nature as it is 'in itself'. As a theory of the conditions under which we have access to Nature itself, it seeks to preserve the changelessness of the laws of motion by ascertaining all relativities, and thus comes up against the question of the structure of its own given area of study—the problem of matter. In *biology* there is an awakening tendency to inquire beyond the definitions which mechanism and vitalism have given for "life" and "organism", and to define anew the kind of Being which belongs to the living as such. In those *humane sciences which are historiological in character*,[1] the urge towards historical actuality itself has been strengthened in the course of time by tradition and by the way tradition has been presented and handed down: the history of literature is to become the history of problems. *Theology* is seeking a more primordial interpretation of man's Being towards God, prescribed by the meaning of faith itself and remaining within it. It is slowly beginning to understand once more Luther's insight that the 'foundation' on which its system of dogma rests has not arisen from an inquiry in which faith is primary, and that conceptually this 'foundation' not only is inadequate for the problematic of theology, but conceals and distorts it.

Basic concepts determine the way in which we get an understanding beforehand of the area of subject-matter underlying all the objects a science takes as its theme, and all positive investigation is guided by this understanding. Only after the area itself has been explored beforehand in a corresponding manner do these concepts become genuinely demonstrated and 'grounded'. But since every such area is itself obtained from the domain of entities themselves, this preliminary research, from which the basic concepts are drawn, signifies nothing else than an interpretation of those entities with regard to their basic state of Being. Such research must run ahead of the positive sciences, and it *can*. Here the work of Plato and Aristotle is evidence enough. Laying the foundations for the sciences in this way is different in principle from the kind of 'logic' which limps along after, investigating the status of some science as it chances to find it, in order to discover its 'method'. Laying the foundations, as we have described it, is rather a productive logic—in the sense that it leaps ahead,

_____

[1] 'In den *historischen Geisteswissenschaften* . . .' Heidegger makes much of the distinction between 'Historie' and 'Geschichte' and the corresponding adjectives 'historisch' and 'geschichtlich'. 'Historie' stands for what Heidegger calls a 'science of history'. (See H. 375, 378.) 'Geschichte' usually stands for the kind of 'history' that actually *happens*. We shall as a rule translate these respectively as 'historiology' and 'history', following similar conventions in handling the two adjectives. See especially Sections 6 and 76 below.

as it were, into some area of Being, discloses it for the first time in the constitution of its Being, and, after thus arriving at the structures within it, makes these available to the positive sciences as transparent assignments for their inquiry.[1] To give an example, what is philosophically primary is neither a theory of the concept-formation of historiology nor the theory of historiological knowledge, nor yet the theory of history as the Object of historiology; what is primary is rather the Interpretation of authentically historical entities as regards their historicality.[2] Similarly the positive outcome of Kant's *Critique of Pure Reason* lies in what it has contributed towards the working out of what belongs to any Nature   11 whatsoever, not in a 'theory' of knowledge. His transcendental logic is an *a priori* logic for the subject-matter of that area of Being called "Nature".

But such an inquiry itself—ontology taken in the widest sense without favouring any particular ontological directions or tendencies—requires a further clue. Ontological inqury is indeed more primordial, as over against the ontical[3] inquiry of the positive sciences. But it remains itself naïve and opaque if in its researches into the Being of entities it fails to discuss the meaning of Being in general. And the ontological task of a genealogy of the different possible ways of Being (which is not to be constructed deductively) is precisely of such a sort as to require that we first come to an understanding of 'what we really mean by this expression "Being" '.

The question of Being aims therefore at ascertaining the *a priori* conditions not only for the possibility of the sciences which examine entities as entities of such and such a type, and, in so doing, already operate with an understanding of Being, but also for the possibility of those ontologies themselves which are prior to the ontical sciences and which provide their foundations. *Basically, all ontology, no matter how rich and firmly compacted a system of categories it has at its disposal, remains blind and perverted from its ownmost aim, if it has not first adequately clarified the meaning of Being, and conceived this clarification as its fundamental task.*

Ontological research itself, when properly understood, gives to the question of Being an ontological priority which goes beyond mere resumption of a venerable tradition and advancement with a problem that has hitherto been opaque. But this objectively scientific priority is not the only one.

[1] '. . . als durchsichtige Anweisungen des Fragens . . .'

[2] '. . . sondern die Intepretation des eigentlich geschichtlich Seienden auf seine Geschichtlichkeit'. We shall translate the frequently occurring term 'Geschichtlichkeit' as 'historicality'. Heidegger very occasionally uses the term 'Historizität', as on H. 20 below, and this will be translated as 'historicity'.

[3] While the terms 'ontisch' ('ontical') and 'ontologisch' ('ontological') are not explicitly defined, their meanings will emerge rather clearly. Ontological inquiry is concerned primarily with *Being*; ontical inquiry is concerned primarily with *entities* and the facts about them.

¶ *4. The Ontical Priority of the Question of Being*

Science in general may be defined as the totality established through an interconnection of true propositions.[1] This definition is not complete, nor does it reach the meaning of science. As ways in which man behaves, sciences have the manner of Being which this entity—man himself— possesses. This entity we denote by the term *"Dasein"*. Scientific research is not the only manner of Being which this entity can have, nor is it the one which lies closest. Moreover, Dasein itself has a special distinctiveness as compared with other entities, and it is worth our while to bring this to view in a provisional way. Here our discussion must anticipate later analyses, in which our results will be authentically exhibited for the first time.

Dasein is an entity which does not just occur among other entities. Rather it is ontically distinguished by the fact that, in its very Being, that Being is an *issue* for it. But in that case, this is a constitutive state of Dasein's Being, and this implies that Dasein, in its Being, has a relationship towards that Being—a relationship which itself is one of Being.[2] And this means further that there is some way in which Dasein understands itself in its Being, and that to some degree it does so explicitly. It is peculiar to this entity that with and through its Being, this Being is disclosed to it. *Understanding of Being is itself a definite characteristic of Dasein's Being.* Dasein is ontically distinctive in that it *is* ontological.[3]

Here "Being-ontological" is not yet tantamount to "developing an ontology". So if we should reserve the term "ontology" for that theoretical inquiry which is explicitly devoted to the meaning of entities, then what we have had in mind in speaking of Dasein's "Being-ontological" is to be designated as something "pre-ontological". It does not signify simply "being-ontical", however, but rather "being in such a way that one has an understanding of Being".

That kind of Being towards which Dasein can comport itself in one way or another, and always does comport itself somehow, we call "*existence*" [*Existenz*]. And because we cannot define Dasein's essence by citing a "what" of the kind that pertains to a subject-matter [eines sachhaltigen Was], and because its essence lies rather in the fact that in each case it

---

[1] '. . . das Ganze eines Begründungszusammenhanges wahrer Sätze . . .' See H. 357 below.

[2] 'Zu dieser Seinsverfassung des Daseins gehört aber dann, dass es in seinem Sein zu diesem Sein ein Seinsverhältnis hat.' This passage is ambiguous and might also be read as: '. . . and this implies that Dasein, in its Being towards this Being, has a relationship of Being.'

[3] '. . . dass es ontologisch *ist*'. As 'ontologisch' may be either an adjective or an adverb, we might also write: '. . . that it *is* ontologically'. A similar ambiguity occurs in the two following sentences, where we read 'Ontologisch-sein' and 'ontisch-seiend' respectively.

has its Being to be, and has it as its own,[1] we have chosen to designate this entity as "Dasein", a term which is purely an expression of its Being [als reiner Seinsausdruck].

Dasein always understands itself in terms of its existence—in terms of a possibility of itself: to be itself or not itself. Dasein has either chosen these possibilities itself, or got itself into them, or grown up in them already. Only the particular Dasein decides its existence, whether it does so by taking hold or by neglecting. The question of existence never gets straightened out except through existing itself. The understanding of oneself which leads *along this way* we call "*existentiell*".[2] The question of existence is one of Dasein's ontical 'affairs'. This does not require that the ontological structure of existence should be theoretically transparent. The question about that structure aims at the analysis [Auseinanderlegung] of what constitutes existence. The context [Zusammenhang] of such structures we call "*existentiality*". Its analytic has the character of an understanding which is not existentiell, but rather *existential.* The task of an existential analytic of Dasein has been delineated in advance, as regards both its possibility and its necessity, in Dasein's ontical constitution.

So far as existence is the determining character of Dasein, the ontological analytic of this entity always requires that existentiality be considered beforehand. By "existentiality" we understand the state of Being that is constitutive for those entities that exist. But in the idea of such a constitutive state of Being, the idea of Being is already included. And thus even the possibility of carrying through the analytic of Dasein depends on working out beforehand the question about the meaning of Being in general. Sciences are ways of Being in which Dasein comports itself towards entities which it need not be itself. But to Dasein, Being in a world is something that belongs essentially. Thus Dasein's understanding of Being pertains with equal primordiality both to an understanding of something like a 'world', and to the understanding of the Being of those entities which become accessible within the world.[3] So whenever an ontology takes for its theme entities whose character of Being is other than that of Dasein, it has its own foundation and motivation in Dasein's own ontical structure, in which a pre-ontological understanding of Being is comprised as a definite characteristic.

13

---

[1] '. . . dass es je sein Sein als seiniges zu sein hat . . .'
[2] We shall translate 'existenziell' by 'existentiell', and 'existenzial' by 'existential' There seems to be little reason for resorting to the more elaborate neologisms proposed by other writers.
[3] '. . . innerhalb der Welt . . .' Heidegger uses at least three expressions which might be translated as 'in the world': 'innerhalb der Welt', 'in der Welt', and the adjective (or adverb) 'innerweltlich'. We shall translate these respectively by 'within the world', 'in the world', and 'within-the-world'.

Therefore *fundamental ontology*, from which alone all other ontologies can take their rise, must be sought in the *existential analytic of Dasein*.

Dasein accordingly takes priority over all other entities in several ways. The first priority is an *ontical* one: Dasein is an entity whose Being has the determinate character of existence. The second priority is an *ontological* one: Dasein is in itself 'ontological', because existence is thus determinative for it. But with equal primordiality Dasein also possesses—as constitutive for its understanding of existence—an understanding of the Being of all entities of a character other than its own. Dasein has therefore a third priority as providing the ontico-ontological condition for the possibility of any ontologies. Thus Dasein has turned out to be, more than any other entity, the one which must first be interrogated ontologically.

But the roots of the existential analytic, on its part, are ultimately *existentiell, that is, ontical.* Only if the inquiry of philosophical research is itself seized upon in an existentiell manner as a possibility of the Being of each existing Dasein, does it become at all possible to disclose the existentiality of existence and to undertake an adequately founded onto-**14** logical problematic. But with this, the ontical priority of the question of being has also become plain.

Dasein's ontico-ontological priority was seen quite early, though Dasein itself was not grasped in its genuine ontological structure, and did not even become a problem in which this structure was sought. Aristotle says: ἡ ψυχὴ τὰ ὄντα πώς ἐστιν.ⱽⁱ "Man's soul is, in a certain way, entities." The 'soul' which makes up the Being of man has αἴσθησις and νόησις among its ways of Being, and in these it discovers all entities, both in the fact that they are, and in their Being as they are—that is, always in their Being. Aristotle's principle, which points back to the ontological thesis of Parmenides, is one which Thomas Aquinas has taken up in a characteristic discussion. Thomas is engaged in the task of deriving the '*transcendentia*'—those characters of Being which lie beyond every possible way in which an entity may be classified as coming under some generic kind of subject-matter (every *modus specialis entis*), and which belong necessarily to anything, whatever it may be. Thomas has to demonstrate that the *verum* is such a *transcendens*. He does this by invoking an entity which, in accordance with its very manner of Being, is properly suited to 'come together with' entities of any sort whatever. This distinctive entity, the *ens quod natum est convenire cum omni ente*, is the soul (*anima*).ⱽⁱⁱ Here the priority of 'Dasein' over all other entities emerges, although it has not been ontologically clarified. This priority has obviously nothing in common with a vicious subjectivizing of the totality of entities.

By indicating Dasein's ontico-ontological priority in this provisional manner, we have grounded our demonstration that the question of Being is ontico-ontologically distinctive. But when we analysed the structure of this question as such (Section 2), we came up against a distinctive way in which this entity functions in the very formulation of that question. Dasein then revealed itself as that entity which must first be worked out in an ontologically adequate manner, if the inquiry is to become a transparent one. But now it has been shown that the ontological analytic of Dasein in general is what makes up fundamental ontology, so that Dasein functions as that entity which in principle is to be _interrogated_ beforehand as to its Being.

If to Interpret the meaning of Being becomes our task, Dasein is not only the primary entity to be interrogated; it is also that entity which already comports itself, in its Being, towards what we are asking about when we ask this question. But in that case the question of Being is nothing other than the radicalization of an essential tendency-of-Being which belongs to Dasein itself—the pre-ontological understanding of Being.

15

What has been shown has to refer back to the character of the analytic.

II

THE TWOFOLD TASK IN WORKING OUT THE QUESTION OF BEING. METHOD AND DESIGN OF OUR INVESTIGATION

¶ *5. The Ontological Analytic of Dasein as Laying Bare the Horizon for an Interpretation of the Meaning of Being in General*

IN designating the tasks of 'formulating' the question of Being, we have shown not only that we must establish which entity is to serve as our primary object of interrogation, but also that the right way of access to this entity is one which we must explicitly make our own and hold secure. We have already discussed which entity takes over the principal role within the question of Being. But how are we, as it were, to set our sights towards this entity, Dasein, both as something accessible to us and as something to be understood and interpreted?

In demonstrating that Dasein is ontico-ontologically prior, we may have misled the reader into supposing that this entity must also be what is given as ontico-ontologically primary not only in the sense that it can itself be grasped 'immediately', but also in that the kind of Being which it possesses is presented just as 'immediately'. Ontically, of course, Dasein is not only close to us—even that which is closest: we *are* it, each of us, we ourselves. In spite of this, or rather for just this reason, it is ontologically that which is farthest. To be sure, its ownmost Being is such that it has an understanding of that Being, and already maintains itself in each case as if its Being has been interpreted in some manner. But we are certainly not saying that when Dasein's own Being is thus interpreted pre-ontologically in the way which lies closest, this interpretation can be taken over as an appropriate clue, as if this way of understanding Being is what must emerge when one's ownmost state of Being is considered[1] as an onto-logical theme. The kind of Being which belongs to Dasein is rather such that, in understanding its own Being, it has a tendency to do so in terms of that entity towards which it comports itself proximally and in a way which is essentially constant—in terms of the 'world'. In Dasein itself, and therefore in its own understanding of Being, the way the world is

---

[1] 'Besinnung'. The earliest editions have 'Bestimmung' instead.

understood is, as we shall show, reflected back ontologically upon the way   16
in which Dasein itself gets interpreted.

Thus because Dasein is ontico-ontologically prior, its own specific state
of Being (if we understand this in the sense of Dasein's 'categorial
structure') remains concealed from it. Dasein is ontically 'closest' to itself
and ontologically farthest, but pre-ontologically it is surely not a stranger.

Here we have merely indicated provisionally that an Interpretation of
this entity is confronted with peculiar difficulties grounded in the kind of
Being which belongs to the object taken as our theme and to the very
behaviour of so taking it. These difficulties are not grounded in any short-
comings of the cognitive powers with which we are endowed, or in the
lack of a suitable way of conceiving—a lack which seemingly would not
be hard to remedy.

Not only, however, does an understanding of Being belong to Dasein,
but this understanding develops or decays along with whatever kind of
Being Dasein may possess at the time; accordingly there are many ways in
which it has been interpreted, and these are all at Dasein's disposal.
Dasein's ways of behaviour, its capacities, powers, possibilities, and vicissitudes, have been studied with varying extent in philosophical psychology,
in anthropology, ethics, and 'political science', in poetry, biography, and
the writing of history, each in a different fashion. But the question remains
whether these interpretations of Dasein have been carried through with
a primordial existentiality comparable to whatever existentiell primordiality they may have possessed. Neither of these excludes the
other but they do not necessarily go together. Existentiell interpretation can demand an existential analytic, if indeed we conceive of
philosophical cognition as something possible and necessary. Only when
the basic structures of Dasein have been adequately worked out with
explicit orientation towards the problem of Being itself, will what we
have hitherto gained in interpreting Dasein get its existential justification.

Thus an analytic of Dasein must remain our first requirement in the
question of Being. But in that case the problem of obtaining and securing
the kind of access which will lead to Dasein, becomes even more a burning
one. To put it negatively, we have no right to resort to dogmatic constructions and to apply just any idea of Being and actuality to this entity, no
matter how 'self-evident' that idea may be; nor may any of the 'categories' which such an idea prescribes be forced upon Dasein without
proper ontological consideration. We must rather choose such a way of
access and such a kind of interpretation that this entity can show itself in ←——
itself and from itself [an ihm selbst von ihm selbst her]. And this
means that it is to be shown as it is *proximally and for the most part*—

in its average everydayness.[1] In this everydayness there are certain structures which we shall exhibit—not just any accidental structures, but essential ones which, in every kind of Being that factical Dasein may possess, persist as determinative for the character of its Being. Thus by having regard for the basic state of Dasein's everydayness, we shall bring out the Being of this entity in a preparatory fashion.

When taken in this way, the analytic of Dasein remains wholly oriented towards the guiding task of working out the question of Being. Its limits are thus determined. It cannot attempt to provide a complete ontology of Dasein, which assuredly must be constructed if anything like a 'philosophical' anthropology is to have a philosophically adequate basis.[2]

If our purpose is to make such an anthropology possible, or to lay its ontological foundations, our Interpretation will provide only some of the 'pieces', even though they are by no means inessential ones. Our analysis of Dasein, however, is not only incomplete; it is also, in the first instance, *provisional*. It merely brings out the Being of this entity, without Interpreting its meaning. It is rather a preparatory procedure by which the horizon for the most primordial way of interpreting Being may be laid bare. Once we have arrived at that horizon, this preparatory analytic of Dasein will have to be repeated on a higher and authentically ontological basis.

We shall point to *temporality*[3] as the meaning of the Being of that entity which we call "Dasein". If this is to be demonstrated, those structures of Dasein which we shall provisionally exhibit must be Interpreted over again as modes of temporality. In thus interpreting Dasein as temporality, however, we shall not give the answer to our leading question as to the meaning of Being in general. But the ground will have been prepared for obtaining such an answer.

---

[1] 'Und zwar soll sie das Seiende in dem zeigen, wie es *zunächst und zumeist* ist, in seiner durchschnittlichen *Alltäglichkeit*.' The phrase 'zunächst und zumeist' is one that occurs many times, though Heidegger does not explain it until Section 71 (H. 370 below), where 'Alltäglichkeit' too gets explained. On 'zunächst' see our note 1, p. 25, H. 6.

[2] The ambiguity of the pronominal references in this sentence and the one before it, reflects a similar ambiguity in the German. (The English-speaking reader should be reminded that the kind of philosophical 'anthropology' which Heidegger has in mind is a study of man in the widest sense, and is not to be confused with the empirical sciences of 'physical' and 'cultural' anthropology.)

[3] '*Zeitlichkeit*'. While it is tempting to translate the adjective 'zeitlich' and the noun 'Zeitlichkeit' by their most obvious English cognates, 'timely' and 'timeliness', this would be entirely misleading; for 'temporal' and 'temporality' come much closer to what Heidegger has in mind, not only when he is discussing these words in their popular senses (as he does on the following page) but even when he is using them in his own special sense, as in Section 65 below. (See especially H. 326 below, where 'Zeitlichkeit' is defined.) On the other hand, he occasionally uses the noun 'Temporalität' and the adjective 'temporal' in a sense which he will explain later (H. 19). We shall translate these by 'Temporality' and 'Temporal', with initial capitals.

We have already intimated that Dasein has a pre-ontological Being as its ontically constitutive state. Dasein *is* in such a way as to be something which understands something like Being.[1] Keeping this interconnection firmly in mind, we shall show that whenever Dasein tacitly understands and interprets something like Being, it does so with *time* as its standpoint. Time must be brought to light—and genuinely conceived—as the horizon for all understanding of Being and for any way of interpreting it. In order for us to discern this, *time* needs to be *explicated primordially as the horizon for the understanding of Being, and in terms of temporality as the Being of Dasein, which understands Being.* This task as a whole requires that the conception of time thus obtained shall be distinguished from the way in which it is ordinarily understood. This ordinary way of understanding it has become explicit in an interpretation precipitated in the traditional concept of time, which has persisted from Aristotle to Bergson and even later. Here we must make clear that this conception of time and, in general, the ordinary way of understanding it, have sprung from temporality, and we must show how this has come about. We shall thereby restore to the ordinary conception the autonomy which is its rightful due, as against Bergson's thesis that the time one has in mind in this conception is space.

'Time' has long functioned as an ontological—or rather an ontical—criterion for naïvely discriminating various realms of entities. A distinction has been made between 'temporal' entities (natural processes and historical happenings) and 'non-temporal' entities (spatial and numerical relationships). We are accustomed to contrasting the 'timeless' meaning of propositions with the 'temporal' course of propositional assertions. It is also held that there is a 'cleavage' between 'temporal' entities and the 'supra-temporal' eternal, and efforts are made to bridge this over. Here 'temporal' always means simply being [seiend] 'in time'—a designation which, admittedly, is still pretty obscure. The Fact remains that time, in the sense of 'being [sein] in time', functions as a criterion for distinguishing realms of Being. Hitherto no one has asked or troubled to investigate how time has come to have this distinctive ontological function, or with what right anything like time functions as such a criterion; nor has anyone asked whether the authentic ontological relevance which is possible for it, gets expressed when "time" is used in so naïvely ontological a manner. 'Time' has acquired this 'self-evident' ontological function 'of its own accord', so to speak; indeed it has done so within the horizon of the way it is ordinarily understood. And it has maintained itself in this function to this day.

18

---

[1] 'Dasein *ist* in der Weise, seiend so etwas wie Sein zu verstehen.'

In contrast to all this, our treatment of the question of the meaning of Being must enable us to show that *the central problematic of all ontology is rooted in the phenomenon of time, if rightly seen and rightly explained*, and we must show *how* this is the case.

If Being is to be conceived in terms of time, and if, indeed, its various modes and derivatives are to become intelligible in their respective modifications and derivations by taking time into consideration, then Being itself (and not merely entities, let us say, as entities 'in time') is thus made visible in its 'temporal' character. But in that case, 'temporal' can no longer mean simply 'being in time'. Even the 'non-temporal' and the 'supra-temporal' are 'temporal' with regard to their Being, and not just privatively by contrast with something 'temporal' as an entity 'in time', but in a *positive* sense, though it is one which we must first explain. In both pre-philosophical and philosophical usage the expression 'temporal' has been pre-empted by the signification we have cited; in the following investigations, however, we shall employ it for another signification. Thus the way in which Being and its modes and characteristics have their meaning determined primordially in terms of time, is what we shall call its "*Temporal*" determinateness.[1] Thus the fundamental ontological task of Interpreting Being as such includes working out the *Temporality of Being*. In the exposition of the problematic of Temporality the question of the meaning of Being will first be concretely answered.

Because Being cannot be grasped except by taking time into consideration, the answer to the question of Being cannot lie in any proposition that is blind and isolated. The answer is not properly conceived if what it asserts propositionally is just passed along, especially if it gets circulated as a free-floating result, so that we merely get informed about a 'standpoint' which may perhaps differ from the way this has hitherto been treated. Whether the answer is a 'new' one remains quite superficial and is of no importance. Its positive character must lie in its being *ancient* enough for us to learn to conceive the possibilities which the 'Ancients' have made ready for us. In its ownmost meaning this answer tells us that concrete ontological research must begin with an investigative inquiry which keeps within the horizon we have laid bare; and this is all that it tells us.

If, then, the answer to the question of Being is to provide the clues for our research, it cannot be adequate until it brings us the insight that the specific kind of Being of ontology hitherto, and the vicissitudes of its inquiries, its findings, and its failures, have been necessitated in the very character of Dasein.

---

[1] 'seine *temporale* Bestimmtheit'. See our note 3, p. 38, H. 17 above.

¶ *6. The Task of Destroying the History of Ontology*

All research—and not least that which operates within the range of the central question of Being—is an ontical possibility of Dasein. Dasein's Being finds its meaning in temporality. But temporality is also the condition which makes historicality possible as a temporal kind of Being which Dasein itself possesses, regardless of whether or how Dasein is an entity 'in time'. Historicality, as a determinate character, is prior to what is called "history" (world-historical historizing).[1]

"Historicality" stands for the state of Being that is constitutive for Dasein's 'historizing' as such; only on the basis of such 'historizing' is anything like 'world-history' possible or can anything belong historically to world-history. In its factical Being, any Dasein is as it already was, and it is 'what' it already was. It *is* its past, whether explicitly or not. And this is so not only in that its past is, as it were, pushing itself along 'behind' it, and that Dasein possesses what is past as a property which is still present-at-hand and which sometimes has after-effects upon it: Dasein 'is' its past in the way of *its* own Being, which, to put it roughly, 'historizes' out of its future on each occasion.[2] Whatever the way of being it may have at the time, and thus with whatever understanding of Being it may possess, Dasein has grown up both into and in a traditional way of interpreting itself: in terms of this it understands itself proximally and, within a certain range, constantly. By this understanding, the possibilities of its Being are disclosed and regulated. Its own past—and this always means the past of its 'generation'—is not something which *follows along after* Dasein, but something which already goes ahead of it.

This elemental historicality of Dasein may remain hidden from Dasein itself. But there is a way by which it can be discovered and given proper attention. Dasein can discover tradition, preserve it, and study it explicitly. The discovery of tradition and the disclosure of what it 'transmits' and how this is transmitted, can be taken hold of as a task in its own right. In this way Dasein brings itself into the kind of Being which consists in historiological inquiry and research. But historiology—or more precisely historicity[3]—is possible as a kind of Being which the inquiring Dasein may

[1] 'weltgeschichtliches Geschehen'. While the verb 'geschehen' ordinarily means to 'happen', and will often be so translated, Heidegger stresses its etymological kinship to 'Geschichte' or 'history'. To bring out this connection, we have coined the verb 'historize', which might be paraphrased as to 'happen in a historical way'; we shall usually translate 'geschehen' this way in contexts where history is being discussed. We trust that the reader will keep in mind that such 'historizing' is characteristic of all historical entities, and is *not* the sort of thing that is done primarily by historians (as 'philosophizing', for instance, is done by philosophers). (On 'world-historical' see H. 381 ff.)

[2] 'Das Dasein "ist" seine Vergangenheit in der Weise *seines* Seins, das, roh gesagt, jeweils aus seiner Zukunft her "geschieht".'

[3] 'Historizität'. Cf. note 2, p. 31. H. 10 above.

possess, only because historicality is a determining characteristic for Dasein in the very basis of its Being. If this historicality remains hidden from Dasein, and as long as it so remains, Dasein is also denied the possibility of historiological inquiry or the discovery of history. If historiology is wanting, this is not evidence *against* Dasein's historicality; on the contrary, as a deficient mode[1] of this state of Being, it is evidence for it. Only because it is 'historical' can an era be unhistoriological.

On the other hand, if Dasein has seized upon its latent possibility not only of making its own existence transparent to itself but also of inquiring into the meaning of existentiality itself (that is to say, of previously inquiring into the meaning of Being in general), and if by such inquiry its eyes have been opened to its own essential historicality, then one cannot fail to see that the inquiry into Being (the ontico-ontological necessity of which we have already indicated) is itself characterized by historicality. The ownmost meaning of Being which belongs to the inquiry into Being as an historical inquiry, gives us the assignment [Anweisung] of inquiring into the history of that inquiry itself, that is, of becoming historiological. In working out the question of Being, we must heed this assignment, so that by positively making the past our own, we may bring ourselves into full possession of the ownmost possibilities of such inquiry. The question of the meaning of Being must be carried through by explicating Dasein beforehand in its temporality and historicality; the question thus brings itself to the point where it understands itself as historiological.

Our preparatory Interpretation of the fundamental structures of Dasein with regard to the average kind of Being which is closest to it (a kind of Being in which it is therefore proximally historical as well), will make manifest, however, not only that Dasein is inclined to fall back upon its world (the world in which it is) and to interpret itself in terms of that world by its reflected light, but also that Dasein simultaneously falls prey to the tradition of which it has more or less explicitly taken hold.[2] This tradition keeps it from providing its own guidance, whether in

1 'defizienter Modus'. Heidegger likes to think of certain characteristics as occurring in various ways or 'modes', among which may be included certain ways of 'not occurring' or 'occurring only to an inadequate extent' or, in general, occurring 'deficiently'. It is as if zero and the negative integers were to be thought of as representing 'deficient modes of being a positive integer'.

2 '... das Dasein hat nicht nur die Geneigtheit, an seine Welt, in der es ist, zu verfallen und reluzent aus ihr her sich auszulegen, Dasein verfällt in eins damit auch seiner mehr oder minder ausdrücklich ergriffenen Tradition.' The verb 'verfallen' is one which Heidegger will use many times. Though we shall usually translate it simply as 'fall', it has the connotation of *deteriorating, collapsing,* or *falling down.* Neither our 'fall back upon' nor our 'falls prey to' is quite right: but 'fall upon' and 'fall on to', which are more literal, would be misleading for 'an ... zu verfallen'; and though 'falls to the lot of' and 'devolves upon' would do well for 'verfällt' with the dative in other contexts, they will not do so well here.

inquiring or in choosing. This holds true—and by no means least—for that understanding which is rooted in Dasein's ownmost Being, and for the possibility of developing it—namely, for ontological understanding.

When tradition thus becomes master, it does so in such a way that what it 'transmits' is made so inaccessible, proximally and for the most part, that it rather becomes concealed. Tradition takes what has come down to us and delivers it over to self-evidence; it blocks our access to those primordial 'sources' from which the categories and concepts handed down to us have been in part quite genuinely drawn.[1] Indeed it makes us forget that they have had such an origin, and makes us suppose that the necessity of going back to these sources is something which we need not even understand. Dasein has had its historicality so thoroughly uprooted by tradition that it confines its interest to the multiformity of possible types, directions, and standpoints of philosophical activity in the most exotic and alien of cultures; and by this very interest it seeks to veil the fact that it has no ground of its own to stand on. Consequently, despite all its historiological interests and all its zeal for an Interpretation which is philologically 'objective' ["sachliche"], Dasein no longer understands the most elementary conditions which would alone enable it to go back to the past in a positive manner and make it productively its own.

We have shown at the outset (Section 1) not only that the question of the meaning of Being is one that has not been attended to and one that has been inadequately formulated, but that it has become quite forgotten in spite of all our interest in 'metaphysics'. Greek ontology and its history —which, in their numerous filiations and distortions, determine the conceptual character of philosophy even today—prove that when Dasein understands either itself or Being in general, it does so in terms of the 'world', and that the ontology which has thus arisen has deteriorated [verfällt] to a tradition in which it gets reduced to something self-evident —merely material for reworking, as it was for Hegel. In the Middle Ages this uprooted Greek ontology became a fixed body of doctrine. Its systematics, however, is by no means a mere joining together of traditional pieces into a single edifice. Though its basic conceptions of Being have been taken over dogmatically from the Greeks, a great deal of unpretentious work has been carried on further within these limits. With the peculiar character which the Scholastics gave it, Greek ontology has, in its essentials, travelled the path that leads through the *Disputationes metaphysicae* of Suarez to the 'metaphysics' and transcendental philosophy of modern times, determining even the foundations and the aims of Hegel's

22

---

[1] In this passage Heidegger juxtaposes a number of words beginning with the prefix 'über-': 'übergibt' ('transmits'); 'überantwortet' ('delivers over'); 'das Überkommene' ('what has come down to us'); 'überlieferten' ('handed down to us').

'logic'. In the course of this history certain distinctive domains of Being have come into view and have served as the primary guides for subsequent problematics: the *ego cogito* of Descartes, the subject, the "I", reason, spirit, person. But these all remain uninterrogated as to their Being and its structure, in accordance with the thoroughgoing way in which the question of Being has been neglected. It is rather the case that the categorial content of the traditional ontology has been carried over to these entities with corresponding formalizations and purely negative restrictions, or else dialectic has been called in for the purpose of Interpreting the substantiality of the subject ontologically.

If the question of Being is to have its own history made transparent, then this hardened tradition must be loosened up, and the concealments which it has brought about[1] must be dissolved. We understand this task as one in which by taking *the question of Being as our clue*, we are to *destroy* the traditional content of ancient ontology until we arrive at those primordial experiences in which we achieved our first ways of determining the nature of Being—the ways which have guided us ever since.

In thus demonstrating the origin of our basic ontological concepts by an investigation in which their 'birth certificate' is displayed, we have nothing to do with a vicious relativizing of ontological standpoints. But this destruction is just as far from having the *negative* sense of shaking off the ontological tradition. We must, on the contrary, stake out the positive possibilities of that tradition, and this always means keeping it within its *limits*; these in turn are given factically in the way the question is formulated at the time, and in the way the possible field for investigation is thus bounded off. On its negative side, this destruction does not relate itself towards the past; its criticism is aimed at 'today' and at the prevalent way of treating the history of ontology, whether it is headed towards doxography, towards intellectual history, or towards a history of problems. But to bury the past in nullity [Nichtigkeit] is not the purpose of this destruction; its aim is *positive*; its negative function remains unexpressed and indirect.

The destruction of the history of ontology is essentially bound up with the way the question of Being is formulated, and it is possible only within such a formulation. In the framework of our treatise, which aims at working out that question in principle, we can carry out this destruction only with regard to stages of that history which are in principle decisive.

In line with the positive tendencies of this destruction, we must in the first instance raise the question whether and to what extent the

---

[1] '. . . der durch sie gezeitigten Verdeckungen.' The verb 'zeitigen' will appear frequently in later chapters. See H. 304 and our note ad loc.

Interpretation of Being and the phenomenon of time have been brought together thematically in the course of the history of ontology, and whether the problematic of Temporality required for this has ever been worked out in principle or ever could have been. The first and only person who has gone any stretch of the way towards investigating the dimension of Temporality or has even let himself be drawn hither by the coercion of the phenomena themselves is Kant. Only when we have established the problematic of Temporality, can we succeed in casting light on the obscurity of his doctrine of the schematism. But this will also show us *why* this area is one which had to remain closed off to him in its real dimensions and its central ontological function. Kant himself was aware that he was venturing into an area of obscurity: 'This schematism of our understanding as regards appearances and their mere form is an art hidden in the depths of the human soul, the true devices of which are hardly ever to be divined from Nature and laid uncovered before our eyes.'[i] Here Kant shrinks back, as it were, in the face of something which must be brought to light as a theme and a principle if the expression "Being" is to have any demonstrable meaning. In the end, those very phenomena which will be exhibited under the heading of 'Temporality' in our analysis, are precisely those *most covert* judgments of the 'common reason' for which Kant says it is the 'business of philosophers' to provide an analytic.

In pursuing this task of destruction with the problematic of Temporality as our clue, we shall try to Interpret the chapter on the schematism and the Kantian doctrine of time, taking that chapter as our point of depar- 24
ture. At the same time we shall show why Kant could never achieve an insight into the problematic of Temporality. There were two things that stood in his way: in the first place, he altogether neglected the problem of Being; and, in connection with this, he failed to provide an ontology with Dasein as its theme or (to put this in Kantian language) to give a preliminary ontological analytic of the subjectivity of the subject. Instead of this, Kant took over Descartes' position quite dogmatically, notwithstanding all the essential respects in which he had gone beyond him. Furthermore, in spite of the fact that he was bringing the phenomenon of time back into the subject again, his analysis of it remained oriented towards the traditional way in which time had been ordinarily understood; in the long run this kept him from working out the phenomenon of a 'transcendental determination of time' in its own structure and function. Because of this double effect of tradition the decisive *connection* between *time* and the '*I think*' was shrouded in utter darkness; it did not even become a problem.

In taking over Descartes' ontological position Kant made an essential omission: he failed to provide an ontology of Dasein. This omission was a decisive one in the spirit [im Sinne] of Descartes' ownmost tendencies. With the '*cogito sum*' Descartes had claimed that he was putting philosophy on a new and firm footing. But what he left undetermined when he began in this 'radical' way, was the kind of Being which belongs to the *res cogitans*, or—more precisely—the *meaning of the Being of the '*sum*'.*[1] By working out the unexpressed ontological foundations of the '*cogito sum*', we shall complete our sojourn at the second station along the path of our destructive retrospect of the history of ontology. Our Interpretation will not only prove that Descartes had to neglect the question of Being altogether; it will also show why he came to suppose that the absolute 'Being-certain' ["Gewisssein"] of the *cogito* exempted him from raising the question of the meaning of the Being which this entity possesses.

Yet Descartes not only continued to neglect this and thus to accept a completely indefinite ontological status for the *res cogitans sive mens sive animus* ['the thing which cognizes, whether it be a mind or spirit']: he regarded this entity as a *fundamentum inconcussum*, and applied the medieval ontology to it in carrying through the fundamental considerations of his *Meditationes*. He defined the *res cogitans* ontologically as an *ens*; and in the medieval ontology the meaning of Being for such an *ens* had been fixed by understanding it as an *ens creatum*. God, as *ens infinitum*, was the *ens i n c r e a t u m*. But createdness [Geschaffenheit] in the widest sense of something's having been produced [Hergestelltheit], was an essential item in the structure of the ancient conception of Being. The seemingly new beginning which Descartes proposed for philosophizing has revealed itself as the implantation of a baleful prejudice, which has kept later generations from making any thematic ontological analytic of the 'mind' ["Gemütes"] such as would take the question of Being as a clue and would at the same time come to grips critically with the traditional ancient ontology.

Everyone who is acquainted with the middle ages sees that Descartes is 'dependent' upon medieval scholasticism and employs its terminology. But with this 'discovery' nothing is achieved philosophically as long as it remains obscure to what a profound extent the medieval ontology has influenced the way in which posterity has determined or failed to determine the ontological character of the *res cogitans*. The full extent of this cannot be estimated until both the meaning and the limitations of the ancient ontology have been exhibited in terms of an orientation directed

---

[1] We follow the later editions in reading '*der Seinssinn des "sum"* '. The earlier editions have an anacoluthic 'den' for 'der'.

towards the question of Being. In other words, in our process of destruction we find ourselves faced with the task of Interpreting the basis of the ancient ontology in the light of the problematic of Temporality. When this is done, it will be manifest that the ancient way of interpreting the Being of entities is oriented towards the 'world' or 'Nature' in the widest sense, and that it is indeed in terms of 'time' that its understanding of Being is obtained. The outward evidence for this (though of course it is *merely* outward evidence) is the treatment of the meaning of Being as παρουσία or οὐσία, which signifies, in ontologico-Temporal terms, 'presence' ["Anwesenheit"].[1] Entities are grasped in their Being as 'presence'; this means that they are understood with regard to a definite mode of time—the '*Present*'[2]

The problematic of Greek ontology, like that of any other, must take its clues from Dasein itself. In both ordinary and philosophical usage, Dasein, man's Being, is 'defined' as the ζῷον λόγον ἔχον—as that living thing whose Being is essentially determined by the potentiality for discourse.[3] λέγειν is the clue for arriving at those structures of Being which belong to the entities we encounter in addressing ourselves to anything or speaking about it [im Ansprechen und Besprechen]. (Cf. Section 7 B.) This is why the ancient ontology as developed by Plato turns into 'dialectic'. As the ontological clue gets progressively worked out—namely, in the 'hermeneutic' of the λόγος—it becomes increasingly possible to grasp the problem of Being in a more radical fashion. The 'dialectic', which has been a genuine philosophical embarrassment, becomes superfluous. That

---

[1] The noun οὐσία is derived from one of the stems used in conjugating the irregular verb εἶναι, ('to be'); in the Aristotelian tradition it is usually translated as 'substance', though translators of Plato are more likely to write 'essence', 'existence', or 'being'. Heidegger suggests that οὐσία is to be thought of as synonymous with the derivative noun παρουσία ('being-at', 'presence'). As he points out, παρουσία has a close etymological correspondence with the German 'Anwesenheit', which is similarly derived from the stem of a verb meaning 'to be' (Cf. O.H.G. 'wesan') and a prefix of the place or time at which ('an-'). We shall in general translate 'Anwesenheit' as 'presence', and the participle 'anwesend' as some form of the expression 'have presence'.

[2] 'die "*Gegenwart*"'. While this noun may, like παρουσία or 'Anwesenheit', mean the *presence* of someone *at* some place or on some occasion, it more often means the *present*, as distinguished from the past and the future. In its etymological root-structure, however, it means a *waiting-towards*. While Heidegger seems to think of all these meanings as somehow fused, we shall generally translate this noun as 'the Present', reserving 'in the present' for the corresponding adjective 'gegenwärtig'.

[3] The phrase ζῷον λόγον ἔχον is traditionally translated as 'rational animal', on the assumption that λόγος refers to the faculty of *reason*. Heidegger, however, points out that λόγος is derived from the same root as the verb λέγειν ('to talk', 'to hold discourse'); he identifies this in turn with νοεῖν ('to cognize', 'to be aware of', 'to know'), and calls attention to the fact that the same stem is found in the adjective διαλεκτικός ('dialectical'). (See also H. 165 below.) He thus interprets λόγος as 'Rede', which we shall usually translate as 'discourse' or 'talk', depending on the context. See Section 7 B below (H. 32 ff.) and Sections 34 and 35, where 'Rede' will be defined and distinguished both from 'Sprache' ('language') and from 'Gerede' ('idle talk') (H. 160 ff.).

is *why* Aristotle 'no longer has any understanding' of it, for he has put it on a more radical footing and raised it to a new level [aufhob]. λέγειν itself—or rather νοεῖν, that simple awareness of something present-at-hand in its sheer presence-at-hand,[1] which Parmenides had already taken to guide him in his own interpretation of Being—has the Temporal structure of a pure 'making-present' of something.[2] Those entities which show themselves in this and for it, and which are understood as entities in the most authentic sense, thus get interpreted with regard to the Present; that is, they are conceived as presence (οὐσία).[3]

Yet the Greeks have managed to interpret Being in this way without any explicit knowledge of the clues which function here, without any acquaintance with the fundamental ontological function of time or even any understanding of it, and without any insight into the reason why this function is possible. On the contrary, they take time itself as one entity among other entities, and try to grasp it in the structure of its Being, though that way of understanding Being which they have taken as their horizon is one which is itself naïvely and inexplicitly oriented towards time.

Within the framework in which we are about to work out the principles of the question of Being, we cannot present a detailed Temporal Interpretation of the foundations of ancient ontology, particularly not of its loftiest and purest scientific stage, which is reached in Aristotle. Instead we shall give an interpretation of Aristotle's essay on time,[ii] which may be chosen as providing a way of *discriminating* the basis and the limitations of the ancient science of Being.

Aristotle's essay on time is the first detailed Interpretation of this

---

[1] '. . . von etwas Vorhandenem in seiner puren Vorhandenheit . . .' The adjective 'vorhanden' means literally 'before the hand', but this signification has long since given way to others. In ordinary German usage it may, for instance, be applied to the stock of goods which a dealer has 'on hand', or to the 'extant' works of an author; and in earlier philosophical writing it could be used, like the word 'Dasein' itself, as a synonym for the Latin '*existentia*'. Heidegger, however, distinguishes quite sharply between 'Dasein' and 'Vorhandenheit', using the latter to designate a kind of Being which belongs to things *other* than Dasein. We shall translate 'vorhanden' as 'present-at-hand', and 'Vorhandenheit' as 'presence-at-hand'. The reader must be careful not to confuse these expressions with our 'presence' ('Anwesenheit') and 'the Present' ('die Gegenwart'), etc., or with a few other verbs and adjectives which we may find it convenient to translate by 'present'.

[2] '. . . des reinen "Gegenwärtigens" von etwas'. The verb 'gegenwärtigen', which is derived from the adjective 'gegenwärtig', is not a normal German verb, but was used by Husserl and is used extensively by Heidegger. While we shall translate it by various forms of 'make present', it does not necessarily mean 'making physically present', but often means something like 'bringing vividly to mind'.

[3] 'Das Seiende, das sich in ihm für es zeigt und das als das eigentliche Seiende verstanden wird, erhält demnach seine Auslegung in Rücksicht auf—Gegen-wart, d.h. es ist als Anwesenheit (οὐσία) begriffen.' The hyphenation of 'Gegen-wart' calls attention to the structure of this word in a way which cannot be reproduced in English. See note 2, p. 47, H. 25 above. The pronouns 'ihm' and 'es' presumably both refer back to λέγειν, though their reference is ambiguous, as our version suggests.

phenomenon which has come down to us. Every subsequent account of time, including Bergson's, has been essentially determined by it. When we analyse the Aristotelian conception, it will likewise become clear, as we go back, that the Kantian account of time operates within the structures which Aristotle has set forth; this means that Kant's basic ontological orientation remains that of the Greeks, in spite of all the distinctions which arise in a new inquiry.

The question of Being does not achieve its true concreteness until we have carried through the process of destroying the ontological tradition. In this way we can fully prove that the question of the meaning of Being is one that we cannot avoid, and we can demonstrate what it means to talk about 'restating' this question.

In any investigation in this field, where 'the thing itself is deeply veiled'[iii] one must take pains not to overestimate the results. For in such an inquiry one is constantly compelled to face the possibility of disclosing an even more primordial and more universal horizon from which we may draw the answer to the question, "What is '*Being*'?" We can discuss such possibilities seriously and with positive results only if the question of Being has been reawakened and we have arrived at a field where we can come to terms with it in a way that can be controlled.

¶ 7. *The Phenomenological Method of Investigation*

In provisionally characterizing the object which serves as the theme of our investigation (the Being of entities, or the meaning of Being in general), it seems that we have also delineated the method to be employed. The task of ontology is to explain Being itself and to make the Being of entities stand out in full relief. And the method of ontology remains questionable in the highest degree as long as we merely consult those ontologies which have come down to us historically, or other essays of that character. Since the term "ontology" is used in this investigation in a sense which is formally broad, any attempt to clarify the method of ontology by tracing its history is automatically ruled out.

When, moreover, we use the term "ontology", we are not talking about some definite philosophical discipline standing in interconnection with the others. Here one does not have to measure up to the tasks of some discipline that has been presented beforehand; on the contrary, only in terms of the objective necessities of definite questions and the kind of treatment which the 'things themselves' require, can one develop such a discipline.

With the question of the meaning of Being, our investigation comes up against the fundamental question of philosophy. This is one that must be treated *phenomenologically*. Thus our treatise does not subscribe to a 'standpoint' or represent any special 'direction'; for phenomenology is nothing of either sort, nor can it become so as long as it understands itself. The expression 'phenomenology' signifies primarily a *methodological conception*. This expression does not characterize the w h a t of the objects of philosophical research as subject-matter, but rather the *how* of that research. The more genuinely a methodological concept is worked out and the more comprehensively it determines the principles on which a science is to be conducted, all the more primordially is it rooted in the way we come to terms with the things themselves,[1] and the farther is it removed from what we call "technical devices", though there are many such devices even in the theoretical disciplines.

Thus the term 'phenomenology' expresses a maxim which can be formulated as 'To the things themselves!' It is opposed to all free-floating constructions and accidental findings; it is opposed to taking over any conceptions which only seem to have been demonstrated; it is opposed to those pseudo-questions which parade themselves as 'problems', often for generations at a time. Yet this maxim, one may rejoin, is abundantly self-evident, and it expresses, moreover, the underlying principle of any scientific knowledge whatsoever. Why should anything so self-evident be taken up explicitly in giving a title to a branch of research? In point of fact, the issue here is a kind of 'self-evidence' which we should like to bring closer to us, so far as it is important to do so in casting light upon the procedure of our treatise. We shall expound only the preliminary conception [Vorbegriff] of phenomenology.

This expression has two components: "phenomenon" and "logos". Both of these go back to terms from the Greek: φαινόμενον and λόγος. Taken superficially, the term "phenomenology" is formed like "theology", "biology", "sociology"—names which may be translated as "science of God", "science of life", "science of society". This would make phenomenology the *science of phenomena*. We shall set forth the preliminary conception of phenomenology by characterizing what one has in mind in the term's two components, 'phenomenon' and 'logos', and by establishing the meaning of the name in which these are *put together*. The history of

---

[1] The appeal to the 'Sachen selbst', which Heidegger presents as virtually a slogan for Husserl's phenomenology, is not easy to translate without giving misleading impressions. What Husserl has in mind is the 'things' that words may be found to signify when their significations are correctly intuited by the right kind of *Anschauung*. (Cf. his *Logische Untersuchungen*, vol. 2, part 1, second edition, Halle, 1913, p. 6.) We have followed Marvin Farber in adopting 'the things themselves'. (Cf. his *The Foundation of Phenomenology*, Cambridge, Mass., 1943, pp. 202-3.) The word 'Sache' will, of course, be translated in other ways also.

the word itself, which presumably arose in the Wolffian school, is here of
no significance.

A. *The Concept of Phenomenon*

The Greek expression φαινόμενον, to which the term 'phenomenon'
goes back, is derived from the verb φαίνεσθαι, which signifies "to show
itself". Thus φαινόμενον means that which shows itself, the manifest [das,
was sich zeigt, das Sichzeigende, das Offenbare]. φαίνεσθαι itself is a
middle-voiced form which comes from φαίνω—to bring to the light of
day, to put in the light. Φαίνω comes from the stem φα—, like φῶς, the
light, that which is bright—in other words, that wherein something can
become manifest, visible in itself. Thus we must *keep in mind* that the expression '*phenomenon*' signifies *that which shows itself in itself*, the manifest.
Accordingly the φαινόμενα or 'phenomena' are the totality of what lies
in the light of day or can be brought to the light—what the Greeks sometimes identified simply with τὰ ὄντα (entities). Now an entity can show
itself f r o m itself [von ihm selbst her] in many ways, depending in each
case on the kind of access we have to it. Indeed it is even possible for an
entity to show itself as something which in itself it is *not*. When it shows
itself in this way, it 'looks like something or other' ["sieht" . . . "so aus
wie . . ."]. This kind of showing-itself is what we call "*seeming*" [Scheinen].   29
Thus in Greek too the expression φαινόμενον ("phenomenon") signifies
that which looks like something, that which is 'semblant', 'semblance'
[das "Scheinbare", der "Schein"]. Φαινόμενον ἀγαθόν means something good which looks like, but 'in actuality' is not, what it gives itself
out to be. If we are to have any further understanding of the concept of
phenomenon, everything depends on our seeing how what is designated
in the first signification of φαινόμενον ('phenomenon' as that which shows
itself) and what is designated in the second ('phenomenon' as semblance)
are structurally interconnected. Only when the meaning of something is
such that it makes a pretension of showing itself—that is, of being a phenomenon—*can* it show itself *as* something which it is *not*; only then *can* it
'merely look like so-and-so'. When φαινόμενον signifies 'semblance', the
primordial signification (the phenomenon as the manifest) is already
included as that upon which the second signification is founded. We shall
allot the term 'phenomenon' to this positive and primordial signification
of φαινόμενον, and distinguish "phenomenon" from "semblance", which
is the privative modification of "phenomenon" as thus defined. But what
both these terms express has proximally nothing at all to do with what is
called an 'appearance', or still less a 'mere appearance'.[1]

---

[1] '. . . was man "Erscheinung" oder gar "blosse Erscheinung" nennt.' Though the
noun 'Erscheinung' and the verb 'erscheinen' behave so much like the English 'appearance' and 'appear' that the ensuing discussion presents relatively few difficulties in this

This is what one is talking about when one speaks of the 'symptoms of a disease' ["Krankheitserscheinungen"]. Here one has in mind certain occurrences in the body which show themselves and which, in showing themselves a s thus showing themselves, 'indicate' ["indizieren"] something which does *not* show itself. The emergence [Auftreten] of such occurrences, their showing-themselves, goes together with the Being-present-at-hand of disturbances which do not show themselves. Thus appearance, as the appearance 'of something', does *not* mean showing-itself; it means rather the announcing-itself by [von] something which does not show itself, but which announces itself through something which does show itself. Appearing is a *not-showing-itself*. But the 'not' we find here is by no means to be confused with the privative "not" which we used in defining the structure of semblance.[1] What appears does *not* show itself; and anything which thus fails to show itself, is also something which can never s e e m.[2] All indications, presentations, symptoms, and symbols have this basic formal structure of appearing, even though they differ among themselves.

respect for the translator, the passage shows some signs of hasty construction, and a few comments may be helpful. We are told several times that 'appearance' and 'phenomenon' are to be sharply distinguished; yet we are also reminded that there is a sense in which they coincide, and even this sense seems to be twofold, though it is not clear that Heidegger is fully aware of this. The whole discussion is based upon two further distinctions: the distinction between 'showing' ('zeigen') and 'announcing' ('melden') and 'bringing forth' ('hervorbringen'), and the distinction between ('x') that which 'shows itself' ('das Sichzeigende') or which 'does the announcing' ('das Meldende') or which 'gets brought forth' ('das Hervorgebrachte'), and ('y') that which 'announces itself' ('das Sichmeldende') or which does the bringing-forth. Heidegger is thus able to introduce the following senses of 'Erscheinung' or 'appearance':

    1a. an observable event *y*, such as a symptom which announces a disease *x* by showing itself, and in or through which *x* announces itself without showing itself;

    1b. *y*'s showing-itself;

    2. *x*'s announcing-itself in or through *y*;

    3a. the 'mere appearance' *y* which *x* may *bring forth* when *x* is of such a kind that its real nature can *never* be made manifest;

    3b. the 'mere appearance' which is the *bringing-forth* of a 'mere appearance' in sense 3a. Heidegger makes abundantly clear that sense 2 is the proper sense of 'appearance' and that senses 3a and 3b are the proper senses of 'mere appearance'. On H. 30 and 31 he concedes that sense 1b corresponds to the primordial sense of 'phenomenon'; but his discussion on H. 28 suggests that sense 1a corresponds to this more accurately, and he reverts to this position towards the end of H. 30.

[1] '. . . als welches es die Struktur des Scheins bestimmt.' (The older editions omit the 'es'.)

[2] 'Was sich in *der* Weise *nicht* zeigt, wie das Erscheinende, kann auch nie scheinen.' This passage is ambiguous, but presumably 'das Erscheinende' is to be interpreted as the *x* of our note 1, p. 51, not our *y*. The reader should notice that our standardized translation of 'scheinen' as 'seem' is one which here becomes rather misleading, even though these words correspond fairly well in ordinary usage. In distinguishing between 'scheinen' and 'erscheinen', Heidegger seems to be insisting that 'scheinen' can be done only by the *y* which 'shows itself' or 'does the announcing', not by the *x* which 'announces itself' in or through *y*, even though German usage does not differentiate these verbs quite so sharply.

In spite of the fact that 'appearing' is never a showing-itself in the sense of "phenomenon", appearing is possible only *by reason of a showing-itself of something*. But this showing-itself, which helps to make possible the appearing, is not the appearing itself. Appearing is an *announcing-itself* [das Sich-*melden*] through something that shows itself. If one then says that with the word 'appearance' we allude to something wherein something appears without being itself an appearance, one has not thereby defined the concept of phenomenon: one has rather *presupposed* it. This presupposition, however, remains concealed; for when one says this sort of thing about 'appearance', the expression 'appear' gets used in two ways. "That wherein something 'appears' " means that wherein something announces itself, and therefore does not show itself; and in the words [Rede] 'without being itself an "appearance" ', "appearance" signifies the *showing-itself.* But this showing-itself belongs essentially to the 'wherein' in which something announces itself. According to this, phenomena are *never appearances*, though on the other hand every appearance is dependent on phenomena. If one defines "phenomenon" with the aid of a conception of 'appearance' which is still unclear, then everything is stood on its head, and a 'critique' of phenomenology on this basis is surely a remarkable undertaking.

So again the expression 'appearance' itself can have a double signification: first, *appearing*, in the sense of announcing-itself, as not-showing-itself; and next, that which does the announcing [das Meldende selbst]—that which in its showing-itself indicates something which does not show itself. And finally one can use "appearing" as a term for the genuine sense of "phenomenon" as showing-itself. If one designates these three different things as 'appearance', bewilderment is unavoidable.

But this bewilderment is essentially increased by the fact that 'appearance' can take on still another signification. That which does the announcing—that which, in its showing-itself, indicates something non-manifest—may be taken as that which emerges in what is itself non-manifest, and which emanates [ausstrahlt] from it in such a way indeed that the non-manifest gets thought of as something that is essentially *never* manifest. When that which does the announcing is taken this way, "appearance" is tantamount to a "bringing forth" or "something brought forth", but something which does not make up the real Being of what brings it forth: here we have an appearance in the sense of 'mere appearance'. That which does the announcing and is brought forth does, of course, show itself, and in such a way that, as an emanation of what it announces, it keeps this very thing constantly veiled in itself. On the other hand, this not-showing which veils is not a semblance. Kant uses the term "appearance" in this twofold way. According to him "appearances" are, in the first place, the 'objects of empirical intuition': they are what shows itself in such intuition. But what thus shows itself (the "phenomenon" in the genuine primordial sense) is at the same time an 'appearance' as an emanation of something which *hides* itself in that appearance—an emanation which announces.

In so far as a phenomenon is constitutive for 'appearance' in the signification of announcing itself through something which shows itself, though such a phenomenon can privatively take the variant form of semblance, appearance too can become mere semblance. In a certain kind of lighting someone can look as if his cheeks were flushed with red; and the redness which shows itself can be taken as an announcement of the Being-present-at-hand of a fever, which in turn indicates some disturbance in the organism.

"*Phenomenon*", the showing-itself-in-itself, signifies a distinctive way in which something can be encountered.[1] "*Appearance*", on the other hand, means a reference-relationship which i s in an entity itself,[2] and which is such that what *does the referring* (or the announcing) can fulfil its possible function only if it shows itself in itself and is thus a 'phenomenon'. Both appearance and semblance are founded upon the phenomenon, though in different ways. The bewildering multiplicity of 'phenomena' designated by the words "phenomenon", "semblance", "appearance", "mere appearance", cannot be disentangled unless the concept of the phenomenon is understood from the beginning as that which shows itself in itself.

If in taking the concept of "phenomenon" this way, we leave indefinite which entities we consider as "phenomena", and leave it open whether what shows itself is an entity or rather some characteristic which an entity may have in its Being, then we have merely arrived at the *formal* conception of "phenomenon". If by "that which shows itself" we understand those entities which are accessible through the empirical "intuition" in, let us say, Kant's sense, then the formal conception of "phenomenon" will indeed be legitimately employed. In this usage "phenomenon" has the signification of the *ordinary* conception of phenomenon. But this ordinary conception is not the phenomenological conception. If we keep within the horizon of the Kantian problematic, we can give an illustration of what is conceived phenomenologically as a "phenomenon", with reservations as to other differences; for we may then say that that which already shows itself in the appearance as prior to the "phenomenon" as

[1] '. . . eine ausgezeichnete Begegnisart von etwas.' The noun 'Begegnis' is derived from the verb 'begegnen', which is discussed in note 2, p. 70, H. 44 below.
[2] '. . . einen seienden Verweisungsbezug im Seienden selbst . . .' The verb 'verweisen', which we shall translate as 'refer' or 'assign', depending upon the context, will receive further attention in Section 17 below. See also our note 2, p. 97, H. 68 below.

ordinarily understood and as accompanying it in every case, can, even though it thus shows itself unthematically, be brought thematically to show itself; and what thus shows itself in itself (the 'forms of the intuition') will be the "phenomena" of phenomenology. For manifestly space and time must be able to show themselves in this way—they must be able to become phenomena—if Kant is claiming to make a transcendental assertion grounded in the facts when he says that space is the *a priori* "inside-which" of an ordering.[1]

If, however, the phenomenological conception of phenomenon is to be understood at all, regardless of how much closer we may come to determining the nature of that which shows itself, this presupposes inevitably that we must have an insight into the meaning of the formal conception of phenomenon and its legitimate employment in an ordinary signification.—But before setting up our preliminary conception of phenomenology, we must also define the signification of λόγος so as to make clear in what sense phenomenology can be a 'science of' phenomena at all.

32

B. *The Concept of the Logos*

In Plato and Aristotle the concept of the λόγος has many competing significations, with no basic signification positively taking the lead. In fact, however, this is only a semblance, which will maintain itself as long as our Interpretation is unable to grasp the basic signification properly in its primary content. If we say that the basic signification of λόγος is "discourse",[2] then this word-for-word translation will not be validated until we have determined what is meant by "discourse" itself. The real signification of "discourse", which is obvious enough, gets constantly covered up by the later history of the word λόγος, and especially by the numerous and arbitrary Interpretations which subsequent philosophy has provided. Λόγος gets 'translated' (and this means that it is always getting interpreted) as "reason", "judgment", "concept", "definition", "ground", or "relationship".[3] But how can 'discourse' be so susceptible of modification that λόγος can signify all the things we have listed, and in good scholarly usage? Even if λόγος is understood in the sense of "assertion", but of "assertion" as 'judgment', this seemingly legitimate translation may still miss the fundamental signification, especially if "judgment" is conceived in a sense taken over from some contemporary 'theory of judgment'. Λόγος does not mean "judgment", and it certainly does not mean this

---

1 Cf. *Critique of Pure Reason*², 'Transcendental Aesthetic', Section I, p. 34.

2 On λόγος, 'Rede', etc., see note 3, p. 47, H. 25 above.

3 '. . . Vernunft, Urteil, Begriff, Definition, Grund, Verhältnis.'

primarily—if one understands by "judgment" a way of 'binding' something with something else, or the 'taking of a stand' (whether by acceptance or by rejection).

Λόγος as "discourse" means rather the same as δηλοῦν: to make manifest what one is 'talking about' in one's discourse.[1] Aristotle has explicated this function of discourse more precisely as ἀποφαίνεσθαι.[iv] The λόγος lets something be seen (φαίνεσθαι), namely, what the discourse is about; and it does so either *for* the one who is doing the talking (the *medium*) or for persons who are talking with one another, as the case may be. Discourse 'lets something be seen' ἀπό . . .: that is, it lets us see something from the very thing which the discourse is about.[2] In discourse (ἀπόφανσις), so far as it is genuine, *what* is said [*was* geredet ist] is drawn *from* what the talk is about, so that discursive communication, in what it says [in ihrem Gesagten], makes manifest what it is talking about, and thus makes this accessible to the other party. This is the structure of the λόγος as ἀπόφανσις. This mode of making manifest in the sense of letting something be seen by pointing it out, does not go with all kinds of 'discourse'. Requesting (εὐχή), for instance, also makes manifest, but in a different way.

When fully concrete, discoursing (letting something be seen) has the character of speaking [Sprechens]—vocal proclamation in words. The λόγος is φωνή, and indeed, φωνὴ μετὰ φαντασίας—an utterance in which something is sighted in each case.

And only *because* the function of the λόγος as ἀπόφανσις lies in letting something be seen by pointing it out, can the λόγος have the structural form of σύνθεσις. Here "synthesis" does not mean a binding and linking together of representations, a manipulation of psychical occurrences where the 'problem' arises of how these bindings, as something inside, agree with something physical outside. Here the συν has a purely apophantical signification and means letting something be seen in its *togetherness* [Beisammen] with something—letting it be seen *as* something.

Furthermore, because the λόγος is a letting-something-be-seen, it can *therefore* be true or false. But here everything depends on our steering clear of any conception of truth which is construed in the sense of 'agreement'. This idea is by no means the primary one in the concept of ἀλήθεια. The 'Being-true' of the λόγος as ἀληθεύειν means that in λέγειν as ἀποφαίνεσθαι the entities *of which* one is talking must be taken out of their hiddenness; one must let them be seen as something unhidden (ἀληθές);

[1] '. . . offenbar machen das, wovon in der Rede "die Rede" ist.'
[2] '. . . von dem selbst her, wovon die Rede ist.'

that is, they must be *discovered*.[1] Similarly, 'Being false' (ψεύδεσθαι) amounts to deceiving in the sense of *covering up* [*verdecken*] : putting something in front of something (in such a way as to let it be seen) and thereby passing it off *as* something which it is *not*.

But because 'truth' has this meaning, and because the λόγος is a definite mode of letting something be seen, the λόγος is just *not* the kind of thing that can be considered as the primary 'locus' of truth. If, as has become quite customary nowadays, one defines "truth" as something that 'really' pertains to judgment,[2] and if one then invokes the support of Aristotle with this thesis, not only is this unjustified, but, above all, the Greek conception of truth has been misunderstood. Αἴσθησις, the sheer sensory perception of something, is 'true' in the Greek sense, and indeed more primordially than the λόγος which we have been discussing. Just as seeing aims at colours, any αἴσθησις aims at its ἴδια (those entities which are genuinely accessible only *through* it and *for* it); and to that extent this perception is always true. This means that seeing always discovers colours, and hearing always discovers sounds. Pure νοεῖν is the perception of the simplest determinate ways of Being which entities as such may possess, and it perceives them just by looking at them.[3] This νοεῖν is what is 'true' in the purest and most primordial sense; that is to say, it merely discovers, and it does so in such a way that it can never cover up. This νοεῖν can never cover up; it can never be false; it can at worst remain a *non-perceiving*, ἀγνοεῖν, not sufficing for straightforward and appropriate access.

When something no longer takes the form of just letting something be seen, but is always harking back to something else to which it points, so that it lets something be seen *as* something, it thus acquires a synthesis-structure, and with this it takes over the possibility of covering up.[4] The 'truth of judgments', however, is merely the opposite of this covering-up, a secondary phenomenon of truth, *with more than one kind of foundation*.[5] Both realism and idealism have—with equal thoroughness—missed the meaning of the Greek conception of truth, in terms of which only the

34

---

[1] The Greek words for 'truth' (ἡ ἀλήθεια, τὸ ἀληθές) are compounded of the privative prefix ἀ- ('not') and the verbal stem -λαθ- ('to escape notice', 'to be concealed'). The truth may thus be looked upon as that which is un-concealed, that which gets discovered or uncovered ('entdeckt').

[2] 'Wenn man . . . Wahrheit als das bestimmt, was "eigentlich" dem Urteil zukommt . . .'

[3] '. . . das schlicht hinsehende Vernehmen der einfachsten Seinsbestimmungen des Seienden als solchen.'

[4] 'Was nicht mehr die Vollzugsform des reinen Sehenlassens hat, sondern je im Aufweisen auf ein anderes rekurriert und so je etwas *als* etwas sehen lässt, das übernimmt mit dieser Synthesisstruktur die Möglichkeit des Verdeckens.'

[5] '. . . ein *mehrfach fundiertes* Phänomen von Wahrheit.' A 'secondary' or 'founded' phenomenon is one which is based upon something else. The notion of 'Fundierung' is one which Heidegger has taken over from Husserl. See our note 1, p. 86, on H. 59 below.

possibility of something like a 'doctrine of ideas' can be understood as philosophical *knowledge*.

And because the function of the λόγος lies in merely letting something be seen, in *letting* entities be *perceived* [im *Vernehmenlassen des Seienden*], λόγος can signify the *reason* [*Vernunft*]. And because, moreover, λόγος is used not only with the signification of λέγειν but also with that of λεγόμενον (that which is exhibited, as such), and because the latter is nothing else than the ὑποκείμενον which, as present-at-hand, already lies at the *bottom* [zum *Grunde*] of any procedure of addressing oneself to it or discussing it, λόγος qua λεγόμενον means the ground, the *ratio*. And finally, because λόγος as λεγόμενον can also signify that which, as something to which one addresses oneself, becomes visible in its relation to something in its 'relatedness', λόγος acquires the signification of *relation* and *relationship*.[1]

This Interpretation of 'apophantical discourse' may suffice to clarify the primary function of the λόγος.

C. *The Preliminary Conception of Phenomenology*

When we envisage concretely what we have set forth in our Interpretation of 'phenomenon' and 'logos', we are struck by an inner relationship between the things meant by these terms. The expression "phenomenology" may be formulated in Greek as λέγειν τὰ φαινόμενα, where λέγειν means ἀποφαίνεσθαι. Thus "phenomenology" means ἀποφαίνεσθαι τὰ φαινόμενα—to let that which shows itself be seen from itself in the very way in which it shows itself from itself. This is the formal meaning of that branch of research which calls itself "phenomenology". But here we are expressing nothing else than the maxim formulated above: 'To the things themselves!'

Thus the term "phenomenology" is quite different in its meaning from expressions such as "theology" and the like. Those terms designate the

[1] Heidegger is here pointing out that the word λόγος is etymologically akin to the verb λέγειν, which has among its numerous meanings those of *laying out, exhibiting, setting forth, recounting, telling a tale, making a statement*. Thus λόγος as λέγειν can be thought of as the faculty of reason ('Vernunft') which makes such activities possible. But λόγος can also mean τὸ λεγόμενον (*that which* is laid out, exhibited, set forth, told); in this sense it is the underlying subject matter (τὸ ὑποκείμενον) to which one addresses oneself and which one discusses ('Ansprechen und Besprechen'); as such it lies 'at the bottom' ('zum Grunde') of what is exhibited or told, and is thus the 'ground' or 'reason' ('Grund') for telling it. But when something is exhibited or told, it is exhibited in its *relatedness* ('in seiner Bezogenheit'); and in this way λόγος as λεγόμενον comes to stand for just such a relation or relationship ('Beziehung und Verhältnis'). The three senses here distinguished correspond to three senses of the Latin '*ratio*', by which λόγος was traditionally translated, though Heidegger explicitly calls attention to only one of these. Notice that 'Beziehung' (which we translate as 'relation') can also be used in some contexts where 'Ansprechen' (our 'addressing oneself') would be equally appropriate. Notice further that 'Verhältnis' (our 'relationship'), which is ordinarily a synonym for 'Beziehung', can, like λόγος and '*ratio*', also refer to the special kind of relationship which one finds in a mathematical proportion. The etymological connection between 'Vernehmen' and 'Vernunft' should also be noted.

objects of their respective sciences according to the subject-matter which they comprise at the time [in ihrer jeweiligen Sachhaltigkeit]. 'Phenomenology' neither designates the object of its researches, nor characterizes the subject-matter thus comprised. The word merely informs us of the "*how*" with which *what* is to be treated in this science gets exhibited and handled. To have a science 'of' phenomena means to grasp its objects *in such a way* that everything about them which is up for discussion must be treated by exhibiting it directly and demonstrating it directly.[1] The expression 'descriptive phenomenology', which is at bottom tautological, has the same meaning. Here "description" does not signify such a procedure as we find, let us say, in botanical morphology; the term has rather the sense of a prohibition—the avoidance of characterizing anything without such demonstration. The character of this description itself, the specific meaning of the λόγος, can be established first of all in terms of the 'thinghood' ["Sachheit"] of what is to be 'described'—that is to say, of what is to be given scientific definiteness as we encounter it phenomenally. The signification of "phenomenon", as conceived both formally and in the ordinary manner, is such that any exhibiting of an entity as it shows itself in itself, may be called "phenomenology" with formal justification.

35

Now what must be taken into account if the formal conception of phenomenon is to be deformalized into the phenomenological one, and how is this latter to be distinguished from the ordinary conception? What is it that phenomenology is to 'let us see'? What is it that must be called a 'phenomenon' in a distinctive sense? What is it that by its very essence is *necessarily* the theme whenever we exhibit something *explicitly*? Manifestly, it is something that proximally and for the most part does *not* show itself at all: it is something that lies *hidden*, in contrast to that which proximally and for the most part does show itself; but at the same time it is something that belongs to what thus shows itself, and it belongs to it so essentially as to constitute its meaning and its ground.

Yet that which remains *hidden* in an egregious sense, or which relapses and gets *covered up* again, or which shows itself only '*in disguise*', is not just this entity or that, but rather the *Being* of entities, as our previous observations have shown. This Being can be covered up so extensively that it becomes forgotten and no question arises about it or about its meaning. Thus that which demands that it become a phenomenon, and which demands this in a distinctive sense and in terms of its ownmost content as a thing, is what phenomenology has taken into its grasp thematically as its object.

[1] . . . in direkter Aufweisung und direkter Ausweisung . . .'

Phenomenology is our way of access to what is to be the theme of ontology, and it is our way of giving it demonstrative precision. *Only as phenomenology, is ontology possible.* In the phenomenological conception of "phenomenon" what one has in mind as that which shows itself is the Being of entities, its meaning, its modifications and derivatives.[1] And this showing-itself is not just any showing-itself, nor is it some such thing as appearing. Least of all can the Being of entities ever be anything such that 'behind it' stands something else 'which does not appear'.

'Behind' the phenomena of phenomenology there is essentially nothing else; on the other hand, what is to become a phenomenon can be hidden. And just because the phenomena are proximally and for the most part *not* given, there is need for phenomenology. Covered-up-ness is the counter-concept to 'phenomenon'.

There are various ways in which phenomena can be covered up. In the first place, a phenomenon can be covered up in the sense that it is still quite *undiscovered*. It is neither known nor unknown.[2] Moreover, a phenomenon can be *buried over* [*verschüttet*]. This means that it has at some time been discovered but has deteriorated [verfiel] to the point of getting covered up again. This covering-up can become complete; or rather—and as a rule—what has been discovered earlier may still be visible, though only as a semblance. Yet so much semblance, so much 'Being'.[3] This covering-up as a 'disguising' is both the most frequent and the most dangerous, for here the possibilities of deceiving and misleading are especially stubborn. Within a 'system', perhaps, those structures of Being—and their concepts—which are still available but veiled in their indigenous character, may claim their rights. For when they have been bound together constructively in a system, they present themselves as something 'clear', requiring no further justification, and thus can serve as the point of departure for a process of deduction.

The covering-up itself, whether in the sense of hiddenness, burying-over, or disguise, has in turn two possibilities. There are coverings-up which are accidental; there are also some which are necessary, grounded in what the thing discovered consists in [der Bestandart des Entdeckten]. Whenever a phenomenological concept is drawn from primordial sources,

---

[1] 'Der phänomenologische Begriff von Phänomen meint als das Sichzeigende das Sein des Seienden, seinen Sinn, seine Modifikationen und Derivate.'

[2] 'Über seinen Bestand gibt es weder Kenntnis noch Unkenntnis.' The earlier editions have 'Erkenntnis' where the latter ones have 'Unkenntnis'. The word 'Bestand' always presents difficulties in Heidegger; here it permits either of two interpretations, which we have deliberately steered between: 'Whether there *is* any such thing, is neither known nor unknown', and 'What it comprises is something of which we have neither knowledge nor ignorance.'

[3] 'Wieviel Schein jedoch, soviel "Sein".'

there is a possibility that it may degenerate if communicated in the form of an assertion. It gets understood in an empty way and is thus passed on, losing its indigenous character, and becoming a free-floating thesis. Even in the concrete work of phenomenology itself there lurks the possibility that what has been primordially 'within our grasp' may become hardened so that we can no longer grasp it. And the difficulty of this kind of research lies in making it self-critical in a positive sense.

The way in which Being and its structures are encountered in the mode of phenomenon is one which must first of all be *wrested* from the objects of phenomenology. Thus the very *point of departure* [*Ausgang*] for our analysis requires that it be secured by the proper method, just as much as does our *access* [*Zugang*] to the phenomenon, or our *passage* [*Durchgang*] through whatever is prevalently covering it up. The idea of grasping and explicating phenomena in a way which is 'original' and 'intuitive' ["*originären*" und "*intuitiven*"] is directly opposed to the *naïveté* of a haphazard, 'immediate', and unreflective 'beholding'. ["*Schauen*"].

Now that we have delimited our preliminary conception of phenomenology, the terms '*phenomenal*' and '*phenomenological*' can also be fixed in their signification. That which is given and explicable in the way the phenomenon is encountered is called 'phenomenal'; this is what we have in mind when we talk about "phenomenal structures". Everything which belongs to the species of exhibiting and explicating and which goes to make up the way of conceiving demanded by this research, is called 'phenomenological'.

Because phenomena, as understood phenomenologically, are never anything but what goes to make up Being, while Being is in every case the Being of some entity, we must first bring forward the entities themselves if it is our aim that Being should be laid bare; and we must do this in the right way. These entities must likewise show themselves with the kind of access which genuinely belongs to them. And in this way the ordinary conception of phenomenon becomes phenomenologically relevant. If our analysis is to be authentic, its aim is such that the prior task of assuring ourselves 'phenomenologically' of that entity which is to serve as our example, has already been prescribed as our point of departure.

With regard to its subject-matter, phenomenology is the science of the Being of entities—ontology. In explaining the tasks of ontology we found it necessary that there should be a fundamental ontology taking as its theme that entity which is ontologico-ontically distinctive, Dasein, in order to confront the cardinal problem—the question of the meaning of Being in general. Our investigation itself will show that the meaning of phenomenological description as a method lies in *interpretation*. The λόγος of the phenomenology of Dasein has the character of a ἑρμηνεύειν, through which the authentic meaning of Being, and also those basic structures of Being which Dasein itself possesses, are *made known* to Dasein's understanding of Being. The phenomenology of Dasein is a *hermeneutic* in the primordial signification of this word, where it designates this business of interpreting. But to the extent that by uncovering the meaning of Being and the basic structures of Dasein in general we may exhibit the horizon for any further ontological study of those entities which do not have the character of Dasein, this hermeneutic also becomes a 'hermeneutic' in the sense of working out the conditions on which the possibility of any onto-logical investigation depends. And finally, to the extent that Dasein, as an entity with the possibility of existence, has ontological priority over every other entity, "hermeneutic", as an interpretation of Dasein's Being, has the third and specific sense of an analytic of the existentiality of existence; and this is the sense which is philosophically *primary*. Then so far as this hermeneutic works out Dasein's historicality ontologically as the ontical condition for the possibility of historiology, it contains the roots of what can be called 'hermeneutic' only in a derivative sense: the methodology of those humane sciences which are historiological in character.

Being, as the basic theme of philosophy, is no class or genus of entities; yet it pertains to every entity. Its 'universality' is to be sought higher up. Being and the structure of Being lie beyond every entity and every possible character which an entity may possess. *Being is the transcendens pure and simple.*[1] And the transcendence of Dasein's Being is distinctive in that it implies the possibility and the necessity of the most radical *individuation*. Every disclosure of Being as the *transcendens* is *transcendental* knowledge. *Phenomenological truth* (*the disclosedness of Being*) *is veritas transcendentalis.*

Ontology and phenomenology are not two distinct philosophical disciplines among others. These terms characterize philosophy itself with regard to its object and its way of treating that object. Philosophy is universal phenomenological ontology, and takes its departure from the hermeneutic of Dasein, which, as an analytic of *existence*, has made fast the guiding-line for all philosophical inquiry at the point where it *arises* and to which it *returns*.

The following investigation would not have been possible if the ground had not been prepared by Edmund Husserl, with whose *Logische Unter-suchungen* phenomenology first emerged. Our comments on the preliminary conception of phenomenology have shown that what is essential in it

---

[1] 'Sein und Seinsstruktur liegen über jedes Seiende and jede mögliche seiende Bestim-mtheit eines Seienden hinaus. *Sein ist das transcendens schlechthin.*'

does not lie in its *actuality* as a philosophical 'movement' ["Richtung"].
Higher than actuality stands *possibility*. We can understand phenomenology only by seizing upon it as a possibility.[v]

With regard to the awkwardness and 'inelegance' of expression in the
analyses to come, we may remark that it is one thing to give a report
in which we tell about *entities*, but another to grasp entities in their *Being*.   39
For the latter task we lack not only most of the words but, above all, the
'grammar'. If we may allude to some earlier researches on the analysis
of Being, incomparable on their own level, we may compare the ontological sections of Plato's *Parmenides* or the fourth chapter of the seventh
book of Aristotle's *Metaphysics* with a narrative section from Thucydides;
we can then see the altogether unprecedented character of those formulations which were imposed upon the Greeks by their philosophers. And
where our powers are essentially weaker, and where moreover the area
of Being to be disclosed is ontologically far more difficult than that which
was presented to the Greeks, the harshness of our expression will be
enhanced, and so will the minuteness of detail with which our concepts
are formed.

¶ 8. *Design of the Treatise*

The question of the meaning of Being is the most universal and the
emptiest of questions, but at the same time it is possible to individualize
it very precisely for any particular Dasein. If we are to arrive at the basic
concept of 'Being' and to outline the ontological conceptions which it
requires and the variations which it necessarily undergoes, we need a clue
which is concrete. We shall proceed towards the concept of Being by way
of an Interpretation of a certain special entity, Dasein, in which we
shall arrive at the horizon for the understanding of Being and for the
possibility of interpreting it; the universality of the concept of Being is
not belied by the relatively 'special' character of our investigation.
But this very entity, Dasein, is in itself 'historical', so that its ownmost ontological elucidation necessarily becomes an 'historiological'
Interpretation.

Accordingly our treatment of the question of Being branches out into
two distinct tasks, and our treatise will thus have two parts:

Part One: the Interpretation of Dasein in terms of temporality, and the
explication of time as the transcendental horizon for the question of
Being.

Part Two: basic features of a phenomenological destruction of the
history of ontology, with the problematic of Temporality as our clue.

Part One has *three divisions*

1. the preparatory fundamental analysis of Dasein;
2. Dasein and temporality;
3. time and Being.[1]

40   Part Two likewise has *three divisions :*[1]

1. Kant's doctrine of schematism and time, as a preliminary stage in a problematic of Temporality;
2. the ontological foundation of Descartes' *'cogito sum'*, and how the medieval ontology has been taken over into the problematic of the *'res cogitans'*;
3. Aristotle's essay on time, as providing a way of discriminating the phenomenal basis and the limits of ancient ontology.

[1] Part Two and the third division of Part One have never appeared.

THE INTERPRETATION OF DASEIN IN TERMS OF TEMPORALITY, AND THE EXPLICATION OF TIME AS THE TRANSCENDENTAL HORIZON FOR THE QUESTION OF BEING

DIVISION ONE

PREPARATORY FUNDAMENTAL ANALYSIS OF DASEIN

In the question about the meaning of Being, what is primarily interrogated is those entities which have the character of Dasein. The preparatory existential analytic of Dasein must, in accordance with its peculiar character, be expounded in outline, and distinguished from other kinds of investigation which seem to run parallel (Chapter 1.) Adhering to the procedure which we have fixed upon for starting our investigation, we must lay bare a fundamental structure in Dasein: Being-in-the-world (Chapter 2). In the interpretation of Dasein, this structure is something '*a priori*'; it is not pieced together, but is primordially and constantly a whole. It affords us, however, various ways of looking at the items which are constitutive for it. The whole of this structure always comes first; but if we keep this constantly in view, these items, as phenomena, will be made to stand out. And thus we shall have as objects for analysis: the world in its worldhood (Chapter 3), Being-in-the-world as Being-with and Being-one's-Self (Chapter 4), and Being-in as such (Chapter 5). By analysis of this fundamental structure, the Being of Dasein can be indicated provisionally. Its existential meaning is *care* (Chapter 6).

I

EXPOSITION OF THE TASK OF A PREPARATORY ANALYSIS OF DASEIN

¶ *9. The Theme of the Analytic of Dasein*

WE are ourselves the entities to be analysed. The Being of any such entity is *in each case mine*.[1] These entities, in their Being, comport themselves towards their Being. As entities with such Being, they are delivered over to their own Being.[2] Being is that which is an issue for every such entity.[3] This way of characterizing Dasein has a double consequence:

1. The 'essence' ["Wesen"] of this entity lies in its "to be" [Zu-sein]. Its Being-what-it-is [Was-sein] (*essentia*) must, so far as we can speak of it at all, be conceived in terms of its Being (*existentia*). But here our ontological task is to show that when we choose to designate the Being of this entity as "existence" [Existenz], this term does not and cannot have the ontological signification of the traditional term "*existentia*"; ontologically, *existentia* is tantamount to *Being-present-at-hand*, a kind of Being which is essentially inappropriate to entities of Dasein's character. To avoid getting bewildered, we shall always use the Interpretative expression "*presence-at-hand*" for the term "*existentia*", while the term "existence", as a designation of Being, will be allotted solely to Dasein.

The 'essence' of Dasein lies in its existence. Accordingly those characteristics which can be exhibited in this entity are not 'properties' present-at-hand of some entity which 'looks' so and so and is itself present-at-hand; they are in each case possible ways for it to be, and no more than that. All the Being-as-it-is [So-sein] which this entity possesses is primarily Being. So when we designate this entity with the term 'Dasein', we are expressing not its "what" (as if it were a table, house or tree) but its Being.

2. That Being which is an *issue* for this entity in its very Being, is in each case mine. Thus Dasein is never to be taken ontologically as an

---

42

[1] 'Das Seiende, dessen Analyse zur Aufgabe steht, sind wir je selbst. Das Sein dieses Seienden ist *je meines*.' The reader must not get the impression that there is anything solipsistic about the second of these sentences. The point is merely that the kind of Being which belongs to Dasein is of a sort which any of us may call his own.

[2] 'Als Seiendes dieses Seins ist es seinem eigenen Sein überantwortet.' The earlier editions read '. . . seinem eigenen Zu-sein . . .'

[3] See note 2, p. 28, H. 8 above.

instance or special case of some genus of entities as things that are present-at-hand.[1] To entities such as these, their Being is 'a matter of indifference';[2] or more precisely, they 'are' such that their Being can be neither a matter of indifference to them, nor the opposite. Because Dasein has *in each case mineness* [*Jemeinigkeit*], one must always use a *personal* pronoun when one addresses it: 'I am', 'you are'.

Furthermore, in each case Dasein is mine to be in one way or another. Dasein has always made some sort of decision as to the way in which it is in each case mine [je meines]. That entity which in its Being has this very Being as an issue, comports itself towards its Being as its ownmost possibility. In each case Dasein *is* its possibility, and it 'has' this possibility, but not just as a property [eigenschaftlich], as something present-at-hand would. And because Dasein is in each case essentially its own possibility, it *can*, in its very Being, 'choose' itself and win itself; it can also lose itself and never win itself; or only 'seem' to do so. But only in so far as it is essentially something which can be *authentic*—that is, something of its own[3] —can it have lost itself and not yet won itself. As modes of Being, *authenticity* and *inauthenticity* (these expressions have been chosen terminologically in a strict sense) ·are both grounded in the fact that any Dasein whatsoever is characterized by mineness.[4] But the inauthenticity of Dasein does not signify any 'less' Being or any 'lower' degree of Being. Rather it is the case that even in its fullest concretion Dasein can be characterized by inauthenticity —when busy, when excited, when interested, when ready for enjoyment.

The two characteristics of Dasein which we have sketched—the priority of '*existentia*' over *essentia*, and the fact that Dasein is in each case mine [die Jemeinigkeit]—have already indicated that in the analytic of this entity we are facing a peculiar phenomenal domain. Dasein does not have the kind of Being which belongs to something merely present-at-hand within the world, nor does it ever have it. So neither is it to be presented thematically as something we come across in the same way as

---

[1] '. . . als Vorhandenem'. The earlier editions have the adjective 'vorhandenem' instead of the substantive.

[2] 'gleichgültig'. This adjective must be distinguished from the German adjective 'indifferent', though they might both ordinarily be translated by the English 'indifferent', which we shall reserve exclusively for the former. In most passages, the latter is best translated by 'undifferentiated' or 'without further differentiation'; occasionally, how-ever, it seems preferable to translate it by 'Indifferent' with an initial capital. We shall follow similar conventions with the nouns 'Gleichgültigkeit' and 'Indifferenz'.

[3] 'Und weil Dasein wesenhaft je seine Möglichkeit ist, *kann* dieses Seiende in seinem Sein sich selbst "wählen", gewinnen, es kann sich verlieren, bzw. nie und nur "scheinbar" gewinnen. Verloren haben kann es sich nur und noch nicht sich gewonnen haben kann es nur, sofern es seinem Wesen nach mögliches *eigentliches*, das heisst sich zueigen ist.' Older editions have 'je wesenhaft' and 'zueigenes'. The connection between 'eigentlich' ('authentic', 'real') and 'eigen' ('own') is lost in translation.

[4] '. . . dass Dasein überhaupt durch Jemeinigkeit bestimmt ist.'

we come across what is present-at-hand. The right way of presenting it is so far from self-evident that to determine what form it shall take is itself an essential part of the ontological analytic of this entity. Only by presenting this entity in the right way can we have any understanding of its Being. No matter how provisional our analysis may be, it always requires the assurance that we have started correctly.

In determining itself as an entity, Dasein always does so in the light of a possibility which it *is* itself and which, in its very Being, it somehow understands. This is the formal meaning of Dasein's existential constitution. But this tells us that if we are to Interpret this entity *ontologically*, the problematic of its Being must be developed from the existentiality of its existence. This cannot mean, however, that "Dasein" is to be construed in terms of some concrete possible idea of existence. At the outset of our analysis it is particularly important that Dasein should not be Interpreted with the differentiated character [Differenz] of some definite way of existing, but that it should be uncovered [aufgedeckt] in the undifferentiated character which it has proximally and for the most part. This undifferentiated character of Dasein's everydayness is *not nothing*, but a positive phenomenal characteristic of this entity. Out of this kind of Being —and back into it again—is all existing, such as it is.[1] We call this everyday undifferentiated character of Dasein "*averageness*" [*Durchschnittlichkeit*].

And because this average everydayness makes up what is ontically proximal for this entity, it has again and again been *passed over* in explicating Dasein. That which is ontically closest and well known, is ontologically the farthest and not known at all; and its ontological signification is constantly overlooked. When Augustine asks: "*Quid autem propinquius meipso mihi?*" and must answer: "*ego certe laboro hic et laboro in meipso: factus sum mihi terra difficultatis et sudoris nimii*",[4] this applies not only to the ontical and pre-ontological opaqueness of Dasein but even more to the ontological task which lies ahead; for not only must this entity not be missed in that kind of Being in which it is phenomenally closest, but it must be made accessible by a positive characterization.

Dasein's average everydayness, however, is not to be taken as a mere 'aspect'. Here too, and even in the mode of inauthenticity, the structure of existentiality lies *a priori*. And here too Dasein's Being is an issue for it in a definite way; and Dasein comports itself towards it in the mode of average everydayness, even if this is only the mode of fleeing *in the face of it* and forgetfulness *thereof*.[2]

[1] 'Aus dieser Seinsart heraus und in sie zurück ist alles Existieren, wie es ist.'
[2] 'Auch in ihr geht es dem Dasein in bestimmter Weise um sein Sein, zu dem es sich im Modus der durchschnittlichen Alltäglichkeit verhält und sei es auch nur im Modus der Flucht *davor* und des Vergessens *seiner*.' For further discussion, see Section 40 below.

But the explication of Dasein in its average everydayness does not give us just average structures in the sense of a hazy indefiniteness. Anything which, taken ontically, *is* in an average way, can be very well grasped ontologically in pregnant structures which may be structurally indistinguishable from certain ontological characteristics [Bestimmungen] of an *authentic* Being of Dasein.

All *explicata* to which the analytic of Dasein gives rise are obtained by considering Dasein's existence-structure. Because Dasein's characters of Being are defined in terms of existentiality, we call them "*e x i s t e n t i a l i a*". These are to be sharply distinguished from what we call "*categories*"— characteristics of Being for entities whose character is not that of Dasein.[1] Here we are taking the expression "category" in its primary ontological signification, and abiding by it. In the ontology of the ancients, the entities we encounter within the world[2] are taken as the basic examples for the interpretation of Being. Noεῖν (or the λόγος, as the case may be) is accepted as a way of access to them.[3] Entities are encountered therein. But the Being of these entities must be something which can be grasped in a distinctive kind of λέγειν (letting something be seen), so that this Being becomes intelligible in advance as that which it is—and as that which it is already in every entity. In any discussion (λόγος) of entities, we have previously addressed ourselves to Being; this addressing is κατηγορεῖσθαι.[4] This signifies, in the first instance, making a public accusation, taking someone to task for something in the presence of everyone. When used ontologically, this term means taking an entity to task, as it were, for whatever it is as an entity—that is to say, letting everyone see it in its Being. The κατηγορίαι are what is sighted and what is visible in such a seeing.[5] They include the various ways in which the nature of those entities which can be addressed and discussed in a λόγος may be

45

----

[1] 'Weil sie sich aus der Existenzialität bestimmen, nennen wir die Seinscharaktere des Daseins *Existenzialien*. Sie sind scharf zu trennen von den Seinsbestimmungen des nicht daseinsmässigen Seienden, die wir *Kategorien* nennen.'

[2] '. . . das innerhalb der Welt begegnende Seiende.' More literally: 'the entity that encounters within the world.' While Heidegger normally uses the verb 'begegnen' in this active intransitive sense, a similar construction with the English 'encounter' is unidiomatic and harsh. We shall as a rule use either a passive construction (as in 'entities encountered') or an active transitive construction (as in 'entities we encounter').

[3] 'Als Zugangsart zu ihm gilt das νοεῖν bzw. der λόγος.' Here we follow the reading of the earlier editions. In the later editions, 'Zugangsart', which is used rather often, is here replaced by 'Zugangsort', which occurs very seldom and is perhaps a misprint. This later version might be translated as follows: 'νοεῖν (or the λόγος, as the case may be) is accepted as the locus of access to such entities.' On νοεῖν and λόγος see Section 7 above, especially H. 32-34.

[4] 'Das je schon vorgängige Ansprechen des Seins im Besprechen (λόγος) des Seienden ist das κατηγορεῖσθαι.'

[5] 'Das in solchem Sehen Gesichtete und Sichtbare . . .' On 'Sehen' and 'Sicht' see H, 147.

determined *a priori*. *Existentialia* and categories are the two basic possibilities for characters of Being. The entities which correspond to them
require different kinds of primary interrogation respectively: any entity
is either a *"who"* (existence) or a *"what"* (presence-at-hand in the broadest
sense). The connection between these two modes of the characters of
Being cannot be handled until the horizon for the question of Being has
been clarified.

In our introduction we have already intimated that in the existential
analytic of Dasein we also make headway with a task which is hardly
less pressing than that of the question of Being itself—the task of laying
bare that *a priori* basis which must be visible before the question of 'what
man is' can be discussed philosophically. The existential analytic of Dasein
comes *before* any psychology or anthropology, and certainly before any
biology. While these too are ways in which Dasein can be investigated, we
can define the theme of our analytic with greater precision if we distinguish it from these. And at the same time the necessity of that analytic
can thus be proved more incisively.

¶ 10. *How the Analytic of Dasein is to be Distinguished from Anthropology, Psychology, and Biology*

After a theme for investigation has been initially outlined in positive
terms, it is always important to show what is to be ruled out, although it
can easily become fruitless to discuss what is not going to happen. We must
show that those investigations and formulations of the question which have
been aimed at Dasein heretofore, have missed the real *philosophical* problem (notwithstanding their objective fertility), and that as long as they
persist in missing it, they have no right to claim that they *can* accomplish
that for which they are basically striving. In distinguishing the existential
analytic from anthropology, psychology, and biology, we shall confine
ourselves to what is in principle the ontological question. Our distinctions
will necessarily be inadequate from the standpoint of 'scientific theory'
simply because the scientific structure of the above-mentioned disciplines
(not, indeed, the 'scientific attitude' of those who work to advance them)
is today thoroughly questionable and needs to be attacked in new ways
which must have their source in ontological problematics.

Historiologically, the aim of the existential analytic can be made
plainer by considering Descartes, who is credited with providing the point   46
of departure for modern philosophical inquiry by his discovery of the
"cogito sum". He investigates the *"cogitare"* of the *"ego"*, at least within
certain limits. On the other hand, he leaves the *"sum"* completely undiscussed, even though it is regarded as no less primordial than the *cogito*. Our

analytic raises the ontological question of the Being of the "*sum*". Not until the nature of this Being has been determined can we grasp the kind of Being which belongs to *cogitationes*.

At the same time it is of course misleading to exemplify the aim of our analytic historiologically in this way. One of our first tasks will be to prove that if we posit an "I" or subject as that which is proximally given, we shall completely miss the phenomenal content [Bestand] of Dasein. *Ontologically*, every idea of a 'subject'—unless refined by a previous onto-logical determination of its basic character—still posits the *subjectum* (ὑποκείμενον) along with it, no matter how vigorous one's ontical protestations against the 'soul substance' or the 'reification of conscious-ness'. The Thinghood itself which such reification implies must have its ontological origin demonstrated if we are to be in a position to ask what we are to understand *positively* when we think of the unreified *Being* of the subject, the soul, the consciousness, the spirit, the person. All these terms refer to definite phenomenal domains which can be 'given form' ["ausformbare"]: but they are never used without a notable failure to see the need for inquiring about the Being of the entities thus designated. So we are not being terminologically arbitrary when we avoid these terms—or such expressions as 'life' and 'man'—in designating those entities which we are ourselves.

On the other hand, if we understand it rightly, in any serious and scientifically-minded 'philosophy of life' (this expression says about as much as "the botany of plants") there lies an unexpressed tendency towards an understanding of Dasein's Being. What is conspicuous in such a philosophy (and here it is defective in principle) is that here 'life' itself as a kind of Being does not become ontologically a problem.

The researches of Wilhelm Dilthey were stimulated by the perennial question of 'life'. Starting from 'life' itself as a whole, he tried to under-stand its 'Experiences'[1] in their structural and developmental inter-connec-tions. His '*geisteswissenschaftliche Psychologie*' is one which no longer seeks to be oriented towards psychical elements and atoms or to piece the life of the soul together, but aims rather at '*Gestalten*' and 'life as a whole'. Its philosophical relevance, however, is not to be sought here, but rather in the fact that in all this he was, *above all*, on his way towards the question 47 of 'life'. To be sure, we can also see here very plainly how limited were both his problematic and the set of concepts with which it had to be put

---

[1] 'Die "Erlebnisse" dieses "Lebens" . . .' The connection between 'Leben' ('life') and 'Erlebnisse' ('Experiences') is lost in translation. An 'Erlebnis' is not just *any* 'experience' ('Erfahrung'), but one which we feel deeply and 'live through'. We shall translate 'Erlebnis' and 'erleben' by 'Experience' with a capital 'E', reserving 'experience' for 'Erfahrung' and 'erfahren'.

into words. These limitations, however, are found not only in Dilthey and Bergson but in all the 'personalistic' movements to which they have given direction and in every tendency towards a philosophical anthropology. The phenomenological Interpretation of personality is in principle more radical and more transparent; but the question of the Being of Dasein has a dimension which this too fails to enter. No matter how much Husserl[ii] and Scheler may differ in their respective inquiries, in their methods of conducting them, and in their orientations towards the world as a whole, they are fully in agreement on the negative side of their Interpretations of personality. The question of 'personal *Being*' itself is one which they no longer raise. We have chosen Scheler's Interpretation as an example, not only because it is accessible in print,[iii] but because he emphasizes personal Being explicitly as such, and tries to determine its character by defining the specific Being of acts as contrasted with anything 'psychical'. For Scheler, the person is never to be thought of as a Thing or a substance; the person 'is rather the *unity* of living-through [Er-lebens] which is immediately experienced in and with our Experiences—not a Thing merely thought of behind and outside what is immediately Experienced'.[iv] The person is no Thinglike and substantial Being. Nor can the Being of a person be entirely absorbed in being a subject of rational acts which follow certain laws.

The person is not a Thing, not a substance, not an object. Here Scheler is emphasizing what Husserl[v] suggests when he insists that the unity of the person must have a Constitution essentially different from that required for the unity of Things of Nature.[1] What Scheler says of the person, he applies to acts as well: 'But an act is never also an object; for it is essential to the Being of acts that they are Experienced only in their performance itself and given in reflection.'[vi] Acts are something non-psychical. Essentially the person exists only in the performance of intentional acts, and is therefore essentially *not* an object. Any psychical Objectification of acts, and hence any way of taking them as something psychical, is tantamount to depersonalization. A person is in any case given as a performer of intentional acts which are bound together by the unity of a meaning. Thus psychical Being has nothing to do with personal Being. Acts get performed; the person is a performer of acts. What, however, is the ontological meaning of 'performance'? How is the kind of Being which belongs to a person to be ascertained ontologically in a positive way? But the critical question cannot stop here. It must face the Being of the whole man, who is customarily taken as a unity of body,

48

---

[1] '. . . wenn er für die Einheit der Person eine wesentlich andere Konstitution fordert als für die der Naturdinge.' The second 'der' appears in the later editions only.

soul, and spirit. In their turn "body", "soul", and "spirit" may designate phenomenal domains which can be detached as themes for definite investigations; within certain limits their ontological indefiniteness may not be important. When, however, we come to the question of man's Being, this is not something we can simply compute[1] by adding together those kinds of Being which body, soul, and spirit respectively possess— kinds of Being whose nature has not as yet been determined. And even if we should attempt such an ontological procedure, some idea of the Being of the whole must be presupposed. But what stands in the way of the basic question of Dasein's Being (or leads it off the track) is an orientation thoroughly coloured by the anthropology of Christianity and the ancient world, whose inadequate ontological foundations have been overlooked both by the philosophy of life and by personalism. There are two important elements in this traditional anthropology:

1. 'Man' is here defined as a ζῷον λόγον ἔχον, and this is Interpreted to mean an *animal rationale*, something living which has reason. But the kind of Being which belongs to a ζῷον is understood in the sense of occurring and Being-present-at-hand. The λόγος is some superior endowment; the kind of Being which belongs to it, however, remains quite as obscure as that of the entire entity thus compounded.

2. The second clue for determining the nature of man's Being and essence is a *theological* one: καὶ εἶπεν ὁ Θεός· ποιήσωμεν ἄνθρωπον κατ' εἰκόνα ἡμετέραν καὶ καθ' ὁμοίωσιν—"*faciamus hominem ad imaginem nostram et similitudinem*"[vii] With this as its point of departure, the anthropology of Christian theology, taking with it the ancient definition, arrives at an interpretation of that entity which we call "man". But just as the Being of God gets Interpreted ontologically by means of the ancient ontology, so does the Being of the *ens finitum*, and to an even greater extent. In modern times the Christian definition has been deprived of its theological character. But the idea of 'transcendence' —that man is something that reaches beyond himself—is rooted in Christian dogmatics, which can hardly be said to have made an ontological problem of man's Being. The idea of transcendence, according to which man is more than a mere something endowed with intelligence, has worked itself out with different variations. The following quotations will illustrate how these have originated: '*His praeclaris dotibus excelluit prima hominis conditio, ut ratio, intelligentia, prudentia, judicium non modo ad terrenae vitae gubernationem suppeterent, sed quibus t r a n s c e n d e r e t usque ad Deum et aeternam felicitatem.*'[viii] '*Denn dass der mensch sin u f s e h e n hat uf Gott und*

---

[1] Reading 'errechnet'. The earliest editions have 'verrechnet', with the correct reading provided in a list of *errata*.

sin wort, zeigt er klarlich an, dass er nach siner natur etwas Gott näher anerborn,
etwas mee n a c h s c h l ä g t, etwas z u z u g s z u jm hat, das alles on zwyfel
*darus flüsst, dass er nach dem b i l d n u s Gottes geschaffen ist'.*ix

The two sources which are relevant for the traditional anthropology—
the Greek definition and the clue which theology has provided—indicate
that over and above the attempt to determine the essence of 'man' as an
entity, the question of his Being has remained forgotten, and that this
Being is rather conceived as something obvious or 'self-evident' in the
sense of the *Being-present-at-hand* of other created Things. These two clues
become intertwined in the anthropology of modern times, where the *res
cogitans*, consciousness, and the interconnectedness of Experience serve as
the point of departure for methodical study. But since even the *cogitationes*
are either left ontologically undetermined, or get tacitly assumed as
something 'self-evidently' 'given' whose 'Being' is not to be questioned,
the decisive ontological foundations of anthropological problematics
remain undetermined.

This is no less true of *'psychology'*, whose anthropological tendencies are
today unmistakable. Nor can we compensate for the absence of ontological foundations by taking anthropology and psychology and building
them into the framework of a general *biology*. In the order which any
possible comprehension and interpretation must follow, biology as a
'science of life' is founded upon the ontology of Dasein, even if not entirely.   50
Life, in its own right, is a kind of Being; but essentially it is accessible only
in Dasein. The ontology of life is accomplished by way of a privative
Interpretation; it determines what must be the case if there can be anything like mere-aliveness [Nur-noch-leben]. Life is not a mere Being-
present-at-hand, nor is it Dasein. In turn, Dasein is never to be defined
ontologically by regarding it as life (in an ontologically indefinite manner)
plus something else.

In suggesting that anthropology, psychology, and biology all fail to
give an unequivocal and ontologically adequate answer to the question
about the *kind of Being* which belongs to those entities which we ourselves
are, we are not passing judgment on the positive work of these disciplines.
We must always bear in mind, however, that these ontological foundations
can never be disclosed by subsequent hypotheses derived from empirical
material, but that they are always 'there' already, even when that
empirical material simply gets *collected*. If positive research fails to see
these foundations and holds them to be self-evident, this by no means
proves that they are not basic or that they are not problematic in a more
radical sense than any thesis of positive science can ever be.x

¶ 11. *The Existential Analytic and the Interpretation of Primitive Dasein. The Difficulties of Achieving a 'Natural Conception of the World'*

The Interpretation of Dasein in its everydayness, however, is not identical with the describing of some primitive stage of Dasein with which we can become acquainted empirically through the medium of anthropology: *Everydayness does not coincide with primitiveness*, but is rather a mode of Dasein's Being, even when that Dasein is active in a highly developed and differentiated culture—and precisely then. Moreover, even primitive Dasein has possibilities of a Being which is not of the everyday kind, and it has a specific everydayness *of its own*. To orient the analysis of Dasein towards the 'life of primitive peoples' can have positive significance [Bedeutung] as a method because 'primitive phenomena' are often less concealed and less complicated by extensive self-interpretation on the part of the Dasein in question. Primitive Dasein often speaks to us more directly in terms of a primordial absorption in 'phenomena' (taken in a pre-phenomenological sense). A way of conceiving things which seems, perhaps, rather clumsy and crude from our standpoint, can be positively helpful in bringing out the ontological structures of phenomena in a genuine way.

But heretofore our information about primitives has been provided by ethnology. And ethnology operates with definite preliminary conceptions and interpretations of human Dasein in general, even in first 'receiving' its material, and in sifting it and working it up. Whether the everyday psychology or even the scientific psychology and sociology which the ethnologist brings with him can provide any scientific assurance that we can have proper access to the phenomena we are studying, and can interpret them and transmit them in the right way, has not yet been established. Here too we are confronted with the same state of affairs as in the other disciplines we have discussed. Ethnology itself already presupposes as its clue an inadequate analytic of Dasein. But since the positive sciences neither 'can' nor should wait for the ontological labours of philosophy to be done, the further course of research will not take the form of an 'advance' but will be accomplished by *recapitulating* what has already been ontically discovered, and by purifying it in a way which is ontologically more transparent.[xi]

No matter how easy it may be to show how ontological problematics differ formally from ontical research there are still difficulties in carrying out an existential analytic, especially in *making a start*. This task includes a *desideratum* which philosophy has long found disturbing but has continually refused to achieve: *to work out the idea of a 'natural conception of the world'*. The rich store of information now available as to the most exotic and manifold cultures and forms of Dasein seems favourable to our setting about this task in a fruitful way. But this is merely a semblance. At bottom this plethora of information can seduce us into failing to recognize the real problem. We shall not get a genuine knowledge of essences simply by the syncretistic activity of universal comparison and classification. Subjecting the manifold to tabulation does not ensure any actual understanding of what lies there before us as thus set in order. If an ordering principle is genuine, it has its own content as a thing [Sachgehalt], which is never to be found by means of such ordering, but is already presupposed in it. So if one is to put various pictures of the world in order, one must have an explicit idea of the world as such. And if the 'world' itself is something constitutive for Dasein, one must have an insight into Dasein's basic structures in order to treat the world-phenomenon conceptually.

In this chapter we have characterized some things positively and taken a negative stand with regard to others; in both cases our goal has been to promote a correct understanding of the tendency which underlies the following Interpretation and the kind of questions which it poses. Ontology can contribute only indirectly towards advancing the positive disciplines as we find them today. It has a goal of its own, if indeed, beyond the acquiring of information about entities, the question of Being is the spur for all scientific seeking.

Hud. would prob. maintain that the fund. understanding can never be achieved w/in the framework of the positive sciences & as a result the philos. project must be undertaken.

II

BEING-IN-THE-WORLD IN GENERAL AS THE BASIC STATE OF DASEIN

¶ *12. A Preliminary Sketch of Being-in-the-World, in terms of an Orientation towards Being-in as such*

IN our preparatory discussions (Section 9) we have brought out some characteristics of Being which will provide us with a steady light for our further investigation, but which will at the same time become structurally concrete as that investigation continues. Dasein is an entity which, in its very Being, comports itself understandingly towards that Being. In saying this, we are calling attention to the formal concept of existence. Dasein exists. Furthermore, Dasein is an entity which in each case I myself am. Mineness belongs to any existent Dasein, and belongs to it as the condition which makes authenticity and inauthenticity possible. In each case Dasein exists in one or the other of these two modes, or else it is modally undifferentiated.[1]

But these are both ways in which Dasein's Being takes on a definite character, and they must be seen and understood *a priori* as grounded upon that state of Being which we have called "*Being-in-the-world*'. An interpretation of this constitutive state is needed if we are to set up our analytic of Dasein correctly.

The compound expression 'Being-in-the-world' indicates in the very way we have coined it, that it stands for a *unitary* phenomenon. This primary datum must be seen as a whole. But while Being-in-the-world cannot be broken up into contents which may be pieced together, this does not prevent it from having several constitutive items in its structure. Indeed the phenomenal datum which our expression indicates is one which may, in fact, be looked at in three ways. If we study it, keeping the whole phenomenon firmly in mind beforehand, the following items may be brought out for emphasis:

First, the '*in-the-world*'. With regard to this there arises the task of inquiring into the ontological structure of the 'world' and defining the idea of *worldhood* as such. (See the third chapter of this Division.)

---

[1] 'Zum existierenden Dasein gehört die Jemeinigkeit als Bedingung der Möglichkeit von Eigentlichkeit und Uneigentlichkeit. Dasein existiert je in einem dieser Modi, bzw. in der modalen Indifferenz ihrer.'

② Second, that *entity* which in every case has Being-in-the-world as the way in which it is. Here we are seeking that which one inquires into when one asks the question 'Who?' By a phenomenological demonstration[1] we shall determine who is in the mode of Dasein's average everydayness. (See the fourth chapter of this Division.)

③ Third, *Being-in* [*In-sein*] as such. We must set forth the ontological Constitution of inhood [Inheit] itself. (See the fifth chapter of this Division.). Emphasis upon any one of these constitutive items signifies that the others are emphasized along with it; this means that in any such case the whole phenomenon gets seen. Of course Being-in-the-world is a state of Dasein[2] which is necessary *a priori*, but it is far from sufficient for completely determining Dasein's Being. Before making these three phenomena the themes for special analyses, we shall attempt by way of orientation to characterize the third of these factors.

What is meant by *"Being-in"*? Our proximal reaction is to round out this expression to "Being-in 'in the world' ", and we are inclined to understand this Being-in as 'Being in something' ["Sein in . . ."]. This   54 latter term designates the kind of Being which an entity has when it is 'in' another one, as the water is 'in' the glass, or the garment is 'in' the cupboard. By this 'in' we mean the relationship of Being which two entities extended 'in' space have to each other with regard to their location in that space. Both water and glass, garment and cupboard, are 'in' space and 'at' a location, and both in the same way. This relationship of Being can be expanded: for instance, the bench is in the lecture-room, the lecture-room is in the university, the university is in the city, and so on, until we can say that the bench is 'in world-space'. All entities whose Being 'in' one another can thus be described have the same kind of Being —that of Being-present-at-hand—as Things occurring 'within' the world. Being-present-at-hand 'in' something which is likewise present-at-hand, and Being-present-at-hand-along-with [Mitvorhandensein] in the sense of a definite location-relationship with something else which has the same kind of Being, are ontological characteristics which we call *"categorial"*: they are of such a sort as to belong to entities whose kind of Being is not of the character of Dasein.

Being-in, on the other hand, is a state of Dasein's Being; it is an existentiale. So one cannot think of it as the Being-present-at-hand of some corporeal Thing (such as a human body) 'in' an entity which is present-at-hand. Nor does the term "Being-in" mean

1 Here we follow the older editions in reading, 'Ausweisung'. The newer editions have 'Aufweisung' ('exhibition').
2 '. . . Verfassung des Daseins . . .' The earliest editions read 'Wesens' instead of 'Daseins'. Correction is made in a list of *errata*.

a spatial 'in-one-another-ness' of things present-at-hand, any more than the word 'in' primordially signifies a spatial relationship of this kind.[1] 'In' is derived from "*innan*"—"to reside",[1] "*habitare*", "to dwell" [sich auf halten]. '*An*' signifies "I am accustomed", "I am familiar with", "I look after something".[2] It has the signification of "*colo*" in the senses of "*habito*" and "*diligo*". The entity to which Being-in in this signification belongs is one which we have characterized as that entity which in each case I myself am [bin]. The expression '*bin*' is connected with '*bei*', and so '*ich bin*' ['I am'] means in its turn "I reside" or "dwell alongside" the world, as that which is familiar to me in such and such a way.[3] "Being" [Sein], as the infinitive of '*ich bin*' (that is to say, when it is understood as an *existentiale*), signifies "to reside alongside . . .", "to be familiar with . . .". "*Being-in*" *is thus the formal existential expression for the Being of Dasein, which has Being-in-the-world as its essential state.*

'Being alongside' the world in the sense of being absorbed in the world[4]

---

[1] Reading '*innan*—*wohnen*'. As Heidegger points out in his footnote, this puzzling passage has its source in Grimm's *Kleinere Schriften*, Vol. VII, pp. 247 ff., where we find two short articles, the first entitled 'IN' and the second 'IN UND BEI'. The first article begins by comparing a number of archaic German words meaning '*domus*', all having a form similar to our English 'inn', which Grimm mentions. He goes on to postulate 'a strong verb "*innan*", which must have meant either "*habitare*", "*domi esse*", or "*recipere in domum*" ' (though only a weak derivative form '*innian*' is actually found), with a surviving strong preterite written either as '*an*' or as '*ann*'. Grimm goes on to argue that the preposition '*in*' is derived from the verb, rather than the verb from the preposition.

[2] '. . . "*an*" bedeutet: ich bin gewohnt, vertraut mit, ich pflege etwas . . .'
In Grimm's second article he adds: 'there was also an anomalous "*ann*" with the plural "*unnum*", which expressed "*amo*", "*diligo*", "*faveo*", and to which our "*gönnen*" and "*Gunst*" are immediately related, as has long been recognized. "*Ann*" really means "ich bin eingewohnt", "pflege zu bauen"; this conceptual transition may be shown with minimal complication in the Latin "*colo*", which stands for "*habito*" as well as "*diligo*".'
It is not entirely clear whether Heidegger's discussion of '*an*' is aimed to elucidate the preposition '*an*' (which corresponds in some of its usages to the English 'at', and which he has just used in remarking that the water and the glass are both *at* a location), or rather to explain the preterite '*an*' of '*innan*'.
The reader should note that while the verb '*wohnen*' normally means 'to reside' or 'to dwell', the expression 'ich bin gewohnt' means 'I am accustomed to', and 'ich bin eingewohnt' means 'I have become accustomed to the place where I reside—to my surroundings'. Similarly 'ich pflege etwas' may mean either 'I am accustomed to do something' or 'I take care of something' or 'I devote myself to it'. (Grimm's 'pflege zu bauen' presumably means 'I am accustomed to putting my trust in something', 'I can build on it'.) The Latin, '*colo*' has the parallel meanings of 'I take care of something' or 'cherish' it ('*diligo*') and 'I dwell' or 'I inhabit' ('*habito*').

[3] '. . . ich wohne, halte mich auf bei . . . der Welt, als dem so und so Vertrauten.' The preposition '*bei*', like '*an*', does not have quite the semantical range of any English preposition. Our 'alongside', with which we shall translate it when other devices seem less satisfactory, especially in the phrase 'Being alongside' ('Sein bei'), is often quite misleading; the sense here is closer to that of 'at' in such expressions as 'at home' or 'at my father's', or that of the French '*chez*'. Here again Heidegger seems to be relying upon Grimm, who proceeds (*loc. cit.*) to connect '*bei*' with '*bauen*' ('build') and '*bin*'.

[4] '. . . in dem . . . Sinne des Aufgehens in der Welt . . .' 'Aufgehen' means literally 'to go up', or 'to rise' in the sense that the sun 'rises' or the dough 'rises'. But when followed by the preposition '*in*', it takes on other meanings. Thus 5 '*geht auf*' into 30 in the sense that

(a sense which calls for still closer interpretation) is an *existentiale* founded upon Being-in. In these analyses the issue is one of *seeing* a primordial structure of Dasein's Being—a structure in accordance with whose phenomenal content the concepts of Being must be Articulated; because of this, and because this structure is in principle one which cannot be grasped by the traditional ontological categories, this 'Being-alongside' must be examined still more closely. We shall again choose the method of contrasting it with a relationship of Being which is essentially different ontologically—*viz.* categorial—but which we express by the same linguistic means. Fundamental ontological distinctions are easily obliterated; and if they are to be envisaged phenomenally in this way, this must be done *explicitly*, even at the risk of discussing the 'obvious'. The status of the ontological analytic shows, however, that we have been far from interpreting these obvious matters with an adequate 'grasp', still less with regard for the meaning of their Being; and we are even farther from possessing a stable coinage for the appropriate structural concepts.

As an *existentiale*, 'Being alongside' the world never means anything like the Being-present-at-hand-together of Things that occur. There is no such thing as the 'side-by-side-ness' of an entity called 'Dasein' with another entity called 'world'. Of course when two things are present-at-hand together alongside one another,[1] we are accustomed to express this occasionally by something like 'The table stands "by" ['bei'] the door' or 'The chair "touches" ['berührt'] the wall'. Taken strictly, 'touching' is never what we are talking about in such cases, not because accurate re-examination will always eventually establish that there is a space between the chair and the wall, but because in principle the chair can never touch the wall, even if the space between them should be equal to zero. If the chair could touch the wall, this would presuppose that the wall is the sort of thing 'for' which a chair would be *encounterable*.[2] An entity present-at-hand within the world can be touched by another entity only if by its very nature the latter entity has Being-in as its own kind of Being—only if, with its Being-there [Da-sein], something like the world is already revealed to it, so that from out of that world another entity can manifest itself in touching, and thus become accessible in its Being-present-at-hand. When two entities are present-at-hand within the world, and furthermore are *worldless* in themselves, they can never 'touch' each other,

it 'goes into' 30 without remainder; a country '*geht auf*' into another country into which it is taken over or absorbed; a person '*geht auf*' in anything to which he devotes himself fully, whether an activity or another person. We shall usually translate '*aufgehen*' by some form of 'absorb'.

[1] 'Das Beisammen zweier Vorhandener . . .'
[2] 'Voraussetzung dafür wäre, dass die Wand "für" den Stuhl *begegnen* könnte.' (Cf. also H. 97 below.)

55

nor can either of them '*be*' '*alongside*' the other. The clause 'furthermore
are worldless' must not be left out; for even entities which are not worldless—Dasein itself, for example—are present-at-hand 'in' the world, or,
more exactly, *can* with some right and within certain limits be *taken* as
merely present-at-hand. To do this, one must completely disregard or just
not see the existential state of Being-in. But the fact that 'Dasein' can be
taken as something which is present-at-hand and just present-at-hand, is
not to be confused with a certain way of 'presence-at-hand' which is Dasein's
own. This latter kind of presence-at-hand becomes accessible not by disregarding Dasein's specific structures but only by understanding them in
advance. Dasein understands its ownmost Being in the sense of a certain
'factual Being-present-at-hand'.[ii] And yet the 'factuality' of the fact
[Tatsache] of one's own Dasein is at bottom quite different ontologically
from the factual occurrence of some kind of mineral, for example. Whenever Dasein i s, it is as a Fact; and the factuality of such a Fact is what we
shall call Dasein's "*facticity*".[1] This is a definite way of Being [Seinsbe-
stimmtheit], and it has a complicated structure which cannot even be
grasped *as a problem* until Dasein's basic existential states have been
worked out. The concept of "facticity" implies that an entity 'within-the-
world' has Being-in-the-world in such a way that it can understand itself
as bound up in its 'destiny' with the Being of those entities which it
encounters within its own world.

In the first instance it is enough to see the ontological difference
between Being-in as an *existentiale* and the category of the 'insideness'
which things present-at-hand can have with regard to one another. By
thus delimiting Being-in, we are not denying every kind of 'spatiality'
to Dasein. On the contrary, Dasein itself has a 'Being-in-space' of its
own; but this in turn is possible only *on the basis of Being-in-the-world in
general*. Hence Being-in is not to be explained ontologically by some
ontical characterization, as if one were to say, for instance, that Being-in
in a world is a spiritual property, and that man's 'spatiality' is a result of
his bodily nature (which, at the same time, always gets 'founded' upon
corporeality). Here again we are faced with the Being-present-at-hand-
together of some such spiritual Thing along with a corporeal Thing,
while the Being of the entity thus compounded remains more obscure

---

[1] 'Die Tatsächlichkeit des Faktums Dasein, als welches jeweilig jedes Dasein ist,
nennen wir seine *Faktizität*.' We shall as a rule translate 'Tatsächlichkeit' as 'factuality',
and 'Faktizität' as 'facticity', following our conventions for 'tatsächlich' and 'faktisch'.
(See note 2, p. 27, H. 7 above.) The present passage suggests a comparable distinction
between the nouns 'Tatsache' and 'Faktum'; so while we find many passages where these
seem to be used interchangeably, we translate 'Faktum' as 'Fact' with an initial capital,
using 'fact' for 'Tatsache' and various other expressions. On 'factuality' and 'facticity'
see also H. 135 below.

than ever. Not until we understand Being-in-the-world as an essential
structure of Dasein can we have any insight into Dasein's *existential
spatiality*. Such an insight will keep us from failing to see this structure or
from previously cancelling it out—a procedure motivated not ontologically but rather 'metaphysically' by the naïve supposition that man is,
in the first instance, a spiritual Thing which subsequently gets misplaced
'into' a space.

Dasein's facticity is such that its Being-in-the-world has always dispersed [zerstreut] itself or even split itself up into definite ways of Being-
in. The multiplicity of these is indicated by the following examples: having
to do with something, producing something, attending to something and
looking after it, making use of something, giving something up and letting
it go, undertaking, accomplishing, evincing, interrogating, considering,
discussing, determining. . . . All these ways of Being-in have *concern*[1] as
their kind of Being—a kind of Being which we have yet to characterize in
detail. Leaving undone, neglecting, renouncing, taking a rest—these too
are ways of concern; but these are all *deficient* modes, in which the possibilities of concern are kept to a 'bare minimum'.[2] The term 'concern'
has, in the first instance, its colloquial [vorwissenschaftliche] signification,
and can mean to carry out something, to get it done [erledigen], to
'straighten it out'. It can also mean to 'provide oneself with something'.[3]
We use the expression with still another characteristic turn of phrase
when we say "I am concerned for the success of the undertaking."[4] Here
'concern' means something like apprehensiveness. In contrast to these
colloquial ontical significations, the expression 'concern' will be used in
this investigation as an ontological term for an *existentiale,* and will designate the Being of a possible way of Being-in-the-world. This term has
been chosen not because Dasein happens to be proximally and to a large
extent 'practical' and economic, but because the Being of Dasein itself

57

---

[1] '*Besorgen*'. As Heidegger points out, he will use this term in a special sense which is to
be distinguished from many of its customary usages. We shall, as a rule, translate it by
'concern', though this is by no means an exact equivalent. The English word 'concern' is
used in many expressions where 'Besorgen' would be inappropriate in German, such as
'This concerns you', 'That is my concern', 'He has an interest in several banking concerns'. 'Besorgen' stands rather for the kind of 'concern' in which we 'concern ourselves'
with activities which we perform or things which we procure.

[2] '. . . alle Modi des "Nur noch" in bezug auf Möglichkeiten des Besorgens.' The point
is that in these cases concern is *just barely* ('nur noch') involved.

[3] '. . . sich etwas besorgen im Sinne von "sich etwas verschaffen".'

[4] '. . . ich besorge, dass das Unternehmen misslingt.' Here it is not difficult to find a
corresponding usage of 'concern', as our version suggests. But the analogy is imperfect.
While we can say that we are 'concerned for the success of the enterprise' or 'concerned
lest the enterprise should fail,' we would hardly follow the German to the extent of
expressing 'concern that' the enterprise should fail; nor would the German express
'Besorgen' at discovering that the enterprise has failed already.

Sorge *fund. meaning* *of the Being of Dasein*

is to be made visible as *care*.[1] This expression too is to be taken as an ontological structural concept. (See Chapter 6 of this Division.) It has nothing to do with 'tribulation', 'melancholy', or the 'cares of life', though ontically one can come across these in every Dasein. These—like their opposites, 'gaiety' and 'freedom from care'—are ontically possible only because Dasein, when understood *ontologically*, is care. Because Being-in-the-world belongs essentially to Dasein, its Being towards the world [Sein zur Welt] is essentially concern.

From what we have been saying, it follows that Being-in is not a 'property' which Dasein sometimes has and sometimes does not have, and *without* which it could *be* just as well as it could with it. It is not the case that man 'is' and then has, by way of an extra, a relationship-of-Being towards the 'world'—a world with which he provides himself occasionally.[2] Dasein is never 'proximally' an entity which is, so to speak, free from Being-in, but which sometimes has the inclination to take up a 'relationship' towards the world. Taking up relationships towards the world is possible only *because* Dasein, as Being-in-the-world, is as it is. This state of Being does not arise just because some other entity is present-at-hand outside of Dasein and meets up with it. Such an entity can 'meet up with' Dasein only in so far as it can, of its own accord, show itself within a *world*.

Nowadays there is much talk about 'man's having an environment [Umwelt]'; but this says nothing ontologically as long as this 'having' is left indefinite. In its very possibility this 'having' is founded upon the existential state of Being-in. Because Dasein is essentially an entity with Being-in, it can explicitly discover those entities which it encounters environmentally, it can know them, it can avail itself of them, it can *have* the 'world'. To talk about 'having an environment' is ontically trivial, but ontologically it presents a problem. To solve it requires nothing else than defining the Being of Dasein, and doing so in a way which is ontologically adequate. Although this state of Being is one of which use has made in biology, especially since K. von Baer, one must not conclude that its philosophical use implies 'biologism'. For the environment is a structure which even biology as a positive science can never find and can never define, but must presuppose and constantly employ. Yet, even as an *a priori* condition for the objects which biology takes for its theme, this structure itself can be explained philosophically only if it has been conceived beforehand as a structure of Dasein. Only in terms of an orientation

----

[1] 'Sorge'. The important etymological connection between 'Besorgen' ('concern') and 'Sorge' ('care') is lost in our translation. On 'Sorge' see especially Sections 41 and 42 below.

[2] 'Der Mensch "ist" nicht und hat überdies noch ein Seinsverhältnis zur "Welt", die er sich gelegentlich zulegt.'

towards the ontological structure thus conceived can 'life' as a state of Being be defined *a priori*, and this must be done in a privative manner.[1] Ontically as well as ontologically, the priority belongs to Being-in-the world as concern. In the analytic of Dasein this structure undergoes a basic Interpretation.

But have we not confined ourselves to negative assertions in all our attempts to determine the nature of this state of Being? Though this Being-in is supposedly so fundamental, we always keep hearing about what it is *not*. Yes indeed. But there is nothing accidental about our characterizing it predominantly in so negative a manner. In doing so we have rather made known what is peculiar to this phenomenon, and our characterization is therefore positive in a genuine sense—a sense appropriate to the phenomenon itself. When Being-in-the-world is exhibited phenomenologically, disguises and concealments are rejected *because* this phenomenon itself always gets 'seen' in a certain way in every Dasein. And it thus gets 'seen' *because* it makes up a basic state of Dasein, and in every case is already disclosed for Dasein's understanding of Being, and disclosed along with that Being itself. But for the most part this phenomenon has been explained in a way which is basically wrong, or interpreted in an ontologically inadequate manner. On the other hand, this 'seeing in a certain way and yet for the most part wrongly explaining' is itself based upon nothing else than this very state of Dasein's Being, which is such that Dasein itself—and this means also its Being-in-the world—gets its ontological understanding of itself in the first instance from those entities which it itself is *not* but which it encounters 'within' its world, and from the Being which they possess.

Both in Dasein and for it, this state of Being is always in some way familiar [bekannt]. Now if it is also to become known [erkannt], the *knowing* which such a task explicitly implies takes *itself* (as a knowing of the world [Welterkennen]) as the chief exemplification of the 'soul's' relationship to the world. Knowing the world (νοεῖν)—or rather addressing oneself to the 'world' and discussing it (λόγος)—thus functions as the primary mode of Being-in-the-world, even though Being-in-the-world does not as such get conceived. But because this structure of Being remains ontologically inaccessible, yet is experienced ontically as a 'relationship' between one entity (the world) and another (the soul), and because one proximally understands Being by taking entities as entities within-the-world for one's ontological foothold, one tries to conceive the relationship between world and soul as grounded in these two entities

59

1 '. . . auf dem Wege der Privation . . .' The point is that in order to understand life merely *as such*, we must make abstraction from the fuller life of Dasein. See H. 50 above.

dissimulation—will come to be seen as Being-fallen & this + facticity + existence will come to be seen as the fund. constit. of D. as care.

themselves and in the meaning of their Being—namely, to conceive it as Being-present-at-hand. And even though Being-in-the-world is something of which one has pre-phenomenological experience and acquaintance [erfahren und gekannt], it becomes *invisible* if one interprets it in a way which is ontologically inappropriate. This state of Dasein's Being is now one with which one is just barely acquainted (and indeed as something obvious), with the stamp of an inappropriate interpretation. So in this way it becomes the 'evident' point of departure for problems of epistemology or the 'metaphysics of knowledge'. For what is more obvious than that a 'subject' is related to an 'Object' and *vice versa*? This 'subject-Object-relationship' must be presupposed. But while this presupposition is unimpeachable in its facticity, this makes it indeed a baleful one, if its ontological necessity and especially its ontological meaning are to be left in the dark.

Thus the phenomenon of Being-in has for the most part been represented exclusively by a single exemplar—knowing the world. This has not only been the case in epistemology; for even practical behaviour has been understood as behaviour which is '*non*-theoretical' and 'atheoretical'. Because knowing has been given this priority, our understanding of its ownmost kind of Being gets led astray, and accordingly Being-in-the-world must be exhibited even more precisely with regard to knowing the world, and must itself be made visible as an existential 'modality' of Being-in.

¶ *13. A Founded Mode in which Being-in is Exemplified.*[1] *Knowing the World.*

If Being-in-the-world is a basic state of Dasein, and one in which Dasein operates not only in general but pre-eminently in the mode of everydayness, then it must also be something which has always been experienced ontically. It would be unintelligible for Being-in-the-world to remain totally veiled from view, especially since Dasein has at its disposal an understanding of its own Being, no matter how indefinitely this understanding may function. But no sooner was the 'phenomenon of knowing the world' grasped than it got interpreted in a 'superficial',

---

[1] '*Die Exemplifizierung des In-Seins an einem fundierten Modus.*' The conception of 'founded' modes is taken from Husserl, who introduces the concept of 'founding' in his *Logische Untersuchungen*, vol. II, Part I, chapter 2 (second edition, Halle, 1913, p. 261). This passage has been closely paraphrased as follows by Marvin Farber in his *The Foundation of Phenomenology*, Cambridge, Massachusetts, 1943, p. 297; 'If in accordance with essential law an a can only exist in a comprehensive unity which connects it with a μ, then we say, an a as such needs foundation through a μ, or also, an a as such is in need of completion by means of a μ. If accordingly a_0, μ_0 are definite particular cases of the pure genera a, or μ, which stand in the cited relationship, and if they are members of one whole, then we say that a_0 is *founded* by μ_0; and it is *exclusively* founded by μ_0 if the need of the completion of a_0 is alone satisfied by μ_0. This terminology can be applied to the species themselves; the equivocation is harmless.' Thus a founded mode of Being-in is simply a mode which can subsist only when connected with something else.

formal manner. The evidence for this is the procedure (still customary today) of setting up knowing as a 'relation between subject and Object' —a procedure in which there lurks as much 'truth' as vacuity. But subject and Object do not coincide with Dasein and the world.

Even if it were feasible to give an ontological definition of "Being-in" primarily in terms of a Being-in-the-world which *knows*, it would still be our first task to show that knowing has the phenomenal character of a Being which is in and towards the world. If one reflects upon this relationship of Being, an entity called "Nature" is given proximally as that which becomes known. Knowing, as such, is not to be met in this entity. If knowing 'is' at all, it belongs solely to those entities which know. But even in those entities, human-Things, knowing is not present-at-hand. In any case, it is not externally ascertainable as, let us say, bodily properties are.[1] Now, inasmuch as knowing belongs to these entities and is not some external characteristic, it must be 'inside'. Now the more unequivocally one maintains that knowing is proximally and really 'inside' and indeed has by no means the same kind of Being as entities which are both physical and psychical, the less one presupposes when one believes that one is making headway in the question of the essence of knowledge and in the clarification of the relationship between subject and Object. For only then can the problem arise of how this knowing subject comes out of its inner 'sphere' into one which is 'other and external', of how knowing can have any object at all, and of how one must think of the object itself so that eventually the subject knows it without needing to venture a leap into another sphere. But in any of the numerous varieties which this approach may take, the question of the kind of Being which belongs to this knowing subject is left entirely unasked, though whenever its knowing gets handled, its way of Being is already included tacitly in one's theme. Of course we are sometimes assured that we are certainly not to think of the subject's "inside" [Innen] and its 'inner sphere' as a sort of 'box' or 'cabinet'. But when one asks for the positive signification of this 'inside' of immanence in which knowing is proximally enclosed, or when one inquires how this 'Being inside' ["Innenseins"] which knowing possesses has its own character of Being grounded in the kind of Being which belongs to the subject, then silence reigns. And no matter how this inner sphere may get interpreted, if one does no more than ask how knowing makes its way 'out of' it and achieves 'transcendence', it becomes evident that the knowing   61 which presents such enigmas will remain problematical unless one has previously clarified how it is and what it is.

---

1 'In jedem Falle ist est nicht so äusserlich feststellbar wie etwa leibliche Eigenschaften.' The older editions have '. . . nicht ist es . . .' and place a comma after 'feststellbar'.

With this kind of approach one remains blind to what is already tacitly implied even when one takes the phenomenon of knowing as one's theme in the most provisional manner: namely, that knowing is a mode of Being of Dasein as Being-in-the-world, and is founded ontically upon this state of Being. But if, as we suggest, we thus find phenomenally that *knowing is a kind of Being which belongs to Being-in-the-world,* one might object that with such an Interpretation of knowing, the problem of knowledge is nullified; for what is left to be asked if one *presupposes* that knowing is already 'alongside' its world, when it is not supposed to reach that world except in the transcending of the subject? In this question the constructivist 'standpoint', which has not been phenomenally demonstrated, again comes to the fore; but quite apart from this, what higher court is to decide *whether* and *in what sense* there is to be any problem of knowledge other than that of the phenomenon of knowing as such and the kind of Being which belongs to the knower?

If we now ask what shows itself in the phenomenal findings about knowing, we must keep in mind that knowing is grounded beforehand in a Being-already-alongside-the-world, which is essentially constitutive for Dasein's Being.[1] Proximally, this Being-already-alongside is not just a fixed staring at something that is purely present-at-hand. Being-in-the-world, as concern, is *fascinated by* the world with which it is concerned.[2] If knowing is to be possible as a way of determining the nature of the present-at-hand by observing it,[3] then there must first be a *deficiency* in our having-to-do with the world concernfully. When concern holds back [Sichenthalten] from any kind of producing, manipulating, and the like, it puts itself into what is now the sole remaining mode of Being-in, the mode of just tarrying alongside. . . . [das Nur-noch-verweilen bei . . .] This kind of Being towards the world is one which lets us encounter entities within-the-world purely in the *way they look* (εἶδος), just that; *on the basis* of this kind of Being, and *as* a mode of it, looking explicitly at what we encounter is possible.[4] Looking *at* something in this way is sometimes a definite way of taking up a direction towards something—of setting our sights towards what is present-at-hand. It takes over a 'view-point' in advance from the entity which it encounters. Such looking-at enters the

---

[1] '. . . dass das Erkennen selbst vorgängig gründet in einem Schon-sein-bei-der-Welt, als welches das Sein von Dasein wesenhaft konstituiert.'

[2] 'Das In-der-Welt-sein ist als Besorgen von der besorgten Welt *benommen.*' Here we follow the older editions. The newer editions have 'das Besorgen' instead of 'als Besorgen'.

[3] 'Damit Erkennen als betrachtendes Bestimmen des Vorhandenen möglich sei . . .' Here too we follow the older editions. The newer editions again have 'das' instead of 'als'.

[4] '*Auf dem Grunde* dieser Seinsart zur Welt, die das innerweltlich begegnende Seiende nur noch in seinem puren *Aussehen* (εἶδος) begegnen lässt, und *als* Modus dieser Seinsart ist ein ausdrückliches Hinsehen auf das so Begegnende möglich.'

mode of dwelling autonomously alongside entities within-the-world.[1] In this kind of '*dwelling*' as a holding-oneself-back from any manipulation or utilization, the *perception* of the present-at-hand is consummated.[2] Per-   62 ception is consummated when one *addresses* oneself to something as something and *discusses* it as such.[3] This amounts to *interpretation* in the broadest sense; and on the basis of such interpretation, perception becomes an act of *making determinate*.[4] What is thus perceived and made determinate can be expressed in propositions, and can be retained and preserved as what has thus been asserted. This perceptive retention of an assertion[5] about something is itself a way of Being-in-the-world; it is not to be Interpreted as a 'procedure' by which a subject provides itself with representations [Vorstellungen] of something which remain stored up 'inside' as having been thus appropriated, and with regard to which the question of how they 'agree' with actuality can occasionally arise.

When Dasein directs itself towards something and grasps it, it does not somehow first get out of an inner sphere in which it has been proximally encapsulated, but its primary kind of Being is such that it is always 'outside' alongside entities which it encounters and which belong to a world already discovered. Nor is any inner sphere abandoned when Dasein dwells alongside the entity to be known, and determines its character; but even in this 'Being-outside' alongside the object, Dasein is still 'inside', if we understand this in the correct sense; that is to say, it is itself 'inside' as a Being-in-the-world which knows. And furthermore, the perceiving of what is known is not a process of returning with one's booty to the 'cabinet' of consciousness after one has gone out and grasped it; even in perceiving, retaining, and preserving, the Dasein which knows *remains outside*, and it does so *as Dasein*. If I 'merely 'know [Wissen] about some way in which the Being of entities is interconnected, if I 'only' represent them, if I 'do no more' than 'think' about them, I am no less

---

[1] 'Solches Hinsehen kommt selbst in den Modus eines eigenständigen Sichaufhaltens bei dem innerweltlichen Seienden.'

[2] 'In sogearteten "*Aufenthalt*"—als dem Sichenthalten von jeglicher Hantierung and Nutzung—vollzieht sich das *Vernehmen* des Vorhandenen.' The word 'Aufenthalt' normally means a stopping-off at some place, a sojourn, an abiding, or even an abode or dwelling. Here the author is exploiting the fact that it includes both the prefixes 'auf-' and 'ent-', which we find in the verbs 'aufhalten' and 'enthalten'. 'Aufhalten' means to hold something at a stage which it has reached, to arrest it, to stop it; when used reflexively it can mean to stay at a place, to dwell there. While 'enthalten' usually means to contain, it preserves its more literal meaning of holding back or refraining, when it is used reflexively. All these meanings are presumably packed into the word 'Aufenthalt' as used here, and are hardly suggested by our 'dwelling'.

[3] 'Das Vernehmen hat die Vollzugsart des *Ansprechens* und *Besprechens* von etwas als etwas.' On 'something as something' see Section 32 below (H. 149), where 'interpretation' is also discussed.

[4] '. . . wird das Vernehmen zum *Bestimmen*.'

[5] 'Aussage'. For further discussion see Section 33 below.

alongside the entities outside in the world than when I *originally* grasp them.[1] Even the forgetting of something, in which every relationship of Being towards what one formerly knew has seemingly been obliterated, must be conceived *as a modification of the primordial Being-in*; and this holds for every delusion and for every error.

We have now pointed out how those modes of Being-in-the-world which are constitutive for knowing the world are interconnected in their foundations; this makes it plain that in knowing, Dasein achieves a new *status of Being [Seinsstand]* towards a world which has already been discovered in Dasein itself. This new possibility of Being can develop itself autonomously; it can become a task to be accomplished, and as scientific knowledge it can take over the guidance for Being-in-the-world. But a '*commercium*' of the subject with a world does not get *created* for the first time by knowing, nor does it *arise* from some way in which the world acts upon a subject. Knowing is a mode of Dasein founded upon Being-in-the-world. Thus Being-in-the-world, as a basic state, must be Interpreted *beforehand*.

[1] '. . . bei einem *originären* Erfassen.'

Task of fund. ontology has emerged as a showing of B-i-t-w. as ground, & in its very func. of grounding.

Sec. 13:
He sketches how B-i-t-w. serves as ground. Is a kind of orient. for the whole forthcoming analysis of B-i-t-w. This also involves destroying trad. preconceptions, espec. those about knowl.

THE WORLDHOOD OF THE WORLD

¶ *14. The Idea of the Worldhood of the World*[1] *in General*

BEING-IN-THE-WORLD shall first be made visible with regard to that item of its structure which is the 'world' itself. To accomplish this task seems easy and so trivial as to make one keep taking for granted that it may be dispensed with. What can be meant by describing 'the world' as a phenomenon? It means to let us see what shows itself in 'entities' within the world. Here the first step is to enumerate the things that are 'in' the world: houses, trees, people, mountains, stars. We can *depict* the way such entities 'look', and we can give an *account* of occurrences in them and with them. This, however, is obviously a pre-phenomenological 'business' which cannot be at all relevant phenomenologically. Such a description is always confined to entities. It is ontical. But what we are seeking is Being. And we have formally defined 'phenomenon' in the phenomenological sense as that which shows itself as Being and as a structure of Being.

Thus, to give a phenomenological description of the 'world' will mean to exhibit the Being of those entities which are present-at-hand within the world, and to fix it in concepts which are categorial. Now the entities within the world are Things—Things of Nature, and Things 'invested with value' ["wertbehaftete" Dinge]. Their Thinghood becomes a problem; and to the extent that the Thinghood of Things 'invested with value' is based upon the Thinghood of Nature, our primary theme is the Being of Things of Nature—Nature as such. That characteristic of Being which belongs to Things of Nature (substances), and upon which

---

1 'Welt', 'weltlich', 'Weltlichkeit', 'Weltmässigkeit'. We shall usually translate 'Welt' as 'the world' or 'a world', following English idiom, though Heidegger frequently omits the article when he wishes to refer to 'Welt' as a 'characteristic' of Dasein. In ordinary German the adjective 'weltlich' and the derivative noun 'Weltlichkeit' have much the same connotations as the English 'worldly' and 'worldliness'; but the meanings which Heidegger assigns to them (H. 65) are quite different from those of their English cognates. At the risk of obscuring the etymological connection and occasionally misleading the reader, we shall translate 'weltlich' as 'worldly', 'Weltlichkeit' as 'worldhood', and 'Weltmässigkeit' as 'worldly character'. The reader must bear in mind, however, that there is no suggestion here of the 'worldliness' of the 'man of the world'.

everything is founded, is substantiality. What is its ontological meaning? By asking this, we have given an unequivocal direction to our inquiry.

But is this a way of asking ontologically about the 'world'? The problematic which we have thus marked out is one which is undoubtedly ontological. But even if this ontology should itself succeed in explicating the Being of Nature in the very purest manner, in conformity with the basic assertions about this entity, which the mathematical natural sciences provide, it will never reach the phenomenon that is the 'world'. Nature is itself an entity which is encountered within the world and which can be discovered in various ways and at various stages.

Should we then first attach ourselves to those entities with which Dasein proximally and for the most part dwells—Things 'invested with value'? Do not these 'really' show us the world in which we live? Perhaps, in fact, they show us something like the 'world' more penetratingly. But these Things too are entities 'within' the world.

Neither the ontical depiction of entities within-the-world nor the ontological Interpretation of their Being is such as to reach the phenomenon of the 'world.' In both of these ways of access to 'Objective Being', the 'world' has already been 'presupposed', and indeed in various ways.

Is it possible that ultimately we cannot address ourselves to 'the world' as determining the nature of the entity we have mentioned? Yet we call this entity one which is "within-the-world". Is 'world' perhaps a characteristic of Dasein's Being? And in that case, does every Dasein 'proximally' have its world? Does not 'world' thus become something 'subjective'? How, then, can there be a 'common' world 'in' which, nevertheless, we *are*? And if we raise the question of the 'world', *what* world do we have in view? Neither the common world nor the subjective world, but *the world-hood of the world as such*. By what avenue do we meet this phenomenon? 'Worldhood' is an ontological concept, and stands for the structure of one of the constitutive items of Being-in-the-world. But we know Being-in-the-world as a way in which Dasein's character is defined existentially. Thus worldhood itself is an *existentiale*. If we inquire ontologically about the 'world', we by no means abandon the analytic of Dasein as a field for thematic study. Ontologically, 'world' is not a way of characterizing those entities which Dasein essentially is *not*; it is rather a characteristic of Dasein itself. This does not rule out the possibility that when we investigate the phenomenon of the 'world' we must do so by the avenue of entities within-the-world and the Being which they possess. The task of 'describing' the world phenomenologically is so far from obvious that even if we do no more than determine adequately what form it shall take, essential ontological clarifications will be needed.

This discussion of the word 'world', and our frequent use of it have made it apparent that it is used in several ways. By unravelling these we can get an indication of the different kinds of phenomena that are signified, and of the way in which they are interconnected.

1. "World" is used as an ontical concept, and signifies the totality of *entities)* those entities which can be present-at-hand within the world.

2. "World" functions as an ontological term, and signifies the Being of those entities which we have just mentioned. And indeed 'world' can become a term for any realm which encompasses a multiplicity of entities: for instance, when one talks of the 'world' of a mathematician, 'world'   65 signifies the realm of possible objects of mathematics.

*3. "World" can be understood in another ontical sense—not, however, as those entities which Dasein essentially is not and which can be en-countered within-the-world, but rather as that *'wherein'* a factical Dasein as such can be said to 'live'. "World" has here a pre-ontological existentiell signification. Here again there are different possibilities: "world" may stand for the 'public' we-world, or one's 'own' closest (domestic) environment.[1]

4. Finally, "world" designates the ontologico-existential concept of *worldhood.* Worldhood itself may have as its modes whatever structural wholes any special 'worlds' may have at the time; but it embraces in itself *worldhood)* the *a priori* character of worldhood in general. We shall reserve the expression "world" as a term for our third signification. If we should sometimes use it in the first of these senses, we shall mark this with single quotation marks.

The derivative form 'worldly' will then apply terminologically to a kind of Being which belongs to Dasein, never to a kind which belongs to entities present-at-hand 'in' the world. We shall designate these latter entities as "belonging to the world" or "within-the-world" [weltzuge-hörig oder innerweltlich].

A glance at previous ontology shows that if one fails to see Being-in-the-world as a state of Dasein, the phenomenon of worldhood likewise gets *passed over*. One tries instead to Interpret the world in terms of the Being of those entities which are present-at-hand within-the-world but which are by no means proximally discovered—namely, in terms of Nature. If one understands Nature ontologico-categorially, one finds that

---

[1] '. . . die "eigene" und nächste (häusliche) Umwelt.' The word 'Umwelt', which is customarily translated as 'environment', means literally the 'world around' or the 'world about'. The prefix 'um-', however, not only may mean 'around' or 'about', but, as we shall see, can also be used in an expression such as 'um zu . . .', which is most easily translated as 'in order to'. Section 15 will be largely devoted to a study of several words in which this same prefix occurs, though this is by no means apparent in the words we have chosen to represent them: 'Umgang' ('dealings'); 'das Um-zu' ('the "in-order-to" '); 'Umsicht' ('circumspection').

Nature is a limiting case of the Being of possible entities within-the-world. Only in some definite mode of its own Being-in-the-world can Dasein discover entities as Nature.[1] This manner of knowing them has the character of depriving the world of its worldhood in a definite way. 'Nature', as the categorial aggregate of those structures of Being which a definite entity encountered within-the-world may possess, can never make *worldhood* intelligible. But even the phenomenon of 'Nature', as it is conceived, for instance, in romanticism, can be grasped ontologically only in terms of the concept of the world—that is to say, in terms of the analytic of Dasein.

When it comes to the problem of analysing the world's worldhood ontologically, traditional ontology operates in a blind alley, if, indeed, it sees this problem at all. On the other hand, if we are to Interpret the worldhood of Dasein and the possible ways in which Dasein is made worldly [Verweltlichung], we must show *why* the kind of Being with which Dasein knows the world is such that it passes over the phenomenon of worldhood both ontically and ontologically. But at the same time the very Fact of this passing-over suggests that we must take special precautions to get the right phenomenal point of departure [Ausgang] for access [Zugang] to the phenomenon of worldhood, so that it will not get passed over.

Our method has already been assigned [Anweisung]. The theme of our analytic is to be Being-in-the-world, and accordingly the very world itself; and these are to be considered within the horizon of average everydayness—the kind of Being which is *closest* to Dasein. We must make a study of everyday Being-in-the-world; with the phenomenal support which this gives us, something like the world must come into view.

That world of everyday Dasein which is closest to it, is the *environment*. From this existential character of average Being-in-the-world, our investigation will take its course [Gang] towards the idea of worldhood in general. We shall seek the worldhood of the environment (environmentality) by going through an ontological Interpretation of those entities within-the-*environment* which we encounter as closest to us. The expression "environment" [Umwelt] contains in the 'environ' ["um"] a suggestion of spatiality. Yet the 'around' ["Umherum"] which is constitutive for the environment does not have a primarily 'spatial' meaning. Instead, the spatial character which incontestably belongs to any environment, can be clarified only in terms of the structure of worldhood. From this point of view, Dasein's spatiality, of which we have given an indication in Section 12, becomes phenomenally visible. In ontology, however, an attempt has

[1] 'Das Seiende als Natur kann das Dasein nur in einem bestimmten Modus seines In-der-Welt-seins entdecken.'

been made to start with spatiality and then to Interpret the Being of the 'world' as *res extensa*. In Descartes we find the most extreme tendency towards such an ontology of the 'world', with, indeed, a counter-orientation towards the *res cogitans*—which does not coincide with Dasein either ontically or ontologically. The analysis of worldhood which we are here attempting can be made clearer if we show how it differs from such an ontological tendency. Our analysis will be completed in three stages: (*A*) the analysis of environmentality and worldhood in general; (*B*) an illustrative contrast between our analysis of worldhood and Descartes' ontology of the 'world'; (*C*) the aroundness [das Umhafte] of the environment, and the 'spatiality' of Dasein.[1]

A. *Analysis of Environmentality and Worldhood in General*

¶ *15. The Being of the Entities Encountered in the Environment*

The Being of those entities which we encounter as closest to us can be exhibited phenomenologically if we take as our clue our everyday Being-in-the-world, which we also call our "dealings"[2] in the world and *with entities within-the-world*. Such dealings have already dispersed themselves into manifold ways of concern.[3] The kind of dealing which is closest to us is as we have shown, not a bare perceptual cognition, but rather that kind of concern which manipulates things and puts them to use; and this has its own kind of 'knowledge'. The phenomenological question applies in the first instance to the Being of those entities which we encounter in such concern. To assure the kind of seeing which is here required, we must first make a remark about method.

In the disclosure and explication of Being, entities are in every case our preliminary and our accompanying theme [das Vor-und Mitthematische]; but our real theme is Being. In the domain of the present analysis, the entities we shall take as our preliminary theme are those which show themselves in our concern with the environment. Such entities are not thereby objects for knowing the 'world' theoretically; they are simply what gets used, what gets produced, and so forth. As entities so encountered, they become the preliminary theme for the purview of a 'knowing' which, as phenomenological, looks primarily towards Being, and which, in thus taking Being as its theme, takes these entities as its accompanying theme. This phenomenological interpretation is accordingly not a way of knowing

---

[1] *A* is considered in Sections 15-18; *B* in Sections 19-21; *C* in Sections 22-24.

[2] 'Umgang'. This word means literally a 'going around' or 'going about', in a sense not too far removed from what we have in mind when we say that someone is 'going about his business'. 'Dealings' is by no means an accurate translation, but is perhaps as convenient as any. 'Intercourse' and 'trafficking' are also possible translations.

[3] See above, H. 57, n. 1, p. 83.

those characteristics of entities which themselves a r e [seiender Beschaff-
enheiten des Seienden]; it is rather a determination of the structure of
the Being which entities possess. But as an investigation of Being, it brings
to completion, autonomously and explicitly, that understanding of Being
which belongs already to Dasein and which 'comes alive' in any of its
dealings with entities. Those entities which serve phenomenologically as
our preliminary theme—in this case, those which are used or which are
to be found in the course of production—become accessible when we put
ourselves into the position of concerning ourselves with them in some
such way. Taken strictly, this talk about "putting ourselves into such a
position" [Sichversetzen] is misleading; for the kind of Being which
belongs to such concernful dealings is not one into which we need to put
ourselves first. This is the way in which everyday Dasein always *is*: when
I open the door, for instance, I use the latch. The achieving of phenomenological access to the entities which we encounter, consists rather in
thrusting aside our interpretative tendencies, which keep thrusting themselves upon us and running along with us, and which conceal not only the
phenomenon of such 'concern', but even more those entities themselves *as*
encountered of their own accord *in* our concern with them. These entangling errors become plain if in the course of our investigation we now ask
which entities shall be taken as our preliminary theme and established as
the pre-phenomenal basis for our study.

One may answer: "Things." But with this obvious answer we have
perhaps already missed the pre-phenomenal basis we are seeking. For in
addressing these entities as 'Things' (*res*), we have tacitly anticipated
their ontological character. When analysis starts with such entities and
goes on to inquire about Being, what it meets is Thinghood and Reality.
Ontological explication discovers, as it proceeds, such characteristics of
Being as substantiality, materiality, extendedness, side-by-side-ness, and
so forth. But even pre-ontologically, in such Being as this, the entities
which we encounter in concern are proximally hidden. When one designates Things as the entities that are 'proximally given', one goes ontologically astray, even though ontically one has something else in mind.
What one really has in mind remains undetermined. But suppose one
characterizes these 'Things' as Things 'invested with value'? What does
"value" mean ontologically? How are we to categorize this 'investing'
and Being-invested? Disregarding the obscurity of this structure of
investiture with value, have we thus met that phenomenal characteristic
of Being which belongs to what we encounter in our concernful dealings?

The Greeks had an appropriate term for 'Things': πράγματα—that is
to say, that which one has to do with in one's concernful dealings

(πρᾶξις). But ontologically, the specifically 'pragmatic' character of the πράγματα is just what the Greeks left in obscurity; they thought of these 'proximally' as 'mere Things'. We shall call those entities which we encounter in concern *"equipment"*.[1] In our dealings we come across equipment for writing, sewing, working, transportation, measurement. The kind of Being which equipment possesses must be exhibited. The clue for doing this lies in our first defining what makes an item of equipment—namely, its equipmentality.

Taken strictly, there 'is' no such thing as *an* equipment. To the Being of any equipment there always belongs a totality of equipment, in which it can be this equipment that it is. Equipment is essentially 'something in-order-to . . .' ["etwas um-zu . . ."]. A totality of equipment is constituted by various ways of the 'in-order-to', such as serviceability, conduciveness, usability, manipulability.

In the 'in-order-to' as a structure there lies an *assignment* or *reference* of something to something.[2] Only in the analyses which are to follow can the phenomenon which this term 'assignment' indicates be made visible in its ontological genesis. Provisionally, it is enough to take a look phenomenally at a manifold of such assignments. Equipment—in accordance with its equipmentality—always is *in terms of* [aus] its belonging to other equipment: ink-stand, pen, ink, paper, blotting pad, table, lamp, furniture, windows, doors, room. These 'Things' never show themselves

---

[1] 'das *Zeug*'. The word 'Zeug' has no precise English equivalent. While it may mean any implement, instrument, or tool, Heidegger uses it for the most part as a collective noun which is analogous to our relatively specific 'gear' (as in 'gear for fishing') or the more elaborate 'paraphernalia', or the still more general 'equipment', which we shall employ throughout this translation. In this collective sense 'Zeug' can sometimes be used in a way which is comparable to the use of 'stuff' in such sentences as 'there is plenty of stuff lying around'. (See H. 74.) In general, however, this pejorative connotation is lacking. For the most part Heidegger uses the term as a collective noun, so that he can say that there is no such thing as '*an* equipment'; but he still uses it occasionally with an indefinite article to refer to some specific tool or instrument—some item or bit of equipment.

[2] 'In der Struktur "Um-zu" liegt eine *Verweisung* von etwas auf etwas.' There is no close English equivalent for the word 'Verweisung', which occurs many times in this chapter. The basic metaphor seems to be that of *turning* something away towards something else, or *pointing* it away, as when one 'refers' or 'commits' or 'relegates' or 'assigns' something to something else, whether one 'refers' a symbol to what it symbolizes, 'refers' a beggar to a welfare agency, 'commits' a person for trial, 'relegates' or 'banishes' him to Siberia, or even 'assigns' equipment to a purpose for which it is to be used. 'Verweisung' thus does some of the work of 'reference', 'commitment', 'assignment', 'relegation', 'banishment'; but it does not do *all* the work of any of these expressions. For a businessman to 'refer' to a letter, for a symbol to 'refer' to what it symbolizes, for a man to 'commit larceny or murder' or merely to 'commit himself' to certain partisan views, for a teacher to give a pupil a long 'assignment', or even for a journalist to receive an 'assignment' to the Vatican, we would have to find some other verb than 'verweisen'. We shall, however, use the verbs 'assign' and 'refer' and their derivatives as perhaps the least misleading substitutes, employing whichever seems the more appropriate in the context, and occasionally using a hendiadys as in the present passage. See Section 17 for further discussion. (When other words such as 'anweisen' or 'zuweisen' are translated as 'assign', we shall usually subjoin the German in brackets.)

proximally as they are for themselves, so as to add up to a sum of *realia* and fill up a room. What we encounter as closest to us (though not as something taken as a theme) is the room; and we encounter it not as something 'between four walls' in a geometrical spatial sense, but as equipment for residing. Out of this the 'arrangement' emerges, and it is in this that any 'individual' item of equipment shows itself. *Before* it does so, a totality of equipment has already been discovered.

Equipment can genuinely show itself only in dealings cut to its own measure (hammering with a hammer, for example); but in such dealings an entity of this kind is *not grasped* thematically as an occurring Thing, nor is the equipment-structure known as such even in the using. The hammering does not simply have knowledge about [um] the hammer's character as equipment, but it has appropriated this equipment in a way which could not possibly be more suitable. In dealings such as this, where something is put to use, our concern subordinates itself to the "in-order-to" which is constitutive for the equipment we are employing at the time; the less we just stare at the hammer-Thing, and the more we seize hold of it and use it, the more primordial does our relationship to it become, and the more unveiledly is it encountered as that which it is—as equipment. The hammering itself uncovers the specific 'manipulability' ["Handlichkeit"] of the hammer. The kind of Being which equipment possesses—in which it manifests itself in its own right—we call "*readiness-to-hand*" [*Zuhandenheit*].[1] Only because equipment has *this* 'Being-in-itself' and does not merely occur, is it manipulable in the broadest sense and at our disposal. No matter how sharply we just *look* [Nur-noch-hinsehen] at the 'outward appearance' ["Aussehen]" of Things in whatever form this takes, we cannot discover anything ready-to-hand. If we look at Things just 'theoretically', we can get along without understanding readiness-to-hand. But when we deal with them by using them and manipulating them, this activity is not a blind one; it has its own kind of sight, by which our manipulation is guided and from which it acquires its specific Thingly character. Dealings with equipment subordinate themselves to the manifold assignments of the 'in-order-to'. And the sight with which they thus accommodate themselves is *circumspection*.[2]

---

[1] Italics only in earlier editions.

[2] The word 'Umsicht', which we translate by 'circumspection', is here presented as standing for a special kind of 'Sicht' ('sight'). Here, as elsewhere, Heidegger is taking advantage of the fact that the prefix 'um' may mean either 'around' or 'in order to'. 'Umsicht' may accordingly be thought of as meaning 'looking around' or 'looking around for something' or 'looking around for a way to get something done'. In ordinary German usage, 'Umsicht' seems to have much the same connotation as our 'circumspection'—a kind of awareness in which one looks around before one decides just what one ought to do next. But Heidegger seems to be generalizing this notion as well as calling attention to

praxis not mindless

'Practical' behaviour is not 'atheoretical' in the sense of "sightlessness".[1] The way it differs from theoretical behaviour does not lie simply in the fact that in theoretical behaviour one observes, while in practical behaviour one *acts* [*gehandelt* wird], and that action must employ theoretical cognition if it is not to remain blind; for the fact that observation is a kind of concern is just as primordial as the fact that action has *its own* kind of sight. Theoretical behaviour is just looking, without circumspection. But the fact that this looking is non-circumspective does not mean that it follows no rules: it constructs a canon for itself in the form of *method*.

The ready-to-hand is not grasped theoretically at all, nor is it itself the sort of thing that circumspection takes proximally as a circumspective theme. The peculiarity of what is proximally ready-to-hand is that, in its readiness-to-hand, it must, as it were, withdraw [zurückzuziehen] in order to be ready-to-hand quite authentically. That with which our everyday dealings proximally dwell is not the tools themselves [die Werkzeuge selbst]. On the contrary, that with which we concern ourselves primarily is the work—that which is to be produced at the time; and this is accordingly ready-to-hand too. The work bears with it that referential totality within which the equipment is encountered.[2]　　　70

The work to be produced, as the "*towards-which*" of such things as the hammer, the plane, and the needle, likewise has the kind of Being that belongs to equipment. The shoe which is to be produced is for wearing (footgear) [Schuhzeug]; the clock is manufactured for telling the time. The work which we chiefly encounter in our concernful dealings—the work that is to be found when one is "at work" on something [das in Arbeit befindliche]—has a usability which belongs to it essentially; in this usability it lets us encounter already the "towards-which" for which *it* is usable. A work that someone has ordered [das bestellte Werk] i s only by reason of its use and the assignment-context of entities which is discovered in using it.

But the work to be produced is not merely usable for something. The

the extent to which circumspection in the narrower sense occurs in our every-day living. (The distinction between 'sight' (Sicht') and 'seeing' ('Sehen') will be developed further in Sections 31 and 36 below.)

[1] '. . . im Sinne der Sichtlosigkeit . . .' The point of this sentence will be clear to the reader who recalls that the Greek verb θεωρεῖν, from which the words 'theoretical' and 'atheoretical' are derived, originally meant 'to see'. Heidegger is pointing out that this is not what we have in mind in the traditional contrast between the 'theoretical' and the 'practical'.

[2] 'Das Werk trägt die Verweisungsganzheit, innerhalb derer das Zeug begegnet.' In this chapter the word 'Werk' ('work') usually refers to the product achieved by working rather than to the process of working as such. We shall as a rule translate 'Verweisungsganzheit' as 'referential totality', though sometimes the clumsier 'totality of assignments' may convey the idea more effectively. (The older editions read 'deren' rather than 'derer'.)

WORLDHOOD = totality of the references

production itself is a using *of* something for something. In the work there is also a reference or assignment to 'materials': the work is dependent on [angewiesen auf] leather, thread, needles, and the like. Leather, moreover is produced from hides. These are taken from animals, which someone else has raised. Animals also occur within the world without having been raised at all; and, in a way, these entities still produce themselves even when they have been raised. So in the environment certain entities become accessible which are always ready-to-hand, but which, in themselves, do not need to be produced. Hammer, tongs, and needle, refer in themselves to steel, iron, metal, mineral, wood, in that they consist of these. In equipment that is used, 'Nature' is discovered along with it by that use—the 'Nature' we find in natural products.

Here, however, "Nature" is not to be understood as that which is just present-at-hand, nor as the *power of Nature*. The wood is a forest of timber, the mountain a quarry of rock; the river is water-power, the wind is wind 'in the sails'. As the 'environment' is discovered, the 'Nature' thus discovered is encountered too. If its kind of Being as ready-to-hand is disregarded, this 'Nature' itself can be discovered and defined simply in its pure presence-at-hand. But when this happens, the Nature which 'stirs and strives', which assails us and enthralls us as landscape, remains hidden. The botanist's plants are not the flowers of the hedgerow; the 'source' which the geographer establishes for a river is not the 'springhead in the dale'.

The work produced refers not only to the "towards-which" of its usability and the "whereof" of which it consists: under simple craft conditions it also has an assignment to the person who is to use it or wear it. The work is cut to his figure; he 'is' there along with it as the work emerges. Even when goods are produced by the dozen, this constitutive assignment is by no means lacking; it is merely indefinite, and points to the random, the average. Thus along with the work, we encounter not only entities ready-to-hand but also entities with Dasein's kind of Being— entities for which, in their concern, the product becomes ready-to-hand; and together with these we encounter the world in which wearers and users live, which is at the same time ours. Any work with which one concerns oneself is ready-to-hand not only in the domestic world of the workshop but also in the *public world*. Along with the public world, the *environing Nature* [*die Umweltnatur*] is discovered and is accessible to everyone. In roads, streets, bridges, buildings, our concern discovers Nature as having some definite direction. A covered railway platform takes account of bad weather; an installation for public lighting takes account of the darkness, or rather of specific changes in the presence or absence of daylight—the 'position of the sun'. In a clock, account is taken of some definite constellation in the world-system. When we look at the clock, we tacitly make use of the 'sun's position', in accordance with which the measurement of time gets regulated in the official astronomical manner. When we make use of the clock-equipment, which is proximally and inconspicuously ready-to-hand, the environing Nature is ready-to-hand along with it. Our concernful absorption in whatever work-world lies closest to us, has a function of discovering; and it is essential to this function that, depending upon the way in which we are absorbed, those entities within-the-world which are brought along [beigebrachte] in the work and with it (that is to say, in the assignments or references which are constitutive for it) remain discoverable in varying degrees of explicitness and with a varying circumspective penetration.

The kind of Being which belongs to these entities is readiness-to-hand. But this characteristic is not to be understood as merely a way of taking them, as if we were talking such 'aspects' into the 'entities' which we proximally encounter, or as if some world-stuff which is proximally present-at-hand in itself[1] were 'given subjective colouring' in this way. Such an Interpretation would overlook the fact that in this case these entities would have to be understood and discovered beforehand as something purely present-at-hand, and must have priority and take the lead in the sequence of those dealings with the 'world' in which something is discovered and made one's own. But this already runs counter to the ontological meaning of cognition, which we have exhibited as a *founded* mode of Being-in-the-world.[2] To lay bare what is just present-at-hand and no more, cognition must first penetrate *beyond* what is ready-to-hand in our concern. *Readiness-to-hand is the way in which entities as they are 'in themselves' are defined ontologico-categorially.* Yet only by reason of something present-at-hand, 'is there' anything ready-to-hand. Does it follow, however, granting this thesis for the nonce, that readiness-to-hand is ontologically founded upon presence-at-hand?

But even if, as our ontological Interpretation proceeds further, readiness-to-hand should prove itself to be the kind of Being characteristic of those entities which are proximally discovered within-the-world, and even if its primordiality as compared with pure presence-at-hand can be demonstrated, have all these explications been of the slightest help towards understanding the phenomenon of the world ontologically? In Interpreting these entities within-the-world, however, we have always

72

---

[1] '. . . ein zunächst an sich vorhandener Weltstoff . . .' The earlier editions have '. . . zunächst ein an sich vorhandener Weltstoff . . .'.

[2] See H. 61 above.

'presupposed' the world. Even if we join them together, we still do not get anything like the 'world' as their sum. If, then, we start with the Being of these entities, is there any avenue that will lead us to exhibiting the phenomenon of the world?[i]

¶ *16. How the Worldly Character of the Environment Announces itself in Entities Within-the-world*[1]

The world itself is not an entity within-the-world; and yet it is so determinative for such entities that only in so far as 'there is' a world can they be encountered and show themselves, in their Being, as entities which have been discovered. But in what way 'is there' a world? If Dasein is ontically constituted by Being-in-the-World, and if an under-standing of the Being of its Self belongs just as essentially to its Being, no matter how indefinite that understanding may be, then does not Dasein have an understanding of the world—a pre-ontological understanding, which indeed can and does get along without explicit ontological insights? With those entities which are encountered within-the-world—that is to say, with their character as within-the-world—does not something like the world show itself for concernful Being-in-the-world? Do we not have a pre-phenomenological glimpse of this phenomenon? Do we not always have such a glimpse of it, without having to take it as a theme for onto-logical Interpretation? Has Dasein itself, in the range of its concernful absorption in equipment ready-to-hand, a possibility of Being in which the worldhood of those entities within-the-world with which it is con-cerned is, in a certain way, lit up for it, *along with* those entities themselves?

If such possibilities of Being for Dasein can be exhibited within its concernful dealings, then the way lies open for studying the phenomenon which is thus lit up, and for attempting to 'hold it at bay', as it were, and to interrogate it as to those structures which show themselves therein.

73   To the everydayness of Being-in-the-world there belong certain modes of concern. These permit the entities with which we concern ourselves to be encountered in such a way that the worldly character of what is within-the-world comes to the fore. When we concern ourselves with something, the entities which are most closely ready-to-hand may be met as something unusable, not properly adapted for the use we have decided upon. The tool turns out to be damaged, or the material unsuitable. In each of these cases *equipment* is here, ready-to-hand. We discover its unusability, how-ever, not by looking at it and establishing its properties, but rather by the circumspection of the dealings in which we use it. When its unusability is thus discovered, equipment becomes conspicuous. This *conspicuousness*

----

[1] '*Die am innerweltlich Seienden sich meldende Weltmässigkeit der Umwelt.*'

presents the ready-to-hand equipment as in a certain un-readiness-to-hand. But this implies that what cannot be used just lies there; it shows itself as an equipmental Thing which looks so and so, and which, in its readiness-to-hand as looking that way, has constantly been present-at-hand too. Pure presence-at-hand announces itself in such equipment, but only to withdraw to the readiness-to-hand of something with which one concerns oneself—that is to say, of the sort of thing we find when we put it back into repair. This presence-at-hand of something that cannot be used is still not devoid of all readiness-to-hand whatsoever; equipment which is present-at-hand *in this way* is still not just a Thing which occurs somewhere. The damage to the equipment is still not a mere alteration of a Thing—not a change of properties which just occurs in something present-at-hand.

In our concernful dealings, however, we not only come up against unusable things *within* what is ready-to-hand already: we also find things which are missing—which not only are not 'handy' ["handlich"] but are not 'to hand' ["zur Hand"] at all. Again, to miss something in this way amounts to coming across something un-ready-to-hand. When we notice what is un-ready-to-hand, that which i s ready-to-hand enters the mode of *obtrusiveness* The more urgently [Je dringlicher] we need what is missing, and the more authentically it is encountered in its un-readiness-to-hand, all the more obtrusive [um so aufdringlicher] does that which is ready-to-hand become—so much so, indeed, that it seems to lose its character of readiness-to-hand. It reveals itself as something just present-at-hand and no more, which cannot be budged without the thing that is missing. The helpless way in which we stand before it is a deficient mode of concern, and as such it uncovers the Being-just-present-at-hand-and-no-more of something ready-to-hand.

In our dealings with the world[1] of our concern, the un-ready-to-hand can be encountered not only in the sense of that which is unusable or simply missing, but as something un-ready-to-hand which is *not* missing at all and *not* unusable, but which 'stands in the way' of our concern. That to which our concern refuses to turn, that for which it has 'no time', is something *un*-ready-to-hand in the manner of what does not belong here, of what has not as yet been attended to. Anything which is un-ready-to-hand in this way is disturbing to us, and enables us to see the *obstinacy* of that with which we must concern ourselves in the first instance before we do anything else. With this obstinacy, the presence-at-hand of the ready-to-hand makes itself known in a new

---

[1] In the earlier editions 'Welt' appears with quotation marks. These are omitted in the later editions.

way as the Being of that which still lies before us and calls for our attending to it.[1]

The modes of conspicuousness, obtrusiveness, and obstinacy all have the function of bringing to the fore the characteristic of presence-at-hand in what is ready-to-hand. But the ready-to-hand is not thereby just *observed* and stared at as something present-at-hand; the presence-at-hand which makes itself known is still bound up in the readiness-to-hand of equipment. Such equipment still does not veil itself in the guise of mere Things. It becomes 'equipment' in the sense of something which one would like to shove out of the way.[2] But in such a Tendency to shove things aside, the ready-to-hand shows itself as still ready-to-hand in its unswerving presence-at-hand.

Now that we have suggested, however, that the ready-to-hand is thus encountered under modifications in which its presence-at-hand is revealed, how far does this clarify the *phenomenon of the world?* Even in analysing these modifications we have not gone beyond the Being of what is within-the-world, and we have come no closer to the world-phenomenon than before. But though we have not as yet grasped it, we have brought ourselves to a point where we can bring it into view.

In conspicuousness, obtrusiveness, and obstinacy, that which is ready-to-hand loses its readiness-to-hand in a certain way. But in our dealings with what is ready-to-hand, this readiness-to-hand is itself understood, though not thematically. It does not vanish simply, but takes its farewell, as it were, in the conspicuousness of the unusable. Readiness-to-hand still shows itself, and it is precisely here that the worldly character of the ready-to-hand shows itself too.

---

[1] Heidegger's distinction between 'conspicuousness' (Auffälligkeit') 'obtrusiveness' ('Aufdringlichkeit'), and 'obstinacy' ('Aufsässigkeit') is hard to present unambiguously in translation. He seems to have in mind three rather similar situations. In each of these we are confronted by a number of articles which are ready-to-hand. In the first situation we wish to use one of these articles for some purpose, but we find that it cannot be used for that purpose. It then becomes 'conspicuous' or 'striking', and *in a way* 'un-ready-to-hand' —in that we are not able to use it. In the second situation we may have precisely the same articles before us, but we want one which is not there. In this case the missing article too is 'un-ready-to-hand', but in another way—in that it is not there to be used. This is annoying, and the articles which are still ready-to-hand before us, thrust themselves upon us in such a way that they become 'obtrusive' or even 'obnoxious'. In the third situation, some of the articles which are ready-to-hand before us are experienced as *obstacles* to the achievement of some purpose; as obstacles they are 'obstinate', 'recalcitrant', 'refractory', and we have to attend to them or dispose of them in some way before we can finish what we want to do. Here again the obstinate objects are un-ready-to-hand, but simply in the way of being obstinate.

In all three situations the articles which are ready-to-hand for us tend to lose their readiness-to-hand in one way or another and reveal their presence-at-hand; only in the second situation, however, do we encounter them as 'just present-at-hand and no more' ('nur noch Vorhandenes').

[2] Here 'Zeug' is used in the pejorative sense of 'stuff'. See our note 1, p. 97 on H. 68.

The structure of the Being of what is ready-to-hand as equipment is determined by references or assignments. In a peculiar and obvious manner, the 'Things' which are closest to us are 'in themselves' ["An-sich"]; and they are encountered as 'in themselves' in the concern which makes use of them without noticing them explicitly—the concern which can come up against something unusable. When equipment cannot be used, this implies that the constitutive assignment of the "in-order-to" to a "towards-this" has been disturbed. The assignments themselves are not observed; they are rather 'there' when we concernfully submit our-selves to them [Sichstellen unter sie]. But *when an assignment has been disturbed*—when something is unusable for some purpose—then the assignment becomes explicit. Even now, of course, it has not become explicit as an ontological structure; but it has become explicit ontically for the circumspection which comes up against the damaging of the tool. When an assignment to some particular "towards-this" has been thus circumspectively aroused, we catch sight of the "towards-this" itself, and along with it everything connected with the work—the whole 'work-shop'—as that wherein concern always dwells. The context of equipment is lit up, not as something never seen before, but as a totality constantly sighted beforehand in circumspection. With this totality, however, the world announces itself.

75

Similarly, when something ready-to-hand is found missing, though its everyday presence [Zugegensein] has been so obvious that we have never taken any notice of it, this makes a *break* in those referential contexts which circumspection discovers. Our circumspection comes up against emptiness, and now sees for the first time *what* the missing article was ready-to-hand *with*, and *what* it was ready-to-hand *for*. The environment announces itself afresh. What is thus lit up is not itself just one thing ready-to-hand among others; still less is it something *present-at-hand* upon which equipment ready-to-hand is somehow founded: it is in the 'there' before anyone has observed or ascertained it. It is itself inaccessible to circumspection, so far as circumspection is always directed towards entities; but in each case it has already been disclosed for cir-cumspection. 'Disclose' and 'disclosedness' will be used as technical terms in the passages that follow, and shall signify 'to lay open' and 'the charac-ter of having been laid open.' Thus 'to disclose' never means anything like 'to obtain indirectly by inference'.[1]

---

[1] In ordinary German usage, the verb 'erschliessen' may mean not only to 'disclose' but also—in certain constructions—to 'infer' or 'conclude' in the sense in which one 'infers' a conclusion from premises. Heidegger is deliberately ruling out this latter interpretation, though on a very few occasions he may use the word in this sense. He explains his own meaning by the cognate verb 'aufschliessen', to 'lay open'. To say that something has been 'disclosed' or 'laid open' in Heidegger's sense, does not mean that one has any

That the world does not 'consist' of the ready-to-hand shows itself in the fact (among others) that whenever the world is lit up in the modes of concern which we have been Interpreting, the ready-to-hand becomes deprived of its worldhood so that Being-just-present-at-hand comes to the fore. If, in our everyday concern with the 'environment', it is to be possible for equipment ready-to-hand to be encountered in its 'Being-in-itself' [in seinem "An-sich-sein"], then those assignments and referential totalities in which our circumspection 'is absorbed' cannot become a theme for that circumspection any more than they can for grasping things 'thematically' but non-circumspectively. If it is to be possible for the ready-to-hand not to emerge from its inconspicuousness, the world *must not announce itself.* And it is in this that the Being-in-itself of entities which are ready-to-hand has its phenomenal structure constituted.

In such privative expressions as "inconspicuousness", "unobtrusiveness", and "non-obstinacy", what we have in view is a positive phenomenal character of the Being of that which is proximally ready-to-hand. With these negative prefixes we have in view the character of the ready-to-hand as "holding itself in"; this is what we have our eye upon in the "Being-in-itself" of something,[1] though 'proximally' we ascribe it to the present-at-hand—to the present-at-hand as that which can be thematically ascertained. As long as we take our orientation primarily and exclusively from the present-at-hand, the 'in-itself' can by no means be ontologically clarified. If, however, this talk about the 'in-itself' has any ontological importance, some interpretation must be called for. This "in-itself" of Being is something which gets invoked with considerable emphasis, mostly in an ontical way, and rightly so from a phenomenal standpoint. But if some *ontological* assertion is supposed to be given when this is *ontically* invoked, its claims are not fulfilled by such a procedure. As the foregoing analysis has already made clear, only on the basis of the phenomenon of the world can the Being-in-itself of entities within-the-world be grasped ontologically.

But if the world can, in a way, be lit up, it must assuredly be disclosed. And it has already been disclosed beforehand whenever what is ready-to-hand within-the-world is accessible for circumspective concern. The world is therefore something 'wherein' Dasein as an entity already *was,* and if in

detailed awareness of the contents which are thus 'disclosed', but rather that they have been 'laid open' to us as implicit in what is given, so that they may be made explicit to our awareness by further analysis or discrimination of the given, rather than by any inference from it.

[1] 'Diese "Un" meinen den Charakter des Ansichhaltens des Zuhandenen, das, was wir mit dem An-sich-sein im Auge haben . . .' The point seems to be that when we speak of something 'as it is "in itself" or "in its own right" ', we think of it as 'holding itself in' or 'holding itself back'—not 'stepping forth' or doing something 'out of character'.

any manner it explicitly comes away from anything, it can never do more than come back to the world.

Being-in-the-world, according to our Interpretation hitherto, amounts to a non-thematic circumspective absorption in references or assignments constitutive for the readiness-to-hand of a totality of equipment. Any concern is already as it is, because of some familiarity with the world. In this familiarity Dasein can lose itself in what it encounters within-the-world and be fascinated with it. What is it that Dasein is familiar with? Why can the worldly character of what is within-the-world be lit up? The presence-at-hand[1] of entities is thrust to the fore by the possible breaks in that referential totality in which circumspection 'operates'; how are we to get a closer understanding of this totality?

These questions are aimed at working out both the phenomenon and the problems of worldhood, and they call for an inquiry into the interconnections with which certain structures are built up. To answer them we must analyse these structures more concretely.

¶ *17. Reference and Signs* – *Deals w. the phenomenal basis for the analysis.*

In our provisional Interpretation of that structure of Being which belongs to the ready-to-hand (to 'equipment'), the phenomenon of reference or assignment became visible; but we merely gave an indication of it, and in so sketchy a form that we at once stressed the necessity of uncovering it with regard to its ontological origin.[2] It became plain, moreover, that assignments and referential totalities could in some sense become constitutive for worldhood itself. Hitherto we have seen the world lit up only in and for certain definite ways in which we concern ourselves environmentally with the ready-to-hand, and indeed it has been lit up only *with* the readiness-to-hand of that concern. So the further we proceed in understanding the Being of entities within-the-world, the broader and   77
firmer becomes the phenomenal basis on which the world-phenomenon may be laid bare.

We shall again take as our point of departure the Being of the ready-to-hand, but this time with the purpose of grasping the phenomenon of *reference* or *assignment* itself more precisely. We shall accordingly attempt an ontological analysis of a kind of equipment in which one may come across such 'references' in more senses than one. We come across 'equipment' in *signs*. The word "sign" designates many kinds of things: not only may it stand for different *kinds* of signs, but Being-a-sign-for can itself be

---

[1] Here the older editions have 'Zuhandenheit' where the newer ones have 'Vorhandenheit'.

[2] Cf. H. 68 above.

formalized as a _universal kind of relation,_ so that the sign-structure itself provides an ontological clue for 'characterizing' any entity whatsoever.

But signs, in the first instance, are themselves items of equipment whose specific character as equipment consists in *showing* or *indicating*.[1] We find such signs in signposts, boundary-stones, the ball for the mariner's storm-warning, signals, banners, signs of mourning, and the like. Indicating can be defined as a 'kind' of referring. Referring is, if we take it as formally as possible, a _relating._ But relation does not function as a genus for 'kinds' or 'species' of references which may somehow become differentiated as sign, symbol, expression, or signification. A relation is something quite formal which may be read off directly by way of 'formalization' from any kind of context, whatever its subject-matter or its way of Being.[ii]

Every reference is a relation, but not every relation is a reference. Every 'indication' is a reference, but not every referring is an indicating. This implies at the same time that every 'indication' is a relation, but not every relation is an indicating. The formally general character of relation is thus brought to light. If we are to investigate such phenomena as references, signs, or even significations, nothing is to be gained by characterizing them as relations. Indeed we shall eventually have to show that 'relations' themselves, *because of* their formally general character, have their ontological source in a reference.

If the present analysis is to be confined to the Interpretation of the sign as distinct from the phenomenon of reference, then even within this limitation we cannot properly investigate the full multiplicity of possible signs. Among signs there are symptoms [Anzeichen], warning signals, signs of things that have happened already [Rückzeichen], signs to mark something, signs by which things are recognized; these have different ways of indicating, regardless of what may be serving as such a sign. From such 'signs' we must distinguish traces, residues, commemorative monuments, documents, testimony, symbols, expressions, appearances, significations. These phenomena can easily be formalized because of their formal relational character; we find it especially tempting nowadays to take such a 'relation' as a clue for subjecting every entity to a kind of 'Interpretation' which always 'fits' because at bottom it says nothing, no more than the facile schema of content and form.

As an example of a sign we have chosen one which we shall use again in a later analysis, though in another regard. Motor cars are sometimes fitted up with an adjustable red arrow, whose position indicates

---

[1] '. . . deren spezifischer Zeugcharakter im *Zeigen* besteht.' While we have often used 'show' and 'indicate' to translate 'zeigen' and 'anzeigen' respectively, in the remainder of this section it seems more appropriate to translate 'zeigen' by 'indicate', or to resort to hendiadys as in the present passage.

the direction the vehicle will take—at an intersection, for instance. The position of the arrow is controlled by the driver. This sign is an item of equipment which is ready-to-hand for the driver in his concern with driving, and not for him alone: those who are not travelling with him—and they in particular—also make use of it, either by giving way on the proper side or by stopping. This sign is ready-to-hand within-the-world in the whole equipment-context of vehicles and traffic regulations. It is equipment for indicating, and as equipment, it is constituted by reference or assignment. It has the character of the "in-order-to", its own definite serviceability; it is for indicating.[1] This indicating which the sign performs can be taken as a kind of 'referring'. But here we must notice that this 'referring' as indicating is not the ontological structure of the sign as equipment.

Instead, 'referring' as indicating is grounded in the Being-structure of equipment, in serviceability for. . . . But an entity may have serviceability without thereby becoming a sign. As equipment, a 'hammer' too is constituted by a serviceability, but this does not make it a sign. Indicating, as a 'reference', is a way in which the "towards-which" of a serviceability becomes ontically concrete; it determines an item of equipment as for this "towards-which" [und bestimmt ein Zeug zu diesem]. On the other hand, the kind of reference we get in 'serviceability-for', is an ontologico-categorial attribute of equipment *as* equipment. That the "towards-which" of serviceability should acquire its concreteness in indicating, is an accident of its equipment-constitution as such. In this example of a sign, the difference between the reference of serviceability and the reference of indicating becomes visible in a rough and ready fashion. These are so far from coinciding that only when they are united does the concreteness of a definite kind of equipment become possible. Now it is certain that indicating differs in principle from reference as a constitutive state of equipment; it is just as incontestable that the sign in its turn is related in a peculiar and even distinctive way to the kind of Being which belongs to whatever equipmental totality may be ready-to-hand in the environment, and to its worldly character. In our concernful

79

---

[1] 'Es hat den Charakter des Um-zu, seine bestimmte Dienlichkeit, es ist zum Zeigen.' The verb 'dienen', is often followed by an infinitive construction introduced by the preposition 'zu'. Similarly the English 'serve' can be followed by an infinitive in such expressions as 'it serves to indicate . . .' In Heidegger's German the 'zu' construction is carried over to the noun 'Dienlichkeit'; the corresponding noun 'serviceability', however, is not normally followed by an infinitive, but rather by an expression introduced by 'for' *e.g.* 'serviceability for indicating . . .' Since the preposition 'zu' plays an important role in this section and the next, it would be desirable to provide a uniform translation for it. We shall, however, translate it as 'for' in such expressions as 'Dienlichkeit zu', but as 'towards' in such expressions as 'Wozu' ('towards-which') and 'Dazu' ('towards-this'), retaining 'in-order-to' for 'Um-zu'.

dealings, equipment for indicating [Zeig-zeug] gets used in a *very special* way. But simply to establish this Fact is ontologically insufficient. The basis and the meaning of this special status must be clarified.

What do we mean when we say that a sign "indicates"? We can answer this only by determining what kind of dealing is appropriate with equipment for indicating. And we must do this in such a way that the readiness-to-hand of that equipment can be genuinely grasped. What is the appropriate way of having-to-do with signs? Going back to our example of the arrow, we must say that the kind of behaving (Being) which corresponds to the sign we encounter, is either to 'give way' or to 'stand still' *vis-à-vis* the car with the arrow. Giving way, as taking a direction, belongs essentially to Dasein's Being-in-the-world. Dasein is always somehow directed [ausgerichtet] and on its way; standing and waiting are only limiting cases of this directional 'on-its-way'. The sign addresses itself to a Being-in-the-world which is specifically 'spatial'. The sign is *not* authentically 'grasped' ["erfasst"] if we just stare at it and identify it as an indicator-Thing which occurs. Even if we turn our glance in the direction which the arrow indicates, and look at something present-at-hand in the region indicated, even then the sign is not authentically encountered. Such a sign addresses itself to the circumspection of our concernful dealings, and it does so in such a way that the circumspection which goes along with it, following where it points, brings into an explicit 'survey' whatever aroundness the environment may have at the time. This circumspective survey does not *grasp* the ready-to-hand; what it achieves is rather an orientation within our environment. There is also another way in which we can experience equipment: we may encounter the arrow simply as equipment which belongs to the car. We can do this without discovering what character it specifically has as equipment: what the arrow is to indicate and how it is to do so, may remain completely undetermined; yet what we are encountering is not a mere Thing. The experiencing of a Thing requires a *definiteness* of its own [ihre eigene *Bestimmtheit*], and must be contrasted with coming across a manifold of equipment, which may often be quite indefinite, even when one comes across it as especially close.

Signs of the kind we have described let what is ready-to-hand be encountered; more precisely, they let some context of it become accessible in such a way that our concernful dealings take on an orientation and hold it secure. A sign is not a Thing which stands to another Thing in the relationship of indicating; it is rather *an item of equipment which explicitly raises a totality of equipment into our circumspection so that together with it the worldly character of the ready-to-hand announces itself.* In a symptom or a warning-signal, 'what is coming' 'indicates itself', but not in the sense of something

80

merely occurring, which comes as an addition to what is already present-at-hand; 'what is coming' is the sort of thing which we are ready for, or which we 'weren't ready for' if we have been attending to something else.[1] In signs of something that has happened already, what has come to pass and run its course becomes circumspectively accessible. A sign to mark something indicates what one is 'at' at any time. Signs always indicate primarily 'wherein' one lives, where one's concern dwells, what sort of involvement there is with something.[2]

The peculiar character of signs as equipment becomes especially clear in 'establishing a sign' ["Zeichenstiftung"]. This activity is performed in a circumspective fore-sight [Vorsicht] out of which it arises, and which requires that it be possible for one's particular environment to announce itself for circumspection at any time by means of something ready-to-hand, and that this possibility should itself be ready-to-hand. But the Being of what is most closely ready-to-hand within-the-world possesses the character of holding-itself-in and not emerging, which we have described above.[3] Accordingly our circumspective dealings in the environment require some equipment ready-to-hand which in its character as equipment takes over the 'work' of *letting* something ready-to-hand *become conspicuous*. So when such equipment (signs) gets produced, its conspicuousness must be kept in mind. But even when signs are thus conspicuous, one does not let them be present-at-hand at random; they get 'set up' ["angebracht"] in a definite way with a view towards easy accessibility.

In establishing a sign, however, one does not necessarily have to produce equipment which is not yet ready-to-hand at all. Signs also arise when one *takes as a sign* [Zum-Zeichen-nehmen] something that is ready-to-hand already. In this mode, signs "get established" in a sense which is even more primordial. In indicating, a ready-to-hand equipment totality, and even the environment in general, can be provided with an availability which is circumspectively oriented; and not only this: establishing a sign can, above all, reveal. What gets taken as a sign becomes accessible only through its readiness-to-hand. If, for instance, the south wind 'is accepted' ["gilt"] by the farmer as a sign of rain, then this 'acceptance' ["Geltung"] —or the 'value' with which the entity is 'invested'—is not a sort of bonus over and above what is already present-at-hand in itself—*viz*, the flow of air in a definite geographical direction. The south wind may be meteorologically accessible as something which just occurs; but it is *never* present-

---

[1] '. . . das "was kommt" ist solches, darauf wir uns gefasst machen, bzw. "nicht gefasst waren", sofern wir uns mit anderem befassten.'

[2] 'Das Merkzeichen zeigt, "woran" man jeweils ist. Die Zeichen zeigen primär immer das, "worin" man lebt, wobei das Besorgen sich aufhält, welche Bewandtnis es damit hat.' On 'Bewandtnis', see note 2, p. 115 H. 84 below.

[3] See H. 75-76 above.

81 at-hand *proximally* in such a way as this, only occasionally taking over the function of a warning signal. On the contrary, only by the circumspection with which one takes account of things in farming, is the south wind discovered in its Being.

But, one will protest, *that which* gets taken as a sign must first have become accessible in itself and been apprehended *before* the sign gets established. Certainly it must in any case be such that in some way we can come across it. The question simply remains as to *how* entities are discovered in this previous encountering, whether as mere Things which occur, or rather as equipment which has not been understood—as something ready-to-hand with which we have hitherto not known 'how to begin', and which has accordingly kept itself veiled from the purview of circumspection. *And here again, when the equipmental characters of the ready-to-hand are still circumspectively undiscovered, they are not to be Interpreted as bare Thinghood presented for an apprehension of what is just present-at-hand and no more.*

The Being-ready-to-hand of signs in our everyday dealings, and the conspicuousness which belongs to signs and which may be produced for various purposes and in various ways, do not merely serve to document the inconspicuousness constitutive for what is most closely ready-to-hand; the sign itself gets its conspicuousness from the inconspicuousness of the equipmental totality, which is ready-to-hand and 'obvious' in its everydayness. The knot which one ties in a handkerchief [der bekannte "Knopf im Taschentuch"] as a sign to mark something is an example of this. What such a sign is to indicate is always something with which one has to concern oneself in one's everyday circumspection. Such a sign can indicate many things, and things of the most various kinds. The wider the extent to which it can indicate, the narrower its intelligibility and its usefulness. Not only is it, for the most part, ready-to-hand as a sign only for the person who 'establishes' it, but it can even become inaccessible to him, so that another sign is needed if the first is to be used circumspectively at all. So when the knot cannot be used as a sign, it does not lose its sign-character, but it acquires the disturbing obtrusiveness of something most closely ready-to-hand.

One might be tempted to cite the abundant use of 'signs' in primitive Dasein, as in fetishism and magic, to illustrate the remarkable role which they play in everyday concern when it comes to our understanding of the world. Certainly the establishment of signs which underlies this way of using them is not performed with any theoretical aim or in the course of theoretical speculation. This way of using them always remains completely within a Being-in-the-world which is 'immediate'. But on

closer inspection it becomes plain that to interpret fetishism and
magic by taking our clue from the idea of signs in general, is not enough   82
to enable us to grasp the kind of 'Being-ready-to-hand' which belongs to
entities encountered in the primitive world. With regard to the sign-
phenomenon, the following Interpretation may be given: for primitive
man, the sign coincides with that which is indicated. Not only can the
sign represent this in the sense of serving as a substitute for what it indicates, but it can do so in such a way that the sign itself always *is* what it
indicates. This remarkable coinciding does not mean, however, that the
sign-Thing has already undergone a certain 'Objectification'—that it has
been experienced as a mere Thing and misplaced into the same realm of
Being of the present-at-hand as what it indicates. This 'coinciding' is not
an identification of things which have hitherto been isolated from each
other: it consists rather in the fact that the sign has not as yet become free
from that of which it is a sign. Such a use of signs is still absorbed completely in Being-towards what is indicated, so that a sign as such cannot
detach itself at all. This coinciding is based not on a prior Objectification
but on the fact that such Objectification is completely lacking. This means,
however, that signs are not discovered as equipment at all—that ultimately
what is 'ready-to-hand' within-the-world just does not have the kind of
Being that belongs to equipment. Perhaps even readiness-to-hand and
equipment have nothing to contribute [nichts auszurichten] as ontological
clues in Interpreting the primitive world; and certainly the ontology of
Thinghood does even less. But if an understanding of Being is constitutive
for primitive Dasein and for the primitive world in general, then it is all
the more urgent to work out the 'formal' idea of worldhood—or at least
the idea of a phenomenon modifiable in such a way that all ontological
assertions to the effect that in a given phenomenal context something is
not yet such-and-such or *no longer* such-and-such, may acquire a *positive*
phenomenal meaning in terms of what it is *not*.[1]

The foregoing Interpretation of the sign should merely provide phenomenal support for our characterization of references or assignments.
The relation between sign and reference is threefold. 1. Indicating, as a
way whereby the "towards-which" of a serviceability can become concrete, is founded upon the equipment-structure as such, upon the "in-
order-to" (assignment). 2. The indicating which the sign does is an
equipmental character of something ready-to-hand, and as such it belongs
to a totality of equipment, to a context of assignments or references.
3. The sign is not only ready-to-hand with other equipment, but in its
readiness-to-hand the environment becomes in each case explicitly

---

[1] '. . . aus dem, was es *nicht* ist.' The older editions write 'was' for 'was'.

accessible for circumspection. *A sign is something ontically ready-to-hand,*
which functions both as this definite equipment and as something indicative of
[was . . . anzeigt] the ontological structure of readiness-to-hand, of referential
totalities, and of worldhood. Here is rooted the special status of the sign as
something ready-to-hand in that environment with which we concern
ourselves circumspectively. Thus the reference or the assignment itself
cannot be conceived as a sign if it is to serve ontologically as the foundation upon which signs are based. Reference is not an ontical characteristic
of something ready-to-hand, when it is rather that by which readiness-
to-hand itself is constituted.

In what sense, then, is reference 'presupposed' ontologically in the
ready-to-hand, and to what extent is it, as such an ontological foundation,
at the same time constitutive for worldhood in general?

¶ *18. Involvement and Significance; the Worldhood of the World*

The ready-to-hand is encountered within-the-world. The Being of this
entity, readiness-to-hand, thus stands in some ontological relationship
towards the world and towards worldhood. In anything ready-to-hand
the world is always 'there'. Whenever we encounter anything, the world
has already been previously discovered, though not thematically. But it
can also be lit up in certain ways of dealing with our environment. The
world is that in terms of which the ready-to-hand is ready-to-hand. How
can the world let the ready-to-hand be encountered? Our analysis
hitherto has shown that what we encounter within-the-world has, in its
very Being, been freed[1] for our concernful circumspection, for taking
account. What does this previous freeing amount to, and how is this to
be understood as an ontologically distinctive feature of the world? What
problems does the question of the worldhood of the world lay before us?

We have indicated that the state which is constitutive for the ready-to-
hand as equipment is one of reference or assignment. How can entities
with this kind of Being be freed by the world with regard to their Being?
Why are these the first entities to be encountered? As definite kinds of
references we have mentioned serviceability-for-, detrimentality [Abträg-
lichkeit], usability, and the like. The "towards-which" [das Wozu] of a
serviceability and the "for-which" [das Wofür] of a usability prescribed
the ways in which such a reference or assignment can become concrete.
But the 'indicating' of the sign and the 'hammering' of the hammer are
not properties of entities. Indeed, they are not properties at all, if the
ontological structure designated by the term 'property' is that of some

---

[1] 'freigegeben'. The idea seems to be that what we encounter has, as it were, been
released, set free, given its freedom, or given free rein, so that our circumspection can take
account of it.

definite character which it is possible for Things to possess [einer möglichen Bestimmtheit von Dingen]. Anything ready-to-hand is, at the worst, appropriate for some purposes and inappropriate for others; and its 'properties' are, as it were, still bound up in these ways in which it is appropriate or inappropriate,[1] just as presence-at-hand, as a possible kind of Being for something ready-to-hand, is bound up in readiness-to-hand. Serviceability too, however, as a constitutive state of equipment (and serviceability is a reference), is not an appropriateness of some entity; it is rather the condition (so far as Being is in question) which makes it possible for the character of such an entity to be defined by its appropriatenesses. But what, then, is "reference" or "assignment" to mean? To say that the Being of the ready-to-hand has the structure of assignment or reference means that it has in itself the character of *having been assigned or referred* [*Verwiesenheit*]. An entity is discovered when it has been assigned or referred to something, and referred as that entity which it is. *With* any such entity there is an involvement which it has *in* something.[2] The character of Being which belongs to the ready-to-hand is just such an *involvement.* If something has an involvement, this implies letting it be involved in something. The relationship of the "with ... in ..." shall be indicated by the term "assignment" or "reference".[3]

84

---

[1] The words 'property' and 'appropriateness' reflect the etymological connection of Heidegger's 'Eigenschaft' and "Geeignetheit'.

[2] 'Es hat *mit* ihm *bei* etwas sein Bewenden.' The terms 'Bewenden' and 'Bewandtnis' are among the most difficult for the translator. Their root meaning has to do with the way something is already '*turning*' when one lets it 'go its own way', 'run its course', follow its 'bent' or 'tendency', or finish 'what it is about', 'what it is up to' or 'what it is involved in'. The German expressions, however, have no simple English equivalents, but are restricted to a rather special group of idioms such as the following, which we have taken from Wildhagen and Héraucourt's admirable *English-German, German-English Dictionary* (Volume II, Wiesbaden 1953): 'es dabei bewenden lassen'—'to leave it at that, to let it go at that, to let it rest there'; 'und dabei hatte es sein Bewenden'—'and there the matter ended'; 'dabei muss es sein Bewenden haben'—'there the matter must rest'—'that must suffice'; 'die Sache hat eine ganz andere Bewandtnis'—'the case is quite different'; 'damit hat es seine besondere Bewandtnis'—'there is something peculiar about it; thereby hangs a tale'; 'damit hat est folgende Bewandtnis'—'the matter is as follows'.

We have tried to render both 'Bewenden' and 'Bewandtnis' by expressions including either 'involve' or 'involvement'. But the contexts into which these words can easily be fitted in ordinary English do not correspond very well to those which are possible for 'Bewenden' and 'Bewandtnis'. Our task is further complicated by the emphasis which Heidegger gives to the prepositions 'mit' and 'bei' in connection with 'Bewenden' and 'Bewandtnis'. In passages such as the present one, it would be more idiomatic to leave these prepositions untranslated and simply write: 'Any such entity is involved in doing something', or 'Any such entity is involved in some activity'. But 'mit' and 'bei' receive so much attention in this connection that in contexts such as this we shall sometimes translate them as 'with' and 'in', though elsewhere we shall handle 'bei' very differently. (The reader must bear in mind that the kind of 'involvement' with which we are here concerned is always an involvement of equipment in 'what it is up to' or what it is 'doing', not a person's involvement in circumstances in which he is 'caught' or 'entangled'.

[3] 'In Bewandtnis liegt: bewenden lassen mit etwas bei etwas. Der Bezug des "mit

When an entity within-the-world has already been proximally freed for its Being, that Being is its "involvement". With any such entity as entity, there is some involvement. The fact that it has such an involvement is *ontologically* definitive for the Being of such an entity, and is not an ontical assertion about it. That in which it is involved is the "towards-which" of serviceability, and the "for-which" of usability.[1] With the "towards-which" of serviceability there can again be an involvement: *with* this thing, for instance, which is ready-to-hand, and which we accordingly call a "hammer", there is an involvement in hammering; with hammering, there is an involvement in making something fast; with making something fast, there is an involvement in protection against bad weather; and this protection 'is' for the sake of [um-willen] providing shelter for Dasein—that is to say, for the sake of a possibility of Dasein's Being. Whenever something ready-to-hand has an involvement with it, *what* involvement this is, has in each case been outlined in advance in terms of the totality of such involvements. In a workshop, for example, the totality of involvements which is constitutive for the ready-to-hand in its readiness-to-hand, is 'earlier' than any single item of equipment; so too for the farmstead with all its utensils and outlying lands. But the totality of involvements itself goes back ultimately to a "towards-which" in which there is *no* further involvement: this "towards-which" is not an entity with the kind of Being that belongs to what is ready-to-hand within a world; it is rather an entity whose Being is defined as Being-in-the-world, and to whose state of Being, worldhood itself belongs. This primary "towards-which" is not just another "towards-this" as something in which an involvement is possible. The primary 'towards-which' is a "for-the-sake-of-which".[2] But the 'for-the-sake-of' always pertains to the Being of

... bei ..." soll durch den Terminus Verweisung angezeigt werden.' Here the point seems to be that if something *has* an 'involvement' in the sense of 'Bewandtnis' (or rather, if there is such an involvement 'with' it), the thing which has this involvement has been 'assigned' or 'referred' for a certain activity or purpose 'in' which it may be said to be involved.

[1] 'Bewandtnis ist das Sein des innerweltlichen Seienden, darauf es je schon zunächst freigegeben ist. Mit ihm als Seiendem hat es je eine Bewandtnis. Dieses, dass es eine Bewandtnis hat, ist die *ontologische* Bestimmung des Seins dieses Seienden, nicht eine ontische Aussage über das Seiende. Das Wobei es die Bewandtnis hat, ist das Wozu der Dienlichkeit, das Wofür der Verwendbarkeit.' This passage and those which follow are hard to translate because Heidegger is using three carefully differentiated prepositions ('zu', 'für', and 'auf') where English idiom needs only 'for'. We can say that something is serviceable, usable, or applicable '*for*' a purpose. and that it may be freed or given free rein 'for' some kind of activity. In German, however, it will be said to have 'Dienlichkeit *zu* . . .', 'Verwendbarkeit *für* . . .'; and it will be 'freigegeben *auf* . . .'. In the remainder of this section we shall use 'for' both for 'für' and for 'auf' as they occur in these expressions; we shall, however, continue to use 'towards-which' for the 'Wozu' of 'Dienlichkeit'. See note 1, p. 109, H. 78 above.

[2] 'Dieses primäre Wozu ist kein Dazu als mögliches Wobei einer Bewandtnis. Das primäre "Wozu" ist ein Worum-willen.'

Dasein, for which, in its Being, that very Being is essentially an *issue*. We have thus indicated the interconnection by which the structure of an involvement leads to Dasein's very Being as the sole authentic "for-the-sake-of-which"; for the present, however, we shall pursue this no further. 'Letting something be involved' must first be clarified enough to give the phenomenon of worldhood the kind of definiteness which makes it possible to formulate any problems about it.

Ontically, "letting something be involved" signifies that within our factical concern we let something ready-to-hand *be* so-and-so *as* it is already and *in order that* it be such.[1] The way we take this ontical sense of 'letting be' is, in principle, ontological. And therewith we Interpret the meaning of previously freeing what is proximally ready-to-hand within-the-world. Previously letting something 'be' does not mean that we must first bring it into its Being and produce it; it means rather that something which is already an 'entity' must be discovered in its readiness-to-hand, and that we must thus let the entity which has this Being be encountered. This '*a priori*' letting-something-be-involved is the condition for the possibility of encountering anything ready-to-hand, so that Dasein, in its ontical dealings with the entity thus encountered, can thereby let it be involved in the ontical sense.[2] On the other hand, if letting something be involved is understood ontologically, what is then pertinent is the freeing of *everything* ready-to-hand as ready-to-hand, no matter whether, taken ontically, it is involved thereby, or whether it is rather an entity of precisely such a sort that ontically it is *not* involved thereby. Such entities are, proximally and for the most part, those with which we concern ourselves when we do not let them 'be' as we have discovered that they are, but work upon them, make improvements in them, or smash them to pieces.

When we speak of having already let something be involved, so that it has been freed for that involvement, we are using a *perfect* tense *a priori* which characterizes the kind of Being belonging to Dasein itself.[3] Letting an entity be involved, if we understand this ontologically, consists in previously freeing it for [auf] its readiness-to-hand within the environment. When we let something be involved, it must be involved in something; and in terms of this "in-which", the "with-which" of this involvement

85

---

[1] 'Bewendenlassen bedeutet ontisch; innerhalb eines faktischen Besorgens ein Zuhandenes so und so *sein* lassen, *wie* es nunmehr ist und *damit* es so ist.'

[2] '. . . es im ontischen Sinne dabei bewenden lassen kann.' While we have translated 'dabei' simply as 'thereby' in this context, it is possible that it should have been construed rather as an instance of the special use of 'bei' with 'bewenden lassen'. A similar ambiguity occurs in the following sentence.

[3] 'Das auf Bewandtnis hin freigebende Je-schon-haben-bewenden-lassen ist ein apriorisches Perfekt, das die Seinsart des Daseins selbst charakterisiert.'

is freed.[1] Our concern encounters it as this thing that is ready-to-hand. To the extent that any *entity shows itself to concern*[2]—that is, to the extent that it is discovered in its Being—it is already something ready-to-hand environmentally; it just is not 'proximally' a 'world-stuff' that is merely present-at-hand.

As the Being of something ready-to-hand, an involvement is itself discovered only on the basis of the prior discovery of a totality of involvements. So in any involvement that has been discovered (that is, in anything ready-to-hand which we encounter), what we have called the "worldly character" of the ready-to-hand has been discovered beforehand. In this totality of involvements which has been discovered beforehand, there lurks an ontological relationship to the world. In letting entities be involved so that they are freed for a totality of involvements, one must have disclosed already that for which [woraufhin] they have been freed. But that for which something environmentally ready-to-hand has thus been freed (and indeed in such a manner that it becomes accessible *as* an entity within-the-world first of all), cannot itself be conceived as an entity with this discovered kind of Being. It is essentially not discoverable, if we henceforth reserve "*discoveredness*" as a term for a possibility of Being which every entity *without* the character of Dasein may possess.

But what does it mean to say that that for which[3] entities within-the-world are proximally freed must have been previously disclosed? To Dasein's Being, an understanding of Being belongs. Any understanding [Verständnis] has its Being in an act of understanding [Verstehen]. If Being-in-the-world is a kind of Being which is essentially befitting to Dasein, then to understand Being-in-the-world belongs to the essential content of its understanding of Being. The previous disclosure of that for which what we encounter within-the-world is subsequently freed,[4] amounts to nothing else than understanding the world—that world towards which Dasein as an entity always comports itself.

Whenever we let there be an involvement with something in something beforehand, our doing so is grounded in our understanding such things as letting something be involved, and such things as the "with-which" and the "in-which" of involvements. Anything of this sort, and anything else

---

[1] 'Aus dem Wobei des Bewendenlassens her ist das Womit der Bewandtnis freigegeben.'
[2] Here we follow the newer editions in reading: 'Sofern sich ihm überhaupt ein *Seiendes* zeigt . . .'. The older editions read 'Sofern sich mit ihm . . .', which is somewhat ambiguous but suggests that we should write: 'To the extent that with what is ready-to-hand any *entity* shows itself . . .'.
[3] 'worauf'. The older editions have 'woraufhin'.
[4] 'Das vorgängige Erschliessen dessen, woraufhin die Freigabe des innerweltlichen Begegnenden erfolgt . . .'

that is basic for it, such as the "towards-this" as that in which there is an involvement, or such as the "for-the-sake-of-which" to which every "towards-which" ultimately goes back[1]—all these must be disclosed beforehand with a certain intelligibility [Verständlichkeit]. And what is that wherein Dasein as Being-in-the-world understands itself pre-onto-logically? In understanding a context of relations such as we have mentioned, Dasein has assigned itself to an "in-order-to" [Um-zu], and it has done so in terms of a potentiality-for-Being for the sake of which it itself is—one which it may have seized upon either explicitly or tacitly, and which may be either authentic or inauthentic. This "in-order-to" prescribes a "towards-this" as a possible "in-which" for letting something be involved; and the structure of letting it be involved implies that this is an involvement which something *has*—an involvement which is *with* something. Dasein always assigns itself from a "for-the-sake-of-which" to the "with-which" of an involvement; that is to say, to the extent that it is, it always lets entities be encountered as ready-to-hand.[2] *That wherein* [*Worin*] Dasein understands itself beforehand in the mode of assigning itself is *that for which* [das *Woraufhin*] it has let entities be encountered beforehand. *The "wherein" of an act of understanding which assigns or refers itself, is that for which one lets entities be encountered in the kind of Being that belongs to involvements; and this "wherein" is the phenomenon of the world.*[3] And the structure of that to which [woraufhin] Dasein assigns itself is what makes up the *worldhood* of the world.

That wherein Dasein already understands itself in this way is always something with which it is primordially familiar. This familiarity with the world does not necessarily require that the relations which are constitutive for the world as world should be theoretically transparent. However, the possibility of giving these relations an explicit ontologico-existential Interpretation, is grounded in this familiarity with the world; and this familiarity, in turn, is constitutive for Dasein, and goes to make up Dasein's understanding of Being. This possibility is one which can be seized upon explicitly in so far as Dasein has set itself the task of giving a primordial Interpretation for its own Being and for the possibilities of that Being, or indeed for the meaning of Being in general.

---

[1] '. . . wie das Dazu, als wobei es die Bewandtnis hat, das Worum-willen, darauf letztlich alles Wozu zurückgeht.' The older editions have '. . . als wobei es je die Bewandtnis hat . . .' and omit the hyphen in 'Worum-willen'.

[2] 'Dieses zeichnet ein Dazu vor, als mögliches Wobei eines Bewendenlassens, das strukturmässig *mit* etwas bewenden lässt. Dasein verweist sich je schon immer aus einem Worum-willen her an das Womit einer Bewandtnis, d. h. es lässt je immer schon, sofern es ist, Seiendes als Zuhandenes begegnen.'

[3] '*Das Worin des sichverweisenden Verstehens als Woraufhin des Begegnenlassens von Seiendem in der Seinsart der Bewandtnis ist das Phänomen der Welt.*'

But as yet our analyses have done no more than lay bare the horizon within which such things as the world and worldhood are to be sought. If we are to consider these further, we must, in the first instance, make it still more clear how the context of Dasein's assigning-itself is to be taken ontologically.

In the _act of understanding_ [*Verstehen*], which we shall analyse more thoroughly later (Compare Section 31), the relations indicated above must have been previously disclosed; the act of understanding holds them in this disclosedness. It holds itself in them with familiarity; and in so doing, it holds them *before* itself, for it is in these that its assignment operates.[1] The understanding lets itself make assignments both i n these relationships themselves and o f them.[2] The relational character which these relationships of assigning possess, we take as one of _signifying_.[3] In its familiarity with these relationships, Dasein 'signifies' to itself: in a primordial manner it gives itself both its Being and its potentiality-for-Being as something which it is to understand with regard to its Being-in-the-world. The "for-the-sake-of-which" signifies an "in-order-to"; this in turn, a "towards-this"; the latter, an "in-which" of letting something be involved; and that in turn, the "with-which" of an involvement. These relationships are bound up with one another as a primordial totality; they are what they are a s this signifying [Be-deuten] in which Dasein gives itself beforehand its Being-in-the-world as something to be understood. The relational totality of this signifying we call _"significance"._ This is what makes up the structure of the world—the structure of that wherein Dasein as such already is. *Dasein, in its familiarity with significance, is the ontical condition for the possibility of discovering entities which are encountered in a world with involvement (readiness-to-hand) as their kind of Being, and which can thus make themselves known as they are in themselves [in seinem An-sich].* Dasein as such is always something of this sort; along with its Being, a context of the ready-to-hand is already essentially discovered: Dasein, in so far as it

---

[1] 'Das . . . Verstehen . . . hält die angezeigten Bezüge in einer vorgängigen Erschlossenheit. Im vertrauten Sich-darin-halten hält es sich diese *vor* als das, worin sich sein Verweisen bewegt.' The context suggests that Heidegger's 'diese' refers to the relationships (Bezüge) rather than to the disclosedness (Erschlossenheit), though the latter interpretation seems a bit more plausible grammatically.

[2] 'Das Verstehen lässt sich in und von diesen Bezügen selbst verweisen.' It is not entirely clear whether 'von' should be translated as 'of', 'from', or 'by'.

[3] *'be-deuten'*. While Heidegger ordinarily writes this word without a hyphen (even, for instance, in the next sentence), he here takes pains to hyphenate it so as to suggest that etymologically it consists of the intensive prefix 'be-' followed by the verb 'deuten'—to 'interpret', 'explain' or 'point to' something. We shall continue to follow our convention of usually translating 'bedeuten' and 'Bedeutung' by 'signify' and 'signification' respectively, reserving 'significance' for 'Bedeutsamkeit' (or, in a few cases, for 'Bedeutung'). But these translations obscure the underlying meanings which Heidegger is emphasizing in this passage.

is, has always submitted[1] itself already to a 'world' which it encounters, and this *submission*[1] belongs essentially to its Being.

But in significance itself, with which Dasein is always familiar, there lurks the ontological condition which makes it possible for Dasein, as something which understands and interprets, to disclose such things as 'significations'; upon these, in turn, is founded the Being of words and of language.

The significance thus disclosed is an existential state of Dasein—of its Being-in-the-world; and as such it is the ontical condition for the possibility that a totality of involvements can be discovered.

If we have thus determined that the Being of the ready-to-hand (involvement) is definable as a context of assignments or references, and that even worldhood may so be defined, then has not the 'substantial Being' of entities within-the-world been volatilized into a system of Relations? And inasmuch as Relations are always 'something thought', has not the Being of entities within-the-world been dissolved into 'pure thinking'?

88

Within our present field of investigation the following structures and dimensions of ontological problematics, as we have repeatedly emphasized, must be kept in principle distinct: 1. the Being of those entities within-the-world which we proximally encounter—readiness-to-hand; 2. the Being of those entities which we can come across and whose nature we can determine if we discover them in their own right by going through the entities proximally encountered—presence-at-hand; 3. the Being of that ontical condition which makes it possible for entities within-the-world to be discovered at all—the worldhood of the world. This third kind of Being gives us an *existential* way of determining the nature of Being-in-the-world, that is, of Dasein. The other two concepts of Being are *categories*, and pertain to entities whose Being is not of the kind which Dasein possesses. The context of assignments or references, which, as significance, is constitutive for worldhood, can be taken formally in the sense of a system of Relations. But one must note that in such formalizations the phenomena get levelled off so much that their real phenomenal content may be lost, especially in the case of such 'simple' relationships as those which lurk in significance. The phenomenal content of these 'Relations' and 'Relata'

---

[1] 'angewiesen'; '*Angewiesenheit*'. The verb 'anweisen', like 'verweisen', can often be translated as 'assign', particularly in the sense in which one assigns or allots a place to something, or in the sense in which one gives an 'assignment' to someone by instructing him how to proceed. The past participle 'angewiesen' can thus mean 'assigned' in either of these senses; but it often takes on the connotation of 'being dependent on' something or even 'at the mercy' of something. In this passage we have tried to compromise by using the verb 'submit'. Other passages call for other idioms, and no single standard translation seems feasible.

—the "in-order-to", the "for-the-sake-of", and the "with-which" of an
involvement—is such that they resist any sort of mathematical function-
alization; nor are they merely something thought, first posited in an 'act
of thinking.' They are rather relationships in which concernful circumspection as such already dwells. This 'system of Relations', as something
constitutive for worldhood, is so far from volatilizing the Being of the
ready-to-hand within-the-world, that the worldhood of the world provides the basis on which such entities can for the first time be discovered
as they are 'substantially' 'in themselves'. And only if entities within-the-
world can be encountered at all, is it possible, in the field of such entities,
to make accessible what is just present-at-hand and no more. By reason of
their Being-just-present-at-hand-and-no-more, these latter entities can
have their 'properties' defined mathematically in 'functional concepts.'
Ontologically, such concepts are possible only in relation to entities whose
Being has the character of pure substantiality. Functional concepts are
never possible except as formalized substantial concepts.

In order to bring out the specifically ontological problematic of worldhood even more sharply, we shall carry our analysis no further until we
have clarified our Interpretation of worldhood by a case at the opposite
extreme.

89   *B. A Contrast between our Analysis of Worldhood and Descartes'*
Interpretation of the World

Only step by step can the concept of worldhood and the structures
which this phenomenon embraces be firmly secured in the course of our
investigation. The Interpretation of the world begins, in the first instance,
with some entity within-the-world, so that the phenomenon of the world
in general no longer comes into view; we shall accordingly try to clarify
this approach ontologically by considering what is perhaps the most
extreme form in which it has been carried out. We not only shall
present briefly the basic features of Descartes' ontology of the 'world', but
shall inquire into its presuppositions and try to characterize these in the
light of what we have hitherto achieved. The account we shall give of
these matters will enable us to know upon what basically undiscussed
ontological 'foundations' those Interpretations of the world which have
come after Descartes—and still more those which preceded him—have
operated.

Descartes sees the *extensio* as basically definitive ontologically for the
world. In so far as extension is one of the constituents of spatiality (according to Descartes it is even identical with it), while in some sense spatiality
remains constitutive for the world, a discussion of the Cartesian ontology

of the 'world' will provide us likewise with a negative support for a positive explication of the spatiality of the environment and of Dasein itself. With regard to Descartes' ontology there are three topics which we shall treat: 1. the definition of the 'world' as *res extensa* (Section 19); 2. the foundations of this ontological definition (Section 20); 3. a hermeneutical discussion of the Cartesian ontology of the 'world' (Section 21). The considerations which follow will not have been grounded in full detail until the '*cogito sum*' has been phenomenologically destroyed. (See Part Two, Division 2.)[1]

¶ *19. The Definition of the 'World' as* r e s e x t e n s a.

Descartes distinguishes the '*ego cogito*' from the '*res corporea*'. This distinction will thereafter be determinative ontologically for the distinction between 'Nature' and 'spirit'. No matter with how many variations of content the opposition between 'Nature' and 'spirit' may get set up ontically, its ontological foundations, and indeed the very poles of this opposition, remain unclarified; this unclarity has its proximate [nächste] roots in Descartes' distinction. What kind of understanding of Being does he have when he defines the Being of these entities? The term for the Being of an entity that is in itself, is "*substantia*". Sometimes this expression means the *Being* of an entity as substance, *substantiality*; at other times it means the entity itself, *a substance*. That "*substantia*" is used in these two ways is not accidental; this already holds for the ancient conception of οὐσία.

    To determine the nature of the *res corporea* ontologically, we must explicate the substance of this entity as a substance—that is, its substantiality. What makes up the authentic Being-in-itself [An-ihm-selbst-sein] of the *res corporea*? How is it at all possible to grasp a substance as such, that is, to grasp its substantiality? "*Et quidem ex quolibet attributo substantia cognoscitur; sed una tamen est cuiusque substantiae praecipua proprietas, quae ipsius naturam essentiamque constituit, et ad quam aliae omnes referuntur.*"[iii] Substances become accessible in their 'attributes', and every substance has some distinctive property from which the essence of the substantiality of that definite substance can be read off. Which property is this in the case of the *res corporea*? "*Nempe e x t e n s i o in longum, latum et profundum, substantiae corporeae naturam constituit.*"[iv] Extension—namely, in length, breadth, and thickness—makes up the real Being of that corporeal substance which we call the 'world'. What gives the *extensio* this distinctive status? "*Nam omne aliud quod corpori tribui potest, extensionem praesupponit . . .*"[v] Extension is a state-of-Being constitutive for the entity we are talking about; it is that

90

<hr/>

[1] This portion of *Being and Time* has never been published.

which must already 'be' before any other ways in which Being is determined, so that these can 'be' what they are. Extension must be 'assigned'
["zugewiesen"] primarily to the corporeal Thing. The 'world's' extension
and substantiality (which itself is characterized by extension) are accordingly demonstrated by showing how all the other characteristics which
this substance definitely possesses (especially *divisio, figura, motus*), can be
conceived only as *modi* of *extensio*, while, on the other hand, *extensio sine
figura vel motu* remains quite intelligible.

Thus a corporeal Thing that maintains its total extension can still
undergo many changes in the ways in which that extension is distributed
in the various dimensions, and can present itself in manifold shapes as
one and the same Thing. ". . . *atque unum et idem corpus, retinendo suam
eandem quantitatem, pluribus diversis modis potest extendi: nunc scilicet magis
secundum longitudinem, minusque secundum latitudinem vel profunditatem, ac paulo
post e contra magis secundum latitudinem, et minus secundum longitudinem.*"vi

91   Shape is a *modus* of *extensio*, and so is motion: for *motus* is grasped only
"*si de nullo nisi locali cogitemus, ac de vi a qua excitatur . . . non inquiramus.*"vii
If the motion is a property of the *res corporea*, and a property which i s,
then in order for it to be experienceable in its Being, it must be conceived
in terms of the Being of this entity itself, in terms of *extensio*; this means
that it must be conceived as mere change of location. So nothing like
'force' counts for anything in determining what the *Being* of this entity is.
Matter may have such definite characteristics as hardness, weight, and
colour; (*durities, pondus, color*); but these can all be taken away from it,
and it still remains what it is. These do not go to make up its real Being;
and in so far as they *are*, they turn out to be modes of *extensio*. Descartes
tries to show this in detail with regard to 'hardness': "*Nam, quantum ad
duritiem, nihil aliud de illa sensus nobis indicat, quam partes durorum corporum
resistere motui manuum nostrarum, cum in illas incurrant. Si enim, quotiescunque
manus nostrae versus aliquam partem moventur, corpora omnia ibi existentia recederent eadem celeritate qua illae accedunt, nullam unquam duritiem sentiremus. Nec
ullo modo potest intelligi, corpora quae sic recederent, idcirco naturam corporis esse
amissura; nec proinde ipsa in duritie consistit.*"viii Hardness is experienced
when one feels one's way by touch [Tasten]. What does the sense of touch
'tell' us about it? The parts of the hard Thing 'resist' a movement of the
hand, such as an attempt to push it away. If, however, hard bodies, those
which do not give way, should change their locations with the same
velocity as that of the hand which 'strikes at' them, nothing would ever
get touched [Berühren], and hardness would not be experienced and
would accordingly never *be*. But it is quite incomprehensible that bodies
which give way with such velocity should thus forfeit any of their

corporeal Being. If they retain this even under a change in velocity which makes it impossible for anything like 'hardness' to be, then hardness does not belong to the Being of entities of this sort. *"Eademque ratione ostendi potest, et pondus, et colorem, et alias omnes eiusmodi qualitates, quae in materia corporea sentiuntur, ex ea tolli posse, ipsa integra remanente: unde sequitur, a nulla ex illis eius ⟨sc. extensionis⟩ naturam dependere."*ix Thus what makes up the Being of the *res corporea* is the *extensio*: that which is *omnimodo divisibile, figurabile et mobile* (that which can change itself by being divided, shaped, or moved in any way), that which is *capax mutationum*—that which main-   92 tains itself (*remanet*) through all these changes. In any corporeal Thing the real entity is what is suited for thus *remaining constant* [*ständigen Verbleib*], so much so, indeed that this is how the substantiality of such a substance gets characterized.

¶ *20. Foundations of the Ontological Definition of the 'World'*

Substantiality is the idea of Being to which the ontological characterization of the *res extensa* harks back. *"Per substantiam nihil aliud intelligere possumus, quam rem quae ita existit, ut nulla alia re indigeat ad existendum."* "By substance we can understand nothing else than an entity which *is* in such a way that it needs no other entity in order to *be*."x The Being of a 'substance' is characterized by not needing anything. That whose Being is such that it has no need at all for any other entity satisfies the idea of substance in the authentic sense; this entity is the *ens perfectissimum*. *". . . substantia quae nulla plane re indigeat, unica tantum potest intelligi, nempe Deus."*xi Here 'God' is a purely ontological term, if it is to be understood as *ens perfectissimum*. At the same time, the 'self-evident' connotation of the concept of God is such as to permit an ontological interpretation for the characteristic of not needing anything—a constitutive item in substantiality. *"Alias vero omnes ⟨res⟩, non nisi ope concursus Dei existere posse percipimus."*xii All entities other than God need to be "produced" in the widest sense and also to be sustained. 'Being' is to be understood within a horizon which ranges from the production of what is to be present-at-hand to something which has no need of being produced. Every entity which is not God is an *ens creatum*. The Being which belongs to one of these entities is 'infinitely' different from that which belongs to the other; yet we still consider creation and creator alike *as entities*. We are thus using "Being" in so wide a sense that its meaning embraces an 'infinite' difference. So even created entities can be called "substance" with some right. Relative to God, of course, these entities need to be produced and sustained; but within the realm of created entities—the 'world' in the sense of *ens creatum*—there are things which 'are in need of no other entity' relatively to the creaturely production and sustentation that we find, for instance, in man. Of these substances there are two kinds: the *res cogitans* and the *res extensa*.

93   The Being of that substance whose distinctive *proprietas* is presented by *extensio* thus becomes definable in principle ontologically if we clarify the *meaning* of Being which is '*common*' to the three kinds of substances, one of them infinite, the others both finite. But ". . . *nomen substantiae non convenit Deo et illis u n i v o c e ut dici solet in Scholis, hoc est . . . quae Deo et creaturis sit communis.*"ˣⁱⁱⁱ Here Descartes touches upon a problem with which medieval ontology was often busied—the question of how the signification of "Being" signifies any entity which one may on occasion be considering. In the assertions 'God is' and 'the world is', we assert Being. This word 'is', however, cannot be meant to apply to these entities in the same sense (συνωνύμως, *univoce*), when between them there is an *infinite* difference of Being; if the signification of 'is' were univocal, then what is created would be viewed as if it were uncreated, or the uncreated would be reduced to the status of something created. But neither does 'Being' function as a mere name which is the same in both cases: in both cases 'Being' is understood. This positive sense in which 'Being' signifies is one which the Schoolmen took as a signification 'by analogy', as distinguished from one which is univocal or merely homonymous. Taking their departure from Aristotle, in whom this problem is foreshadowed in prototypical form just as at the very outset of Greek ontology, they established various kinds of analogy, so that even the 'Schools' have different ways of taking the signification-function of "Being". In working out this problem ontologically, Descartes is always far behind the Schoolmen;ˣⁱᵛ indeed he evades the question. ". . . *nulla eius ⟨substantiae⟩ nominis significatio potest distincte intelligi, quae Deo et creaturis sit communis.*"ˣᵛ This evasion is tantamount to his failing to discuss the meaning of Being which the idea of substantiality embraces, or the character of the 'universality' which belongs to this signification. Of course even the ontology of the medievals has gone no further than that of the ancients in inquiring into what "Being" itself may mean. So it is not surprising if no headway is made with a question like that of the way in which "Being" signifies, as long as this has to be discussed on the basis of an unclarified meaning of Being which this signification 'expresses'. The meaning remains unclarified because it is held to be 'self-evident'.

94   Descartes not only evades the ontological question of substantiality altogether; he also emphasizes explicitly that substance as such—that is to say, its substantiality—is in and for itself inaccessible from the outset [vorgängig]. "*Verumtamen non potest substantia primum animadverti ex hoc solo,*

quod sit res existens, quia hoc solum per se nos non afficit . . .".[xvi] 'Being' itself does not 'affect' us, and therefore cannot be perceived. 'Being is not a Real predicate,' says Kant,[1] who is merely repeating Descartes' principle. Thus the possibility of a pure problematic of Being gets renounced in principle, and a way is sought for arriving at those definite characteristics of substance which we have designated above. Because 'Being' is not in fact accessible *as an entity*, it is expressed through attributes—definite characteristics of the entities under consideration, characteristics which themselves are.[2] Being is not expressed through just any such characteristics, but rather through those satisfying in the purest manner that meaning of "Being" and "substantiality", which has still been tacitly presupposed. To the *substantia finita* as *res corporea*, what must primarily be 'assigned' ["Zuweisung"] is the *extensio*. "*Quin et facilius intelligimus substantiam extensam, vel substantiam cogitantem, quam substantiam solam, omisso eo quod cogitet vel sit extensa*";[xvii] for substantiality is detachable *ratione tantum*; it is not detachable *realiter*, nor can we come across it in the way in which we come across those entities themselves which are substantially.

Thus the ontological grounds for defining the 'world' as *res extensa* have been made plain: they lie in the idea of substantiality, which not only remains unclarified in the meaning of its Being, but gets passed off as something incapable of clarification, and gets represented indirectly by way of whatever substantial property belongs most pre-eminently to the particular substance. Moreover, in this way of defining "substance" through some substantial entity, lies the reason why the term "substance" is used in two ways. What is here intended is substantiality; and it gets understood in terms of a characteristic of substance—a characteristic which is itself an entity.[3] Because something ontical is made to underlie the ontological, the expression "*substantia*" functions sometimes with a signification which is ontological, sometimes with one which is ontical, but mostly with one which is hazily ontico-ontological. Behind this slight difference of signification, however, there lies hidden a failure to master the basic problem of Being. To treat this adequately, we must 'track down' the equivocations *in the right way*. He who attempts this sort of thing does not just 'busy himself' with 'merely verbal significations'; he must venture forward into the most primordial problematic of the 'things themselves' to get such 'nuances' straightened out.   **95**

---

[1] Immanuel Kant, *Critique of Pure Reason, Transcendental Dialectic*, Book II, chapter III, Section 4.

[2] '. . . seiende Bestimmtheiten des betreffenden Seienden . . .'

[3] '. . . aus einer seienden Beschaffenheit der Substanz.'

¶ *21. Hermeneutical Discussion of the Cartesian Ontology of the 'World'*

The critical question now arises: does this ontology of the 'world' seek the phenomenon of the world at all, and if not, does it at least define some entity within-the-world fully enough so that the worldly character of this entity can be made visible in it? *To both questions we must answer "No".* The entity which Descartes is trying to grasp ontologically and in principle with his *"extensio"*, is rather such as to become discoverable first of all by going through an entity within-the-world which is proximally ready-to-hand—Nature. Though this is the case, and though any ontological characterization of this *latter* entity within-the-world may lead us into obscurity, even if we consider both the idea of substantiality and the meaning of the *"existit"* and *"ad existendum"* which have been brought into the definition of that idea, it still remains possible that through an ontology based upon a radical separation of God, the "I", and the 'world', the ontological problem of the world will in some sense get formulated and further advanced. If, however, this is not possible, we must then demonstrate explicitly not only that Descartes' conception of the world is ontologically defective, but that his Interpretation and the foundations on which it is based have led him to *pass over* both the phenomenon of the world and the Being of those entities within-the-world which are proximally ready-to-hand.

In our exposition of the problem of worldhood (Section 14), we suggested the importance of obtaining proper access to this phenomenon. So in criticizing the Cartesian point of departure, we must ask which kind of Being that belongs to Dasein we should fix upon as giving us an appropriate way of access to those entities with whose Being as *extensio* Descartes equates the Being of the 'world'. The only genuine access to them lies in knowing [Erkennen], *intellectio*, in the sense of the kind of knowledge [Erkenntnis] we get in mathematics and physics. Mathematical knowledge is regarded by Descartes as the one manner of apprehending entities which can always give assurance that their Being has been securely grasped. If anything measures up in its own kind of Being to the Being that is accessible in mathematical knowledge, then it *is* in the authentic sense. Such entities are those *which always are what they are.* Accordingly, that which can be shown to have the character of something that *constantly remains* (as *remanens capax mutationum*), makes up the real Being of those entities of the world which get experienced. That which enduringly remains, really *is*. This is the sort of thing which mathematics knows. That which is accessible in an entity *through mathematics*, makes up its Being. Thus the Being of the 'world' is, as it were, dictated to it in terms of a definite idea of Being which lies veiled in the concept of substantiality, and in terms of the idea of a knowledge by which *such* entities are cognized. The kind of Being which belongs to entities within-the-world is something which they themselves might have been permitted to present; but Descartes does not let them do so.[1] Instead he prescribes for the world its 'real' Being, as it were, on the basis of an idea of Being whose source has not been unveiled and which has not been demonstrated in its own right—an idea in which Being is equated with constant presence-at-hand. Thus his ontology of the world is not primarily determined by his leaning towards mathematics, a science which he chances to esteem very highly, but rather by his ontological orientation in principle towards Being as constant presence-at-hand, which mathematical knowledge is exceptionally well suited to grasp. In this way Descartes explicitly switches over philosophically from the development of traditional ontology to modern mathematical physics and its transcendental foundations.

The problem of how to get appropriate access to entities within-the-world is one which Descartes feels no need to raise. Under the unbroken ascendance of the traditional ontology, the way to get a genuine grasp of what really is [des eigentlichen Seienden] has been decided in advance: it lies in νοεῖν—'beholding' in the widest sense [der "Anschauung" im weitesten Sinne]; διανοεῖν or 'thinking' is just a more fully achieved form of νοεῖν and is founded upon it. *Sensatio* (αἴσθησις), as opposed to *intellectio*, still remains possible as a way of access to entities by a beholding which is perceptual in character; but Descartes presents his 'critique' of it because he is oriented ontologically by these principles.

Descartes knows very well that entities do not proximally show themselves in their real Being. What is 'proximally' given is this waxen Thing which is coloured, flavoured, hard, and cold in definite ways, and which gives off its own special sound when struck. But this is not of any importance ontologically, nor, in general, is anything which is given through the senses. "*Satis erit, si advertamus sensuum perceptiones non referri, nisi ad istam corporis humani cum mente coniunctionem, et nobis quidem ordinarie exhibere, quid ad illam externa corpora prodesse possint aut nocere . . .*"[xviii] The senses do not enable us to cognize any entity in its Being; they merely serve to announce the ways in which 'external' Things within-the-world are useful or harmful for human creatures encumbered with bodies. "*. . . non . . . nos docere, qualia ⟨ corpora ⟩ in seipsis existant*";[xix] they tell us nothing about entities in their Being. "*Quod agentes, percipiemus naturam materiae, sive corporis in universum spectati, non consistere in eo quod sit res dura, vel ponderosa, vel colorata,*

97

---

1 'Descartes lässt sich nicht die Seinsart des innerweltlichen Seienden von diesem vorgeben . . .'

*vel alio aliquo modo sensus afficiens : sed tantum in eo quod sit res extensa in longum, latum et profundum."*xx

If we subject Descartes' Interpretation of the experience of hardness and resistance to a critical analysis, it will be plain how unable he is to let what shows itself in sensation present itself in its own kind of Being,[1] or even to determine its character (Cf. Section 19).

Hardness gets taken as resistance. But neither hardness nor resistance is understood in a phenomenal sense, as something experienced in itself whose nature can be determined in such an experience. For Descartes, resistance amounts to no more than not yielding place—that is, not undergoing any change of location. So if a Thing resists, this means that it stays in a definite location relatively to some other Thing which is changing its location, or that it is changing its own location with a velocity which permits the other Thing to 'catch up' with it. But when the experience of hardness is Interpreted this way, the kind of Being which belongs to sensory perception is obliterated, and so is any possibility that the entities encountered in such perception should be grasped in their Being. Descartes takes the kind of Being which belongs to the perception of something, and translates it into the only kind he knows: the perception of something becomes a definite way of Being-present-at-hand-side-by-side of two *res extensae* which are present-at-hand; the way in which their movements are related is itself a mode of that *extensio* by which the presence-at-hand of the corporeal Thing is primarily characterized. Of course no behaviour in which one feels one's way by touch [eines tastenden Verhaltens] can be 'completed' unless what can thus be felt [des Betastbaren] has 'closeness' of a very special kind. But this does not mean that touching [Berührung] and the hardness which makes itself known in touching consist ontologically in different velocities of two corporeal Things. Hardness and resistance do not show themselves at all unless an entity has the kind of Being which Dasein—or at least something living—possesses.

Thus Descartes' discussion of possible kinds of *access* to entities within-the-world is dominated by an idea of Being which has been gathered from a definite realm of these entities themselves.

98   The idea of Being as permanent presence-at-hand not only gives Descartes a motive for identifying entities within-the-world with the world in general, and for providing so extreme a definition of their Being; it also keeps him from bringing Dasein's ways of behaving into view in a manner which is ontologically appropriate. But thus the road is completely

---

[1] '. . . das in der Sinnlichkeit sich Zeigende in seiner eigenen Seinsart sich vorgeben zu lassen . . .'

blocked to seeing the founded character of all sensory and intellective awareness, and to understanding these as possibilities of Being-in-the-world.[1] On the contrary, he takes the Being of 'Dasein' (to whose basic constitution Being-in-the-world belongs) in the very same way as he takes the Being of the *res extensa*—namely, as substance.

But with these criticisms, have we not fobbed off on Descartes a task altogether beyond his horizon, and then gone on to 'demonstrate' that he has failed to solve it? If Descartes does not know the phenomenon of the world, and thus knows no such thing as within-the-world-ness, how can he identify the world itself with certain entities within-the-world and the Being which they possess?

In controversy over principles, one must not only attach oneself to theses which can be grasped doxographically; one must also derive one's orientation from the objective tendency of the problematic, even if it does not go beyond a rather ordinary way of taking things. In his doctrine of the *res cogitans* and the *res extensa*, Descartes not only *wants to formulate* the problem of 'the "I" and the world'; he claims to have solved it in a radical manner. His *Meditations* make this plain. (See especially Meditations I and VI.) By taking his basic ontological orientation from traditional sources and not subjecting it to positive criticism, he has made it impossible to lay bare any primordial ontological problematic of Dasein; this has inevitably obstructed his view of the phenomenon of the world, and has made it possible for the ontology of the 'world' to be compressed into that of certain entities within-the-world. The foregoing discussion should have proved this.

One might retort, however, that even if in point of fact both the problem of the world and the Being of the entities encountered environmentally as closest to us remain concealed, Descartes has still laid the basis for characterizing ontologically that entity within-the-world upon which, in its very Being, every other entity is founded—material Nature. This would be the fundamental stratum upon which all the other strata of actuality within-the-world are built up. The extended Thing as such would serve, in the first instance, as the ground for those definite characters which show themselves, to be sure, as qualities, but which 'at bottom' are quantitative modifications of the modes of the *extensio* itself. These qualities, which are themselves reducible, would provide the footing for such specific qualities as "beautiful", "ugly", "in keeping", "not in   99

[1] 'Damit ist aber vollends der Weg dazu verlegt, gar auch noch den fundierten Charakter alles sinnlichen und verstandesmässigen Vernehmens zu sehen und sie als eine Möglichkeit des In-der-Welt-seins zu verstehen.' While we have construed the pronoun 'sie' as referring to the two kinds of awareness which have just been mentioned, it would be grammatically more plausible to interpret it as referring either to 'Dasein's ways of behaving' or to 'the idea of Being as permanent presence-at-hand'.

keeping," "useful", "useless". If one is oriented primarily by Thinghood, these latter qualities must be taken as non-quantifiable value-predicates by which what is in the first instance just a material Thing, gets stamped as something good. But with this stratification, we come to those entities which we have characterized ontologically as equipment ready-to-hand The Cartesian analysis of the 'world' would thus enable us for the first time to build up securely the structure of what is proximally ready-to-hand; all it takes is to round out the Thing of Nature until it becomes a full-fledged Thing of use, and this is easily done.

But quite apart from the specific problem of the world itself, can the Being of what we encounter proximally within-the-world be reached ontologically by this procedure? When we speak of material Thinghood, have we not tacitly posited a kind of Being—the constant presence-at hand of Things—which is so far from having been rounded out ontologically by subsequently endowing entities with value-predicates, that these value-characters themselves are rather just ontical characteristics of those entities which have the kind of Being possessed by Things? Adding on value-predicates cannot tell us anything at all new about the Being of goods, *but would merely presuppose again that goods have pure presence-at-hand as their kind of Being.* Values would then be determinate characteristics which a Thing possesses, and they would be *present-at-hand.* They would have their sole ultimate ontological source in our previously laying down the actuality of Things as the fundamental stratum. But even pre-phenomenological experience shows that in an entity which is supposedly a Thing, there is something that will not become fully intelligible through Thinghood alone. Thus the Being of Things has to be rounded out. What, then does the Being of values or their 'validity' ["Geltung"] (which Lotze took as a mode of 'affirmation') really amount to ontologically? And what does it signify ontologically for Things to be 'invested' with values in this way? As long as these matters remain obscure, to reconstruct the Thing of use in terms of the Thing of Nature is an ontologically questionable undertaking, even if one disregards the way in which the problematic has been perverted in principle. And if we are to reconstruct this Thing of use, which supposedly comes to us in the first instance 'with its skin off', does not this always require *that we previously take a positive look at the phenomenon whose totality such a reconstruction is to restore?* But if we have not given a proper explanation beforehand of its ownmost state of Being, are we not building our reconstruction without a plan? Inasmuch as this reconstruction and 'rounding-out' of the traditional ontology of the 'world' results in our reaching the same *entities* with which we started when we

100   analysed the readiness-to-hand of equipment and the totality of

involvements, it seems as if the *Being* of these entities has in fact been clarified or has at least become a *problem*. But by taking *extensio* as a *proprietas*, Descartes can hardly reach the Being of substance; and by taking refuge in 'value'-characteristics ["wertlichen" Beschaffenheiten] we are just as far from even catching a glimpse of Being as readiness-to-hand, let alone permitting it to become an ontological theme.

Descartes has narrowed down the question of the world to that of Things of Nature [Naturdinglichkeit] as those entities within-the-world which are proximally accessible. He has confirmed the opinion that to *know* an entity in what is supposedly the most rigorous ontical manner is our only possible access to the primary Being of the entity which such knowledge reveals. But at the same time we must have the insight to see that in principle the 'roundings-out' of the Thing-ontology also operate on the same dogmatic basis as that which Descartes has adopted.

We have already intimated in Section 14 that passing over the world and those entities which we proximally encounter is not accidental, not an oversight which it would be simple to correct, but that it is grounded in a kind of Being which belongs essentially to Dasein itself. When our analytic of Dasein has given some transparency to those main structures of Dasein which are of the most importance in the framework of this problematic, and when we have assigned [zugewiesen] to the concept of Being in general the horizon within which its intelligibility becomes possible, so that readiness-to-hand and presence-at-hand also become primordially intelligible ontologically for the first time, only then can our critique of the Cartesian ontology of the world (an ontology which, in principle, is still the usual one today) come philosophically into its own.

To do this, we must show several things. (See Part One, Division Three.)[1]

1. Why was the phenomenon of the world passed over at the beginning of the ontological tradition which has been decisive for us (explicitly in the case of Parmenides), and why has this passing-over kept constantly recurring?

2. Why is it that, instead of the phenomenon thus passed over, entities within-the-world have intervened as an ontological theme?[2]

3. Why are these entities found in the first instance in 'Nature'?

4. Why has recourse been taken to the phenomenon of value when it has seemed necessary to round out such an ontology of the world?

---

1 This Division has never been published.

2 'Warum springt für das übersprungene Phänomen das innerweltlich Seiende als ontologisches Thema ein?' The verbal play on 'überspringen' ('pass over') and 'einspringen' ('intervene' or 'serve as a deputy') is lost in translation. On 'einspringen' see our note 1, p. 158, H. 122 below.

In the answers to these questions a positive understanding of the *problematic* of the world will be reached for the first time, the sources of our failure to recognize it will be exhibited, and the ground for rejecting the traditional ontology of the world will have been demonstrated.

101   The world and Dasein and entities within-the-world are the ontologically constitutive states which are closest to us; but we have no guarantee that we can achieve the basis for meeting up with these as phenomena by the seemingly obvious procedure of starting with the Things of the world, still less by taking our orientation from what is supposedly the most rigorous knowledge of entities. Our observations on Descartes should have brought us this insight.

But if we recall that spatiality is manifestly one of the constituents of entities within-the-world, then in the end the Cartesian analysis of the 'world' can still be 'rescued'. When Descartes was so radical as to set up the *extensio* as the *praesuppositum* for every definite characteristic of the *res corporea*, he prepared the way for the understanding of something *a priori* whose content Kant was to establish with greater penetration. Within certain limits the analysis of the *extensio* remains independent of his neglecting to provide an explicit interpretation for the Being of extended entities. There is some phenomenal justification for regarding the *extensio* as a basic characteristic of the 'world', even if by recourse to this neither the spatiality of the world nor that of the entities we encounter in our environment (a spatiality which is proximally discovered) nor even that of Dasein itself, can be conceived ontologically.

C. *The Aroundness of the Environment*[1] *and Dasein's Spatiality*

In connection with our first preliminary sketch of Being-in (See Section 12), we had to contrast Dasein with a way of Being in space which we call "insideness" [Inwendigkeit]. This expression means that an entity which is itself extended is closed round [umschlossen] by the extended boundaries of something that is likewise extended. The entity inside [Das inwendig Seiende] and that which closes it round are both present-at-hand in space. Yet even if we deny that Dasein has any such insideness in a spatial receptacle, this does not in principle exclude it from having any spatiality at all, but merely keeps open the way for seeing the kind of spatiality which is constitutive for Dasein. This must now be set forth. But inasmuch as any entity within-the-*world* is likewise in space, its spatiality will have an ontological connection with the world. We must therefore determine in what sense space is a constituent for that world which has in turn been characterized as an item in the structure of Being-in-the-world. In particular

---

1 '*Das Umhafte der Umwelt*'. See our note 1, p. 93, H. 65 above.

we must show how the aroundness of the environment, the specific spatiality of entities encountered in the environment, is founded upon the worldhood of the world, while contrariwise the world, on its part, is   102 not present-at-hand in space. Our study of Dasein's spatiality and the way in which the world is spatially determined will take its departure from an analysis of what is ready-to-hand in space within-the-world. We shall consider three topics: 1. the spatiality of the ready-to-hand within-the-world (Section 22); 2. the spatiality of Being-in-the-world (Section 23); 3. space and the spatiality of Dasein (Section 24).

¶ *22. The Spatiality of the Ready-to-hand Within-the-world*

If space is constitutive for the world in a sense which we have yet to determine, then it cannot surprise us that in our foregoing ontological characterization of the Being of what is within-the-world we have had to look upon this as something that is also within space. This spatiality of the ready-to-hand is something which we have not yet grasped explicitly as a phenomenon; nor have we pointed out how it is bound up with the structure of Being which belongs to the ready-to-hand. This is now our task.

To what extent has our characterization of the ready-to-hand already come up against its spatiality? We have been talking about what is *proximally* ready-to-hand. This means not only those entities which we encounter *first* before any others, but also those which are 'close by'.[1] What is ready-to-hand in our everyday dealings has the character of *closeness*. To be exact, this closeness of equipment has already been intimated in the term 'readiness-to-hand', which expresses the Being of equipment. Every entity that is 'to hand' has a different closeness, which is not to be ascertained by measuring distances. This closeness regulates itself in terms of circumspectively 'calculative' manipulating and using. At the same time what is close in this way gets established by the circumspection of concern, with regard to the direction in which the equipment is accessible at any time. When this closeness of the equipment has been given directionality,[2] this signifies not merely that the equipment has its

---

[1] 'in der Nähe.' While the noun 'Nähe' often means the *'closeness'* or *'nearness'* of something that is close to us, it can also stand for our immediate *'vicinity'*, as in the present expression, and in many passages it can be interpreted either way. We shall in general translate it as 'closeness', but we shall translate 'in der Nähe' and similar phrases as 'close by'.

[2] 'Die ausgerichtete Nähe des Zeugs . . .' The verb 'ausrichten' has many specialized meanings—to 'align' a row of troops, to 'explore' a mine, to 'make arrangements' for something, to 'carry out' a commission, etc. Heidegger, however, keeps its root meaning in mind and associates it with the word 'Richtung' ('direction', 'route to be taken', etc.). We shall accordingly translate it as a rule by some form of the verb 'direct' (which will also be used occasionally for the verb 'richten'), or by some compound expression involving the word 'directional'. For further discussion, see H. 108 ff. below.

position [Stelle] in space as present-at-hand somewhere, but also that as equipment it has been essentially fitted up and installed, set up, and put to rights. Equipment has its *place* [*Platz*], or else it 'lies around'; this must be distinguished in principle from just occurring at random in some spatial position. When equipment for something or other has its place, this place defines itself as the place of this equipment—as one place out of a whole totality of places directionally lined up with each other and belonging to the context of equipment that is environmentally ready-to-hand. Such a place and such a muliplicity of places are not to be interpreted as the "where" of some random Being-present-at-hand of Things. In each case the place is the definite 'there' or 'yonder' ["Dort" und "Da"] of an item of equipment which *belongs somewhere*. Its belonging-somewhere at the time [Die jeweilige Hingehörigheit] corresponds to the equipmental character of what is ready-to-hand; that is, it corresponds to the belonging-to [Zugehörigkeit] which the ready-to-hand has towards a totality of equipment in accordance with its involvements. But in general the "whither" to which the totality of places for a context of equipment gets allotted, is the underlying condition which makes possible the belonging-somewhere of an equipmental totality as something that can be placed. This "whither", which makes it possible for equipment to belong somewhere, and which we circumspectively keep in view ahead of us in our concernful dealings, we call the "*region*".[1]

'In the region of' means not only 'in the direction of' but also within the range [Umkreis] of something that lies in that direction. The kind of place which is constituted by direction and remoteness[2] (and closeness is only a mode of the latter) is already oriented towards a region and oriented within it. Something like a region must first be discovered if there is to be any possibility of allotting or coming across places for a totality of equipment that is circumspectively at one's disposal. The regional orientation of the multiplicity of places belonging to the ready-to-hand goes to make up the aroundness—the "round-about-us" [das Um-uns-herum]—of those entities which we encounter as closest environmentally. A three-dimensional multiplicity of possible positions which gets filled up with Things present-at-hand is never proximally given. This dimensionality of space is still veiled in the spatiality of the ready-to-hand. The 'above' is what is 'on the ceiling'; the 'below' is what is 'on the floor';

103 (margin)

---

[1] 'Gegend'. There is no English word which quite corresponds to 'Gegend'. 'Region' and 'whereabouts' perhaps come the closest, and we have chosen the former as the more convenient. (Heidegger himself frequently uses the word 'Region', but he does so in contexts where 'realm' seems to be the most appropriate translation; we have usually so translated it, leaving the English 'region' for 'Gegend'.)

[2] 'Entferntheit'. For further discussion, see Section 23 and our note 2, p. 138, H. 105.

the 'behind' is what is 'at the door'; all "wheres" are discovered and circumspectively interpreted as we go our ways in everyday dealings; they are not ascertained and catalogued by the observational measurement of space.

Regions are not first formed by things which are present-at-hand together; they always are ready-to-hand already in individual places. Places themselves either get allotted to the ready-to-hand in the circumspection of concern, or we come across them. Thus anything constantly ready-to-hand of which circumspective Being-in-the-world takes account beforehand, has its place. The "where" of its readiness-to-hand is put to account as a matter for concern, and oriented towards the rest of what is ready-to-hand. Thus the sun, whose light and warmth are in everyday use, has its own places—sunrise, midday, sunset, midnight; these are discovered in circumspection and treated distinctively in terms of changes in the usability of what the sun bestows. Here we have something which is ready-to-hand with uniform constancy, although it keeps changing; its places become accentuated 'indicators' of the regions which lie in them. These celestial regions, which need not have any geographical meaning as yet, provide the "whither" beforehand for every[1] special way of giving form to the regions which places can occupy. The house has its sunny side and its shady side; the way it is divided up into 'rooms' ["Räume"] is oriented towards these, and so is the 'arrangement' ["Einrichtung"] within them, according to their character as equipment. Churches and graves, for instance, are laid out according to the rising and the setting of the sun—the regions of life and death, which are determinative for Dasein itself with regard to its ownmost possibilities of Being in the world. Dasein, in its very Being, has this Being as an issue; and its concern discovers beforehand those regions in which some involvement is decisive. This discovery of regions beforehand is co-determined [mitbestimmt] by the totality of involvements for which the ready-to-hand, as something encountered, is freed.

The readiness-to-hand which belongs to any such region beforehand has the *character of inconspicuous familiarity*, and it has it in an even more primordial sense than does the Being of the ready-to-hand.[2] The region itself becomes visible in a conspicuous manner only when one discovers

104

---

1 Reading 'jede' with the later editions. The earliest editions have 'je', which has been corrected in the list of *errata*.

2 'Die vorgängige Zuhandenheit der jeweiligen Gegend hat in einem noch ursprünglicheren Sinne als das Sein des Zuhandenen den *Charakter der unauffälligen Vertrautheit.*' Here the phrase 'als das Sein des Zuhandenen' is ambiguously placed. In the light of Section 16 above, we have interpreted 'als' as 'than' rather than 'as', and have treated 'das Sein' as a nominative rather than an accusative. But other readings are grammatically just as possible.

the ready-to-hand circumspectively and does so in the deficient modes of concern.[1] Often the region of a place does not become accessible explicitly as such a region until one fails to find something in *its* place. The space which is discovered in circumspective Being-in-the-world as the spatiality of the totality of equipment, always belongs to entities themselves as the place of that totality. The bare space itself is still veiled over. Space has been split up into places. But this spatiality has its own unity through that totality-of-involvements in-accordance-with-the-world [weltmässige] which belongs to the spatially ready-to-hand. The 'environment' does not arrange itself in a space which has been given in advance; but its specific worldhood, in its significance, Articulates the context of involvements which belongs to some current totality of circumspectively allotted places. The world at such a time always reveals the spatiality of the space which belongs to it. To encounter the ready-to-hand in its environmental space remains ontically possible only because Dasein itself is 'spatial' with regard to its Being-in-the-world.

¶ 23. *The Spatiality of Being-in-the-world*

If we attribute spatiality to Dasein, then this 'Being in space' must manifestly be conceived in terms of the kind of Being which that entity possesses. Dasein is essentially not a Being-present-at-hand; and its "spatiality" cannot signify anything like occurrence at a position in 'world-space', nor can it signify Being-ready-to-hand at some place. Both of these are kinds of Being which belong to entities encountered within-the-world. Dasein, however, is 'in' the world in the sense that it deals with entities encountered within-the-world, and does so concernfully and with familiarity. So if spatiality belongs to it in any way, that is possible only because of this Being-in. But its spatiality shows the characters of *de-severance* and *directionality*.[2]

105

[1] 'Sie wird selbst nur sichtbar in der Weise des Auffallens bei einem umsichtigen Entdecken des Zuhandenen und zwar in den defizienten Modi des Besorgens.' This sentence too is ambiguous. The pronoun 'Sie' may refer either to the *region*, as we have suggested, or to its *readiness-to-hand*. Furthermore, while we have taken 'nur sichtbar in der Weise des Auffallens' as a unit, it is possible that 'in der Weise des Auffallens' should be construed as going with the words that follow. In this case we should read: '. . . becomes visible only when it becomes conspicuous in our circumspective discovery of the ready-to-hand, and indeed in the deficient modes of concern.'

[2] '*Ent-fernung und Ausrichtung.*' The nouns 'Entfernung' and 'Entfernheit' can usually be translated by 'removing', 'removal', 'remoteness', or even 'distance'. In this passage, however, Heidegger is calling attention to the fact that these words are derived from the stem 'fern-' ('far' or 'distant') and the privative prefix 'ent-'. Usually this prefix would be construed as merely intensifying the notion of separation or distance expressed in the 'fern-'; but Heidegger chooses to construe it as more strictly privative, so that the verb 'entfernen' will be taken to mean *abolishing* a distance or farness rather than enhancing it. It is as if by the very act of recognizing the 'remoteness' of something, we have in a sense brought it closer and made it less 'remote'.

Apparently there is no word in English with an etymological structure quite parallel

When we speak of deseverance as a kind of Being which Dasein has with regard to its Being-in-the-world, we do not understand by it any such thing as remoteness (or closeness) or even a distance.[1] We use the expression "deseverance"* in a signification which is both active and transitive. It stands for a constitutive state of Dasein's Being—a state with regard to which removing something in the sense of putting it away is only a determinate factical mode. "De-severing"* amounts to making the farness vanish—that is, making the remoteness of something disappear, bringing it close.[2] Dasein is essentially de-severant: it lets any entity be encountered close by as the entity which it is. De-severance discovers remoteness; and remoteness, like distance, is a determinate categorial characteristic of entities whose nature is not that of Dasein. De-severance*, however, is an *existentiale*; this must be kept in mind. Only to the extent that entities are revealed for Dasein in their deseveredness [Entferntheit], do 'remotenesses' ["Entfernungen"] and distances with regard to other things become accessible in entities within-the-world themselves. Two points are just as little desevered from one another as two Things, for neither of these types of entity has the kind of Being which would make it capable of desevering. They merely have a measurable distance between them, which we can come across in our de-severing.

Proximally and for the most part, de-severing[3] is a circumspective

to that of 'entfernen'; perhaps 'dissever' comes the nearest, for this too is a verb of separation in which a privative prefix is used as an intensive. We have coined the similar verb 'desever' in the hope that this will suggest Heidegger's meaning when 'remove' and its derivatives seem inappropriate. But with 'desever', one cannot slip back and forth from one sense to another as easily as one can with 'entfernen'; so we have resorted to the expedient of using both 'desever' and 'remove' and their derivatives, depending upon the sense we feel is intended. Thus 'entfernen' will generally be rendered by 'remove' or 'desever', 'entfernt' by 'remote' or 'desevered'. Since Heidegger is careful to distinguish 'Entfernung' and 'Entferntheit', we shall usually translate these by 'deseverance' and 'remoteness' respectively; in the few cases where these translations do not seem appropriate, we shall subjoin the German word in brackets.

Our problem is further complicated by Heidegger's practise of occasionally putting a hyphen after the prefix 'ent-', presumably to emphasize its privative character. In such cases we shall write 'de-sever', 'de-severance', etc. Unfortunately, however, there are typographical discrepancies between the earlier and later editions. Some of the earlier hyphens occur at the ends of lines and have been either intentionally or inadvertently omitted in resetting the type; some appear at the end of the line in the later editions, but not in the earlier ones; others have this position in both editions. We shall indicate each of these ambiguous cases with an asterisk, supplying a hyphen only if there seems to be a good reason for doing so.

On 'Ausrichtung' see our note 2, p. 135, H. 102 above.

[1] 'Abstand'. Heidegger uses three words which might be translated as 'distance': 'Ferne' (our 'farness'), 'Entfernung' (our 'deseverance'), and 'Abstand' ('distance' in the sense of a measurable interval). We shall reserve 'distance' for 'Abstand'.

[2] 'Entfernen* besagt ein Verschwindenmachen der Ferne, d. h. der Entferntheit von etwas, Näherung.'

[3] This hyphen is found only in the later editions.

bringing-close—bringing something close by, in the sense of procuring it, putting it in readiness, having it to hand. But certain ways in which entities are discovered in a purely cognitive manner also have the character of bringing them close. *In Dasein there lies an essential tendency towards closeness.* All the ways in which we speed things up, as we are more or less compelled to do today, push us on towards the conquest of remoteness. With the 'radio', for example, Dasein has so expanded its everyday environment that it has accomplished a de-severance of the 'world'— a de-severance which, in its meaning for Dasein, cannot yet be visualized.

De-severing does not necessarily imply any explicit estimation of the farness of something ready-to-hand in relation to Dasein. Above all, remoteness* never gets taken as a distance. If farness is to be estimated, this is done relatively to deseverances in which everyday Dasein maintains itself. Though these estimates may be imprecise and variable if we try to compute them, in the everydayness of Dasein they have their *own definiteness* which is thoroughly intelligible. We say that to go over yonder is "a good walk", "a stone's throw", or 'as long as it takes to smoke a pipe'. These measures express not only that they are not intended to 'measure' anything but also that the remoteness* here estimated belongs to some entity to which one goes with concernful circumspection. But even when we avail ourselves of a fixed measure and say 'it is half an hour to the house', this measure must be taken as an estimate. 'Half an hour' is not thirty minutes, but a duration [Dauer] which has no 'length' at all in the sense of a quantitative stretch. Such a duration is always interpreted in terms of well-accustomed everyday ways in which we 'make provision' ["Besorgungen"]. Remotenesses* are estimated proximally by circumspection, even when one is quite familiar with 'officially' calculated measures. Since what is de-severed in such estimates is ready-to-hand, it retains its character as specifically within-the-world. This even implies that the pathways we take towards desevered entities in the course of our dealings will vary in their length from day to day. What is ready-to-hand in the environment is certainly not present-at-hand for an eternal observer exempt from Dasein: but it is encountered in Dasein's circumspectively concernful everydayness. As Dasein goes along its ways, it does not measure off a stretch of space as a corporeal Thing which is present-at-hand; it does not 'devour the kilometres'; bringing-close or de-severance is always a kind of concernful Being towards what is brought close and de-severed. A pathway which is long 'Objectively' can be much shorter than one which is 'Objectively' shorter still but which is perhaps 'hard going' and comes before us[1] as interminably long. *Yet only in thus 'coming before us'[1] is the current world authentically ready-to-hand.* The Objective distances of Things present-at-hand do not coincide with the remoteness and closeness of what is ready-to-hand within-the-world. Though we may know these distances exactly, this knowledge still remains blind; it does not have the function of discovering the environment circumspectively and bringing it close; this knowledge is used only in and for a concernful Being which does not measure stretches—a Being towards the world that 'matters' to one [. . . Sein zu der einen "angehenden" Welt].

When one is oriented beforehand towards 'Nature' and 'Objectively' measured distances of Things, one is inclined to pass off such estimates and interpretations of deseverance as 'subjective'. Yet this 'subjectivity' perhaps uncovers the 'Reality' of the world at its most Real; it has nothing to do with 'subjective' arbitrariness or subjectivistic 'ways of taking' an entity which 'in itself' is otherwise. *The circumspective de-severing of Dasein's everydayness reveals the Being-in-itself of the 'true world'—of that entity which Dasein, as something existing, is already alongside.*[2]

When one is primarily and even exclusively oriented towards remotenesses as measured distances, the primordial spatiality of Being-in is concealed. That which is presumably 'closest' is by no means that which is at the smallest distance 'from us'. It lies in that which is desevered to an average extent when we reach for it, grasp it, or look at it. Because Dasein is essentially spatial in the way of de-severance, its dealings always keep within an 'environment' which is desevered from it with a certain leeway [Spielraum]; accordingly our seeing and hearing always go proximally beyond what is distantially 'closest'. Seeing and hearing are distance-senses [Fernsinne] not because they are far-reaching, but because it is in them that Dasein as deseverant mainly dwells. When, for instance, a man wears a pair of spectacles which are so close to him distantially that they are 'sitting on his nose', they are environmentally more remote from him than the picture on the opposite wall. Such equipment has so little closeness that often it is proximally quite impossible to find. Equipment for seeing—and likewise for hearing, such as the telephone receiver—has what we have designated as the inconspicuousness of the proximally ready-to-hand. So too, for instance, does the street, as equipment for walking. One feels the touch of it at every step as one walks; it is seemingly the closest and Realest of all that is ready-to-hand, and it slides itself, as it

---

[1] 'vorkommt'; ' "Vorkommen" '. In general 'vorkommen' may be translated as 'occur', and is to be thought of as applicable strictly to the present-at-hand. In this passage, however, it is applied to the ready-to-hand; and a translation which calls attention to its etymological structure seems to be called for.

[2] 'Das umsichtige Ent-fernen der Alltäglichkeit des Daseins entdeckt das An-sich-sein der "wahren Welt", des Seienden, bei dem Dasein als existierendes je schon ist.'

were, along certain portions of one's body—the soles of one's feet. And yet it is farther remote than the acquaintance whom one encounters 'on the street' at a 'remoteness' ["Entfernung"] of twenty paces when one is taking such a walk. Circumspective concern decides as to the closeness and farness of what is proximally ready-to-hand environmentally. Whatever this concern dwells alongside beforehand is what is closest, and this is what regulates our de-severances.

If Dasein, in its concern, brings something close by, this does not signify that it fixes something at a spatial position with a minimal distance from some point of the body. When something is close by, this means that it is within the range of what is proximally ready-to-hand for circumspection. Bringing-close is not oriented towards the I-Thing encumbered with a body, but towards concernful Being-in-the-world—that is, towards whatever is proximally encountered in such Being. It follows, moreover, that Dasein's spatiality is not to be defined by citing the position at which some corporeal Thing is present-at-hand. Of course we say that even Dasein always occupies a place. But this 'occupying' must be distinguished in principle from Being-ready-to-hand at a place in some particular region. Occupying a place must be conceived as a desevering of the environmentally ready-to-hand into a region which has been circumspectively discovered in advance. Dasein understands its "here" [Hier] in terms of its environmental "yonder". The "here" does not mean the "where" of something present-at-hand, but rather the "whereat" [Wobei] of a de-severant Being-alongside, together with this de-severance. Dasein, in accordance with its spatiality, is proximally never here but yonder; from this "yonder" it comes back to its "here"; and it comes back to its "here" only in the way in which it interprets its concernful Being-towards in terms of what is ready-to-hand yonder. This becomes quite plain if we consider a certain phenomenal peculiarity of the de-severance structure of Being-in.

As Being-in-the-world, Dasein maintains itself essentially in a de-severing. This de-severance—the farness of the ready-to-hand from Dasein itself—is something that Dasein can *never cross over*. Of course the remoteness of something ready-to-hand from Dasein can show up as a distance from it,[1] if this remoteness is determined by a relation to some Thing which gets thought of as present-at-hand at the place Dasein has formerly occupied. Dasein can subsequently traverse the "between" of this distance, but only in such a way that the distance itself becomes one which has been desevered*. So little has Dasein crossed over its de-severance that it has rather taken it along with it and keeps doing so constantly; for

[1] '... kann zwar selbst von diesem als Abstand vorfindlich werden ...'

Dasein is essentially de-severance—that is, it is spatial. It cannot wander about within the current range of its de-severances; it can never do more than change them. Dasein is spatial in that it discovers space circumspectively, so that indeed it constantly comports itself de-severantly* towards the entities thus spatially encountered.

As de-severant Being-in, Dasein has likewise the character of *direction-ality.* Every bringing-close [Näherung] has already taken in advance a direction towards a region out of which what is de-severed brings itself close [sich nähert], so that one can come across it with regard to its place. Circumspective concern is de-severing which gives directionality. In this concern —that is, in the Being-in-the-world of Dasein itself—a supply of 'signs' is presented. Signs, as equipment, take over the giving of directions in a way which is explicit and easily manipulable. They keep explicitly open those regions which have been used circumspectively—the particular "whithers" to which something belongs or goes, or gets brought or fetched. If Dasein *is*, it already has, as directing and desevering, its own discovered region. Both directionality and de-severance, as modes of Being-in-the-world, are guided beforehand *by the circumspection* of concern.

Out of this directionality arise the fixed directions of right and left. Dasein constantly takes these directions along with it, just as it does its de-severances. Dasein's spatialization in its 'bodily nature' is likewise marked out in accordance with these directions. (This 'bodily nature' hides a whole problematic of its own, though we shall not treat it here.) Thus things which are ready-to-hand and used for the body—like gloves, for example, which are to move with the hands—must be given direction-ality towards right and left. A craftsman's tools, however, which are held in the hand and are moved with it, do not share the hand's specifically 'manual' ["handliche"] movements. So although hammers are handled just as much with the hand as gloves are, there are no right- or left-handed hammers.

One must notice, however, that the directionality which belongs to de-severance is founded upon Being-in-the-world. Left and right are not something 'subjective' for which the subject has a feeling; they are directions of one's directedness into a world that is ready-to-hand already. 'By the mere feeling of a difference between my two sides'xxi I could never find my way about in a world. The subject with a 'mere feeling' of this difference is a construct posited in disregard of the state that is truly constitutive for any subject—namely, that whenever Dasein has such a 'mere feeling', it is in a world already *and must be* in it to be able to orient itself at all. This becomes plain from the example with which Kant tries to clarify the phenomenon of orientation.

109

Suppose I step into a room which is familiar to me but dark, and which has been rearranged [umgeräumt] during my absence so that everything which used to be at my right is now at my left. If I am to orient myself the 'mere feeling of the difference' between my two sides will be of no help at all as long as I fail to apprehend some definite object 'whose position', as Kant remarks casually, 'I have in mind'. But what does this signify except that whenever this happens I necessarily orient myself both in and from my being already alongside a world which is 'familiar'?[1] The equipment-context of a world must have been presented to Dasein. That I am already in a world is no less constitutive for the possibility of orientation than is the feeling for right and left. While this state of Dasein's Being is an obvious one, we are not thereby justified in suppressing the ontologically constitutive role which it plays. Even Kant does not suppress it, any more than any other Interpretation of Dasein. Yet the fact that this is a state of which we constantly make use, does not exempt us from providing a suitable ontological explication, but rather demands one. The psychological Interpretation according to which the "I" has something 'in the memory' ["im Gedächtnis"] is at bottom a way of alluding to the existentially constitutive state of Being-in-the-world. Since Kant fails to see this structure, he also fails to recognize all the interconnections which the Constitution of any possible orientation implies. Directedness with regard to right and left is based upon the essential directionality of Dasein in general, and this directionality in turn is essentially co-determined by Being-in-the-world. Even Kant, of course, has not taken orientation as a theme for Interpretation. He merely wants to show that every orientation requires a 'subjective principle'. Here 'subjective' is meant to signify that this principle is *a priori*.[2] Nevertheless, the *a priori* character of directedness with regard to right and left is based upon the 'subjective' *a priori* of Being-in-the-world, which has nothing to do with any determinate character restricted beforehand to a worldless subject.

De-severance and directionality, as constitutive characteristics of Being-in, are determinative for Dasein's spatiality—for its being concernfully and circumspectively in space, in a space discovered and within-the-world. Only the explication we have just given for the spatiality of the ready-to-hand within-the-world and the spatiality of Being-in-the-world, will provide the prerequisites for working out the phenomenon of the world's spatiality and formulating the ontological problem of space.

[1] '. . . in und aus einem je schon sein bei einer "bekannten" Welt.' The earlier editions have 'Sein' for 'sein'.

[2] Here we follow the later editions in reading '. . . bedeuten wollen: a priori.' The earlier editions omit the colon, making the passage ambiguous.

¶ *24. Space and Dasein's Spatiality*

As Being-in-the-world, Dasein has already discovered a 'world' at any time. This discovery, which is founded upon the worldhood of the world, is one which we have characterized as freeing entities for a totality of involvements. Freeing something and letting it be involved, is accomplished by way of referring or assigning oneself circumspectively, and this in turn is based upon one's previously understanding significance. We have now shown that circumspective Being-in-the-world is spatial. And only because Dasein is spatial in the way of de-severance and directionality can what is ready-to-hand within-the-world be encountered in its spatiality. To free a totality of involvements is, equiprimordially, to let something be involved at a region, and to do so by de-severing and giving directionality; this amounts to freeing the spatial belonging-somewhere of the ready-to-hand. In that significance with which Dasein (as concernful Being-in) is familiar, lies the essential co-disclosedness of space.[1]

The space which is thus disclosed with the worldhood of the world still lacks the pure multiplicity of the three dimensions. In this disclosedness which is closest to us, space, as the pure "wherein" in which positions are ordered by measurement and the situations of things are determined, still remains hidden. In the phenomenon of the region we have already indicated that on the basis of which space is discovered beforehand in Dasein. By a 'region" we have understood the "whither" to which an equipment-context ready-to-hand might possibly belong, when that context is of such a sort that it can be encountered as directionally desevered—that is, as having been placed.[2] This belongingness [Gehörigkeit] is determined   111 in terms of the significance which is constitutive for the world, and it Articulates the "hither" and "thither" within the possible "whither". In general the "whither" gets prescribed by a referential totality which has been made fast in a "for-the-sake-of-which" of concern, and within which letting something be involved by freeing it, assigns itself. *With* anything encountered as ready-to-hand there is always an involvement in [bei] a region. To the totality of involvements which makes up the Being of the ready-to-hand within-the-world, there belongs a spatial involvement which has the character of a region. By reason of such an involvement, the ready-to-hand becomes something which we can come across and ascertain as having form and direction.[3] With the factical Being of

---

[1] '. . . die wesenhafte Mitserschlossenheit des Raumes.'

[2] 'Wir verstehen sie als das Wohin der möglichen Zugehörigkeit des zuhandenen Zeugzusammenhanges, der als ausgerichtet entfernter, d. h. platzierter soll begegnen können.'

[3] 'Auf deren Grunde wird das Zuhandene nach Form und Richtung vorfindlich und bestimmbar'. The earliest editions have 'erfindlich', which has been corrected to 'vorfindlich' in a list of *errata*.

Dasein, what is ready-to-hand within-the-world is desevered* and given directionality, depending upon the degree of transparency that is possible for concernful circumspection.

When we let entities within-the-world be encountered in the way which is constitutive for Being-in-the-world, we 'give them space'. This 'giving space', which we also call '*making room*' for them,[1] consists in freeing the ready-to-hand for its spatiality. As a way of discovering and presenting a possible totality of spaces determined by involvements, this making-room is what makes possible one's factical orientation at the time. In concerning itself circumspectively with the world, Dasein can move things around or out of the way or 'make room' for them [um—, weg—, und "einräumen"] only because making-room—understood as an *existentiale*—belongs to its Being-in-the-world. But neither the region previously discovered nor in general the current spatiality is explicitly in view. In itself it is present [zugegen] for circumspection in the inconspicuousness of those ready-to-hand things in which that circumspection is concernfully absorbed. With Being-in-the-world, space is proximally discovered in this spatiality. On the basis of the spatiality thus discovered, space itself becomes accessible for cognition.

Space is not in the subject, nor is the world in space. Space is rather 'in' the world in so far as space has been disclosed by that Being-in-the-world which is constitutive for Dasein. Space is not to be found in the subject, nor does the subject observe the world 'as if' that world were in a space; but the 'subject' (Dasein), if well understood ontologically, is spatial. And because Dasein is spatial in the way we have described, space shows itself as *a priori*. This term does not mean anything like previously belonging to a subject which is proximally still worldless and which emits a space out of itself. Here "*apriority*" means the previousness with which space has been encountered (as a region) whenever the ready-to-hand is encountered environmentally.

The spatiality of what we proximally encounter in circumspection can become a theme for circumspection itself, as well as a task for calculation and measurement, as in building and surveying. Such thematization of the spatiality of the environment is still predominantly an act of circumspection by which space in itself already comes into view in a certain way. The space which thus shows itself can be studied purely by looking at it, if one gives up what was formerly the only possibility of access to it—circumspective calculation. When space is 'intuited formally', the pure

112

---

[1] Both 'Raum-geben' (our 'giving space') and 'Einräumen' (our 'making room') are often used in the metaphorical sense of 'yielding', 'granting', or 'making concessions'. 'Einräumen' may also be used for 'arranging' furniture, 'moving it in', or 'stowing it away'.

possibilities of spatial relations are discovered. Here one may go through a series of stages in laying bare pure homogeneous space, passing from the pure morphology of spatial shapes to *analysis situs* and finally to the purely metrical science of space. In our present study we shall not consider how all these are interconnected.[xxii] Our problematic is merely designed to establish ontologically the phenomenal basis upon which one can take the discovery of pure space as a theme for investigation, and work it out.

When space is discovered non-circumspectively by just looking at it, the environmental regions get neutralized to pure dimensions. Places— and indeed the whole circumspectively oriented totality of places belonging to equipment ready-to-hand—get reduced to a multiplicity of positions for random Things. The spatiality of what is ready-to-hand within-the-world loses its involvement-character, and so does the ready-to-hand. The world loses its specific aroundness; the environment becomes the world of Nature. The 'world', as a totality of equipment ready-to-hand, becomes spatialized [verräumlicht] to a context of extended Things which are just present-at-hand and no more. The homogeneous space of Nature shows itself only when the entities we encounter are discovered in such a way that the worldly character of the ready-to-hand gets specifically *deprived of its worldhood.*[1]

In accordance with its Being-in-the-world, Dasein always has space presented as already discovered, though not thematically. On the other hand, space in itself, so far as it embraces the mere possibilities of the pure spatial Being of something, remains proximally still concealed. The fact that space essentially *shows* itself *in a world* is not yet decisive for the kind of Being which it possesses. It need not have the kind of Being characteristic of something which is itself spatially ready-to-hand or present-at-hand. Nor does the Being of space have the kind of Being which belongs to Dasein. Though the Being of space itself cannot be conceived as the kind of Being which belongs to a *res extensa*, it does not follow that it must be defined onto-logically as a 'phenomenon' of such a *res.* (In its Being, it would not be distinguished from such a *res.*) Nor does it follow that the Being of space can be equated to that of the *res cogitans* and conceived as merely 'subjective', quite apart from the questionable character of the *Being* of such a subject.   113

The Interpretation of the Being of space has hitherto been a matter of perplexity, not so much because we have been insufficiently acquainted with the content of space itself as a thing [des Sachgehaltes des Raumes

---

[1] '. . . die den Charakter einer spezifischen *Entweltlichung* der Weltmässigkeit des Zuhandenen hat.'

selbst], as because the possibilities of Being in general have not been in principle transparent, and an Interpretation of them in terms of ontological concepts has been lacking. If we are to understand the ontological problem of space, it is of decisive importance that the question of Being must be liberated from the narrowness of those concepts of Being which merely chance to be available and which are for the most part rather rough; and the problematic of the Being of space (with regard to that phenomenon itself and various phenomenal spatialities) must be turned in such a direction as to clarify the possibilities of Being in general.

In the phenomenon of space the primary ontological character of the Being of entities within-the-world is not to be found, either as unique or as one among others. Still less does space constitute the phenomenon of the world. Unless we go back to the world, space cannot be conceived. Space becomes accessible only if the environment is deprived of its worldhood; and spatiality is not discoverable at all except on the basis of the world. Indeed space is still *one* of the things that is constitutive for the world, just as Dasein's own spatiality is essential to its basic state of Being-in-the-world.[1]

---

[1] '. . . so zwar, dass der Raum die Welt doch *mit*konstituiert, entsprechend der wesenhaften Räumlichkeit des Daseins selbst hinsichtlich seiner Grundverfassung des In-der-Welt-seins.'

IV

BEING-IN-THE-WORLD AS BEING-WITH AND BEING-ONE'S-SELF. THE "THEY"

Our analysis of the worldhood of the world has constantly been bringing the whole phenomenon of Being-in-the-world into view, although its constitutive items have not all stood out with the same phenomenal distinctness as the phenomenon of the world itself. We have Interpreted the world ontologically by going through what is ready-to-hand within-the-world; and this Interpretation has been put first, because Dasein, in its everydayness (with regard to which Dasein remains a constant theme for study), not only is in a world but comports itself towards that world with one predominant kind of Being. Proximally and for the most part Dasein is fascinated with its world. Dasein is thus absorbed in the world; the kind of Being which it thus possesses, and in general the Being-in which underlies it, are essential in determining the character of a phenomenon which we are now about to study. We shall approach this phenomenon by asking *who* it is that Dasein is in its everydayness. All the structures of Being which belong to Dasein, together with the phenomenon which provides the answer to this question of the "who", are ways of its Being. To characterize these ontologically is to do so existentially. We must therefore pose the question correctly and outline the procedure for bringing into view a broader phenomenal domain of Dasein's everydayness. By directing our researches towards the phenomenon which is to provide us with an answer to the question of the "who", we shall be led to certain structures of Dasein which are equiprimordial with Being-in-the-world: *Being-with* and *Dasein-with* [*Mitsein* und *Mitdasein*]. In this kind of Being is grounded the mode of everyday Being-one's-Self [Selbstsein]; the explication of this mode will

---

1 'Das Man'. In German one may write 'man glaubt' where in French one would write '*on croit*', or in English 'they believe', 'one believes', or 'it is believed'. But the German 'man' and the French '*on*' are specialized for such constructions in a way in which the pronouns 'they', 'one', and 'it' are not. There is accordingly no single idiomatic translation for the German 'man' which will not sometimes lend itself to ambiguity, and in general we have chosen whichever construction seems the most appropriate in its context. But when Heidegger introduces this word with a definite article and writes 'das Man', as he does very often in this chapter, we shall translate this expression as 'the "they" ', trusting that the reader will not take this too literally.

enable us to see what we may call the 'subject' of everydayness—the *"they"*. Our chapter on the 'who' of the average Dasein will thus be divided up as follows: 1. an approach to the existential question of the "who" of Dasein (Section 25); 2. the Dasein-with of Others, and everyday Being-with (Section 26); 3. everyday Being-one's-Self and the "they" (Section 27).

¶ *25. An Approach to the Existential Question of the "Who" of Dasein*

The answer to the question of who Dasein is, is one that was seemingly given in Section 9, where we indicated formally the basic characteristics of Dasein. Dasein is an entity which is in each case I myself; its Being is in each case mine. This definition *indicates* an *ontologically* constitutive state, but it does no more than indicate it. At the same time this tells us *ontically* (though in a rough and ready fashion) that in each case an "I"—not Others— is this entity. The question of the "who" answers itself in terms of the "I" itself, the 'subject', the 'Self'.[1] The "who" is what maintains itself as something identical throughout changes in its Experiences and ways of behaviour, and which relates itself to this changing multiplicity in so doing. Ontologically we understand it as something which is in each case already constantly present-at-hand, both in and for a closed realm, and which lies at the basis, in a very special sense, as the *subjectum*. As something selfsame in manifold otherness,[2] it has the character of the *Self*. Even if one rejects the "soul substance" and the Thinghood of consciousness, or denies that a person is an object, ontologically one is still positing something whose Being retains the meaning of present-at-hand, whether it does so explicitly or not. Substantiality is the ontological clue for determining which entity is to provide the answer to the question of the "who". Dasein is tacitly conceived in advance as something present-at-hand. This meaning of Being is always implicated in any case where the Being of Dasein has been left indefinite. Yet presence-at-hand is the kind of Being which belongs to entities whose character is not that of Dasein.

The assertion that it is I who in each case Dasein is, is ontically obvious; but this must not mislead us into supposing that the route for an ontological Interpretation of what is 'given' in this way has thus been unmistakably prescribed. Indeed it remains questionable whether even the mere ontical content of the above assertion does proper justice to the stock of phenomena belonging to everyday Dasein. It could be that the "who" of everyday Dasein just is *not* the "I myself".

[1] 'dem "Selbst" '. While we shall ordinarily translate the *intensive* 'selbst' by the corresponding English intensives 'itself', 'oneself', 'myself', etc., according to the context, we shall translate the *substantive* 'Selbst' by the substantive 'Self' with a capital.

[2] '. . . als Selbiges in der vielfältigen Andersheit . . .' While the words 'identisch' and 'selbig' are virtually synonyms in ordinary German, Heidegger seems to be intimating a distinction between them. We shall accordingly translate the former by 'identical' and the latter by 'selfsame' to show its etymological connection with 'selbst'. Cf. H. 130 below.

If, in arriving at ontico-ontological assertions, one is to exhibit the phenomena in terms of the kind of Being which the entities themselves possess, and if this way of exhibiting them is to retain its priority over even the most usual and obvious of answers and over whatever ways of formulating problems may have been derived from those answers, then the phenomenological Interpretation of Dasein must be defended against a perversion of our problematic when we come to the question we are about to formulate.

But is it not contrary to the rules of all sound method to approach a problematic without sticking to what is given as evident in the area of our theme? And what is more indubitable than the givenness of the "I"? And does not this givenness tell us that if we aim to work this out primordially, we must disregard everything else that is 'given'—not only a 'world' that is [einer seienden "Welt"], but even the Being of other 'I's? The kind of "giving" we have here is the mere, formal, reflective awareness of the "I"; and perhaps what it gives is indeed evident.[1] This insight even affords access to a phenomenological problematic in its own right, which has in principle the signification of providing a framework as a 'formal phenomenology of consciousness'.

In this context of an existential analytic of factical Dasein, the question arises whether giving the "I" in the way we have mentioned discloses Dasein in its everydayness, if it discloses Dasein at all. Is it then obvious *a priori* that access to Dasein must be gained only by mere reflective awareness of the "I" of actions? What if this kind of 'giving-itself' on the part of Dasein should lead our existential analytic astray and do so, indeed, in a manner grounded in the Being of Dasein itself? Perhaps when Dasein addresses itself in the way which is closest to itself, it always says "I am this entity", and in the long run says this loudest when it is 'not' this entity. Dasein is in each case mine, and this is its constitution; but what if this should be the very reason why, proximally and for the most part, Dasein *is not itself*? What if the aforementioned approach, starting with the givenness of the "I" to Dasein itself, and with a rather patent self-interpretation of Dasein, should lead the existential analytic, as it were, into a pitfall? If that which is accessible by mere "giving" can be determined, there is presumably an ontological horizon for determining it; but what if this horizon should remain in principle undetermined? It may well be that it is always ontically correct to say of this entity that 'I' am it. Yet the ontological analytic which makes use of such assertions must make certain reservations about them in principle. The word 'I' is to be

116

---

[1] 'Vielleicht ist in der Tat das, was diese Art von Gebung, das schlichte, formale, reflektive Ichvernehmen gibt, evident.'

understood only in the sense of a non-committal *formal indicator,* indicating
something which may perhaps reveal itself as its 'opposite' in some particular phenomenal context of Being. In that case, the 'not-I' is by no means
tantamount to an entity which essentially lacks 'I-hood' ["Ichheit"],
but is rather a definite kind of Being which the 'I' itself possesses, such as
having lost itself [Selbstverlorenheit].

Yet even the positive Interpretation of Dasein which we have so far
given, already forbids us to start with the formal givenness of the "I", if our
purpose is to answer the question of the "who" in a way which is phenomenally adequate. In clarifying Being-in-the-world we have shown that
a bare subject without a world never 'is' proximally, nor is it ever given.
And so in the end an isolated "I" without Others is just as far from being
proximally given.[1] If, however, 'the Others' already *are there with us* [*mit
da sind*] in Being-in-the-world, and if this is ascertained phenomenally, even
this should not mislead us into supposing that the *ontological* structure of
what is thus 'given' is obvious, requiring no investigation. Our task is to
make visible phenomenally the species to which this Dasein-with in closest
everydayness belongs, and to Interpret it in a way which is ontologically
appropriate.

Just as the ontical obviousness of the Being-in-itself of entities within-
the-world misleads us into the conviction that the meaning of this Being
is obvious ontologically, and makes us overlook the phenomenon of the
world, the ontical obviousness of the fact that Dasein is in each case mine,
also hides the possibility that the ontological problematic which belongs
to it has been led astray. *Proximally* the "who" of Dasein is not only a
problem *ontologically*; even *ontically* it remains concealed.

But does this mean that there are no clues whatever for answering the
question of the "who" by way of existential analysis? Certainly not. Of
the ways in which we formally indicated the constitution of Dasein's Being
in Sections 9 and 12 above, the one we have been discussing does not, of
course, function so well as such a clue as does the one according to which
Dasein's 'Essence' is grounded in its existence.[1] *If the 'I' is an Essential
characteristic of Dasein, then it is one which must be Interpreted existentially.* In
that case the "Who?" is to be answered only by exhibiting phenomenally
a definite kind of Being which Dasein possesses. If in each case Dasein is
its Self only in *existing*, then the constancy of the Self no less than the

---

[1] 'as such a clue': here we read 'als solcher', following the later editions. The earliest
editions have 'als solche', which has been corrected in the list of *errata*.

"Essence": while we ordinarily use 'essence' and 'essential' to translate 'Wesen' and
'wesenhaft', we shall use 'Essence' and "Essential' (with initial capitals) to translate the
presumably synonymous but far less frequent 'Essenz' and 'essentiell'.

The two 'formal indications' to which Heidegger refers are to be found on H. 42 above.

possibility of its 'failure to stand by itself'[1] requires that we formulate the question existentially and ontologically as the sole appropriate way of access to its problematic.

But if the Self is conceived 'only' as a way of Being of this entity, this seems tantamount to volatilizing the real 'core' of Dasein. Any apprehensiveness however which one may have about this gets its nourishment from the perverse assumption that the entity in question has at bottom the kind of Being which belongs to something present-at-hand, even if one is far from attributing to it the solidity of an occurrent corporeal Thing. Yet man's *'substance'* is not spirit as a synthesis of soul and body; it is rather *existence.*

¶ *26. The Dasein-with of Others and Everyday Being-with*

The answer to the question of the "who" of everyday Dasein is to be obtained by analysing that kind of Being in which Dasein maintains itself proximally and for the most part. Our investigation takes its orientation from Being-in-the-world—that basic state of Dasein by which every mode of its Being gets co-determined. If we are correct in saying that by the foregoing explication of the world, the remaining structural items of Being-in-the-world have become visible, then this must also have prepared us, in a way, for answering the question of the "who".

In our 'description' of that environment which is closest to us—the work-world of the craftsman, for example,—the outcome was that along with the equipment to be found when one is at work [in Arbeit], those Others for whom the 'work' ["Werk"] is destined are 'encountered too'.[2] If this is ready-to-hand, then there lies in the kind of Being which belongs to it (that is, in its involvement) an essential assignment or reference to possible wearers, for instance, for whom it should be 'cut to the figure'. Similarly, when material is put to use, we encounter its producer or 'supplier' as one who 'serves' well or badly. When, for example, we walk along the edge of a field but 'outside it', the field shows itself as belonging to such-and-such a person, and decently kept up by him; the book we have used was bought at So-and-so's shop and given by such-and-such

118

---

[1] '... die Ständigkeit des Selbst ebensosehr wie seine mögliche "Unselbständigkeit" ...' The adjective 'ständig', which we have usually translated as 'constant' in the sense of 'permanent' or 'continuing', goes back to the root meaning of 'standing', as do the adjectives 'selbständig' ('independent') and 'unselbständig' ('dependent'). These concepts will be discussed more fully in Section 64 below, especially H. 322, where 'Unselbständigkeit' will be rewritten not as 'Un-selbständigkeit' ('failure to stand by one's Self') but as 'Unselbst-ständigkeit' ('constancy to the Unself'). See also H. 128. (The connection with the concept of existence will perhaps be clearer if one recalls that the Latin verb 'existere' may also be derived from a verb of *standing*, as Heidegger points out in his later writings.)

[2] Cf. Section 15 above, especially H. 70f.

a person, and so forth. The boat anchored at the shore is assigned in its Being-in-itself to an acquaintance who undertakes voyages with it; but even if it is a 'boat which is strange to us', it still is indicative of Others. The Others who are thus 'encountered' in a ready-to-hand, environmental context of equipment, are not somehow added on in thought to some Thing which is proximally just present-at-hand; such 'Things' are encountered from out of the world in which they are ready-to-hand for Others—a world which is always mine too in advance. In our previous analysis, the range of what is encountered within-the-world was, in the first instance, narrowed down to equipment ready-to-hand or Nature present-at-hand, and thus to entities with a character other than that of Dasein. This restriction was necessary not only for the purpose of simplifying our explication but above all because the kind of Being which belongs to the Dasein of Others, as we encounter it within-the-world, differs from readiness-to-hand and presence-at-hand. Thus Dasein's world frees entities which not only are quite distinct from equipment and Things, but which also—in accordance with their kind of Being *as Dasein* themselves— are 'in' the world in which they are at the same time encountered within-the-world, and are 'in' it by way of Being-in-the-world.[1] These entities are neither present-at-hand nor ready-to-hand; on the contrary, they are *like* the very Dasein which frees them, in that *they are there too, and there with it*. So if one should want to identify the world in general with entities within-the-world, one would have to say that Dasein too is 'world'.[2]

Thus in characterizing the encountering of *Others*, one is again still oriented by that Dasein which is in each case one's *own*. But even in this characterization does one not start by marking out and isolating the 'I' so that one must then seek some way of getting over to the Others from this isolated subject? To avoid this misunderstanding we must notice in what sense we are talking about 'the Others'. By 'Others' we do not mean everyone else but me—those over against whom the "I" stands out. They are rather those from whom, for the most part, one does *not* distinguish oneself—those among whom one is too. This Being-there-too [Auch-dasein] with them does not have the ontological character of a Being-present-at-hand-along-'with' them within a world. This 'with' is something of the character of Dasein; the 'too' means a sameness of Being as circumspectively concernful Being-in-the-world. 'With' and 'too' are to be

---

[1] '. . . sondern gemäss seiner Seinsart *als Dasein* selbst in der Weise des In-der-Welt-seins "in" der Welt ist, in der es zugleich innerweltlich begegnet.'

[2] 'Dieses Seiende ist weder vorhanden noch zuhanden, sondern ist *so, wie* das freigebende Dasein selbst—es *ist auch und mit da*. Wollte man denn schon Welt überhaupt mit dem innerweltlich Seienden identifizieren, dann müsste man sagen, "Welt" ist auch Dasein.'

understood *existentially*, not categorially. By reason of this *with-like* [*mithaften*] Being-in-the-world, the world is always the one that I share with Others. The world of Dasein is a *with-world* [*Mitwelt*]. Being-in is *Being-with* Others. Their *Being-in-themselves within-the-world* is *Dasein-with* [*Mit-dasein*].

When Others are encountered, it is not the case that one's own subject is *proximally* present-at-hand and that the rest of the subjects, which are likewise occurrents, get discriminated beforehand and then apprehended; nor are they encountered by a primary act of looking at oneself in such a way that the opposite pole of a distinction first gets ascertained. They are encountered from out of the *world*, in which concernfully circumspective Dasein essentially dwells. Theoretically concocted 'explanations' of the Being-present-at-hand of Others urge themselves upon us all too easily; but over against such explanations we must hold fast to the phenomenal facts of the case which we have pointed out, namely, that Others are encountered *environmentally*. This elemental worldly kind of encountering, which belongs to Dasein and is closest to it, goes so far that even one's *own* Dasein becomes something that it can itself proximally 'come across' only when it *looks away* from 'Experiences' and the 'centre of its actions', or does not as yet 'see' them at all. Dasein finds 'itself' proximally in *what* it does, uses, expects, avoids—in those things environmentally ready-to-hand with which it is proximally *concerned*.

And even when Dasein explicitly addresses itself as "I here", this locative personal designation must be understood in terms of Dasein's existential spatiality. In Interpreting this (See Section 23) we have already intimated that this "I-here" does not mean a certain privileged point—that of an I-Thing—but is to be understood as Being-in in terms of the "yonder" of the world that is ready-to-hand—the "yonder" which is the dwelling-place of Dasein as *concern*.[1]

W. von Humboldt[ii] has alluded to certain languages which express the 'I' by 'here', the 'thou' by 'there', the 'he' by 'yonder', thus rendering the personal pronouns by locative adverbs, to put it grammatically. It is controversial whether indeed the primordial signification of locative expressions is adverbial or pronominal. But this dispute loses its basis if one notes that locative adverbs have a relationship to the "I" *qua* Dasein. The 'here' and the 'there' and the 'yonder' are primarily not mere ways of designating the location of entities present-at-hand within-the-world at positions in space; they are rather characteristics of Dasein's primordial

---

[1] '. . . dass dieses Ich-hier nicht einen ausgezeichneten Punkt des Ichdinges meint, sondern sich versteht als In-sein aus dem Dort der zuhandenen Welt, bei dem Dasein als *Besorgen* sich aufhält.' The older editions have 'In-Sein' for 'In-sein', and 'dabei' for 'bei dem'.

spatiality. These supposedly locative adverbs are Dasein-designations; they have a signification which is primarily existential, not categorial. But they are not pronouns either; their signification is prior to the differentiation of locative adverbs and personal pronouns: these expressions have a Dasein-signification which is authentically spatial, and which serves as evidence that when we interpret Dasein without any theoretical distortions we can see it immediately as 'Being-alongside' the world with which it concerns itself, and as Being-alongside it spatially—that is to say, as desevering* and giving directionality. In the 'here', the Dasein which is absorbed in its world speaks not towards itself but away from itself towards the 'yonder' of something circumspectively ready-to-hand; yet it still has *itself* in view in its existential spatiality.

Dasein understands itself proximally and for the most part in terms of its world; and the Dasein-with of Others is often encountered in terms of what is ready-to-hand within-the-world. But even if Others become themes for study, as it were, in their own Dasein, they are not encountered as person-Things present-at-hand: we meet them 'at work', that is, primarily in their Being-in-the-world. Even if we see the Other 'just standing around', he is never apprehended as a human-Thing present-at-hand, but his 'standing-around' is an existential mode of Being—an unconcerned, uncircumspective tarrying alongside everything and nothing [Verweilen bei Allem und Keinem]. The Other is encountered in his Dasein-with in the world.

The expression 'Dasein', however, shows plainly that 'in the first instance' this entity is unrelated to Others, and that of course it can still be 'with' Others afterwards. Yet one must not fail to notice that we use the term "Dasein-with" to designate that Being for which the Others who are [die seienden Anderen] are freed within-the-world. This Dasein-with of the Others is disclosed within-the-world for a Dasein, and so too for those who are Daseins with us [die Mitdaseienden], only because Dasein in itself is essentially Being-with. The phenomenological assertion that "Dasein is essentially Being-with" has an existential-ontological meaning. It does not seek to establish ontically that factically I am not present-at-hand alone, and that Others of my kind occur. If this were what is meant by the proposition that Dasein's Being-in-the-world is essentially constituted by Being-with, then Being-with would not be an existential attribute which Dasein, of its own accord, has coming to it from its own kind of Being. It would rather be something which turns up in every case by reason of the occurrence of Others. Being-with is an existential characteristic of Dasein even when factically no Other is present-at-hand or perceived. Even Dasein's Being-alone is Being-with in the world. The Other can *be missing* only *in*[1] and *for*[1] a Being-with. Being-alone is a deficient mode of Being-with; its very possibility is the proof of this. On the other hand, factical Being-alone is not obviated by the occurrence of a second example of a human being 'beside' me, or by ten such examples. Even if these and more are present-at-hand, Dasein can still be alone. So Being-with and the facticity of Being with one another are not based on the occurrence together of several 'subjects'. Yet Being-alone 'among' many does not mean that with regard to their Being they are merely present-at-hand there alongside us. Even in our Being 'among them' they are *there with* us; their Dasein-with is encountered in a mode in which they are indifferent and alien. Being missing and 'Being away' [Das Fehlen und "Fortsein"] are modes of Dasein-with, and are possible only because Dasein as Being-with lets the Dasein of Others be encountered in its world. Being-with is in every case a characteristic of one's own Dasein; Dasein-with characterizes the Dasein of Others to the extent that it is freed by its world for a Being-with. Only so far as one's own Dasein has the essential structure of Being-with, is it Dasein-with as encounterable for Others.[2]

    If Dasein-with remains existentially constitutive for Being-in-the-world, then, like our circumspective dealings with the ready-to-hand within-the-world (which, by way of anticipation, we have called 'concern'), it must be Interpreted in terms of the phenomenon of *care*; for as "care" the Being of Dasein in general is to be defined.[3] (Compare Chapter 6 of this Division.) Concern is a character-of-Being which Being-with cannot have as its own, even though Being-with, like concern, is a *Being towards* entities encountered within-the-world. But those entities towards which Dasein as Being-with comports itself do not have the kind of Being which belongs to equipment ready-to-hand; they are themselves Dasein. These entities are not objects of concern, but rather of *solicitude.*[4]

the comportment in which we come across others f. out of the world.

    [1] Italics supplied in the later editions.
    [2] '. . . Mitdasein charakterisiert das Dasein anderer, sofern es für ein Mitsein durch dessen Welt freigegeben ist. Das eigene Dasein ist, sofern es die Wesensstruktur des Mitseins hat, als für Andere begegnend Mitdasein.'
    [3] '. . . als welche das Sein des Daseins überhaupt bestimmt wird.' The older editions omit 'wird'.
    [4] 'Dieses Seiende wird nicht besorgt, sondern steht in der *Fürsorge*.' There is no good English equivalent for 'Fürsorge', which we shall usually translate by 'solicitude'. The more literal 'caring-for' has the connotation of 'being fond of', which we do not want here; 'personal care' suggests personal hygiene; 'personal concern' suggests one's personal business or affairs. 'Fürsorge' is rather the kind of care which we find in 'prenatal care' or 'taking care of the children', or even the kind of care which is administered by welfare agencies. Indeed the word 'Fürsorge' is regularly used in contexts where we would speak of 'welfare work' or 'social welfare'; this is the usage which Heidegger has in mind in his discussion of 'Fürsorge' as 'a factical social arrangement'. (The etymological connection between 'Sorge ('care'), 'Fürsorge' ('solicitude'), and 'Besorgen ('concern'), is entirely lost in our translation.)

Even 'concern' with food and clothing, and the nursing of the sick body, are forms of solicitude. But we understand the expression "solicitude" in a way which corresponds to our use of "concern" as a term for an *existentiale*. For example, 'welfare work.' ["Fürsorge"], as a factical social arrangement, is grounded in Dasein's state of Being as Being-with. Its factical urgency gets its motivation in that Dasein maintains itself proximally and for the most part in the deficient modes of solicitude. Being for, against, or without one another, passing one another by, not "mattering" to one another—these are possible ways of solicitude. And it is precisely these last-named deficient and Indifferent modes that characterize everyday, average Being-with-one-another. These modes of Being show again the characteristics of inconspicuousness and obviousness which belong just as much to the everyday Dasein-with of Others within-the-world as to the readiness-to-hand of the equipment with which one is daily concerned. These Indifferent modes of Being-with-one-another may easily mislead ontological Interpretation into interpreting this kind of Being, in the first instance, as the mere Being-present-at-hand of several subjects. It seems as if only negligible variations of the same kind of Being lie before us; yet ontologically there is an essential distinction between the 'indifferent' way in which Things at random occur together and the way in which entities who are with one another do not "matter" to one another.

With regard to its positive modes, solicitude has two extreme possibilities. It can, as it were, take away 'care' from the Other and put itself in his position in concern: it can *leap in* for him.[1] This kind of solicitude takes over for the Other that with which he is to concern himself. The Other is thus thrown out of his own position; he steps back so that afterwards, when the matter has been attended to, he can either take it over as something finished and at his disposal,[2] or disburden himself of it completely. In such solicitude the Other can become one who is dominated and dependent, even if this domination is a tacit one and remains hidden from him. This kind of solicitude, which leaps in and takes away 'care', is to a large extent determinative for Being with one another, and pertains for the most part to our concern with the ready-to-hand.

In contrast to this, there is also the possibility of a kind of solicitude which does not so much leap in for the Other as *leap ahead* of him [ihm

122

---

[1] '... sich an seine Stelle setzen, für ihn *einspringen*.' Here, as on H. 100 (See our note 2, p. 133), it would be more idiomatic to translate 'für ihn einspringen' as 'intervene for him', 'stand in for him' or 'serve as deputy for him'; but since 'einspringen' is to be contrasted with 'vorspringen', 'vorausspringen' and perhaps even 'entspringen' in the following paragraphs, we have chosen a translation which suggests the etymological connection.

[2] '... um nachträglich das Besorgte als fertig Verfügbares zu übernehmen ...'

solicitude leaps in & dominates

vorausspringt] in his existentiell potentiality-for-Being, not in order to take away his 'care' but rather to give it back to him authentically as such for the first time. This kind of solicitude pertains essentially to authentic care —that is, to the existence of the Other, not to a "*what*" with which he is concerned; it helps the Other to become transparent to himself *in* his care and to become *free for* it.

Solicitude proves to be a state of Dasein's Being—one which, in accordance with its different possibilities, is bound up with its Being towards the world of its concern, and likewise with its authentic Being towards itself. Being with one another is based proximally and often exclusively upon what is a matter of common concern in such Being. A Being-with-one-another which arises [entspringt] from one's doing the same thing as someone else, not only keeps for the most part within the outer limits, but enters the mode of distance and reserve. The Being-with-one-another of those who are hired for the same affair often thrives only on mistrust. On the other hand, when they devote themselves to the same affair in common, their doing so is determined by the manner in which their Dasein, each in its own way, has been taken hold of.[1] They thus become *authentically* bound together, and this makes possible the right kind of objectivity [die rechte Sachlichkeit], which frees the Other in his freedom for himself.

Everyday Being-with-one-another maintains itself between the two extremes of positive solicitude—that which leaps in and dominates, and that which leaps forth and liberates [vorspringend-befreienden]. It brings numerous mixed forms to maturity;[2] to describe these and classify them would take us beyond the limits of this investigation.

Just as *circumspection* belongs to concern as a way of discovering what is ready-to-hand, solicitude is guided by *considerateness* and *forbearance*.[3] Like solicitude, these can range through their respective deficient and Indifferent modes up to the point of *inconsiderateness* or the perfunctoriness for which indifference leads the way.[4]

                             123

[1] 'Umgekehrt ist das gemeinsame Sicheinsetzen für dieselbe Sache aus dem je eigens ergriffenen Dasein bestimmt.'

[2] Reading '. . . und zeitigt mannigfache Mischformen . . .' with the older editions. The later editions have 'zeigt' ('shows') instead of 'zeitigt' ('brings to maturity'). On 'zeitigen' see H. 304 and our note ad loc.

[3] 'Wie dem Besorgen als Weise des Entdeckens des Zuhandenen die *Umsicht* zugehört, so ist die Fürsorge geleitet durch die *Rücksicht* und *Nachsicht*.' Heidegger is here calling attention to the etymological kinship of the three words which he italicizes, each of which stands for a special kind of *sight* or *seeing* ('Sicht').
The italicization of 'Umsicht' ('circumspection') is introduced in the newer editions.

[4] '. . . bis zur *Rücksichtslosigkeit* und dem Nachsehen, das die Gleichgültigkeit leitet.' This passage is ambiguous both syntactically and semantically. It is not clear, for instance, whether the subject of the relative clause is 'die Gleichgültigkeit' or the pronoun 'das', though we prefer the former interpretation. 'Nachsehen', which is etymologically

The world not only frees the ready-to-hand as entities encountered within-the-world; it also frees Dasein—the Others in their Dasein-with. But Dasein's ownmost meaning of Being is such that this entity (which has been freed environmentally) is Being-in in the same world in which, as encounterable for Others, it is there with them. We have interpreted worldhood as that referential totality which constitutes significance (Section 18). In Being-familiar with this significance and previously understanding it, Dasein lets what is ready-to-hand be encountered as discovered in its involvement. In Dasein's Being, the context of references or assignments which significance implies is tied up with Dasein's ownmost Being—a Being which essentially can have no involvement, but which is rather that Being *for the sake of which* Dasein itself is as it is.

According to the analysis which we have now completed, Being with Others belongs to the Being of Dasein, which is an issue for Dasein in its very Being.[1] Thus as Being-with, Dasein 'is' essentially for the sake of Others. This must be understood as an existential statement as to its essence. Even if the particular factical Dasein does *not* turn to Others, and supposes that it has no need of them or manages to get along without them, it *is* in the way of Being-with. In Being-with, as the existential "for-the-sake-of" of Others, these have already been disclosed in their Dasein. With their Being-with, their disclosedness has been constituted beforehand; accordingly, this disclosedness also goes to make up significance—that is to say, worldhood. And, significance, as worldhood, is tied up with the existential "for-the-sake-of-which".[2] Since the worldhood of that world in which every Dasein essentially is already, is thus constituted, it accordingly lets us encounter what is environmentally ready-to-hand as something with which we are circumspectively concerned, and it does so in such a way that together with it we encounter the Dasein-with of Others. The structure of the world's worldhood is such that Others are not proximally present-at-hand as free-floating subjects along with other Things, but show themselves in the world in their special environmental Being, and do so in terms of what is ready-to-hand in that world.

Being-with is such that the disclosedness of the Dasein-with of Others

---

akin to 'Nachsicht', means to 'inspect' or 'check' something; but it often means to do this in a very perfunctory manner, and this latter sense may well be the one which Heidegger has in mind.

[1] '. . . zum Sein des Daseins, um das es ihm in seinem Sein selbst geht . . .' The older editions have 'darum' instead of 'um das'.

[2] 'Diese mit dem Mitsein vorgängig konstituierte Erschlossenheit der Anderen macht demnach auch die Bedeutsamkeit, d.h. die Weltlichkeit mit aus, als welche sie im existenzialen Worum-willen festgemacht ist.' The word 'sie' appears only in the later editions.

belongs to it; this means that because Dasein's Being is Being-with, its understanding of Being already implies the understanding of Others. This understanding, like any understanding, is not an acquaintance derived from knowledge about them, but a primordially existential kind of Being, which, more than anything else, makes such knowledge and acquaintance possible.[1] Knowing oneself [Sichkennen] is grounded in Being-with, which understands primordially. It operates proximally in accordance with the kind of Being which is closest to us—Being-in-the-world as Being-with; and it does so by an acquaintance with that which Dasein, along with the Others, comes across in its environmental circumspection and concerns itself with—an acquaintance in which Dasein understands. Solicitous concern is understood in terms of what we are concerned with, and along with our understanding of it. Thus in concernful solicitude the Other is proximally disclosed.

124

But because solicitude dwells proximally and for the most part in the deficient or at least the Indifferent modes (in the indifference of passing one another by), the kind of knowing-oneself which is essential and closest, demands that one become acquainted with oneself.[2] And when, indeed, one's knowing-oneself gets lost in such ways as aloofness, hiding oneself away, or putting on a disguise, Being-with-one-another must follow special routes of its own in order to come close to Others, or even to 'see through them' ["hinter sie" zu kommen].

But just as opening oneself up [Sichoffenbaren] or closing oneself off is grounded in one's having Being-with-one-another as one's kind of Being at the time, and indeed *is* nothing else but this, even the explicit disclosure of the Other in solicitude grows only out of one's primarily Being with him in each case. Such a disclosure of the Other (which is indeed thematic, but not in the manner of theoretical psychology) easily becomes the phenomenon which proximally comes to view when one considers the theoretical problematic of understanding the 'psychical life of Others' ["fremden Seelenlebens"]. In this phenomenally 'proximal' manner it thus presents a way of Being with one another understandingly; but at the same time it gets taken as that which, primordially and 'in the beginning', constitutes Being towards Others and makes it possible at all.

---

[1] 'Dieses Verstehen ist, wie Verstehen überhaupt, nicht eine aus Erkennen erwachsene Kenntnis, sondern eine ursprünglich existenziale Seinsart die Erkennen und Kenntnis allererst möglich macht'. While we have here translated 'Kenntnis' as 'acquaintance' and 'Erkennen' as 'knowledge about', these terms must not be understood in the special senses exploited by Lord Russell and C. L. Lewis. The 'acquaintance' here involved is of the kind which may be acquired whenever one is well informed about something, whether one has any direct contact with it or not.

[2] '. . . bedarf das nächste und wesenhafte Sichkennen eines Sichkennenlernens.' 'Sichkennen' ('knowing oneself') is to be distinguished sharply from 'Selbsterkenntnis' ('knowledge of the Self'), which will be discussed on H. 146. See our note 1, p. 186.

This phenomenon, which is none too happily designated as *'empathy'* [*"Einfühlung"*], is then supposed, as it were, to provide the first onto-logical bridge from one's own subject, which is given proximally as alone, to the other subject, which is proximally quite closed off.

Of course Being towards Others is ontologically different from Being towards Things which are present-at-hand. The entity which is 'other' has itself the same kind of Being as Dasein. In Being with and towards Others, there is thus a relationship of Being [Seinsverhältnis] from Dasein to Dasein. But it might be said that this relationship is already constitutive for one's own Dasein, which, in its own right, has an understanding of Being, and which thus relates itself[1] towards Dasein. The relationship-of-Being which one has towards Others would then become a Projection[2] of one's own Being-towards-oneself 'into something else'. The Other would be a duplicate of the Self.

But while these deliberations seem obvious enough, it is easy to see that they have little ground to stand on. The presupposition which this argu-ment demands—that Dasein's Being towards itself is Being towards an Other—fails to hold. As long as the legitimacy of this presupposition has not turned out to be evident, one may still be puzzled as to how Dasein's relationship to itself is thus to be disclosed to the Other as Other.

Not only is Being towards Others an autonomous, irreducible relation-ship of Being: this relationship, as Being-with, is one which, with Dasein's Being, already is.[3] Of course it is indisputable that a lively mutual acquaintanceship on the basis of Being-with, often depends upon how far one's own Dasein has understood itself at the time; but this means that it depends only upon how far one's essential Being with Others has made itself transparent and has not disguised itself.[4] And that is possible only if Dasein, as Being-in-the-world, already is with Others. 'Empathy' does not first constitute Being-with; only on the basis of Being-with does 'empathy' become possible: it gets its motivation from the unsociability of the dominant modes of Being-with.[5]

[1] '. . . sich . . . verhält . . .' We have often translated this expression as 'comports' itself', compromising between two other possible meanings: 'relates itself' and 'behaves or 'conducts itself'. In this passage, however, and in many others where this expression is tied up with 'Verhältnis' ('relationship') rather than with 'Verhalten' ('behaviour or 'conduct'), only 'relates itself' seems appropriate.

[2] 'Projektion'. Here we are dealing with 'projection' in the familiar psychological sense, not in the sense which would be expressed by 'Entwurf'. See H. 145 ff.

[3] 'Das Sein zu Anderen ist nicht nur ein eigenständiger, irreduktibler Seinsbezug, er ist als Mitsein mit dem Sein des Daseins schon seiend.'

[4] '. . . wie weit es das wesenhafte Mitsein mit anderen sich durchsichtig gemacht und nicht verstellt hat . . .' (The older editions have '. . . sich nicht undurchsichtig gemacht und verstellt hat . . .'.)

[5] ' "Einfühlung" konstituiert nicht erst das Mitsein, sondern ist auf dessen Grunde erst möglich und durch die vorherrschenden defizienten Modi des Mitseins in ihrer Unumgänglichkeit motiviert.'

But the fact that 'empathy' is not a primordial existential phenomenon, any more than is knowing in general, does not mean that there is nothing problematical about it. The special hermeneutic of empathy will have to show how Being-with-one-another and Dasein's knowing of itself are led astray and obstructed by the various possibilities of Being which Dasein itself possesses, so that a genuine 'understanding' gets suppressed, and Dasein takes refuge in substitutes; the possibility of understanding the stranger correctly presupposes such a hermeneutic as its positive existential condition.[1] Our analysis has shown that Being-with is an existential constituent of Being-in-the-world. Dasein-with has proved to be a kind of Being which entities encountered within-the-world have as their own. So far as Dasein *is* at all, it has Being-with-one-another as its kind of Being. This cannot be conceived as a summative result of the occurrence of several 'subjects'. Even to come across a number of 'subjects' [einer Anzahl von "Subjekten"] becomes possible only if the Others who are concerned proximally in their Dasein-with are treated merely as 'numerals' ["Nummer"]. Such a number of 'subjects' gets discovered only by a definite Being-with-and-towards-one-another. This 'inconsiderate' Being-with 'reckons' ["rechnet"] with the Others without seriously 'counting on them' ["auf sie zählt"], or without even wanting to 'have anything to do' with them.

One's own Dasein, like the Dasein-with of Others, is encountered proximally and for the most part in terms of the with-world with which we are environmentally concerned. When Dasein is absorbed in the world of its concern—that is, at the same time, in its Being-with towards Others—it is not itself. *Who* is it, then, who has taken over Being as everyday Being-with-one-another?

¶ *27. Everyday Being-one's-Self and the "They"*

The *ontologically* relevant result of our analysis of Being-with is the insight that the 'subject character' of one's own Dasein and that of Others is to be defined existentially—that is, in terms of certain ways in which one may be. In that with which we concern ourselves environmentally the Others are encountered as what they are; they *are* what they do [sie sind das, was sie betreiben].

In one's concern with what one has taken hold of, whether with, for, or against, the Others, there is constant care as to the way one differs from them, whether that difference is merely one that is to be evened out, whether one's own Dasein has lagged behind the Others and wants to

---

[1] '... welche positive existenziale Bedingung rechtes Fremdverstehen für seine Möglichkeit voraussetzt.' We have construed 'welche' as referring back to 'Hermeneutik', though this is not entirely clear.

126

catch up in relationship to them, or whether one's Dasein already has some priority over them and sets out to keep them suppressed. The care about this distance between them is disturbing to Being-with-one-another, though this disturbance is one that is hidden from it. If we may express this existentially, such Being-with-one-another has the character of *distantiality* [*Abständigkeit*]. The more inconspicuous this kind of Being is to everyday Dasein itself, all the more stubbornly and primordially does it work itself out.

But this distantiality which belongs to Being-with, is such that Dasein, as everyday Being-with-one-another, stands in *subjection* [*Botmässigkeit*] to Others. It itself *is* not;[1] its Being has been taken away by the Others. Dasein's everyday possibilities of Being are for the Others to dispose of as they please. These Others, moreover, are not *definite* Others. On the contrary, any Other can represent them. What is decisive is just that inconspicuous domination by Others which has already been taken over unawares from Dasein as Being-with. One belongs to the Others oneself and enhances their power. 'The Others' whom one thus designates in order to cover up the fact of one's belonging to them essentially oneself, are those who proximally and for the most part *'are there'* in everyday Being-with-one-another. The "who" is not this one, not that one, not oneself [man selbst], not some people [einige], and not the sum of them all. The 'who' is the neuter, *the "they"* [*das Man*].

We have shown earlier how in the environment which lies closest to us, the public 'environment' already is ready-to-hand and is also a matter of concern [mitbesorgt]. In utilizing public means of transport and in making use of information services such as the newspaper, every Other is like the next. This Being-with-one-another dissolves one's own Dasein completely into the kind of Being of 'the Others', in such a way, indeed, that the Others, as distinguishable and explicit, vanish more and more. In this inconspicuousness and unascertainability, the real dictatorship of the "they" is unfolded. We take pleasure and enjoy ourselves as *they* [man] take pleasure; we read, see, and judge about literature and art as *they* see and judge; likewise we shrink back from the 'great mass' as *they* shrink back; we find 'shocking' what *they* find shocking. The "they", which is nothing definite, and which all are, though not as the sum, prescribes the kind of Being of everydayness.

The "they" has its own ways in which to be. That tendency of Being-with which we have called "distantiality" is grounded in the fact that Being-with-one-another concerns itself as such with *averageness*, which is an existential characteristic of the "they". The "they", in its Being,

127

---

[1] 'Nicht es selbst *ist*; . . .'

essentially makes an issue of this. Thus the "they" maintains itself factically in the averageness of that which belongs to it, of that which it regards as valid and that which it does not, and of that to which it grants success and that to which it denies it. In this averageness with which it prescribes what can and may be ventured, it keeps watch over everything exceptional that thrusts itself to the fore. Every kind of priority gets noiselessly suppressed. Overnight, everything that is primordial gets glossed over as something that has long been well known. Everything gained by a struggle becomes just something to be manipulated. Every secret loses its force. This care of averageness reveals in turn an essential tendency of Dasein which we call the "levelling down" [*Einebnung*] of all possibilities of Being.

Distantiality, averageness, and levelling down, as ways of Being for the "they", constitute what we know as 'publicness' ["die Offentlichkeit"]. Publicness proximally controls every way in which the world and Dasein get interpreted, and it is always right—not because there is some distinctive and primary relationship-of-Being in which it is related to 'Things', or because it avails itself of some transparency on the part of Dasein which it has explicitly appropriated, but because it is insensitive to every difference of level and of genuineness and thus never gets to the 'heart of the matter' ["auf die Sachen"]. By publicness everything gets obscured, and what has thus been covered up gets passed off as something familiar and accessible to everyone.

The "they" is there alongside everywhere [ist überall dabei], but in such a manner that it has always stolen away whenever Dasein presses for a decision. Yet because the "they" presents every judgment and decision as its own, it deprives the particular Dasein of its answerability. The "they" can, as it were, manage to have 'them' constantly invoking it.[1] It can be answerable for everything most easily, because it is not someone who needs to vouch for anything. It 'was' always the "they" who did it, and yet it can be said that it has been 'no one'. In Dasein's everydayness the agency through which most things come about is one of which we must say that "it was no one".

Thus the particular Dasein in its everydayness is *disburdened* by the "they". Not only that; by thus disburdening it of its Being, the "they" accommodates Dasein [kommt . . . dem Dasein entgegen] if Dasein has any tendency to take things easily and make them easy. And because the "they" constantly accommodates the particular Dasein by disburdening it of its Being, the "they" retains and enhances its stubborn dominion.

Everyone is the other, and no one is himself. The "*they*", which supplies

128

---

[1] 'Das Man kann es sich gleichsam leisten, dass "man" sich ständig auf es beruft.'

the answer to the question of the *"who"* of everyday Dasein, is the *"nobody"* to whom every Dasein has already surrendered itself in Being-among-one-other [Untereinandersein].

In these characters of Being which we have exhibited—everyday Being-among-one-another, distantiality, averageness, levelling down, public-ness, the disburdening of one's Being, and accommodation—lies that 'constancy' of Dasein which is closest to us. This "constancy" pertains not to the enduring Being-present-at-hand of something, but rather to Dasein's kind of Being as Being-with. Neither the Self of one's own Dasein nor the Self of the Other has as yet found itself or lost itself as long as it is [seiend] in the modes we have mentioned. In these modes one's way of Being is that of inauthenticity and failure to stand by one's Self.[1] To be in this way signifies no lessening of Dasein's facticity, just as the "they", as the "nobody", is by no means nothing at all. On the contrary, in this kind of Being, Dasein is an *ens realissimum*, if by 'Reality' we understand a Being that has the character of Dasein.

Of course, the "they" is as little present-at-hand as Dasein itself. The more openly the "they" behaves, the harder it is to grasp, and the slier it is, but the less is it nothing at all. If we 'see' it ontico-ontologically with an unprejudiced eye, it reveals itself as the 'Realest subject' of everyday-ness. And even if it is not accessible like a stone that is present-at-hand, this is not in the least decisive as to its kind of Being. One may neither decree prematurely that this "they" is 'really' nothing, nor profess the opinion that one can Interpret this phenomenon ontologically by some-how 'explaining' it as what results from taking the Being-present-at-hand-together of several subjects and then fitting them together. On the contrary, in working out concepts of Being one must direct one's course by these phenomena, which cannot be pushed aside.

Furthermore, the "they" is not something like a 'universal subject' which a plurality of subjects have hovering above them. One can come to take it this way only if the Being of such 'subjects' is understood as having a character other than that of Dasein, and if these are regarded as cases of a genus of occurrents—cases which are factually present-at-hand. With this approach, the only possibility ontologically is that everything which is not a case of this sort is to be understood in the sense of genus and species. The "they" is not the genus to which the individual Dasein belongs, nor can we come across it in such entities as an abiding characteristic. That even the traditional logic fails us when confronted with these phenomena, is not surprising if we bear in mind that it has its foundation in an

129

---

[1] 'Man ist in der Weise der Unselbständigkeit und Uneigentlichkeit.' On 'Ständigkeit' and 'Unselbständigkeit' see our note 1, p. 153, H. 117 above.

ontology of the present-at-hand—an ontology which, moreover, is still a rough one. So no matter in how many ways this logic may be improved and expanded, it cannot in principle be made any more flexible. Such reforms of logic, oriented towards the 'humane sciences', only increase the ontological confusion.

The "they" is an e x i s t e n t i a l e; and as a primordial phenomenon, it belongs to ⨏ *Dasein's positive constitution.* It itself has, in turn, various possibilities of becoming concrete as something characteristic of Dasein [seiner daseins-mässigen Konkretion]. The extent to which its dominion becomes com-pelling and explicit may change in the course of history.

The Self of everyday Dasein is the *they-self*,[1] which we distinguish from the *authentic Self*—that is, from the Self which has been taken hold of in its own way [eigens ergriffenen]. As they-self, the particular Dasein has been *dispersed* into the "they", and must first find itself. This dispersal characterizes the 'subject' of that kind of Being which we know as con-cernful absorption in the world we encounter as closest to us. If Dasein is familiar with itself as they-self, this means at the same time that the "they" itself prescribes that way of interpreting the world and Being-in-the-world which lies closest. Dasein is for the sake of the "they" in an everyday manner, and the "they" itself Articulates the referential context of significance.[2] When entities are encountered, Dasein's world frees them for a totality of involvements with which the "they" is familiar, and within the limits which have been established with the "they's" averageness. *Proxi-mally*, factical Dasein is in the with-world, which is discovered in an average way. *Proximally*, it is not 'I', in the sense of my own Self, that 'am', but rather the Others, whose way is that of the "they".[3] In terms of the "they", and as the "they", I am 'given' proximally to 'myself' [mir "selbst"]. Proximally Dasein is "they", and for the most part it remains so. If Dasein discovers the world in its own way [eigens] and brings it close, if it discloses to itself its own authentic Being, then this discovery of the 'world' and this disclosure of Dasein are always accomplished as a clearing-away of concealments and obscurities, as a breaking up of the disguises with which Dasein bars its own way.

With this Interpretation of Being-with and Being-one's-Self in the

[1] '. . . das Man-selbst . . .' This expression is also to be distinguished from 'das Man selbst' ('the "they" itself'), which appears elsewhere in this paragraph. In the first of these expressions 'selbst' appears as a substantive, in the second as a mere intensive.

[2] 'Das Man selbst, worum-willen das Dasein alltäglich ist, artikuliert den Verweisungs-zusammenhang der Bedeutsamkeit.' It is also possible to construe 'alltäglich' as a pre-dicate adjective after 'ist'; in that case we should read: 'Dasein is everyday for the sake of the "they".'

[3] '*Zunächst* "bin" nicht "ich" im Sinne des eigenen Selbst, sondern die Anderen in der Weise des Man.' In the earlier editions there are commas after ' "ich" ' and 'Anderen', which would suggest a somewhat different interpretation.

"they", the question of the "who" of the everydayness of Being-with-one-another is answered. These considerations have at the same time brought us a concrete understanding of the basic constitution of Dasein: Being-in-the-world, in its everydayness and its averageness, has become visible.

From the kind of Being which belongs to the "they"—the kind which is closest—everyday Dasein draws its pre-ontological way of interpreting its Being. In the first instance ontological Interpretation follows the tendency to interpret it this way: it understands Dasein in terms of the world and comes across it as an entity within-the-world. But that is not all: even that meaning of Being on the basis of which these 'subject' entities [diese seienden "Subjekte"] get understood, is one which that ontology of Dasein which is 'closest' to us lets itself present in terms of the 'world'. But because the phenomenon of the world itself gets passed over in this absorption in the world, its place gets taken [tritt an seine Stelle] by what is present-at-hand within-the-world, namely, Things. The Being of those entities which *are there with us*, gets conceived as presence-at-hand. Thus by exhibiting the positive phenomenon of the closest everyday Being-in-the-world, we have made it possible to get an insight into the reason why an ontological Interpretation of this state of Being has been missing. *This very state of Being,*[1] *in its everyday kind of Being, is what proximally misses itself and covers itself up.*

If the Being of everyday Being-with-one-another is already different in principle from pure presence-at-hand—in spite of the fact that it is seemingly close to it ontologically—still less can the Being of the authentic Self be conceived as presence-at-hand. *Authentic Being-one's-Self* does not rest upon an exceptional condition of the subject, a condition that has been detached from the "they"; *it is rather an existentiell modification of the "they"— of the "they" as an essential existentiale.*

But in that case there is ontologically a gap separating the selfsameness of the authentically existing Self from the identity of that "I" which maintains itself throughout its manifold Experiences.

[1] We interpret Heidegger's pronoun 'Sie' as referring to 'Seinsverfassung' ('state of Being'); but there are other words in the previous sentence to which it might refer with just as much grammatical plausibility, particularly 'Interpretation'.

V

BEING-IN AS SUCH

¶ 28. The Task of a Thematic Analysis of Being-in

IN the preparatory stage of the existential analytic of Dasein, we have for our leading theme this entity's basic state, Being-in-the-World. Our first aim is to bring into relief phenomenally the unitary primordial structure of Dasein's Being, in terms of which its possibilities and the ways for it 'to be' are ontologically determined. Up till now, our phenomenal characterization of Being-in-the-world has been directed towards the world, as a structural item of Being-in-the-world, and has attempted to provide an answer to the question about the "who" of this entity in its everydayness. But even in first marking out the tasks of a preparatory fundamental analysis of Dasein, we have already provided an advance orientation as to *Being-in as such*,[1] and have illustrated it in the concrete mode of knowing the world.[ii]

The fact that we foresaw this structural item which carries so much weight, arose from our aim of setting the analysis of single items, from the outset, within the frame of a steady preliminary view of the structural whole, and of guarding against any disruption or fragmentation of the unitary phenomenon. Now, keeping in mind what has been achieved in the concrete analysis of the world and the "who", we must turn our Interpretation back to the phenomenon of Being-in. By considering this more penetratingly, however, we shall not only get a new and surer phenomenological view of the structural totality of Being-in-the-world, but shall also pave the way to grasping the primordial Being of Dasein itself—namely, care.

But what more is there to point out in Being-in-the-world, beyond the essential relations of Being alongside the world (concern), Being-with (solicitude), and Being-one's-Self ("who")? If need be, there still remains the possibility of broadening out the analysis by characterizing comparatively the variations of concern and its circumspection, of solicitude and the considerateness which goes with it; there is also the possibility of contrasting Dasein with entities whose character is not that of Dasein by a more precise explication of the Being of all possible entities within-the-world. Without question, there are unfinished tasks still lying in this field. What we have hitherto set forth needs to be rounded out in many ways by working out fully the existential *a priori* of philosophical anthropology and taking a look at it. But this is not the aim of our investigation. *Its aim is one of* fundamental ontology. Consequently, if we inquire about Being-in as our theme, we cannot indeed consent to nullify the primordial character of this phenomenon by deriving it from others—that is to say, by an inappropriate analysis, in the sense of a dissolving or breaking up. But the fact that something primordial is underivable does not rule out the possibility that a multiplicity of characteristics of Being may be constitutive for it. If these show themselves, then existentially they are equiprimordial. The phenomenon of the equiprimordiality of constitutive items has often been disregarded in ontology, because of a methodologically unrestrained tendency to derive everything and anything from some simple 'primal ground'.

In which direction must we look, if we are to characterize Being-in, as such, phenomenally? We get the answer to this question by recalling what we were charged with keeping phenomenologically in view when we called attention to this phenomenon: Being-in is distinct from the present-at-hand insideness of something present-at-hand 'in' something else that is present-at-hand; Being-in is not a characteristic that is effected, or even just elicited, in a present-at-hand subject by the 'world's' Being-present-at-hand; Being-in is rather an essential kind of Being of this entity itself. But in that case, what else is presented with this phenomenon than the *commercium* which is present-at-hand *between* a subject present-at-hand and an Object present-at-hand? Such an interpretation would come closer to the phenomenal content if we were to say that *Dasein is the Being* of this 'between'. Yet to take our orientation from this 'between' would still be misleading. For with such an orientation we would also be covertly assuming the entities between which this "between", as such, 'is', and we would be doing so in a way which is ontologically vague. The "between" is already conceived as the result of the *convenientia* of two things that are present-at-hand. But to assume these beforehand always *splits* the phenomenon asunder, and there is no prospect of putting it together again from the fragments. Not only do we lack the 'cement'; even the 'schema' in accordance with which this joining-together is to be accomplished, has been split asunder, or never as yet unveiled. What is decisive for ontology is to prevent the splitting of the phenomenon—in other words, to hold its positive phenomenal content secure. To say that for this we need far-reaching and detailed study, is simply to express the fact that something which was ontically self-evident in the traditional way of treating the 'problem of knowledge' has often been ontologically disguised to the point where it has been lost sight of altogether.

The entity which is essentially constituted by Being-in-the-world *is* itself in every case its 'there'. According to the familiar signification of the word, the 'there' points to a 'here' and a 'yonder'. The 'here' of an 'I-here' is always understood in relation to a 'yonder' ready-to-hand, in the sense of a Being towards this 'yonder'—a Being which is de-severant, directional, and concernful. Dasein's existential spatiality, which thus determines its 'location', is itself grounded in Being-in-the-world. The "yonder" belongs definitely to something encountered within-the-*world*. 'Here' and 'yonder' are possible only in a 'there'—that is to say, only if there is an entity which has made a disclosure of spatiality as the Being of the 'there'. This entity carries in its ownmost Being the character of not being closed off. In the expression 'there' we have in view this essential disclosedness. By reason of this disclosedness, this entity (Dasein), together with the Being-there[1] of the world, is 'there' for itself.

When we talk in an ontically figurative way of the *lumen naturale* in man, we have in mind nothing other than the existential-ontological structure of this entity, that it *is* in such a way as to be its "there". To say that it is 'illuminated' ["erleuchtet"] means that *as* Being-in-the-world it is cleared [gelichtet] in itself, not through any other entity, but in such a way that it *is* itself the clearing.[2] Only for an entity which is existentially cleared in this way does that which is present-at-hand become accessible in the light or hidden in the dark. By its very nature, Dasein brings its "there" along with it. If it lacks its "there", it is not factically the entity which is essentially Dasein; indeed, it is not this entity at all. *Dasein is its disclosedness.*

We are to set forth the Constitution of this Being. But in so far as the essence of this entity is existence, the existential proposition, 'Dasein *is* its disclosedness', means at the same time that the Being which is an issue for this entity in its very Being is to be its 'there'. In addition to characterizing the primary Constitution of the Being of disclosedness, we will require, in conformity with the course of the analysis, an Interpretation of the kind of Being in which this entity is its "there" in an *everyday* manner.

This chapter, in which we shall undertake the explication of Being-in as such (that is to say, of the Being of the "there"), breaks up into two parts: A. the existential Constitution of the "there"; B. the everyday Being of the "there", and the falling of Dasein.

In *understanding* and *state-of-mind*, we shall see the two constitutive ways

---

[1] '*Da-sein*'. See our note 1, p. 27, H. 7 above.

[2] '*Lichtung*'. This word is customarily used to stand for a 'clearing' in the woods, not for a 'clarification'; the verb 'lichten' is similarly used. The force of this passage lies in the fact that these words are cognates of the noun 'Licht' ('light').

of being the "there"; and these are equiprimordial. If these are to be analysed, some phenomenal confirmation is necessary; in both cases this will be attained by Interpreting some concrete mode which is important for the subsequent problematic. State-of-mind and understanding are characterized equiprimordially by discourse.

Under A (the existential Constitution of the "there") we shall accordingly treat: Being-there as state-of-mind (Section 29); fear as a mode of state-of-mind (Section 30); Being-there as understanding (Section 31); understanding and interpretation (Section 32); assertion as a derivative mode of interpretation (Section 33); Being-there, discourse, and language (Section 34).

The analysis of the characteristics of the Being of Being-there is an existential one. This means that the characteristics are not properties of something present-at-hand, but essentially existential ways to be. We must therefore set forth their kind of Being in everydayness.

Under B (the everyday Being of the "there", and the falling of Dasein) we shall analyse idle talk (Section 35), curiosity (Section 36), and ambiguity (Section 37) as existential modes of the everyday Being of the "there"; we shall analyse them as corresponding respectively to the constitutive phenomenon of discourse, the sight which lies in understanding, and the interpretation (or explaining [Deutung]) which belongs to understanding. In these phenomenal modes a basic kind of Being of the "there" will become visible—a kind of Being which we Interpret as *falling*; and this 'falling' shows a movement [Bewegtheit] which is existentially its own.[1]

A. The *Existential Constitution* of the "There"

¶ 29. *Being there as State-of-mind* Mood

What we indicate *ontologically* by the term "state-of-mind"[2] is *ontically* the most familiar and everyday sort of thing; our mood, our Being-attuned.[3] Prior to all psychology of moods, a field which in any case still

[1] While we shall ordinarily reserve the word 'falling' for 'Verfallen' (see our note 2, p. 42, H. 21 above), in this sentence it represents first 'Verfallen' and then 'Fallen', the usual German word for 'falling'. 'Fallen' and 'Verfallen' are by no means strictly synonymous; the latter generally has the further connotation of 'decay' or 'deterioration', though Heidegger will take pains to point out that in his own usage it 'does not express any negative evaluation'. See Section 38 below.

[2] 'Befindlichkeit'. More literally: 'the state in which one may be found'. (The common German expression 'Wie befinden Sie sich?' means simply 'How are you?' or 'How are you feeling?') Our translation, 'state-of-mind', comes fairly close to what is meant; but it should be made clear that the 'of-mind' belongs to English idiom, has no literal counterpart in the structure of the German word, and fails to bring out the important connotation of finding oneself. *a kind of self-finding w. connotation of Mood.*

[3] '. . . die Stimmung, das Gestimmtsein.' The noun 'Stimmung' originally means the tuning of a musical instrument, but it has taken on several other meanings and is the usual word for one's mood or humour. We shall usually translate it as 'mood', and we shall generally translate both 'Gestimmtsein' and 'Gestimmtheit' as 'having a mood', though sometimes, as in the present sentence, we prefer to call attention to the root metaphor of 'Gestimmtsein' by writing 'Being-attuned', etc.

lies fallow, it is necessary to see this phenomenon as a fundamental *existentiale*, and to outline its structure.

Both the undisturbed equanimity and the inhibited ill-humour of our everyday concern, the way we slip over from one to the other, or slip off into bad moods, are by no means nothing ontologically,[1] even if these phenomena are left unheeded as supposedly the most indifferent and fleeting in Dasein. The fact that moods can deteriorate [verdorben werden] and change over means simply that in every case Dasein always has some mood [gestimmt ist]. The pallid, evenly balanced lack of mood [Ungestimmtheit], which is often persistent and which is not to be mistaken for a bad mood, is far from nothing at all. Rather, it is in this that Dasein becomes satiated with itself. Being has become manifest as a burden. Why that should be, one does not *know*. And Dasein cannot know anything of the sort because the possibilities of disclosure which belong to cognition reach far too short a way compared with the primordial disclosure belonging to moods, in which Dasein is brought before its Being as "there". Furthermore, a mood of elation can alleviate the manifest burden of Being; that such a mood is possible also discloses the burdensome character of Dasein, even while it alleviates the burden. A mood makes manifest 'how one is, and how one is faring' ["wie einem ist und wird"]. In this 'how one is', having a mood brings Being to its "there".

In having a mood, Dasein is always disclosed moodwise as that entity to which it has been delivered over in its Being; and in this way it has been delivered over to the Being which, in existing, it has to be. "To be disclosed" does not mean "to be known as this sort of thing". And even in the most indifferent and inoffensive everydayness the Being of Dasein can burst forth as a naked 'that it is and has to be' [als nacktes "Dass es es ist und zu sein hat"]. The pure 'that it is' shows itself, but the "whence" and the "whither" remain in darkness. The fact that it is just as everyday a matter for Dasein not to 'give in' ["nachgibt"] to such moods—in other words, not to follow up [nachgeht] their disclosure and allow itself to be brought before that which is disclosed—is no evidence *against* the phenomenal facts of the case, in which the Being of the "there" is disclosed moodwise in its "that-it-is";[2] it is rather evidence for it. In an

---

[1] In this sentence 'equanimity' represents 'Gleichmut', 'ill-humour' represents 'Missmut', and 'bad moods' represents 'Verstimmungen'.

[2] '. . . den phänomenalen Tatbestand der stimmungsmässigen Erschlossenheit des Seins des Da in seinem Dass . . .' It would be more literal to write simply 'in its "that" '; but to avoid a very natural confusion between the conjunction 'that' and pronoun 'that', we shall translate 'das Dass' as 'the "that-it-is" ', even though we use the same expression *unhyphenated* for 'das "Dass es ist" ' in this paragraph and in that which follows. (The striking contrast between the 'Da' and the 'Dass' is of course lost in translation.)

135

ontico-existentiell sense, Dasein for the most part evades the Being which is disclosed in the mood. In an *ontologico*-existential sense, this means that even in that to which such a mood pays no attention, Dasein is unveiled in its Being-delivered-over to the "there". In the evasion itself the "there" *is* something disclosed.

This characteristic of Dasein's Being—this 'that it is'—is veiled in its "whence" and "whither", yet disclosed in itself all the more unveiledly; we call it the "*throwness*"[1] of this entity into its "there"; indeed, it is thrown in such a way that, as Being-in-the-world, it is the "there". The expression "throwness" is meant to suggest the *facticity of its being delivered over.*[2] The 'that it is and has to be' which is disclosed in Dasein's state-of-mind is not the same 'that-it-is' which expresses ontologico-categorially the factuality belonging to presence-at-hand. This factuality becomes accessible only if we ascertain it by looking at it. The "that-it-is" which is disclosed in Dasein's state-of-mind must rather be conceived as an existential attribute of the entity which has Being-in-the-world as its way of Being. *Facticity is not the factuality of the factum brutum of something present-at-hand, but a characteristic of Dasein's Being—one which has been taken up into existence, even if proximally it has been thrust aside.* The "that-it-is" of facticity never becomes something that we can come across by beholding it.

An entity of the character of Dasein is its "there" in such a way that, whether explicitly or not, it finds itself [sich befindet] in its throwness. In a state-of-mind Dasein is always brought before itself, and has always found itself, not in the sense of coming across itself by perceiving itself, but in the sense of finding itself in the mood that it has.[3] As an entity which has been delivered over to its Being, it remains also delivered over to the fact that it must always have found itself—but found itself in a way of finding which arises not so much from a direct seeking as rather from a fleeing. The way in which the mood discloses is not one in which we look at throwness, but one in which we turn towards or turn away [An- und Abkehr]. For the most part the mood does not turn towards the burdensome character of Dasein which is manifest in it, and least of all does it do so in the mood of elation when this burden has been alleviated. It is always by way of a state-of-mind that this turning-away is what it is.

---

[1] '*Geworfenheit*'. This important term, which Heidegger introduces here, is further discussed in Section 38.

[2] 'Der Ausdruck Geworfenheit soll die *Faktizität der Überantwortung andeuten*.' On the distinction between 'facticity' and 'factuality', see H. 56 above.

[3] In this sentence there is a contrast between 'wahrnehmendes Sich-vorfinden' ('coming across itself by perceiving') and 'gestimmtes Sichbefinden' ('finding itself in the mood that it has'). In the next sentence, on the other hand, 'found' and 'finding' represent 'gefunden' and 'Finden'.

Phenomenally, we would wholly fail to recognize both *what* mood discloses and *how* it discloses, if that which is disclosed were to be compared with what Dasein is acquainted with, knows, and believes 'at the same time' when it has such a mood. Even if Dasein is 'assured' in its belief about its 'whither', or if, in rational enlightenment, it supposes itself to know about its "whence", all this counts for nothing as against the phenomenal facts of the case: for the mood brings Dasein before the "that-it-is" of its "there", which, as such, stares it in the face with the inexorability of an enigma.[1] From the existential-ontological point of view, there is not the slightest justification for minimizing what is 'evident' in states-of-mind, by measuring it against the apodictic certainty of a theoretical cognition of something which is purely present-at-hand. However the phenomena are no less falsified when they are banished to the sanctuary of the irrational. When irrationalism, as the counterplay of rationalism, talks about the things to which rationalism is blind, it does so only with a squint.

Factically, Dasein can, should, and must, through knowledge and will, become master of its moods; in certain possible ways of existing, this may signify a priority of volition and cognition. Only we must not be misled by this into denying that ontologically mood is a primordial kind of Being for Dasein, in which Dasein is disclosed to itself *prior to* all cognition and volition, and *beyond* their range of disclosure. And furthermore, when we master a mood, we do so by way of a counter-mood; we are never free of moods. Ontologically, we thus obtain as the *first* essential characteristic of states-of-mind that *they disclose Dasein in its thrownness, and—proximally and for the most part—in the manner of an evasive turning-away.*

From what has been said we can see already that a state-of-mind is very remote from anything like coming across a psychical condition by the kind of apprehending which first turns round and then back. Indeed it is so far from this, that only because the "there" has already been disclosed in a state-of-mind can immanent reflection come across 'Experiences' at all. The 'bare mood' discloses the "there" more primordially, but correspondingly it *closes it off* more stubbornly than any *not*-perceiving.

This is shown by *bad moods*. In these, Dasein becomes blind to itself, the environment with which it is concerned veils itself, the circumspection of concern gets led astray. States-of-mind are so far from being reflected upon, that precisely what they do is to assail Dasein in its unreflecting devotion to the 'world' with which it is concerned and on which it expends

136

---

[1] '. . . so verschlägt das alles nichts gegen den phänomenalen Tatbestand, dass die Stimmung das Dasein vor das Dass seines Da bringt, als welches es ihm in unerbittlicher Rätselhaftigkeit entgegenstarrt.' The pronoun 'es' (the reference of which is not entirely unambiguous) appears only in the later editions.

itself. A mood assails us. It comes neither from 'outside' nor from 'inside', but arises out of Being-in-the-world, as a way of such Being. But with the negative distinction between state-of-mind and the reflective apprehending of something 'within', we have thus reached a positive insight into their character as disclosure. *The mood has already disclosed, in every case, Being-in-the-world as a whole, and makes it possible first of all to direct oneself towards something.* Having a mood is not related to the psychical in the first instance, and is not itself an inner condition which then reaches forth in an enigmatical way and puts its mark on Things and persons. It is in this that the *second* essential characteristic of states-of-mind shows itself. We have seen that the world, Dasein-with, and existence are *equiprimordially disclosed*; and state-of-mind is a basic existential species of their disclosedness, because this disclosedness itself is essentially Being-in-the-world.[1]

Besides these two essential characteristics of states-of-mind which have been explained—the disclosing of thrownness and the current disclosing of Being-in-the-world as a whole—we have to notice a *third*, which contributes above all towards a more penetrating understanding of the worldhood of the world. As we have said earlier,[iii] the world which has already been disclosed beforehand permits what is within-the-world to be encountered. This prior disclosedness of the world belongs to Being-in and is partly constituted by one's state-of-mind. Letting something be encountered is primarily *circumspective*; it is not just sensing something, or staring at it. It implies circumspective concern, and has the character of becoming affected in some way [Betroffenwerdens]; we can see this more precisely from the standpoint of state-of-mind. But to be affected by the unserviceable, resistant, or threatening character [Bedrohlichkeit] of that which is ready-to-hand, becomes ontologically possible only in so far as Being-in as such has been determined existentially beforehand in such a manner that what it encounters within-the-world can "*matter*" to it in this way. The fact that this sort of thing can "matter" to it is grounded in one's state-of-mind; and as a state-of-mind it has already disclosed the world—as something by which it can be threatened, for instance.[2] Only something which is in the state-of-mind of fearing (or fearlessness) can discover that what is environmentally ready-to-hand is threatening. Dasein's openness to the world is constituted existentially by the attunement of a state-of-mind.

And only because the 'senses' [die "Sinne"] belong ontologically to an

---

[1] '. . . weil diese selbst wesenhaft In-der-Welt-sein ist.' It is not clear whether the antecedent of 'diese' is 'Existenz' ('existence') or '*Erschlossenheit*' ('*disclosedness*').

[2] 'Diese Angänglichkeit gründet in der Befindlichkeit, als welche sie die Welt zum Beispiel auf Bedrohbarkeit hin erschlossen hat.' The pronoun 'sie' appears only in the newer editions.

entity whose kind of Being is Being-in-the-world with a state-of mind,[1] can they be 'touched' by anything or 'have a sense for' ["Sinn haben für"] something in such a way that what touches them shows itself in an affect.[2] Under the strongest pressure and resistance, nothing like an affect would come about, and the resistance itself would remain essentially undiscovered, if Being-in-the-world, with its state-of-mind, had not already submitted itself [sich schon angewiesen] to having entities within-the-world "matter" to it in a way which its moods have outlined in advance. *Existentially, a state-of-mind implies a disclosive submission to the world, out of* ③ *which we can encounter something that matters to us.* Indeed *from the ontological* 138 *point of view* we must as a general principle leave the primary discovery of the world to 'bare mood'. Pure beholding, even if it were to penetrate to the innermost core of the Being of something present-at-hand, could never discover anything like that which is threatening.

The fact that, even though states-of-mind are primarily disclosive, everyday circumspection goes wrong and to a large extent succumbs to delusion because of them, is a μὴ ὄν [non-being] when measured against the idea of knowing the 'world' absolutely. But if we make evaluations which are so unjustified ontologically, we shall completely fail to recognize the existentially positive character of the capacity for delusion. It is precisely when we see the 'world' unsteadily and fitfully in accordance with our moods, that the ready-to-hand shows itself in its specific worldhood, which is never the same from day to day. By looking at the world theoretically, we have already dimmed it down to the uniformity of what is purely present-at-hand, though admittedly this uniformity comprises a new abundance of things which can be discovered by simply characterizing them. Yet even the purest θεωρία [theory] has not left all moods behind it; even when we look theoretically at what is just present-at-hand, it does not show itself purely as it looks unless this θεωρία lets it come towards us in a *tranquil* tarrying alongside . . . , in ραστώνη and διαγωγή.[iv] Any cognitive determining has its existential-ontological Constitution in the state-of-mind of Being-in-the-world; but pointing this out is not to be confused with attempting to surrender science ontically to 'feeling'.

[1] 'befindlichen In-der-Welt-seins'. In previous chapters we have usually translated 'befindlich' by such expressions as 'which is to be found', etc. See, for instance, H. 67, 70, 117 above, where this adjective is applied to a number of things which are hardly of the character of Dasein. In the present chapter, however, the word is tied up with the special sense of 'Befindlichkeit' as 'state-of-mind', and will be translated by expressions such as 'with a state-of-mind', 'having a state-of-mind', etc.

[2] In this sentence Heidegger has been calling attention to two ways of using the word 'Sinn' which might well be expressed by the word 'sense' but hardly by the word 'meaning': (1) 'die Sinne' as 'the five senses' or the 'senses' one has when one is 'in one's senses'; (2) 'der Sinn' as the 'sense' one has 'for' something—one's 'sense for clothes', one's 'sense of beauty', one's 'sense of the numinous', etc. Cf. the discussion of 'Sinn' on H. 151 f. below.

The different modes of state-of-mind and the ways in which they are interconnected in their foundations cannot be Interpreted within the problematic of the present investigation. The phenomena have long been well-known ontically under the terms "affects" and "feelings" and have always been under consideration in philosophy. It is not an accident that the earliest systematic Interpretation of affects that has come down to us is not treated in the framework of 'psychology'. Aristotle investigates the πάθη [affects] in the second book of his *Rhetoric*. Contrary to the traditional orientation, according to which rhetoric is conceived as the kind of thing we 'learn in school', this work of Aristotle must be taken as the first systematic hermeneutic of the everydayness of Being with one another. Publicness, as the kind of Being which belongs to the "they" (Cf. Section 27), not only has in general its own way of having a mood, but needs moods and 'makes' them for itself. It is into such a mood and out of such a mood that the orator speaks. He must understand the possibilities of moods in order to rouse them and guide them aright.

139

How the Interpretation of the affects was carried further in the Stoa, and how it was handed down to modern times through patristic and scholastic theology, is well known. What has escaped notice is that the basic ontological Interpretation of the affective life in general has been able to make scarcely one forward step worthy of mention since Aristotle. On the contrary, affects and feelings come under the theme of psychical phenomena, functioning as a third class of these, usually along with ideation [Vorstellen] and volition. They sink to the level of accompanying phenomena.

It has been one of the merits of phenomenological research that it has again brought these phenomena more unrestrictedly into our sight. Not only that: Scheler, accepting the challenges of Augustine and Pascal,[v] has guided the problematic to a consideration of how acts which 'represent' and acts which 'take an interest' are interconnected in their foundations. But even here the existential-ontological foundations of the phenomenon of the act in general are admittedly still obscure.

A state-of-mind not only discloses Dasein in its thrownness and its submission to that world which is already disclosed with its own Being; it is itself the existential kind of Being in which Dasein constantly surrenders itself to the 'world' and lets the 'world' "matter" to it in such a way that somehow Dasein evades its very self. The existential constitution of such evasion will become clear in the phenomenon of falling.

A state-of-mind is a basic existential way in which Dasein is its "there". It not only characterizes Dasein ontologically, but, because of what it discloses, it is at the same time methodologically significant in principle

for the existential analytic. Like any ontological Interpretation whatsoever, this analytic can only, so to speak, "listen in" to some previously
disclosed entity as regards its Being. And it will attach itself to Dasein's
distinctive and most far-reaching possibilities of disclosure, in order to
get information about this entity from these. Phenomenological Inter-   140
pretation must make it possible for Dasein itself to disclose things primordially; it must, as it were, let Dasein interpret itself. Such Interpretation
takes part in this disclosure only in order to raise to a conceptual level the
phenomenal content of what has been disclosed, and to do so existentially.

Later (Cf. Section 40)[1] we shall provide an Interpretation of anxiety
as such a basic state-of-mind of Dasein, and as one which is significant from
the existential-ontological standpoint; with this in view, we shall now
illustrate the phenomenon of state-of-mind even more concretely in its
determinate mode of *fear*.

¶ 30. *Fear as a Mode of State-of-Mind* vi

There are three points of view from which the phenomenon of fear may
be considered. We shall analyse: (1) that in the face of which we fear,
(2) fearing, and (3) that about which we fear. These possible ways of
looking at fear are not accidental; they belong together. With them the
general structure of states-of-mind comes to the fore. We shall complete
our analysis by alluding to the possible ways in which fear may be
modified; each of these pertains to different items in the structure of fear.

That in the face of which we fear, the 'fearsome',[2] is in every case something which we encounter within-the-world and which may have either
readiness-to-hand, presence-at-hand, or Dasein-with as its kind of Being.
We are not going to make an ontical report on those entities which can
often and for the most part be 'fearsome': we are to define the fearsome
phenomenally in its fearsomeness. What do we encounter in fearing that
belongs to the fearsome as such? That in the face of which we fear can
be characterized as threatening. Here several points must be considered.
1. What we encounter has detrimentality as its kind of involvement. It
shows itself within a context of involvements. 2. The target of this detrimentality is a definite range of what can be affected by it; thus the detrimentality is itself made definite, and comes from a definite region. 3. The
region itself is well known as such, and so is that which is coming from it;
but that which is coming from it has something 'queer' about it.[3] 4. That
which is detrimental, as something that threatens us, is not yet within

---

[1] The earliest editions cite Section 39 rather than Section 40. This has been corrected
in the list of *errata*.
[2] 'Das *Wovor* der Furcht, das Furchtbare . . .'
[3] '. . . mit dem es nicht "geheuer" ist.'

striking distance [in beherrschbarer Nähe], but it is coming close. In such a drawing-close, the detrimentality radiates out, and therein lies its threatening character. 5. This drawing-close is within what is close by. Indeed, something may be detrimental in the highest degree and may even be coming constantly closer; but if it is still far off, its fearsomeness remains veiled. If, however, that which is detrimental draws close and is close by, then it is threatening: it can reach us, and yet it may not. As it draws close, this 'it can, and yet in the end it may not' becomes aggravated. We say, "It is fearsome". 6. This implies that what is detrimental as coming-close close by carries with it the patent possibility that it may stay away and pass us by; but instead of lessening or extinguishing our fearing, this enhances it.

141

In *fearing as such*, what we have thus characterized as threatening is freed and allowed to matter to us. We do not first ascertain a future evil (*malum futurum*) and then fear it. But neither does fearing first take note of what is drawing close; it discovers it beforehand in its fearsomeness. And in fearing, fear can then look at the fearsome explicitly, and 'make it clear' to itself. Circumspection sees the fearsome because it has fear as its state-of-mind. Fearing, as a slumbering possibility of Being-in-the-world in a state-of-mind (we call this possibility 'fearfulness' ["Furchtsamkeit"]), has already disclosed the world, in that out of it something like the fearsome may come close. The potentiality for coming close is itself freed by the essential existential spatiality of Being-in-the-world.

That which fear fears *about* is that very entity which is afraid—Dasein.[1] Only an entity for which in its Being this very Being is an issue, can be afraid. Fearing discloses this entity as endangered and abandoned to itself. Fear always reveals Dasein in the Being of its "there", even if it does so in varying degrees of explicitness. If we fear about our house and home, this cannot be cited as an instance contrary to the above definition of what we fear about; for as Being-in-the-world, Dasein is in every case concernful Being-alongside.[2] Proximally and for the most part, Dasein *is*

---

[1] 'Das *Worum* die Furcht fürchtet, ist das sich fürchtende Seiende selbst, das Dasein.' While it is convenient to translate 'das Worum der Furcht' as 'that which one fears about', this expression must be taken in a narrower sense than one would ordinarily expect in English. What Heidegger generally has in mind is rather the person *on whose behalf* or *for whose sake* one fears. (Cf. our remarks on 'um' in note 1, p. 93, H. 65, and note 2, p. 98, H. 69 above.) Thus 'fürchten um' comes closer to the ordinary meaning of 'fear for' than it does to that of 'fear about'. We shall soon see, however, that Heidegger also uses the expression 'fürchten für', for which 'fear for' would seem to be the natural translation. Notice that what he then has in mind—namely, our fearing for Others—is only a special case of 'fearing for' in the ordinary English sense, and likewise only a special case of what we shall call 'fearing about' in this translation.

[2] 'Sein bei'. Here our usual translation, 'Being-alongside', fails to bring out the connection. A German reader would recall at once that 'bei' may mean, 'at the home of' like the French *'chez'*. See our note 3, p. 80, H. 54 above.

in terms of *what* it is concerned with. When this is endangered, Being-alongside is threatened. Fear discloses Dasein predominantly in a privative way. It bewilders us and makes us 'lose our heads'. Fear closes off our endangered Being-in, and yet at the same time lets us see it, so that when the fear has subsided, Dasein must first find its way about again.

Whether privatively or positively, fearing about something, as being-afraid in the face of something, always discloses equiprimordially entities within-the-world and Being-in—the former as threatening and the latter as threatened. Fear is a mode of state-of-mind.

One can also fear about Others, and we then speak of "fearing for" them [Fürchten für sie]. This fearing for the Other does not take away his fear. Such a possibility has been ruled out already, because the Other, *for* whom we fear, need not fear at all on his part. It is precisely when the Other is *not* afraid and charges recklessly at what is threatening him that we fear most *for* him. Fearing-for is a way of having a co-state-of-mind   142 with Others, but not necessarily a being-afraid-with or even a fearing-with-one-another.[1] One can "fear about" without "being-afraid". Yet when viewed more strictly, fearing-about is "being-afraid-for-*oneself*".[2] Here what one "is apprehensive about" is one's Being-with with the Other, who might be torn away from one.[3] That which is fearsome is not aimed directly at him who fears with someone else. Fearing-about knows that in a certain way it is unaffected, and yet it is co-affected in so far as the Dasein-with for which it fears is affected. Fearing-about is therefore not a weaker form of being-afraid. Here the issue is one of existential modes, not of degrees of 'feeling-tones'. Fearing-about does not lose its specific genuiness even if it is not 'really' afraid.

There can be variations in the constitutive items of the full phenomenon of fear. Accordingly, different possibilities of Being emerge in fearing. Bringing-close close by, belongs to the structure of the threatening as encounterable. If something threatening breaks in suddenly upon concernful Being-in-the-world (something threatening in its 'not right away, but any moment'), fear becomes *alarm* [*Erschrecken*]. So, in what is threatening we must distinguish between the closest way in which it brings itself close, and the manner in which this bringing-close gets encountered—its suddenness. That in the face of which we are alarmed is proximally something well known and familiar. But if, on the other hand,

[1] 'Fürchten für . . . ist eine Weise der Mitbefindlichkeit mit den Anderen, aber nicht notwendig ein Sich-mitfürchten oder gar ein Miteinanderfürchten.'

[2] 'ein *Sich*fürchten'. We have hitherto translated 'sich fürchten' with various forms of 'be afraid', which is its usual signification in ordinary German. In this passage, however, the emphasis on the reflexive pronoun 'sich' clearly calls for 'being-afraid-for-*oneself*'.

[3] ' "Befürchtet" ist dabei das Mitsein mit dem Anderen, der einem entrissen werden könnte.'

that which threatens has the character of something altogether unfamiliar, then fear becomes *dread* [*Grauen*]. And where that which threatens is laden with dread, and is at the same time encountered with the suddenness of the alarming, then fear becomes *terror* [*Entsetzen*]. There are further variations of fear, which we know as timidity, shyness, misgiving, becoming startled. All modifications of fear, as possibilities of having a state-of-mind, point to the fact that Dasein as Being-in-the-world is 'fearful' ["furchtsam"]. This 'fearfulness' is not to be understood in an ontical sense as some factical 'individualized' disposition,[1] but as an existential possibility of the essential state-of-mind of Dasein in general, though of course it is not the only one.

¶ *31. Being-there as Understanding*

State-of-mind is *one* of the existential structures in which the Being of the 'there' maintains itself. Equiprimordial with it in constituting this Being is *understanding*. A state-of-mind always has its understanding, even if it merely keeps it suppressed. Understanding always has its mood. If we Interpret understanding as a fundamental *existentiale*, this indicates that this phenomenon is conceived as a basic mode of Dasein's *Being*. On the other hand, 'understanding' in the sense of *one* possible kind of cognizing among others (as distinguished, for instance, from 'explaining'), must, like explaining, be Interpreted as an existential derivative of that primary understanding which is one of the constituents of the Being of the "there" in general.

We have, after all, already come up against this primordial understanding in our previous investigations, though we did not allow it to be included explicitly in the theme under discussion. To say that in existing, Dasein is its "there", is equivalent to saying that the world is 'there'; its *Being-there* is Being-in. And the latter is likewise 'there', as that for the sake of which Dasein is. In the "for-the-sake-of-which", existing Being-in-the-world is disclosed as such, and this disclosedness we have called "understanding".[vii] In the understanding of the "for-the-sake-of-which", the significance which is grounded therein, is disclosed along with it. The disclosedness of understanding, as the disclosedness of the "for-the-sake-of-which" and of significance equiprimordially, pertains to the entirety of Being-in-the-world. Significance is that on the basis of which the world is disclosed as such. To say that the "for-the-sake-of-which" *and* significance are both disclosed in Dasein, means that Dasein is that entity which, as Being-in-the-world, is an issue for itself.

---

[1] '. . . im ontischen Sinne einer faktischen, "vereinzelten" Veranlagung . . .' While the verb 'vereinzeln' often means 'to isolate', Heidegger does not ordinarily use it in this sense. Indeed he contrasts it with the verb 'isolieren'. Cf. H. 188 below.

Sec. 18

When we are talking ontically we sometimes use the expression 'understanding something' with the signification of 'being able to manage something', 'being a match for it', 'being competent to do something'.[1] In understanding, as an *existentiale*, that which we have such competence over is not a "what", but Being as existing. The kind of Being which Dasein has, as potentiality-for-Being, lies existentially in understanding. Dasein is not something present-at-hand which possesses its competence for something by way of an extra; it is primarily Being-possible. Dasein is in every case what it can be, and in the way in which it is its possibility. The Being-possible which is essential for Dasein, pertains to the ways of its solicitude for Others and of its concern with the 'world', as we have characterized them; and in all these, and always, it pertains to Dasein's potentiality-for-Being towards itself, for the sake of itself. The Being-possible which Dasein is existentially in every case, is to be sharply distinguished both from empty logical possibility and from the contingency of something present-at-hand, so far as with the present-at-hand this or that can 'come to pass'.[2] As a modal category of presence-at-hand, possibility signifies what is *not yet* actual and what is *not at any time* necessary. It characterizes the *merely* possible. Ontologically it is on a lower level than actuality and necessity. On the other hand, possibility as an *existentiale* is the most primordial and ultimate positive way in which Dasein is characterized ontologically. As with existentiality in general, we can, in the first instance, only prepare for the problem of possibility. The phenomenal basis for seeing it at all is provided by the understanding as a disclosive potentiality-for-Being.

144

Possibility, as an *existentiale*, does not signify a free-floating potentiality-for-Being in the sense of the 'liberty of indifference' (*libertas indifferentiae*). In every case Dasein, as essentially having a state-of-mind, has already got itself into definite possibilities. As the potentiality-for-Being which is *is*, it has let such possibilities pass by; it is constantly waiving the possibilities of its Being, or else it seizes upon them and makes mistakes.[3] But this means that Dasein is Being-possible which has been delivered over to itself—*thrown possibility* through and through. Dasein is the possibility of Being-free *for* its ownmost potentiality-for-Being. Its Being-possible is transparent to itself in different possible ways and degrees.

Understanding is the Being of such potentiality-for-Being, which is

---

[1] '. . . in der Bedeutung von "einer Sache vorstehen können", "ihr gewachsen sein", "etwas können".' The expression 'vorstehen' ('to manage', 'to be in charge') is here connected with 'verstehen' ('to understand').

[2] '. . . von der Kontingenz eines Vorhandenen, sofern mit diesem das und jenes "passieren" kann.'

[3] '. . . ergreift sie und vergreift sich.'

never something still outstanding as not yet present-at-hand, but which, as something which is essentially never present-at-hand, '*is*' with the Being of Dasein, in the sense of existence. Dasein is such that in every case it has understood (or alternatively, not understood) that it is to be thus or thus. As such understanding it 'knows' *what* it is capable of—that is, what its potentiality-for-Being is capable of.[1] This 'knowing' does not first arise from an immanent self-perception, but belongs to the Being of the "there", which is essentially understanding. And only *because* Dasein, in understanding, is its "there", *can* it go astray and fail to recognize itself. And in so far as understanding is *accompanied by* state-of-mind and as such is existentially surrendered to thrownness, Dasein has in every case already gone astray and failed to recognize itself. In its potentiality-for-Being it is therefore delivered over to the possibility of first finding itself again in its possibilities.

Understanding is the existential Being of Dasein's own potentiality-for-Being; and it is so in such a way that this Being discloses in itself what its Being is capable of.[2] We must grasp the structure of this *existentiale* more precisely.

As a disclosure, understanding always pertains to the whole basic state of Being-in-the-world. As a potentiality-for-Being, any Being-in is a potentiality-for-Being-in-the-world. Not only is the world, *qua* world, disclosed as possible significance, but when that which is within-the-world is itself freed, this entity is freed for *its own* possibilities. That which is ready-to-hand is discovered as such in its service*ability*, its us*ability*, and its detriment*ality*. The totality of involvements is revealed as the categorial whole of a *possible* interconnection of the ready-to-hand. But even the 'unity' of the manifold present-at-hand, of Nature, can be discovered only if a *possibility* of it has been disclosed. Is it accidental that the question about the *Being* of Nature aims at the 'conditions of its *possibility*'? On what is such an inquiry based? When confronted with this inquiry, we cannot leave aside the question: *why* are entities which are not of the character of Dasein understood in their Being, if they are disclosed in accordance with the conditions of their possibility? Kant presupposes something of the sort, perhaps rightly. But this presupposition itself is something that cannot be left without demonstrating how it is justified.

Why does the understanding—whatever may be the essential dimensions of that which can be disclosed in it—always press forward into possibilities? It is because the understanding has in itself the existential

145

[1] 'Als solches Verstehen "weiss" es, *woran* es mit ihm selbst, das heisst seinem Sein-können ist.'

[2] '. . . *so zwar, dass dieses Sein an ihm selbst das Woran des mit ihm selbst Seins erschliesst.*'

structure which we call "*projection*".[1] With equal primordiality the under-. standing projects Dasein's Being both upon its "for-the-sake-of-which" and upon significance, as the worldhood of its current world. The character of understanding as projection is constitutive for Being-in-the-world with regard to the disclosedness of its existentially constitutive state-of-Being by which the factical potentiality-for-Being gets its leeway [Spielraum]. And as thrown, Dasein is thrown into the kind of Being which we call "projecting". Projecting has nothing to do with comporting oneself towards a plan that has been thought out, and in accordance with which Dasein arranges its Being. On the contrary, any Dasein has, as Dasein, already projected itself; and as long as it is, it is projecting. As long as it is, Dasein always has understood itself and always will understand itself in terms of possibilities. Furthermore, the character of understanding as projection is such that the understanding does not grasp thematically that upon which it projects—that is to say, possibilities. Grasping it in such a manner would take away from what is projected its very character as a possibility, and would reduce it to the given contents which we have in mind; whereas projection, in throwing, throws before itself the possibility as possibility, and lets it *be* as such.[2] As projecting, understanding is the kind of Being of Dasein in which it *is* its possibilities as possibilities. *DAsein is mirrored back to itself.*

Because of the kind of Being which is constituted by the *existentiale* of projection, Dasein is constantly 'more' than it factually is, supposing that one might want to make an inventory of it as something-at-hand and list the contents of its Being, and supposing that one were able to do so. But Dasein is never more than it factically is, for to its facticity its potentiality-for-Being belongs essentially. Yet as Being-possible, moreover, Dasein is never anything less; that is to say, it *is* existentially that which, in its

---

[1] '*Entwurf*'. The basic meaning of this noun and the cognate verb 'entwerfen' is that of 'throwing' something 'off' or 'away' from one; but in ordinary German usage, and often in Heidegger, they take on the sense of 'designing' or 'sketching' some 'project' which is to be carried through; and they may also be used in the more special sense of 'projection' in which a geometer is said to 'project' a curve 'upon' a plane. The words 'projection' and 'project' accordingly lend themselves rather well to translating these words in many contexts, especially since their root meanings are very similar to those of 'Entwurf' and 'entwerfen'; but while the root meaning of 'throwing off' is still very much alive in Heidegger's German, it has almost entirely died out in the ordinary English usage of 'projection' and 'project', which in turn have taken on some connotations not felt in the German. Thus when in the English translation Dasein is said to 'project' entities, or possibilities, or even its own Being 'upon' something, the reader should bear in mind that the root meaning of 'throwing' is more strongly felt in the German than in the translation.

[2] '. . . zieht es herab zu einem gegebenen, gemeinten Bestand, während der Entwurf im Werfen die Möglichkeit als Möglichkeit sich vorwirft und als solche *sein* lässt.' The expression 'einem etwas vorwerfen' means literally to 'throw something forward to someone', but often has the connotation of 'reproaching him with something', or 'throwing something in his teeth'. Heidegger may have more than one of these significations in mind.

potentiality-for-Being, it is *not yet.* Only because the Being of the "there"
receives its Constitution through understanding and through the character of understanding as projection, only because it *is* what it becomes (or
alternatively, does not become), can it say to itself 'Become what you are',
and say this with understanding.

146 →Projection always pertains to the full disclosedness of Being-in-the-
world; as potentiality-for-Being, understanding has itself possibilities,
which are sketched out beforehand within the range of what is essentially
disclosable in it. Understanding *can* devote itself primarily to the disclosedness of the world; that is, Dasein can, proximally and for the most
part, understand itself in terms of its world. Or else understanding throws
itself primarily into the "for-the-sake-of-which"; that is, Dasein exists as
itself. Understanding is either authentic, arising out of one's own Self as
such, or inauthentic. The 'in-' of "inauthentic" does not mean that
Dasein cuts itself off from its Self and understands 'only' the world. The
world belongs to Being-one's-Self as Being-in-the-world. On the other
hand, authentic understanding, no less than that which is inauthentic,
can be either genuine or not genuine. As potentiality-for-Being, understanding is altogether permeated with possibility. When one is diverted
into [Sichverlegen in] one of these basic possibilities of understanding, the
other is not laid aside [legt . . . nicht ab]. *Because understanding, in every case,*
pertains rather to Dasein's full disclosedness as Being-in-the-world, this diversion
of the understanding is an existential modification of projection as a whole. In understanding the world, Being-in is always understood along with it, while
understanding of existence as such is always an understanding of the world.

As factical Dasein, any Dasein has already diverted its potentiality-for-
Being into a possibility of understanding.

In its projective character, understanding goes to make up existentially
what we call Dasein's "*sight*" [*Sicht*]. With the disclosedness of the "there",
this sight is existentially [existenzial seiende]; and Dasein *is* this sight
equiprimordially in each of those basic ways of its Being which we have
already noted: as the circumspection [Umsicht] of concern, as the considerateness [Rücksicht] of solicitude, and as that sight which is directed
upon Being as such [Sicht auf das Sein als solches], for the sake of which
any Dasein is as it is. The sight which is related primarily and on the whole
to existence we call "*transparency*" [*Durchsichtigkeit*]. We choose this term
to designate 'knowledge of the Self'[1] in a sense which is well understood,

---

[1] ' "Selbsterkenntnis" '. This should be carefully distinguished from the 'Sichkennen'
discussed on H. 124-125. Perhaps this distinction can be expressed—though rather crudely
—by pointing out that we are here concerned with a full and sophisticated knowledge of
the Self in all its implications, while in the earlier passage we were concerned with the
kind of 'self-knowledge' which one loses when one 'forgets oneself' or does something so
out of character that one 'no longer knows oneself'.

so as to indicate that here it is not a matter of perceptually tracking down and inspecting a point called the "Self", but rather one of seizing upon the full disclosedness of Being-in-the-world *throughout all* the constitutive items which are essential to it, and doing so with understanding. In existing, entities sight 'themselves' [sichtet "sich"] only in so far as they have become transparent to themselves with equal primordiality in those items which are constitutive for their existence: their Being-alongside the world and their Being-with Others.

On the other hand, Dasein's opaqueness [Undurchsichtigkeit] is not rooted primarily and solely in 'egocentric' self-deceptions; it is rooted just as much in lack of acquaintance with the world.

We must, to be sure, guard against a misunderstanding of the expression 'sight'. It corresponds to the "clearedness" [Gelichtetheit] which we took as characterizing the disclosedness of the "there". 'Seeing' does not mean just perceiving with the bodily eyes, but neither does it mean pure non-sensory awareness of something present-at-hand in its presence-at-hand. In giving an existential signification to "sight", we have merely drawn upon the peculiar feature of seeing, that it lets entities which are accessible to it be encountered unconcealedly in themselves. Of course, every 'sense' does this within that domain of discovery which is genuinely its own. But from the beginning onwards the tradition of philosophy has been oriented primarily towards 'seeing' as a way of access to entities *and to Being.* To keep the connection with this tradition, we may formalize "sight" and "seeing" enough to obtain therewith a universal term for characterizing any access to entities or to Being, as access in general.

By showing how all sight is grounded primarily in understanding (the circumspection of concern is understanding as *common sense* [*Verständig-keit*]), we have deprived pure intuition [Anschauen] of its priority, which corresponds noetically to the priority of the present-at-hand in traditional ontology. 'Intuition' and 'thinking' are both derivatives of understanding, and already rather remote ones. Even the phenomenological 'intuition of essences' ["Wesensschau"] is grounded in existential understanding. We can decide about this kind of seeing only if we have obtained explicit conceptions of Being and of the structure of Being, such as only phenomena in the phenomenological sense can become.

The disclosedness of the "there" in understanding is itself a way of Dasein's potentiality-for-Being. In the way in which its Being is projected both upon the "for-the-sake-of-which" and upon significance (the world), there lies the disclosedness of Being in general. Understanding of Being has already been taken for granted in projecting upon possibilities. In projection, Being is understood, though not ontologically conceived. An entity whose kind of Being is the essential projection of Being-in-the-world has understanding of Being, and has this as constitutive for its Being. What was posited dogmatically at an earlier stage[viii] now gets exhibited in terms of the Constitution of the Being in which Dasein as understanding is its "there". The existential meaning of this understanding of Being cannot be satisfactorily clarified within the limits of this investigation except on the basis of the Temporal Interpretation of Being.

148   As *existentialia*, states-of-mind and understanding characterize the primordial disclosedness of Being-in-the-world. By way of having a mood, Dasein 'sees' possibilities, in terms of which it is. In the projective disclosure of such possibilities, it already has a mood in every case. The projection of its ownmost potentiality-for-Being has been delivered over to the Fact of its thrownness into the "there". Has not Dasein's Being become more enigmatical now that we have explicated the existential constitution of the Being of the "there" in the sense of thrown projection? It has indeed. We must first let the full enigmatical character of this Being emerge, even if all we can do is to come to a genuine break-down over its 'solution', and to formulate anew the question about the Being of thrown projective Being-in-the-world.

But in the first instance, even if we are just to bring into view the every-day kind of Being in which there is understanding with a state-of-mind, and if we are to do so in a way which is phenomenally adequate to the full disclosedness of the "there", we must work out these *existentialia* concretely.[1]

¶ 32. *Understanding and Interpretation*[2]

As understanding, Dasein projects its Being upon possibilities. This *Being-towards-possibilities* which understands is itself a potentiality-for-Being, and it is so because of the way these possibilities, as disclosed, exert their counter-thrust [Rückschlag] upon Dasein. The projecting of the understanding has its own possibility—that of developing itself [sich auszubilden]. This development of the understanding we call "interpretation".[3] In it the understanding appropriates understandingly that which is understood by it. In interpretation, understanding does not become something different. It becomes itself. Such interpretation is grounded existentially in understanding; the latter does not arise from the former. Nor is interpretation the acquiring of information about what is

---

1 'konkreten'. The earlier editions have 'konkreteren' ('more concretely').
2 '*Auslegung*'. See our note 3, p. 19, H. 1 above.
3 'Auslegung'. The older editions have 'A u s l e g u n g'.

understood; it is rather the working-out of possibilities projected in understanding. In accordance with the trend of these preparatory analyses of everyday Dasein, we shall pursue the phenomenon of interpretation in understanding the world—that is, in inauthentic understanding, and indeed in the mode of its genuineness.

In terms of the significance which is disclosed in understanding the world, concernful Being-alongside the ready-to-hand gives itself to understand whatever involvement that which is encountered can have.[1] To say that "circumspection discovers" means that the 'world' which has already been understood comes to be interpreted. The ready-to-hand comes *explicitly* into the sight which understands. All preparing, putting to rights, repairing, improving, rounding-out, are accomplished in the following way: we take apart[2] in its "in-order-to" that which is circum-   149 spectively ready-to-hand, and we concern ourselves with it in accordance with what becomes visible through this process. That which has been circumspectively taken apart with regard to its "in-order-to", and taken apart as such—that which is *explicitly* understood—has the structure of *something as something*. The circumspective question as to what this particular thing that is ready-to-hand may be, receives the circumspectively interpretative answer that it is for such and such a purpose [es ist zum . . .]. If we tell what it is for [des Wozu], we are not simply designating something; but that which is designated is understood *as* that *as* which we are to take the thing in question. That which is disclosed in understanding— that which is understood—is already accessible in such a way that its 'as which' can be made to stand out explicitly. The 'as' makes up the structure of the explicitness of something that is understood. It constitutes the interpretation. In dealing with what is environmentally ready-to-hand by interpreting it circumspectively, we 'see' it *as* a table, a door, a carriage, or a bridge; but what we have thus interpreted [Ausgelegte] need not necessarily be also taken apart [auseinander zu legen] by making an assertion which definitely characterizes it. Any mere pre-predicative seeing of the ready-to-hand is, in itself, something which already understands and interprets. But does not the absence of such an 'as' make up the mereness of any pure perception of something? Whenever we see with this kind of sight, we already do so understandingly and interpretatively. In the mere encountering of something, it is understood in terms of a totality of involvements; and such seeing hides in itself the explicitness of the assignment-relations (of the "in-order-to") which belong to that totality.

---

[1] '. . . gibt sich . . . zu verstehen, welche Bewandtnis es je mit dem Begegnenden haben kann.'

[2] 'auseinandergelegt'. Heidegger is contrasting the verb 'auslegen' (literally, 'lay out') with the cognate 'auseinanderlegen' ('lay asunder' or 'take apart').

go to 201

That which is understood gets Articulated when the entity to be understood is brought close interpretatively by taking as our clue the 'something as something'; and this Articulation lies *before* [liegt *vor*] our making any thematic assertion about it. In such an assertion the 'as' does not turn up for the first time; it just gets expressed for the first time, and this is possible only in that it lies before us as something expressible.[1] The fact that when we look at something, the explicitness of assertion can be absent, does not justify our denying that there is any Articulative interpretation in such mere seeing, and hence that there is any as-structure in it. When we have to do with anything, the mere seeing of the Things which are closest to us bears in itself the structure of interpretation, and in so primordial a manner that just to grasp something *free*, as it were, *of the "as"*, requires a certain readjustment. When we merely stare at something, our just-having-it-before-us lies before us *as a failure to understand it any more*. This grasping which is free of the "as", is a privation of the kind of seeing in which one *merely* understands. It is not more primordial than that kind of seeing, but is derived from it. If the 'as' is ontically unexpressed, this must not seduce us into overlooking it as a constitutive state for understanding, existential and *a priori*.

But if we never perceive equipment that is ready-to-hand without already understanding and interpreting it, and if such perception lets us circumspectively encounter something as something, does this not mean that in the first instance we have experienced something purely present-at-hand, and then taken it *as* a door, *as* a house? This would be a misunderstanding of the specific way in which interpretation functions as disclosure. In interpreting, we do not, so to speak, throw a 'signification' over some naked thing which is present-at-hand, we do not stick a value on it; but when something within-the-world is encountered as such, the

150

---

[1] '. . . was allein so möglich ist, dass es als Aussprechbares vor-liegt.' Here we follow the reading of the earlier editions. The hyphen in 'vor-liegt' comes at the end of the line in the later editions, but is undoubtedly meant to suggest (like the italicization of the 'vor' in the previous sentence) that this verb is to be interpreted with unusual literalness.

This paragraph is noteworthy for an exploitation of the prefix 'aus' ('out'), which fails to show up in our translation. Literally an 'Aussage' ('assertion') is something which is 'said out'; an 'Auslegung' ('interpretation') is a 'laying-out'; that which is 'ausdrücklich' ('explicit') is something that has been 'pressed out'; that which is 'aussprechbar' (our 'expressible') is something that can be 'spoken out'.

The verbs 'ausdrücken' and 'aussprechen' are roughly synonymous; but 'aussprechen' often has the more specific connotations of 'pronunciation', 'pronouncing oneself', 'speaking one's mind', 'finishing what one has to say', etc. While it would be possible to reserve 'express' for 'ausdrücken' and translate 'aussprechen' by some such phrase as 'speak out', it is more convenient to use 'express' for both verbs, especially since 'aussprechen' and its derivatives have occurred very seldom before the present chapter, in which 'ausdrücken' rarely appears. On the other hand, we can easily distinguish between the more frequent 'ausdrücklich' and 'ausgesprochen' by translating the latter as 'expressed' or 'expressly', and reserving 'explicit' for both 'ausdrücklich' and 'explizit'.

thing in question already has an involvement which is disclosed in our understanding of the world, and this involvement is one which gets laid out by the interpretation.[1]

The ready-to-hand is always understood in terms of a totality of involvements. This totality need not be grasped explicitly by a thematic interpretation. Even if it has undergone such an interpretation, it recedes into an understanding which does not stand out from the background. And this is the very mode in which it is the essential foundation for everyday circumspective interpretation. In every case this interpretation is grounded in *something we have in advance*—in a *fore-having*.[2] As the appropriation of understanding, the interpretation operates in Being towards a totality of involvements which is already understood—a Being which understands. When something is understood but is still veiled, it becomes unveiled by an act of appropriation, and this is always done under the guidance of a point of view, which fixes that with regard to which what is understood is to be interpreted. In every case interpretation is grounded in *something we see in advance*—in a *fore-sight*. This fore-sight 'takes the first cut' out of what has been taken into our fore-having, and it does so with a view to a definite way in which this can be interpreted.[3] Anything understood which is held in our fore-having and towards which we set our sights 'foresightedly', becomes conceptualizable through the interpretation. In such an interpretation, the way in which the entity we are interpreting is to be conceived can be drawn from the entity itself, or the interpretation can force the entity into concepts to which it is opposed in its manner of Being. In either case, the interpretation has already decided for a definite way of conceiving it, either with finality or with reservations; it is grounded in *something we grasp in advance*—in a *fore-conception*.

Whenever something is interpreted as something, the interpretation will be founded essentially upon fore-having, fore-sight, and fore-conception. An interpretation is never a presuppositionless apprehending of

---

[1] '... die durch die Auslegung herausgelegt wird.'

[2] In this paragraph Heidegger introduces the important words 'Vorhabe', 'Vorsicht', and 'Vorgriff'. 'Vorhabe' is perhaps best translated by some such expression as 'what we have in advance' or 'what we have before us'; but we shall usually find it more convenient to adopt the shorter term 'fore-having', occasionally resorting to hendiadys, as in the present sentence, and we shall handle the other terms in the same manner. 'Vorsicht' ('what we see in advance' or 'fore-sight') is the only one of these expressions which occurs in ordinary German usage, and often has the connotation of 'caution' or 'prudence'; Heidegger, however, uses it in a more general sense somewhat more akin to the English 'foresight', without the connotation of a shrewd and accurate prediction. 'Vorgriff' ('what we grasp in advance' or 'fore-conception') is related to the verb 'vorgreifen' ('to anticipate') as well as to the noun "Begriff".

[3] 'Die Auslegung gründet jeweils in einer *Vorsicht*, die das in Vorhabe Genommene auf eine bestimmte Auslegbarkeit hin "anschneidet".' The idea seems to be that just as the person who cuts off the first slice of a loaf of bread gets the loaf 'started', the fore-sight 'makes a start' on what we have in advance—the fore-having.

something presented to us.[1] If, when one is engaged in a particular concrete kind of interpretation, in the sense of exact textual Interpretation,
one likes to appeal [beruft] to what 'stands there', then one finds that
what 'stands there' in the first instance is nothing other than the obvious
undiscussed assumption [Vormeinung] of the person who does the
interpreting. In an interpretative approach there lies such an assumption,
as that which has been 'taken for granted' ["gesetzt"] with the interpretation as such—that is to say, as that which has been presented in our
fore-having, our fore-sight, and our fore-conception.

How are we to conceive the character of this 'fore'? Have we done so if
we say formally that this is something '*a priori*'? Why does understanding,
which we have designated as a fundamental *existentiale* of Dasein, have
this structure as its own? Anything interpreted, as something interpreted,
has the 'as'-structure as its own; and how is this related to the 'fore'
structure? The phenomenon of the 'as'-structure is manifestly not to be
dissolved or broken up 'into pieces'. But is a primordial analytic for it
thus ruled out? Are we to concede that such phenomena are 'ultimates'?
Then there would still remain the question, "why?" Or do the fore-
structure of understanding and the as-structure of interpretation show an
existential-ontological connection with the phenomenon of projection?
And does this phenomenon point back to a primordial state of Dasein's
Being?

Before we answer these questions, for which the preparation up till now
has been far from sufficient, we must investigate whether what has become
visible as the fore-structure of understanding and the as-structure of
interpretation, does not itself already present us with a unitary phenomenon—one of which copious use is made in philosophical problematics,
though what is used so universally falls short of the primordiality of
ontological explication.

In the projecting of the understanding, entities are disclosed in their
possibility. The character of the possibility corresponds, on each occasion,
with the kind of Being of the entity which is understood. Entities within-
the-world generally are projected upon the world—that is, upon a whole
of significance, to whose reference-relations concern, as Being-in-the-
world, has been tied up in advance. When entities within-the-world are
discovered along with the Being of Dasein—that is, when they have come
to be understood—we say that they have *meaning* [*Sinn*]. But that which
is understood, taken strictly, is not the meaning but the entity, or

---

[1] '. . . eines Vorgegebenen.' Here, as in many other passages, we have translated
'vorgeben' by various forms of the verb 'to present'; but it would perhaps be more in line
with Heidegger's discussion of the prefix 'vor-' to write '. . . of something fore-given'.

alternatively, Being. Meaning is that wherein the intelligibility [Verständlichkeit] of something maintains itself. That which can be Articulated in a disclosure by which we understand, we call "meaning". The *concept of meaning* embraces the formal existential framework of what necessarily belongs to that which an understanding interpretation Articulates. *Meaning is the "upon-which" of a projection in terms of which something becomes intelligible as something; it gets its structure from a fore-having, a fore-sight, and a fore-conception.*[1] In so far as understanding and interpretation make up the existential state of Being of the "there", "meaning" must be conceived as the formal-existential framework of the disclosedness which belongs to understanding. Meaning is an *existentiale* of Dasein, not a property attaching to entities, lying 'behind' them, or floating somewhere as an 'intermediate domain'. Dasein only 'has' meaning, so far as the disclosedness of Being-in-the-world can be 'filled in' by the entities discoverable in that disclosedness.[2] *Hence only Dasein can be meaningful [sinnvoll] or meaningless [sinnlos].* That is to say, its own Being and the entities disclosed with its Being can be appropriated in understanding, or can remain relegated to non-understanding.

This Interpretation of the concept of 'meaning' is one which is ontologico-existential in principle; if we adhere to it, then all entities whose kind of Being is of a character other than Dasein's must be conceived as *unmeaning [unsinniges]*, essentially devoid of any meaning at all. Here 'unmeaning' does not signify that we are saying anything about the value of such entities, but it gives expression to an ontological characteristic. *And only that which is unmeaning can be absurd [widersinnig].* The present-at-hand, as Dasein encounters it, can, as it were, assault Dasein's Being; natural events, for instance, can break in upon us and destroy us.

And if we are inquiring about the meaning of Being, our investigation does not then become a "deep" one [tiefsinnig], nor does it puzzle out what stands behind Being. It asks about Being itself in so far as Being enters into the intelligibility of Dasein. The meaning of Being can never be

---

[1] '*Sinn ist das durch Vorhabe, Vorsicht und Vorgriff strukturierte Woraufhin des Entwurfs, aus dem her etwas als etwas verständlich wird.*' (Notice that our usual translation of 'verständlich, and 'Verständlichkeit' as 'intelligible' and 'intelligibility', fails to show the connection of the words with 'Verständnis', etc. This connection could have been brought out effectively by writing 'understandable,' 'understandability', etc., but only at the cost of awkwardness.)

[2] '*Sinn "hat" nur das Dasein, sofern die Erschlossenheit des In-der-Welt-seins durch das in ihr entdeckbare Seiende "erfüllbar" ist.*' The point of this puzzling and ambiguous sentence may become somewhat clearer if the reader recalls that here as elsewhere (see H. 75 above) the verb 'erschliessen' ('disclose') is used in the sense of 'opening something up' so that its contents can be 'discovered'. What thus gets 'opened up' will then be 'filled in' as more and more of its contents get discovered.

contrasted with entities, or with Being as the 'ground' which gives entities support; for a 'ground' becomes accessible only as meaning, even if it is itself the abyss of meaninglessness.[1]

As the disclosedness of the "there", understanding always pertains to the whole of Being-in-the-world. In every understanding of the world, existence is understood with it, and *vice versa*. All interpretation, moreover, operates in the fore-structure, which we have already characterized. Any interpretation which is to contribute understanding, must already have understood what is to be interpreted. This is a fact that has always been remarked, even if only in the area of derivative ways of understanding and interpretation, such as philological Interpretation. The latter belongs within the range of scientific knowledge. Such knowledge demands the rigour of a demonstration to provide grounds for it. In a scientific proof, we may not presuppose what it is our task to provide grounds for. But if interpretation must in any case already operate in that which is understood, and if it must draw its nurture from this, how is it to bring any scientific results to maturity without moving in a circle, especially if, moreover, the understanding which is presupposed still operates within our common information about man and the world? Yet according to the most elementary rules of logic, this *circle* is a *circulus vitiosus*. If that be so, however, the business of historiological interpretation is excluded *a priori* from the domain of rigorous knowledge. In so far as the Fact of this circle in understanding is not eliminated, historiology must then be resigned to less rigorous possibilities of knowing. Historiology is permitted to compensate for this defect to some extent through the 'spiritual signification' of its 'objects'. But even in the opinion of the historian himself, it would admittedly be more ideal if the circle could be avoided and if there remained the hope of creating some time a historiology which would be as independent of the standpoint of the observer as our knowledge of Nature is supposed to be.

153   *But if we see this circle as a vicious one and look out for ways of avoiding it, even if we just 'sense' it as an inevitable imperfection, then the act of understanding has been misunderstood from the ground up.* The assimilation of understanding and interpretation to a definite ideal of knowledge is not the issue here. Such an ideal is itself only a subspecies of understanding—a subspecies which has strayed into the legitimate task of grasping the present-at-hand in its essential unintelligibility [Unverständlichkeit]. If the basic conditions which make interpretation possible are to be fulfilled, this must

---

[1] 'Der Sinn von Sein kann nie in Gegensatz gebracht werden zum Seienden oder zum Sein als tragenden "Grund" des Seienden, weil "Grund" nur als Sinn zugänglich wird, und sei er selbst der Abgrund der Sinnlosigkeit.' Notice the etymological kinship between 'Grund' ('ground') and 'Abgrund' ('abyss').

rather be done by not failing to recognize beforehand the essential conditions under which it can be performed. What is decisive is not to get out of the circle but to come into it in the right way. This circle of understanding is not an orbit in which any random kind of knowledge may move; it is the expression of the existential *fore-structure* of Dasein itself. It is not to be reduced to the level of a vicious circle, or even of a circle which is merely tolerated. In the circle is hidden a positive possibility of the most primordial kind of knowing. To be sure, we genuinely take hold of this possibility only when, in our interpretation, we have understood that our first, last, and constant task is never to allow our fore-having, fore-sight, and fore-conception to be presented to us by fancies and popular conceptions, but rather to make the scientific theme secure by working out these fore-structures in terms of the things themselves. Because understanding, in accordance with its existential meaning, is Dasein's own potentiality-for-Being, the ontological presuppositions of historiological knowledge transcend in principle the idea of rigour held in the most exact sciences. Mathematics is not more rigorous than historiology, but only narrower, because the existential foundations relevant for it lie within a narrower range.

The 'circle' in understanding belongs to the structure of meaning, and the latter phenomenon is rooted in the existential constitution of Dasein— that is, in the understanding which interprets. An entity for which, as Being-in-the-world, its Being is itself an issue, has, ontologically, a circular structure. If, however, we note that 'circularity' belongs ontologically to a kind of Being which is present-at-hand (namely, to subsistence [Bestand]), we must altogether avoid using this phenomenon to characterize anything like Dasein ontologically.

¶ *33. Assertion as a Derivative Mode of Interpretation*

All interpretation is grounded on understanding. That which has been articulated[1] as such in interpretation and sketched out beforehand in the understanding in general as something articulable, is the meaning. In so far as assertion ('judgment')[2] is grounded on understanding and presents us with a derivative form in which an interpretation has been carried out, it *too* 'has' a meaning. Yet this meaning cannot be defined as something which occurs 'in' ["an"] a judgment along with the judging itself. In our

154

---

[1] 'Gegliederte'. The verbs 'artikulieren' and 'gliedern' can both be translated by 'articulate' in English; even in German they are nearly synonymous, but in the former the emphasis is presumably on the 'joints' at which something gets divided, while in the latter the emphasis is presumably on the 'parts' or 'members'. We have distinguished between them by translating 'artikulieren' by 'Articulate' (with a capital 'A'), and 'gliedern' by 'articulate' (with a lower-case initial).

[2] '. . . die Aussage (das "Urteil") . . .'

present context, we shall give an explicit analysis of assertion, and this analysis will serve several purposes.

For one thing, it can be demonstrated, by considering assertion, in what ways the structure of the 'as', which is constitutive for understanding and interpretation, can be modified. When this has been done, both understanding and interpretation will be brought more sharply into view. For another thing, the analysis of assertion has a special position in the problematic of fundamental ontology, because in the decisive period when ancient ontology was beginning, the λόγος functioned as the only clue for obtaining access to that which authentically i s [zum eigentlich Seienden], and for defining the Being of such entities. Finally assertion has been accepted from ancient times as the primary and authentic 'locus' of *truth*. The phenomenon of truth is so thoroughly coupled with the problem of Being that our investigation, as it proceeds further, will necessarily come up against the problem of truth; and it already lies within the dimensions of that problem, though not explicitly. The analysis of assertion will at the same time prepare the way for this latter problematic.

In what follows, we give three significations to the term "*assertion*". These are drawn from the phenomenon which is thus designated, they are connected among themselves, and in their unity they encompass the full structure of assertion.

1. The primary signification of "assertion" is "*pointing out*" [*Aufzeigen*]. In this we adhere to the primordial meaning of λόγος as ἀπόφανσις—letting an entity be seen from itself. In the assertion 'The hammer is too heavy', what is discovered for sight is not a 'meaning', but an entity in the way that it is ready-to-hand. Even if this entity is not close enough to be grasped and 'seen', the pointing-out has in view the entity itself and not, let us say, a mere "representation" [Vorstellung] of it—neither something 'merely represented' nor the psychical condition in which the person who makes the assertion "represents" it.

2. "Assertion" means no less than "*predication*". We 'assert' a 'predicate' of a 'subject', and the 'subject' is *given a definite character* [*bestimmt*] by the 'predicate'. In this signification of "assertion", that which is put forward in the assertion [Das Ausgesagte] is not the predicate, but 'the hammer itself'. On the other hand, that which does the asserting [Das Aussagende] (in other words, that which gives something a definite character) lies in the 'too heavy'. That which is put forward in the assertion in the second signification of "assertion" (that which is given a definite character, as such) has undergone a narrowing of content as compared with what is put forward in the assertion in the first signification

155

of this term. Every predication is what it is, only as a pointing-out. The second signification of "assertion" has its foundation in the first. Within this pointing-out, the elements which are Articulated in predication—the subject and predicate—arise. It is not by giving something a definite character that we first discover that which shows itself—the hammer—as such; but when we give it such a character, our seeing gets *restricted* to it in the first instance, so that by this explicit *restriction*[1] of our view, that which is already manifest may be made *explicitly* manifest in its definite character. In giving something a definite character, we must, in the first instance, take a step back when confronted with that which is already manifest—the hammer that is too heavy. In 'setting down the subject', we dim entities down to focus in 'that hammer there', so that by thus dimming them down we may let that which is manifest be seen *in* its own definite character as a character that can be determined.[2] Setting down the subject, setting down the predicate, and setting down the two together, are thoroughly 'apophantical' in the strict sense of the word.

3. "Assertion" means "*communication*" [*Mitteilung*], speaking forth [Heraussage]. As communication, it is directly related to "assertion" in the first and second significations. It is letting someone see with us what we have pointed out by way of giving it a definite character. Letting someone see with us shares with [teilt . . . mit] the Other that entity which has been pointed out in its definite character. That which is 'shared' is our *Being towards* what has been pointed out—a Being in which we see it in common. One must keep in mind that this Being-towards is Being-in-the-world, and that from out of this very world what has been pointed out gets encountered. Any assertion, as a communication understood in this existential manner, must have been expressed.[3] As something communicated, that which has been put forward in the assertion is something that Others can 'share' with the person making the assertion, even though the entity which he has pointed out and to which he has given a definite character is not close enough for them to grasp and see it. That which is put forward in the assertion is something which can be passed along in 'further retelling'. There is a widening of the range of that mutual sharing which sees. But at the same time, what has been pointed out may become veiled again in this further retelling, although even the kind of knowing which arises in such hearsay (whether knowledge that

---

[1] '*Einschränkung*'. The older editions have 'Entschränkung'.

[2] '. . . die "Subjektsetzung" blendet das Seiende ab auf "der Hammer da", um durch den Vollzug der Entblendung das Offenbare *in* seiner bestimmbaren Bestimmtheit sehen zu lassen.'

[3] 'Zur Aussage als der so existenzial verstandenen Mit-teilung gehört die Ausgesprochenheit.'

something is the case [Wissen] or merely an acquaintance with something [Kennen]) always has the entity itself in view and does not 'give assent' to some 'valid meaning' which has been passed around. Even hearsay is a Being-in-the-world, and a Being towards what is heard.

There is prevalent today a theory of 'judgment' which is oriented to the phenomenon of 'validity'.[1] We shall not give an extensive discussion of it here. It will be sufficient to allude to the very questionable character of this phenomenon of 'validity', though since the time of Lotze people have been fond of passing this off as a 'primal phenomenon' which cannot be traced back any further. The fact that it can play this role is due only to its ontologically unclarified character. The 'problematic' which has established itself round this idolized word is no less opaque. In the first place, validity is viewed as the *'form' of actuality* which goes with the content of the judgment, in so far as that content remains unchanged as opposed to the changeable 'psychical' process of judgment. Considering how the status of the question of Being in general has been characterized in the introduction to this treatise, we would scarcely venture to expect that 'validity' as 'ideal Being' is distinguished by special ontological clarity. In the second place, "validity" means at the same time the validity of the meaning of the judgment, which is valid of the 'Object' it has in view; and thus it attains the signification of an *'Objectively valid character'* and of Objectivity in general. In the third place, the meaning which is thus 'valid' *of* an entity, and which is valid 'timelessly' in itself, is said to be 'valid' also in the sense of being valid *for* everyone who judges rationally. "Validity" now means a *bindingness*, or 'universally valid' character.[2] Even if one were to advocate a 'critical' epistemological theory, according to which the subject does not 'really' 'come out' to the Object, then this valid character, as the validity of an Object (Objectivity), is grounded upon that stock of true (!) meaning which is itself valid. The three significations of 'being valid' which we have set forth—the way of Being of the ideal, Objectivity, and bindingness—not only are opaque in themselves but constantly get confused with one another. Methodological fore-sight

[1] Heidegger uses three words which might conveniently be translated as 'validity': 'Geltung' (our 'validity'), 'Gültigkeit' (our 'valid character'), and 'Gelten' (our 'being valid', etc.). The reader who has studied logic in English and who accordingly thinks of 'validity' as merely a property of arguments in which the premises imply the conclusion, must remember that in German the verb 'gelten' and its derivatives are used much more broadly, so as to apply to almost anything that is commonly (or even privately) accepted, so that one can speak of the 'validity' of legal tender, the 'validity' of a ticket for so many weeks or months, the 'validity' of that which 'holds' for me or for you, the 'validity' of anything that is the case. While Heidegger's discussion does not cover as many of these meanings as will be listed in any good German dictionary, he goes well beyond the narrower usage of the English-speaking logician. Of course, we shall often translate 'gelten' in other ways.

[2] '. . . *Verbindlichkeit*, "Allgemeingültigkeit".'

demands that we do not choose such unstable concepts as a clue to Interpretation. We make no advance restriction upon the concept of "meaning" which would confine it to signifying the 'content of judgment', but we understand it as the existential phenomenon already characterized, in which the formal framework of what can be disclosed in understanding and Articulated in interpretation becomes visible.

If we bring together the three significations of 'assertion' which we have analysed, and get a unitary view of the full phenomenon, then we may define *"assertion"* as *"a pointing-out which gives something a definite character and which communicates"*. It remains to ask with what justification we have taken assertion as a mode of interpretation at all. If it is something of this sort, then the essential structures of interpretation must recur in it. The pointing-out which assertion does is performed on the basis of what has already been disclosed in understanding or discovered circumspectively. Assertion is not a free-floating kind of behaviour which, in its own right, might be capable of disclosing entities in general in a primary way: on the contrary it always maintains itself on the basis of Being-in-the-world. What we have shown earlier[ix] in relation to knowing the world, holds just as well as assertion. Any assertion requires a fore-having of whatever has been disclosed; and this is what it points out by way of giving something a definite character. Furthermore, in any approach when one gives something a definite character, one is already taking a look directionally at what is to be put forward in the assertion. When an entity which has been presented is given a definite character, the function of giving it such a character is taken over by that with regard to which we set our sights towards the entity.[1] Thus any assertion requires a fore-sight; in this the predicate which we are to assign [zuzuweisende] and make stand out, gets loosened, so to speak, from its unexpressed inclusion in the entity itself. To any assertion as a communication which gives something a definite character there belongs, moreover, an Articulation of what is pointed out, and this Articulation is in accordance with significations. Such an assertion will operate with a definite way of conceiving: "The hammer is heavy", "Heaviness belongs to the hammer", "The hammer has the property of heaviness". When an assertion is made, some fore-conception is always implied; but it remains for the most part inconspicuous, because the language already hides in itself a developed way of conceiving. Like any interpretation whatever, assertion necessarily has a fore-having, a fore-sight, and a fore-conception as its existential foundations.

157

---

1 'Woraufhin das vorgegebene Seiende anvisiert wird, das übernimmt im Bestimmungsvollzug die Funktion des Bestimmenden.'

But to what extent does it become a *derivative* mode of interpretation? What has been modified in it? We can point out the modification if we stick to certain limiting cases of assertion which function in logic as normal cases and as examples of the 'simplest' assertion-phenomena. Prior to all analysis, logic has already understood 'logically' what it takes as a theme under the heading of the "categorical statement"—for instance, 'The hammer is heavy'. The unexplained presupposition is that the 'meaning' of this sentence is to be taken as: "This Thing—a hammer—has the property of heaviness". In concernful circumspection there are no such assertions 'at first'. But such circumspection has of course its specific ways of interpreting, and these, as compared with the 'theoretical judgment' just mentioned, may take some such form as 'The hammer is too heavy', or rather just 'Too heavy!', 'Hand me the other hammer!' Interpretation is carried out primordially not in a theoretical statement but in an action of circumspective concern—laying aside the unsuitable tool, or exchanging it, 'without wasting words'. From the fact that words are absent, it may not be concluded that interpretation is absent. On the other hand, the kind of interpretation which is circumspectively *expressed* is not necessarily already an assertion in the sense we have defined. *By what existential-ontological modifications does assertion arise from circumspective interpretation?*

The entity which is held in our fore-having—for instance, the hammer —is proximally ready-to-hand as equipment. If this entity becomes the 'object' of an assertion, then as soon as we begin this assertion, there is already a change-over in the fore-having. Something *ready-to-hand with which* we have to do or perform something, turns into something '*about which*' the assertion that points it out is made. Our fore-sight is aimed at something present-at-hand in what is ready-to-hand. Both *by* and *for* this way of looking at it [Hin-sicht], the ready-to-hand becomes veiled as ready-to-hand. Within this discovering of presence-at-hand, which is at the same time a covering-up of readiness-to-hand, something present-at-hand which we encounter is given a definite character in its Being-present-at-hand-in-such-and-such-a-manner. Only now are we given any access to *properties* or the like. When an assertion has given a definite character to something present-at-hand, it says something about it *as* a "what"; and this "what" is drawn *from that* which is present-at-hand as such. The as-structure of interpretation has undergone a modification. In its function of appropriating what is understood, the 'as' no longer reaches out into a totality of involvements. As regards its possibilities for Articulating reference-relations, it has been cut off from that significance which, as such, constitutes environmentality. The 'as' gets pushed back into the

158

uniform plane of that which is merely present-at-hand. It dwindles to the structure of just letting one see what is present-at-hand, and letting one see it in a definite way. This levelling of the primordial 'as' of circumspective interpretation to the "as" with which presence-at-hand is given a definite character is the specialty of assertion. Only so does it obtain the possibility of exhibiting something in such a way that we just look at it.

Thus assertion cannot disown its ontological origin from an interpretation which understands. The primordial 'as' of an interpretation (ἑρμηνεία) which understands circumspectively we call the "existential-*hermeneutical* 'as' " in distinction from the "*apophantical* 'as' " of the assertion.

Between the kind of interpretation which is still wholly wrapped up in concernful understanding and the extreme opposite case of a theoretical assertion about something present-at-hand, there are many intermediate gradations: assertions about the happenings in the environment, accounts of the ready-to-hand, 'reports on the Situation', the recording and fixing of the 'facts of the case', the description of a state of affairs, the narration of something that has befallen. We cannot trace back these 'sentences' to theoretical statements without essentially perverting their meaning. Like the theoretical statements themselves, they have their 'source' in circumspective interpretation.

With the progress of knowledge about the structure of the λόγος, it was inevitable that this phenomenon of the apophantical 'as' should come into view in some form or other. The manner in which it was proximally seen was not accidental, and did not fail to work itself out in the subsequent history of logic.

When considered philosophically, the λόγος itself is an entity, and, according to the orientation of ancient ontology, it is something present-at-hand. Words are proximally present-at-hand; that is to say, we come across them just as we come across Things; and this holds for any sequence of words, as that in which the λόγος expresses itself. In this first search for the structure of the λόγος as thus present-at-hand, what was found was the *Being-present-at-hand-together* of several words. What establishes the unity of this "together"? As Plato knew, this unity lies in the fact that the λόγος is always λόγος τινός. In the λόγος an entity is manifest, and with a view to this entity, the words are put together in *one* verbal whole. Aristotle saw this more radically: every λόγος is both σύνθεσις and διαίρεσις, not just the one (call it 'affirmative judgment') or the other (call it 'negative judgment'). Rather, every assertion, whether it affirms or denies, whether it is true or false, is *σύνθεσις and διαίρεσις* equiprimordially. To exhibit anything is to take it together and take it apart. It is

159

true, of course, that Aristotle did not pursue the analytical question as far as the problem of which phenomenon within the structure of the λόγος is the one that permits and indeed obliges us to characterize every statement as synthesis and diaeresis.

Along with the formal structures of 'binding' and 'separating'—or, more precisely, along with the unity of these—we should meet the phenomenon of the 'something as something', and we should meet this as a phenomenon. In accordance with this structure, something is understood with regard to something: it is taken together with it, yet in such a way that this confrontation which *understands* will at the same time take apart what has been taken together, and will do so by Articulating it *interpretatively*. If the phenomenon of the 'as' remains covered up, and, above all, if its existential source in the hermeneutical 'as' is veiled, then Aristotle's phenomenological approach to the analysis of the λόγος collapses to a superficial 'theory of judgment', in which judgment becomes the binding or separating of representations and concepts.

Binding and separating may be formalized still further to a 'relating'. The judgment gets dissolved logistically into a system in which things are 'co-ordinated' with one another; it becomes the object of a 'calculus'; but it does not become a theme for ontological Interpretation. The possibility and impossibility of getting an analytical understanding of σύνθεσις and διαίρεσις—of the 'relation' in judgment generally—is tightly linked up with whatever the current status of the ontological problematic and its principles may be.

How far this problematic has worked its way into the Interpretation of the λόγος, and how far on the other hand the concept of 'judgment' has (by a remarkable counter-thrust) worked its way into the ontological problematic, is shown by the phenomenon of the *copula*. When we consider this 'bond', it becomes clear that proximally the synthesis-structure is regarded as self-evident, and that it has also retained the function of serving as a standard for Interpretation. But if the formal characteristics of 'relating' and 'binding' can contribute nothing phenomenally towards the structural analysis of the λόγος as subject-matter, then in the long run the phenomenon to which we allude by the term "copula" has nothing to do with a bond or binding. The Interpretation of the 'is', whether it be expressed in its own right in the language or indicated in the verbal ending, leads us therefore into the context of problems belonging to the existential analytic, if assertion and the understanding of Being are existential possibilities for the Being of Dasein itself. When we come to work out the question of Being (cf. Part I, Division 3),[1] we shall thus

----

[1] This Division has never appeared.

encounter again this peculiar phenomenon of Being which we meet within the λόγος.

By demonstrating that assertion is derived from interpretation and understanding, we have made it plain that the 'logic' of the λόγος is rooted in the existential analytic of Dasein; and provisionally this has been sufficient. At the same time, by knowing that the λόγος has been Interpreted in a way which is ontologically inadequate, we have gained a sharper insight into the fact that the methodological basis on which ancient ontology arose was not a primordial one. The λόγος gets experienced as something present-at-hand and Interpreted as such, while at the same time the entities which it points out have the meaning of presence-at-hand. This meaning of Being is left undifferentiated and uncontrasted with other possibilities of Being, so that Being in the sense of a formal Being-something becomes fused with it simultaneously, and we are unable even to obtain a clear-cut division between these two realms.

¶ *34. Being-there and Discourse. Language*

The fundamental *existentialia* which constitute the Being of the "there", the disclosedness of Being-in-the-world, are states-of-mind and understanding. In understanding, there lurks the possibility of interpretation— that is, of appropriating what is understood. In so far as a state-of-mind is equiprimordial with an act of understanding, it maintains itself in a certain understanding. Thus there corresponds to it a certain capacity for getting interpreted. We have seen that assertion is derived from interpretation, and is an extreme case of it. In clarifying the third signification of assertion as communication (speaking forth), we were led to the concepts of "saying" and "speaking", to which we had purposely given no attention up to that point. The fact that language *now* becomes our theme *for the first time* will indicate that this phenomenon has its roots in the existential constitution of Dasein's disclosedness. _The existential-ontological foundation of language is discourse or talk._[1] This phenomenon is one of which we have been making constant use already in our foregoing Interpretation of state-of-mind, understanding, interpretation, and assertion; but we have, as it were, kept it suppressed in our thematic analysis.   161

Discourse is existentially equiprimordial with state-of-mind and understanding. The intelligibility of something has always been articulated, even before there is any appropriative interpretation of it. Discourse is the Articulation

---

[1] '*Rede*'. As we have pointed out earlier (see our note 3, p. 47, H. 25 above), we have translated this word either as 'discourse' or 'talk', as the context seems to demand, sometimes compromising with the hendiadys 'discourse or talk'. But in some contexts 'discourse' is too formal while 'talk' is too colloquial; the reader must remember that there is no good English equivalent for 'Rede'. For a previous discussion see Section 7 B above (H. 32-34).

of intelligibility. Therefore it underlies both interpretation and assertion. That which can be Articulated in interpretation, and thus even
more primordially in discourse, is what we have called "meaning". That
which gets articulated as such in discursive Articulation, we call the
"totality-of-significations" [Bedeutungsganze]. This can be dissolved or
broken up into significations. Significations, as what has been Articulated
from that which can be Articulated, always carry meaning [. . . sind . . .
sinnhaft]. If discourse, as the Articulation of the intelligibility of the
"there", is a primordial *existentiale* of disclosedness, and if disclosedness is
primarily constituted by Being-in-the-world, then discourse too must have
essentially a kind of Being which is specifically *worldly*. The intelligibility
of Being-in-the-world—an intelligibility which goes with a state-of-mind
—*expresses itself as discourse*. The totality-of-significations of intelligibility
is *put into words*. To significations, words accrue. But word-Things do not
get supplied with significations.   *as system*

The way in which discourse gets expressed is language.[1] Language is a
totality of words—a totality in which discourse has a 'worldly' Being of
its own; and as an entity within-the-world, this totality thus becomes
something which we may come across as ready-to-hand. Language can
be broken up into word-Things which are present-at-hand. Discourse is
existentially language, because that entity whose disclosedness it Articulates according to significations, has, as its kind of Being, Being-in-the-
world—a Being which has been thrown and submitted to the 'world'.

As an existential state in which Dasein is disclosed, discourse is constitutive for Dasein's existence. *Hearing* and *keeping silent* [*Schweigen*] are
possibilities belonging to discursive speech. In these phenomena the constitutive function of discourse for the existentiality of existence becomes
entirely plain for the first time. But in the first instance the issue is one of
working out the structure of discourse as such.

Discoursing or talking is the way in which we articulate 'significantly'
the intelligibility of Being-in-the-world. Being-with belongs to Being-
in-the-world, which in every case maintains itself in some definite way
of concernful Being-with-one-another. Such Being-with-one-another is
discursive as assenting or refusing, as demanding or warning, as pronouncing, consulting, or interceding, as 'making assertions', and as
talking in the way of 'giving a talk'.[2] Talking is talk about something.
That which the discourse is *about* [das *Worüber* der Rede] does not necessarily or even for the most part serve as the theme for an assertion in

---

[1] 'Die Hinausgesprochenheit der Rede ist die Sprache.'
[2] 'Dieses ist redend als zu- und absagen, auffordern, warnen, als Aussprache, Rück-
sprache, Fürsprache, ferner als "Aussagen machen" und als reden in der Weise des
"Redenhaltens".'

which one gives something a definite character. Even a command is given about something; a wish is about something. And so is intercession. What the discourse is about is a structural item that it necessarily possesses; for discourse helps to constitute the disclosedness of Being-in-the-world, and in its own structure it is modelled upon this basic state of Dasein. What is talked about [das Beredete] in talk is always 'talked to' ["an-geredet"] in a definite regard and within certain limits. In any talk or discourse, there is *something said-in-the-talk* as such [ein *Geredetes* as solches]—something said as such [das . . . Gesagte als solches] whenever one wishes, asks, or expresses oneself about something. In this "something said", discourse communicates.

As we have already indicated in our analysis of assertion,[1] the phenomenon of *communication* must be understood in a sense which is ontologically broad. 'Communication' in which one makes assertions—giving information, for instance—is a special case of that communication which is grasped in principle existentially. In this more general kind of communication, the Articulation of Being with one another understandingly is constituted. Through it a co-state-of-mind [Mitbefindlichkeit] gets 'shared', and so does the understanding of Being-with. Communication is never anything like a conveying of experiences, such as opinions or wishes, from the interior of one subject into the interior of another. Dasein-with is already essentially manifest in a co-state-of-mind and a co-understanding. In discourse Being-with becomes 'explicitly' *shared*; that is to say, it *is* already, but it is unshared as something that has not been taken hold of and appropriated.[2]

Whenever something is communicated in what is said-in-the-talk, all talk about anything has at the same time the character of *expressing itself* [Sichaussprechens]. In talking, Dasein *expresses* itself [spricht sich . . . *aus*] not because it has, in the first instance, been encapsulated as something 'internal' over against something outside, but because as Being-in-the-world it is already 'outside' when it understands. What is expressed is precisely this Being-outside—that is to say, the way in which one currently has a state-of-mind (mood), which we have shown to pertain to the full disclosedness of Being-in. Being-in and its state-of-mind are made known in discourse and indicated in language by intonation, modulation, the tempo of talk, 'the way of speaking'. In 'poetical' discourse, the communication of the existential possibilities of one's state-of-mind can become an aim in itself, and this amounts to a disclosing of existence.

---

[1] Reading '. . . bei der Analyse der Aussage . . .' with the older editions. The words 'der Aussage' have been omitted in the newer editions.

[2] 'Das Mitsein wird in der Rede "ausdrücklich" *geteilt*, das heisst es *ist* schon, nur ungeteilt als nicht ergriffenes und zugeeignetes.'

In discourse the intelligibility of Being-in-the-world (an intelligibility which goes with a state-of-mind) is articulated according to significations; and discourse is this articulation. The items constitutive for discourse are: what the discourse is about (what is talked about); what is said-in-the-talk, as such; the communication; and the making-known. These are not properties which can just be raked up empirically from language. They are existential characteristics rooted in the state of Dasein's Being, and it is they that first make anything like language ontologically possible. In the factical linguistic form of any definite case of discourse, some of these items may be lacking, or may remain unnoticed. The fact that they often do *not* receive 'verbal' expression, is merely an index of some definite kind of discourse which, in so far as it is discourse, must in every case lie within the totality of the structures we have mentioned.

Attempts to grasp the 'essence of language' have always taken their orientation from one or another of these items; and the clues to their conceptions of language have been the ideas of 'expression', of 'symbolic form', of communication as 'assertion',[1] of the 'making-known' of experiences, of the 'patterning' of life. Even if one were to put these various fragmentary definitions together in syncretistic fashion, nothing would be achieved in the way of a fully adequate definition of "language". We would still have to do what is decisive here—to work out in advance the ontologico-existential whole of the structure of discourse on the basis of the analytic of Dasein.

We can make clear the connection of discourse with understanding and intelligibility by considering an existential possibility which belongs to talking itself—hearing. If we have not heard 'aright', it is not by accident that we say we have not 'understood'. Hearing is constitutive for discourse. And just as linguistic utterance is based on discourse, so is acoustic perception on hearing. Listening to . . . is Dasein's existential way of Being-open as Being-with for Others. Indeed, hearing constitutes the primary and authentic way in which Dasein is open for its ownmost potentiality-for-Being—as in hearing the voice of the friend whom every Dasein carries with it. Dasein hears, because it understands. As a Being-in-the-world with Others, a Being which understands, Dasein is 'in thrall' to Dasein-with and to itself; and in this thraldom it "belongs" to these.[2] Being-with develops in listening to one another [Aufeinander-hören], which can be done in several possible ways: following,[3] going along with,

---

[1] '. . . der Mitteilung als "Aussage" . . .' The quotation marks around 'Aussage' appear only in the newer editions.

[2] 'Als verstehendes In-der-Welt-sein mit den Anderen ist es dem Mitdasein und ihm selbst "hörig" und in dieser Hörigkeit zugehörig.' In this sentence Heidegger uses some cognates of 'hören' ('hearing') whose interrelations disappear in our version.

[3] '. . . des Folgens . . .' In the earlier editions there are quotation marks around 'Folgens'.

and the privative modes of not-hearing, resisting, defying, and turning away.

It is on the basis of this potentiality for hearing, which is existentially primary, that anything like *hearkening* [*Horchen*] becomes possible. Hearkening is phenomenally still more primordial than what is defined 'in the first instance' as "hearing" in psychology—the sensing of tones and the perception of sounds. Hearkening too has the kind of Being of the hearing which understands. What we 'first' hear is never noises or complexes of sounds, but the creaking waggon, the motor-cycle. We hear the column on the march, the north wind, the woodpecker tapping, the fire crackling.

It requires a very artificial and complicated frame of mind to 'hear' a 'pure noise'. The fact that motor-cycles and waggons are what we proximally hear is the phenomenal evidence that in every case Dasein, as Being-in-the-world, already dwells *alongside* what is ready-to-hand within-the-world; it certainly does not dwell proximally alongside 'sensations'; nor would it first have to give shape to the swirl of sensations to provide the springboard from which the subject leaps off and finally arrives at a 'world'. Dasein, as essentially understanding, is proximally alongside what is understood.

Likewise, when we are explicitly hearing the discourse of another, we proximally understand what is said, or—to put it more exactly—we are already with him, in advance, alongside the entity which the discourse is about. On the other hand, what we proximally hear is *not* what is expressed in the utterance. Even in cases where the speech is indistinct or in a foreign language, what we proximally hear is *unintelligible* words, and not a multiplicity of tone-data.[1]

Admittedly, when what the discourse is about is heard 'naturally', we can at the same time hear the 'diction', the way in which it is said [die Weise des Gesagtseins], but only if there is some co-understanding beforehand of what is said-in-the-talk; for only so is there a possibility of estimating whether the way in which it is said is appropriate to what the discourse is about thematically.

In the same way, any answering counter-discourse arises proximally and directly from understanding what the discourse is about, which is already 'shared' in Being-with.

Only where talking and hearing are existentially possible, can anyone hearken. The person who 'cannot hear' and 'must feel'[2] may perhaps be one who is able to hearken very well, and precisely because of this. Just

---

[1] Here we follow the reading of the newer editions: '. . . nicht eine Mannigfaltigkeit von Tondaten.' The older editions have 'reine' instead of 'eine'.

[2] The author is here alluding to the German proverb, 'Wer nicht hören kann, muss fühlen.' (I.e. he who cannot heed, must suffer.)

hearing something "all around" [Das Nur-herum-hören] is a privation of the hearing which understands. Both talking and hearing are based upon understanding. And understanding arises neither through talking at length [vieles Reden] nor through busily hearing something "all around". Only he who already understands can listen [zuhören].

Keeping silent is another essential possibility of discourse, and it has the same existential foundation. In talking with one another, the person who keeps silent can 'make one understand' (that is, he can develop an understanding), and he can do so more authentically than the person who is never short of words. Speaking at length [Viel-sprechen] about something does not offer the slightest guarantee that thereby under-standing is advanced. On the contrary, talking extensively about some-thing, covers it up and brings what is understood to a sham clarity—the unintelligibility of the trivial. But to keep silent does not mean to be dumb. On the contrary, if a man is dumb, he still has a tendency to 'speak'. Such a person has not proved that he can keep silence; indeed, he entirely lacks the possibility of proving anything of the sort. And the person who is accustomed by Nature to speak little is no better able to show that he is keeping silent or that he is the sort of person who can do so. He who never says anything cannot keep silent at any given moment. Keeping silent authentically is possible only in genuine discoursing. To be able to keep silent, Dasein must have something to say—that is, it must have at its disposal an authentic and rich disclosedness of itself. In that case one's reticence [Verschwiegenheit] makes something manifest, and does away with 'idle talk' ["Gerede"]. As a mode of discoursing, reticence Articulates the intelligibility of Dasein in so primordial a manner that it gives rise to a potentiality-for-hearing which is genuine, and to a Being-with-one-another which is transparent.

Because discourse is constititutive for the Being of the "there" (that is, for states-of-mind and understanding), while "Dasein" means Being-in-the-world, Dasein as discursive Being-in, has already expressed itself. Dasein has language. Among the Greeks, their everyday existing was largely diverted into talking with one another, but at the same time they 'had eyes' to see. Is it an accident that in both their pre-philosophical and their philosophical ways of interpreting Dasein, they defined the essence of man as ζῷον λόγον ἔχον? The later way of interpreting this definition of man in the sense of the *animal rationale*, 'something living which has reason', is not indeed 'false', but it covers up the phenomenal basis for this definition of "Dasein". Man shows himself as the entity which talks. This does not signify that the possibility of vocal utterance is peculiar to him, but rather that he is the entity which is such as to discover the world and

Dasein itself. The Greeks had no word for "language"; they understood this phenomenon 'in the first instance' as discourse. But because the λόγος came into their philosophical ken primarily as assertion, *this* was the kind of *logos* which they took as their clue for working out the basic structures of the forms of discourse and its components. Grammar sought its foundations in the 'logic' of this *logos*. But this logic was based upon the ontology of the present-at-hand. The basic stock of 'categories of signification', which passed over into the subsequent science of language, and which in principle is still accepted as the standard today, is oriented towards discourse as assertion. But if on the contrary we take this phenomenon to have in principle the primordiality and breadth of an *existentiale*, then there emerges the necessity of re-establishing the science of language on foundations which are ontologically more primordial. The task of *liberating* grammar from logic requires *beforehand* a *positive* understanding of the basic *a priori* structure of discourse in general as an *existentiale*. It is not a task that can be carried through later on by improving and rounding out what has been handed down. Bearing this in mind, we must inquire into the basic forms in which it is possible to articulate anything understandable, and to do so in accordance with significations; and this articulation must not be confined to entities within-the-world which we cognize by considering them theoretically, and which we express in sentences. A doctrine of signification will not emerge automatically even if we make a comprehensive comparison of as many languages as possible, and those which are most exotic. To accept, let us say, the philosophical horizon within which W. von Humboldt made language a problem, would be no less inadequate. The doctrine of signification is rooted in the ontology of Dasein. Whether it prospers or decays depends on the fate of this ontology.ˣ

In the last resort, philosophical research must resolve to ask what kind of Being goes with language in general. Is it a kind of equipment ready-to-hand within-the-world, or has it Dasein's kind of Being, or is it neither of these? What kind of Being does language have, if there can be such a thing as a 'dead' language? What do the "rise" and "decline" of a language mean ontologically? We possess a science of language, and the Being of the entities which it has for its theme is obscure. Even the horizon for any investigative question about it is veiled. Is it an accident that proximally and for the most part significations are 'worldly', sketched out beforehand by the significance of the world, that they are indeed often predominantly 'spatial'? Or does this 'fact' have existential-ontological necessity? and if it is necessary, why should it be so? Philosophical research will have to dispense with the 'philosophy of language' if it is to inquire

166

into 'the 'things themselves' and attain the status of a problematic which has been cleared up conceptually.

Our Interpretation of language has been designed merely to point out the ontological 'locus' of this phenomenon in Dasein's state of Being, and especially to prepare the way for the following analysis, in which, taking as our clue a fundamental kind of Being belonging to discourse, in connection with other phenomena, we shall try to bring Dasein's everydayness into view in a manner which is ontologically more primordial.

B. The Everyday Being of the "There", and the Falling of Dasein

In going back to the existential structures of the disclosedness of Being-in-the-world, our Interpretation has, in a way, lost sight of Dasein's everydayness. In our analysis, we must now regain this phenomenal horizon which was our thematical starting-point. The question now arises: what are the existential characteristics of the disclosedness of Being-in-the-world, so far as the latter, as something which is everyday, maintains itself in the kind of Being of the "they"? Does the "they" have a state-of-mind which is specific to it, a special way of understanding, talking, and interpreting? It becomes all the more urgent to answer these questions when we remember that proximally and for the most part Dasein is absorbed in the "they" and is mastered by it. Is not Dasein, as thrown Being-in-the-world, thrown proximally right into the publicness of the "they"? And what does this publicness mean, other than the specific disclosedness of the "they"?

If understanding must be conceived primarily as Dasein's potentiality-for-Being, then it is from an analysis of the way of understanding and interpreting which belongs to the "they" that we must gather which possibilities of its Being have been disclosed and appropriated by Dasein as "they". In that case, however, these possibilities themselves make manifest an essential tendency of Being—one which belongs to everyday-ness. And finally, when this tendency has been explicated in an ontologic-ally adequate manner, it must unveil a primordial kind of Being of Dasein, in such a way, indeed, that from this kind of Being[1] the phenomenon of thrownness, to which we have called attention, can be exhibited in its existential concreteness.

In the first instance what is required is that the disclosedness of the "they"—that is, the everyday kind of Being of discourse, sight, and interpretation—should be made visible in certain definite phenomena. In

---

[1] Reading '. . . von ihr aus . . .'. The earliest editions omit 'aus'; correction is made in a list of errata.

relation to these phenomena, it may not be superfluous to remark that our own Interpretation is purely ontological in its aims, and is far removed from any moralizing critique of everyday Dasein, and from the aspirations of a 'philosophy of culture'.

¶ 35. *Idle Talk*

The expression 'idle talk' ["Gerede"] is not to be used here in a 'disparaging'[1] signification. Terminologically, it signifies a positive phenomenon which constitutes the kind of Being of everyday Dasein's understanding and interpreting. For the most part, discourse is expressed by being spoken out, and has always been so expressed; it is language.[2] But in that case understanding and interpretation already lie in what has thus been expressed. In language, as a way things have been expressed or spoken out [Ausgesprochenheit], there is hidden a way in which the understanding of Dasein has been interpreted. This way of interpreting it is no more just present-at-hand than language is; on the contrary, its Being is itself of the character of Dasein. Proximally, and with certain limits, Dasein is constantly delivered over to this interpretedness, which controls and distributes the possibilities of average understanding and of the state-of-mind belonging to it. The way things have been expressed or spoken out is such that in the totality of contexts of signification into which it has been articulated, it preserves an understanding of the disclosed world and therewith, equiprimordially, an understanding of the Dasein-with of Others and of one's own Being-in. The understanding which has thus already been "deposited" in the way things have been expressed, pertains just as much to any traditional discoveredness of entities which may have been reached, as it does to one's current understanding of Being and to whatever possibilities and horizons for fresh interpretation and conceptual Articulation may be available. But now we must go beyond a bare allusion to the Fact of this interpretedness of Dasein, and must inquire about the existential kind of Being of that discourse which is expressed and which expresses itself. If this cannot be conceived as something present-at-hand, what is its Being, and what does this tell us in principle about Dasein's everyday kind of Being?

168

Discourse which expresses itself is communication. Its tendency of

---

[1] These quotation marks are supplied only in the older editions. (It is not easy to translate 'Gerede' in a way which does not carry disparaging connotations. Fortunately Heidegger makes his meaning quite clear.)

[2] 'Die Rede spricht sich zumeist aus und hat sich schon immer ausgesprochen. Sie ist Sprache.' As we have pointed out earlier (see our note 1, p. 190 H. 149 above), it is often sufficient to translate 'aussprechen' as 'express'. In the present passage, however, the connotation of 'speaking out' or 'uttering' seems especially important; we shall occasionally make it explicit in our translation by hendiadys or other devices.

Being is aimed at bringing the hearer to participate in disclosed Being towards what is talked about in the discourse.

In the language which is spoken when one expresses oneself, there lies an average intelligibility; and in accordance with this intelligibility the discourse which is communicated can be understood to a considerable extent, even if the hearer does not bring himself into such a kind of Being towards what the discourse is about as to have a primordial understanding of it. We do not so much understand the entities which are talked about; we already are listening only to what is said-in-the-talk as such. What is said-in-the-talk gets understood; but what the talk is about is understood only approximately and superficially. We have *the same thing* in view, because it is in *the same* averageness that we have a common understanding of what is said.

Hearing and understanding have attached themselves beforehand to what is said-in-the-talk as such. The primary relationship-of-Being towards the entity talked about is not 'imparted' by communication;[1] but Being-with-one-another takes place in talking with one another and in concern with what is said-in-the-talk. To this Being-with-one-another, the fact that talking is going on is a matter of consequence.[2] The Being-said, the *dictum*, the pronouncement [Ausspruch]—all these now stand surety for the genuineness of the discourse and of the understanding which belongs to it, and for its appropriateness to the facts. And because this discoursing has lost its primary relationship-of-Being towards the entity talked about, or else has never achieved such a relationship, it does not communicate in such a way as to let this entity be appropriated in a primordial manner, but communicates rather by following the route of *gossiping* and *passing the word along*.[3] What is said-in-the-talk as such, spreads in wider circles and takes on an authoritative character. Things are so because one says so. Idle talk is constituted by just such gossiping and passing the word along —a process by which its initial lack of grounds to stand on [Bodenständigkeit] becomes aggravated to complete groundlessness [Bodenlosigkeit]. And indeed this idle talk is not confined to vocal gossip, but even spreads to what we write, where it takes the form of 'scribbling' [das "Geschreibe"]. In this latter case the gossip is not based so much upon hearsay. It feeds upon superficial reading [dem Angelesenen]. The average understanding of the reader will *never be able* to decide what has been drawn from primordial sources with a struggle and how much is just gossip. The average understanding, moreover, will not want any such distinction, and does not need it, because, of course, it understands everything.

---

[1] 'Die Mitteilung "teilt" nicht den primären Seinsbezug zum beredeten Seienden . . .'

[2] 'Ihm liegt daran, dass geredet wird.' We have interpreted 'Ihm' as referring to 'das Miteinandersein', but other interpretations are grammatically possible.

[3] '. . . sondern auf dem Wege des *Weiter-* und *Nachredens.*'

The groundlessness of idle talk is no obstacle to its becoming public; instead it encourages this. Idle talk is the possibility of understanding everything without previously making the thing one's own. If this were done, idle talk would founder; and it already guards against such a danger. Idle talk is something which anyone can rake up; it not only releases one from the task of genuinely understanding, but develops an undifferentiated kind of intelligibility, for which nothing is closed off any longer.

Discourse, which belongs to the essential state of Dasein's Being and has a share in constituting Dasein's disclosedness, has the possibility of becoming idle talk. And when it does so, it serves not so much to keep Being-in-the-world open for us in an articulated understanding, as rather to close it off, and cover up the entities within-the-world. To do this, one need not aim to deceive. Idle talk does not have the kind of Being which belongs to *consciously passing off* something as something else. The fact that something has been said groundlessly, and then gets passed along in further retelling, amounts to perverting the act of disclosing [Erschliessen] into an act of closing off [Verschliessen]. For what is said is always understood proximally as 'saying' something—that is, an uncovering something. Thus, by its very nature, idle talk is a closing-off, since to go back to the ground of what is talked about is something which it *leaves undone*.

This closing-off is aggravated afresh by the fact that an understanding of what is talked about is supposedly reached in idle talk. Because of this, idle talk discourages any new inquiry and any disputation, and in a peculiar way suppresses them and holds them back.

This way in which things have been interpreted in idle talk has already established itself in Dasein. There are many things with which we first become acquainted in this way, and there is not a little which never gets beyond such an average understanding. This everyday way in which things have been interpreted is one into which Dasein has grown in the first instance, with never a possibility of extrication. In it, out of it, and against it, all genuine understanding, interpreting, and communicating, all re-discovering and appropriating anew, are performed. In no case is a Dasein, untouched and unseduced by this way in which things have been interpreted, set before the open country of a 'world-in-itself' so that it just beholds what it encounters. The dominance of the public way in which things have been interpreted has already been decisive even for the possibilities of having a mood—that is, for the basic way in which Dasein 170 lets the world "matter" to it.[1] The "they" prescribes one's state-of-mind, and determines what and how one 'sees'.

[1] '. . . über die Möglichkeiten des Gestimmtseins entschieden, das heisst über die Grundart, in der sich das Dasein von der Welt angehen lässt.' The second 'über' is found only in the later editions.

Idle talk, which closes things off in the way we have designated, is the kind of Being which belongs to Dasein's understanding when that understanding has been uprooted. But idle talk does not occur as a condition which is present-at-hand in something present-at-hand: idle talk has been uprooted existentially, and this uprooting is constant. Ontologically this means that when Dasein maintains itself in idle talk, it is—as Being-in-the-world—cut off from its primary and primordially genuine relationships-of-Being towards the world, towards Dasein-with, and towards its very Being-in. Such a Dasein keeps floating unattached [in einer Schwebe]; yet in so doing, it is always alongside the world, with Others, and towards itself. To be uprooted in this manner is a possibility-of-Being only for an entity whose disclosedness is constituted by discourse as characterized by understanding and states-of-mind—that is to say, for an entity whose disclosedness, in such an ontologically constitutive state, *is* its "there", its 'in-the-world'. Far from amounting to a "not-Being" of Dasein, this uprooting is rather Dasein's most everyday and most stubborn 'Reality'.

Yet the obviousness and self-assurance of the average ways in which things have been interpreted, are such that while the particular Dasein drifts along towards an ever-increasing groundlessness as it floats, the uncanniness of this floating remains hidden from it under their protecting shelter.

¶ 36. *Curiosity*

In our analysis of understanding and of the disclosedness of the "there" in general, we have alluded to the *lumen naturale*, and designated the disclosedness of Being-in as Dasein's "*clearing*", in which it first becomes possible to have something like sight.[1] Our conception of "sight" has been gained by looking at the basic kind of disclosure which is characteristic of Dasein—namely, understanding, in the sense of the genuine appropriation of those entities towards which Dasein can comport itself in accordance with its essential possibilities of Being.

The basic state of sight shows itself in a peculiar tendency-of-Being which belongs to everydayness—the tendency towards 'seeing'. We designate this tendency by the term "*curiosity*" [*Neugier*], which characteristically is not confined to seeing, but expresses the tendency towards a peculiar way of letting the world be encountered by us in perception. Our aim in Interpreting this phenomenon is in principle one which is existential-ontological. We do not restrict ourselves to an orientation towards cognition. Even at an early date (and in Greek philosophy this

[1] See H. 133 above.

was no accident) cognition was conceived in terms of the 'desire to see'.[1] The treatise which stands first in the collection of Aristotle's treatises on ontology begins with the sentence: πάντες ἄνθρωποι τοῦ εἰδέναι ὀρέγονται φύσει.[xi] The care for seeing is essential to man's Being.[2] This remark introduces an investigation in which Aristotle seeks to uncover the source of all learned exploration of entities and their Being, by deriving it from that species of Dasein's Being which we have just mentioned. This Greek Interpretation of the existential genesis of science is not accidental. It brings to explicit understanding what has already been sketched out beforehand in the principle of Parmenides: τὸ γὰρ αὐτὸ νοεῖν ἐστίν τε καὶ εἶναι.[3] Being is that which shows itself in the pure perception which belongs to beholding, and only by such seeing does Being get discovered. Primordial and genuine truth lies in pure beholding. This thesis has remained the foundation of western philosophy ever since. The Hegelian dialectic found in it its motivating conception, and is possible only on the basis of it.

The remarkable priority of 'seeing' was noticed particularly by Augustine, in connection with his Interpretation of *concupiscentia*.[xii] "*Ad oculos enim videre proprie pertinet.*" ("Seeing belongs properly to the eyes.") "*Utimur autem hoc verbo etiam in ceteris sensibus cum eos ad cognoscendum intendimus.*" ("But we even use this word 'seeing' for the other senses when we devote them to cognizing.") "*Neque enim dicimus: audi quid rutilet; aut, olfac quam niteat; aut, gusta quam splendeat; aut, palpa quam fulgeat: videri enim dicuntur haec omnia.*" ("For we do not say 'Hear how it glows', or 'Smell how it glistens', or 'Taste how it shines', or 'Feel how it flashes'; but we say of each, '*See*'; we say that all this is seen.") "*Dicimus autem non solum, vide quid luceat, quod soli oculi sentire possunt.*" ("We not only say, 'See how that shines', when the eyes alone can perceive it;") "*sed etiam, vide quid sonet; vide quid oleat; vide quid sapiat; vide quam durum sit;*" ("but we even say, 'See how that sounds', 'See how that is scented', 'See how that tastes', 'See how hard that is'.") "*Ideoque generalis experientia sensuum concupiscentia sicut dictum est oculorum vocatur, quia videndi officium in quo primatum oculi tenent, etiam ceteri sensus sibi de similitudine usurpant, cum aliquid cognitionis explorant.*" ("Therefore the experience of the senses in general is designated

---

[1] '. . . nicht in der verengten Orientierung am Erkennen, das schon früh und in der griechischen Philosophie nicht zufällig aus der "Lust zu sehen" begriffen wird.' The earlier editions have '. . . am Erkennen, als welches schon früh . . .'

[2] While the sentence from Aristotle is usually translated, 'All men by nature desire to know', Heidegger takes εἰδέναι in its root meaning, 'to see', and connects ὀρέγονται (literally: 'reach out for') with 'Sorge' ('care').

[3] This sentence has been variously interpreted. The most usual version is: 'For thinking and being are the same.' Heidegger, however, goes back to the original meaning of νοεῖν as 'to perceive with the eyes'.

as the 'lust of the eyes'; for when the issue is one of knowing something, the other senses, by a certain resemblance, take to themselves the function of seeing—a function in which the eyes have priority.")

172   What is to be said about this tendency just to perceive? Which existential state of Dasein will become intelligible in the phenomenon of curiosity?

Being-in-the-world is proximally absorbed in the world of concern. This concern is guided by circumspection, which discovers the ready-to-hand and preserves it as thus discovered. Whenever we have something to contribute or perform, circumspection gives us the route for proceeding with it, the means of carrying it out, the right opportunity, the appropriate moment. Concern may come to rest in the sense of one's interrupting the performance and taking a rest, or it can do so by getting it finished. In rest, concern does not disappear; circumspection, however, becomes free and is no longer bound to the world of work. When we take a rest, care subsides into circumspection which has been set free. In the world of work, circumspective discovering has de-severing as the character of its Being. When circumspection has been set free, there is no longer anything ready-to-hand which we must concern ourselves with bringing close. But, as essentially de-severant, this circumspection provides itself with new possibilities of de-severing. This means that it tends away from what is most closely ready-to-hand, and into a far and alien world. Care becomes concern with the possibilities of seeing the 'world' merely as it *looks* while one tarries and takes a rest. Dasein seeks what is far away simply in order to bring it close to itself in the way it looks. Dasein lets itself be carried along [mitnehmen] solely by the looks of the world; in this kind of Being, it concerns itself with becoming rid of itself as Being-in-the-world and rid of its Being alongside that which, in the closest everyday manner, is ready-to-hand.

When curiosity has become free, however, it concerns itself with seeing, not in order to understand what is seen (that is, to come into a Being towards it) but *just* in order to see. It seeks novelty only in order to leap from it anew to another novelty. In this kind of seeing, that which is an issue for care does not lie in grasping something and being knowingly in the truth; it lies rather in its possibilities of abandoning itself to the world. Therefore curiosity is characterized by a specific way of *not tarrying* alongside what is closest. Consequently it does not seek the leisure of tarrying observantly, but rather seeks restlessness and the excitement of continual novelty and changing encounters. In not tarrying, curiosity is concerned with the constant possibility of *distraction*. Curiosity has nothing to do with observing entities and marvelling at them—θαυμάζειν. To be amazed to the point of not understanding is something in which it has no interest.

Rather it concerns itself with a kind of knowing, but just in order to have known. Both this *not tarrying* in the environment with which one concerns oneself, and this *distraction by* new possibilities, are constitutive items for curiosity; and upon these is founded the third essential characteristic of this phenomenon, which we call the character of "*never dwelling anywhere*" [*Aufenthaltslosigkeit*]. Curiosity is everywhere and nowhere. This mode of Being-in-the-world reveals a new kind of Being of everyday Dasein—a kind in which Dasein is constantly uprooting itself.

Idle talk controls even the ways in which one may be curious. It says what one "must" have read and seen. In being everywhere and nowhere, curiosity is delivered over to idle talk. These two everyday modes of Being for discourse and sight are not just present-at-hand side by side in their tendency to uproot, but *either* of these ways-to-be drags the *other* one with it. Curiosity, for which nothing is closed off, and idle talk, for which there is nothing that is not understood, provide themselves (that is, the Dasein which is in this manner [dem so seienden Dasein]) with the guarantee of a 'life' which, supposedly, is genuinely 'lively'. But with this supposition a third phenomenon now shows itself, by which the disclosedness of everyday Dasein is characterized.

¶ *37. Ambiguity*

When, in our everyday Being-with-one-another, we encounter the sort of thing which is accessible to everyone, and about which anyone can say anything, it soon becomes impossible to decide what is disclosed in a genuine understanding, and what is not. This ambiguity [Zweideutigkeit] extends not only to the world, but just as much to Being-with-one-another as such, and even to Dasein's Being towards itself.

Everything looks as if it were genuinely understood, genuinely taken hold of, genuinely spoken, though at bottom it is not; or else it does not look so, and yet at bottom it is. Ambiguity not only affects the way we avail ourselves of what is accessible for use and enjoyment, and the way we manage it; ambiguity has already established itself in the understanding as a potentiality-for-Being, and in the way Dasein projects itself and presents itself with possibilities.[1] Everyone is acquainted with what is up for discussion and what occurs,[2] and everyone discusses it; but everyone also knows already how to talk about what has to happen first— about what is not yet up for discussion but 'really' must be done. Already everyone has surmised and scented out in advance what Others have also surmised and scented out. This Being-on-the scent is of course based upon

---

[1] '. . . sondern sie hat sich schon im Verstehen als Seinkönnen, in der Art des Entwurfs und der Vorgabe von Möglichkeiten des Daseins festgesetzt.'
[2] '. . . was vorliegt und vorkommt . . .'

hearsay, for if anyone is genuinely 'on the scent' of anything, he does not
speak about it; and this is the most entangling way in which ambiguity
presents Dasein's possibilities so that they will already be stifled in their
power.[1]

Even supposing that what "*they*" have surmised and scented out should
some day be actually translated into deeds, ambiguity has already taken
care that interest in what has been Realised will promptly die away. Indeed
this interest persists, in a kind of curiosity and idle talk, only so long as
there is a possibility of a non-committal just-surmising-with-someone-else.
Being "in on it" with someone [das Mit-dabei-sein] when one is on the
scent, and so long as one is on it, precludes one's allegiance when what
has been surmised gets carried out. For in such a case Dasein is in every
case forced back on itself. Idle talk and curiosity lose their power, and are
already exacting their penalty.[2] When confronted with the carrying-
through of what "they" have surmised together, idle talk readily establishes that "they" "could have done that too"—for "they" have indeed
surmised it together. In the end, idle talk is even indignant that what it
has surmised and constantly demanded now *actually* happens. In that case,
indeed, the opportunity to keep on surmising has been snatched away.

But when Dasein goes in for something in the reticence of carrying it
through or even of genuinely breaking down on it, its time is a different
time and, as seen by the public, an essentially slower time than that of
idle talk, which 'lives at a faster rate'. Idle talk will thus long since have
gone on to something else which is currently the very newest thing. That
which was earlier surmise and has now been carried through, has come too
late if one looks at that which is newest. Idle talk and curiosity take care
in their ambiguity to ensure that what is genuinely and newly created is
out of date as soon as it emerges before the public. Such a new creation
can become free in its positive possibilities only if the idle talk which covers
it up has become ineffective, and if the 'common' interest has died away.

In the ambiguity of the way things have been publicly interpreted,
talking about things ahead of the game and making surmises about them
curiously, gets passed off as what is really happening, while taking action
and carrying something through get stamped as something merely subsequent and unimportant. Thus Dasein's understanding in the "they" is
constantly *going wrong* [*versieht sich*] in its projects, as regards the genuine
possibilities of Being. Dasein is always ambiguously 'there'—that is to say,
in that public disclosedness of Being-with-one-another where the loudest

---

[1] '. . . ist die verfänglichste Weise, in der die Zweideutigkeit Möglichkeiten des Daseins
vorgibt, um sie auch schon in ihrer Kraft zu ersticken.' (Notice that 'ihrer' may refer to
'Zweideutigkeit' or to 'Möglichkeiten'.)
[2] 'Und sie rächen sich auch schon.'

idle talk and the most ingenious curiosity keep 'things moving', where, in an everyday manner, everything (and at bottom nothing) is happening.

This ambiguity is always tossing to curiosity that which it seeks; and it gives idle talk the semblance of having everything decided in it.

But this kind of Being of the disclosedness of Being-in-the-world dominates also Being-with-one-another as such. The Other is proximally 'there' in terms of what "they" have heard about him, what "they" say in their talk about him, and what "they" know about him. Into primordial Being-with-one-another, idle talk first slips itself in between. Everyone keeps his eye on the Other first and next, watching how he will 175 comport himself and what he will say in reply. Being-with-one-another in the "they" is by no means an indifferent side-by-side-ness in which everything has been settled, but rather an intent, ambiguous watching of one another, a secret and reciprocal listening-in. Under the mask of "for-one-another", an "against-one-another" is in play.

In this connection, we must notice that ambiguity does not first arise from aiming explicitly at disguise or distortion, and that it is not something which the individual Dasein first conjures up. It is already implied in Being with one another, as *thrown* Being-with-one-another in a world. Publicly, however, it is quite hidden; and *"they"* will always defend themselves against this Interpretation of the kind of Being which belongs to the way things have been interpreted by the "they", lest it should prove correct. It would be a misunderstanding if we were to seek to have the explication of these phenomena confirmed by looking to the "they" for agreement.

The phenomena of idle talk, curiosity, and ambiguity have been set forth in such a manner as to indicate that they are already interconnected in their Being. We must now grasp in an existential-ontological manner the kind of Being which belongs to this interconnection. The basic kind of Being which belongs to everydayness is to be understood within the horizon of those structures of Dasein's Being which have been hitherto obtained.

¶ 38. Falling and Thrownness

Idle talk, curiosity and ambiguity characterize the way in which, in an everyday manner, Dasein is its 'there'—the disclosedness of Being-in-the-world. As definite existential characteristics, these are not present-at-hand in Dasein, but help to make up its Being. In these, and in the way they are interconnected in their Being, there is revealed a basic kind of Being which belongs to everydayness; we call this the *"falling"*[1] of Dasein.

---

[1] '*Verfallen*'. See our note 2, p. 42, H. 21 above, and note 1, p. 172, H. 134 above.

This term does not express any negative evaluation, but is used to signify that Dasein is proximally and for the most part *alongside* the 'world' of its concern. This "absorption in . . ." [Aufgehen bei . . .] has mostly the character of Being-lost in the publicness of the "they". Dasein has, in the first instance, fallen away [abgefallen] from itself as an authentic potentiality for Being its Self, and has fallen into the 'world'.[1] "Fallenness" into the 'world' means an absorption in Being-with-one-another, in so far as the latter is guided by idle talk, curiosity, and ambiguity. Through the Interpretation of falling, what we have called the "inauthenticity" of Dasein[xiii] may now be defined more precisely. On no account, however, do the terms "inauthentic" and "non-authentic" signify 'really not',[2] as if in this mode of Being, Dasein were altogether to lose its Being. "Inauthenticity" does not mean anything like Being-no-longer-in-the-world, but amounts rather to a quite distinctive kind of Being-in-the-world—the kind which is completely fascinated by the 'world' and by the Dasein-with of Others in the "they". Not-Being-its-self [Das Nicht-es-selbst-sein] functions as a *positive* possibility of that entity which, in its essential concern, is absorbed in a world. This kind of *not-Being* has to be conceived as that kind of Being which is closest to Dasein and in which Dasein maintains itself for the most part.

So neither must we take the fallenness of Dasein as a 'fall' from a purer and higher 'primal status'. Not only do we lack any experience of this ontically, but ontologically we lack any possibilities or clues for Interpreting it.

In falling, Dasein *itself* as factical Being-in-the-world, is something *from* which it has already fallen away. And it has not fallen into some entity which it comes upon for the first time in the course of its Being, or even one which it has not come upon at all; it has fallen into the *world*, which itself belongs to its Being. Falling is a definite existential characteristic of Dasein itself. It makes no assertion about Dasein as something present-at-hand, or about present-at-hand relations to entities from which Dasein 'is descended' or with which Dasein has subsequently wound up in some sort of *commercium*.

We would also misunderstand the ontologico-existential structure of falling[3] if we were to ascribe to it the sense of a bad and deplorable ontical property of which, perhaps, more advanced stages of human culture might be able to rid themselves.

---

[1] '. . . und an die "Welt" verfallen.' While we shall follow English idioms by translating 'an die "Welt"' as 'into the "world"' in contexts such as this, the preposition 'into' is hardly the correct one. The idea is rather that of falling *at* the world or collapsing *against* it.
[2] 'Un- und nichteigentlich, bedeutet aber keineswegs "eigentlich nicht" . . .'
[3] 'Die ontologisch-existenziale Struktur des Verfallens . . .' The words 'des Verfallens' do not appear in the earlier editions.

Neither in our first allusion to Being-in-the-world as Dasein's basic state, nor in our characterization of its constitutive structural items, did we go beyond an analysis of the *constitution* of this kind of Being and take note of its character as a phenomenon. We have indeed described concern and solicitude, as the possible basic kinds of Being-in. But we did not discuss the question of the everyday kind of Being of these ways in which one may be. We also showed that Being-in is something quite different from a mere confrontation, whether by way of observation or by way of action; that is, it is not the Being-present-at-hand-together of a subject and an Object. Nevertheless, it must still have seemed that Being-in-the-world has the function of a rigid framework, within which Dasein's possible ways of comporting itself towards its world run their course without touching the 'framework' itself as regards its Being. But this supposed 'framework' itself helps make up the kind of Being which is Dasein's. An *existential mode* of Being-in-the-world is documented in the phenomenon of falling.

Idle talk discloses to Dasein a Being towards its world, towards Others, and towards itself—a Being in which these are understood, but in a mode of groundless floating. Curiosity discloses everything and anything, yet in such a way that Being-in is everywhere and nowhere. Ambiguity hides nothing from Dasein's understanding, but only in order that Being-in-the-world should be suppressed in this uprooted "everywhere and nowhere".

By elucidating ontologically the kind of Being belonging to everyday Being-in-the-world as it shows through in these phenomena, we first arrive at an existentially adequate determination of Dasein's basic state. Which is the structure that shows us the 'movement' of falling?

Idle talk and the way things have been publicly interpreted (which idle talk includes) constitute themselves in Being-with-one-another. Idle talk is not something present-at-hand for itself within the world, as a product detached from Being-with-one-another. And it is just as far from letting itself be volatilized to something 'universal' which, because it belongs essentially to nobody, is 'really' nothing and occurs as 'Real' only in the individual Dasein which speaks. Idle talk is the kind of Being that belongs to Being-with-one-another itself; it does not first arise through certain circumstances which have effects upon Dasein 'from outside'. But if Dasein itself, in idle talk and in the way things have been publicly interpreted, presents to itself the possibility of losing itself in the "they" and falling into groundlessness, this tells us that Dasein prepares for itself a constant temptation towards falling. Being-in-the-world is in itself *tempting* [*versucherisch*].

Since the way in which things have been publicly interpreted has already become a temptation to itself in this manner, it holds Dasein fast in its fallenness. Idle talk and ambiguity, having seen everything, having understood everything, develop the supposition that Dasein's disclosedness, which is so available and so prevalent, can guarantee to Dasein that all the possibilities of its Being will be secure, genuine, and full. Through the self-certainty and decidedness of the "they", it gets spread abroad increasingly that there is no need of authentic understanding or the state-of-mind that goes with it. The supposition of the "they" that one is leading and sustaining a full and genuine 'life', brings Dasein a *tranquillity*, for which everything is 'in the best of order' and all doors are open. Falling Being-in-the-world, which tempts itself, is at the same time *tranquillizing* [*beruhigend*].

However, this tranquillity in inauthentic Being does not seduce one into stagnation and inactivity, but drives one into uninhibited 'hustle' ["Betriebs"]. Being-fallen into the 'world' does not now somehow come to rest. The tempting tranquillization *aggravates* the falling. With special regard to the interpretation of Dasein, the opinion may now arise that understanding the most alien cultures and 'synthesizing' them with one's own may lead to Dasein's becoming for the first time thoroughly and genuinely enlightened about itself. Versatile curiosity and restlessly "knowing it all" masquerade as a universal understanding of Dasein. But at bottom it remains indefinite *what* is really to be understood, and the question has not even been asked. Nor has it been understood that understanding itself is a potentiality-for-Being which must be made free in one's *ownmost* Dasein alone. When Dasein, tranquillized, and 'understanding' everything, thus compares itself with everything, it drifts along towards an alienation [Entfremdung] in which its ownmost potentiality-for-Being is hidden from it. Falling Being-in-the-world is not only tempting and tranquillizing; it is at the same time *alienating*.

Yet this alienation cannot mean that Dasein gets factically torn away from itself. On the contrary, this alienation drives it into a kind of Being which borders on the most exaggerated 'self-dissection', tempting itself with all possibilities of explanation, so that the very 'characterologies' and 'typologies' which it has brought about[1] are themselves already becoming something that cannot be surveyed at a glance. This alienation *closes off* from Dasein its authenticity and possibility, even if only the possibility of genuinely foundering. It does not, however, surrender Dasein to an entity which Dasein itself is not, but forces it into its

---

[1] '. . . die von ihr gezeitigten . . .' We follow the *difficilior lectio* of the earlier editions. The newer editions have '. . . . die von ihr gezeigten . . .' ('. . . which it has shown . . .'). See H. 304 below, and our note ad loc.

inauthenticity—into a possible kind of Being *of itself*. The alienation of falling—at once tempting and tranquillizing—leads by its own movement, to Dasein's getting *entangled* [*verfängt*] in itself.

The phenomena we have pointed out—temptation, tranquillizing, alienation and self-entangling (entanglement)—characterize the specific kind of Being which belongs to falling. This 'movement' of Dasein in its own Being, we call its "*downward plunge*" [*Absturz*]. Dasein plunges out of itself into itself, into the groundlessness and nullity of inauthentic everydayness. But this plunge remains hidden from Dasein by the way things have been publicly interpreted, so much so, indeed, that it gets interpreted as a way of 'ascending' and 'living concretely'.

This downward plunge into and within the groundlessness of the inauthentic Being of the "they", has a kind of motion which constantly tears the understanding away from the projecting of authentic possibilities, and into the tranquillized supposition that it possesses everything, or that everything is within its reach. Since the understanding is thus constantly torn away from authenticity and into the "they" (though always with a sham of authenticity), the movement of falling is characterized by *turbulence* [Wirbel].

Falling is not only existentially determinative for Being-in-the-world. 179 At the same time turbulence makes manifest that the thrownness which can obtrude itself upon Dasein in its state-of-mind, has the character of throwing and of movement. Thrownness is neither a 'fact that is finished' nor a Fact that is settled.[1] Dasein's facticity is such that *as long as* it is what it is, Dasein remains in the throw, and is sucked into the turbulence of the "they's" inauthenticity. Thrownness, in which facticity lets itself be seen phenomenally, belongs to Dasein, for which, in its Being, that very Being is an issue. Dasein exists factically.

But now that falling has been exhibited, have we not set forth a phenomenon which speaks directly *against* the definition we have used in indicating the formal idea of existence? Can Dasein be conceived as an entity for which, in its Being, its potentiality-for-Being is an *issue*, if this entity, in its very everydayness, *has lost itself*, and, in falling, 'lives' *away from itself*? But falling into the world would be phenomenal 'evidence' *against* the existentiality of Dasein only if Dasein were regarded as an isolated "I" or subject, as a self-point from which it moves away. In that case, the world would be an Object. Falling into the world would then have to be re-Interpreted ontologically as Being-present-at-hand in the manner of an entity within-the-world. If, however, we keep in mind

---

[1] 'Die Geworfenheit ist nicht nur nicht eine "fertige Tatsache", sondern auch nicht ein abgeschlossenes Faktum.'

that Dasein's Being is in the state of *Being-in-the-world*, as we have already pointed out, then it becomes manifest that falling, as a *kind of Being of this Being-in*, affords us rather the most elemental evidence *for* Dasein's existentiality. In falling, nothing other than our potentiality-for-Being-in-world is the issue, even if in the mode of inauthenticity. Dasein can fall only *because* Being-in-the-world understandingly with a state-of-mind is an issue for it. On the other hand, *authentic* existence is not something which floats above falling everydayness; existentially, it is only a modified way in which such everydayness is seized upon.

The phenomenon of falling does not give us something like a 'night view' of Dasein, a property which occurs ontically and may serve to round out the innocuous aspects of this entity. Falling reveals an *essential* ontological structure of Dasein itself. Far from determining its nocturnal side, it constitutes all Dasein's days in their everydayness.

It follows that our existential-ontological Interpretation makes no ontical assertion about the 'corruption of human Nature', not because the necessary evidence is lacking, but because the problematic of this Interpretation is *prior* to any assertion about corruption or incorruption. Falling is conceived ontologically as a kind of motion. Ontically, we have not decided whether man is 'drunk with sin' and in the *status corruptionis*, whether he walks in the *status integritatis*, or whether he finds himself in an intermediate stage, the *status gratiae*. But in so far as any faith or 'world view', makes any such assertions, and if it asserts anything about Dasein as Being-in-the-world, it must come back to the existential structures which we have set forth, provided that its assertions are to make a claim to *conceptual* understanding.

The leading question of this chapter has been about the Being of the "there". Our theme has been the ontological Constitution of the disclosedness which essentially belongs to Dasein. The Being of that disclosedness is constituted by states-of-mind, understanding, and discourse. Its everyday kind of Being is characterized by idle talk, curiosity, and ambiguity. These show us the movement of falling, with temptation, tranquillizing, alienation, and entanglement as its essential characteristics.

But with this analysis, the whole existential constitution of Dasein has been laid bare in its principal features, and we have obtained the phenomenal ground for a 'comprehensive' Interpretation of Dasein's Being as care.

VI

CARE AS THE BEING OF DASEIN

Carry through the primordial disclosure of D. as care

¶ 39. The Question of the Primordial Totality of Dasein's Structural Whole

BEING-IN-THE-WORLD is a structure which is primordially and constantly *whole*. In the preceding chapters (Division One, Chapters 2-5) this structure has been elucidated phenomenally as a whole, and also in its constitutive items, though always on this basis. The preliminary glance which we gave to the whole of this phenomenon in the beginning[1] has now lost the emptiness of our first general sketch of it. To be sure, the constitution of the structural whole and its everyday kind of Being, is phenomenally so *manifold* that it can easily obstruct our looking at the whole as such phenomenologically in a way which is *unified*. But we may look at it more freely and our unified view of it may be held in readiness more securely if we now raise the question towards which we have been working in our preparatory fundamental analysis of Dasein in general: *"how is the totality of that structural whole which we have pointed out to be defined in an existential-ontological manner?"*

181

Dasein exists factically. We shall inquire whether existentiality and facticity have an ontological unity, or whether facticity belongs essentially to existentiality. Because Dasein essentially has a state-of-mind belonging to it, Dasein has a kind of Being in which it is brought before itself and becomes disclosed to itself in its thrownness. But thrownness, as a kind of Being, belongs to an entity which in each case *is* its possibilities, and is them in such a way that it understands itself in these possibilities and in terms of them, projecting itself upon them. Being alongside the ready-to-hand, belongs just as primordially to Being-in-the-world as does Being-with Others; and Being-in-the-world is in each case for the sake of itself. The Self, however, is proximally and for the most part inauthentic, the they-self. Being-in-the-world is always fallen. Accordingly *Dasein's* *"average everydayness"* can be defined as *"Being-in-the-world which is falling and disclosed, thrown and projecting, and for which its ownmost potentiality-for-Being is an issue, both in its Being alongside the 'world' and in its Being-with Others"*.

QUESTION. Can we succeed in grasping this structural whole of Dasein's everydayness in its totality? Can Dasein's Being be brought out in such a unitary manner that in terms of it the essential equiprimordiality of the structures we have pointed out, as well as their existential possibilities of modification, will become intelligible? Does our present approach *via* the existential analytic provide us an avenue for arriving at this Being phenomenally?

To put it negatively, it is beyond question that the totality of the structural whole is not to be reached by building it up out of elements. For this we would need an architect's plan. The Being of Dasein, upon which the structural whole as such is ontologically supported, becomes ANSWER accessible to us when we look all the way *through* this whole *to a single* primordially unitary phenomenon which is already in this whole in such a way that it provides the ontological foundation for each structural item in its structural possibility. Thus we cannot Interpret this 'comprehensively' by a process of gathering up what we have hitherto gained and taking it all together. The question of Dasein's basic existential character is essentially different from that of the Being of something present-at-hand. Our everyday environmental experiencing [Erfahren], which remains directed both ontically and ontologically towards entities within-the-world, is not the sort of thing which can present Dasein in an ontically primordial manner for ontological analysis. Similarly our immanent per-
182 ception of Experiences [Erlebnissen] fails to provide a clue which is ontologically adequate. On the other hand, Dasein's Being is not be to deduced from an idea of man. Does the Interpretation of Dasein which we have hitherto given permit us to infer what Dasein, *from its own standpoint*, demands as the only appropriate ontico-ontological way of access to itself?

An understanding of Being belongs to Dasein's ontological structure. As something that is [Seiend], it is disclosed to itself in its Being. The kind of Being which belongs to this disclosedness is constituted by state-of-mind and understanding. Is there in Dasein an understanding state-of-mind in which Dasein has been disclosed to itself in some distinctive way?

If the existential analytic of Dasein is to retain clarity in principle as to its function in fundamental ontology, then in order to master its provisional task of exhibiting Dasein's Being, it must seek for one of the *most far-reaching* and *most primordial* possibilities of disclosure—one that lies in Dasein itself. The way of disclosure in which Dasein brings itself before itself must be such that in it Dasein becomes accessible as *simplified* in a certain manner. With what is thus disclosed, the structural totality of the Being we seek must then come to light in an elemental way.

As a state-of-mind which will satisfy these methodological requirements, the phenemonon of *anxiety*[1] will be made basic for our analysis. In working out this basic state-of-mind and characterizing ontologically what is disclosed in it as such, we shall take the phenomenon of falling as our point of departure, and distinguish anxiety from the kindred phenomenon of fear, which we have analysed earlier. As one of Dasein's possibilities of Being, anxiety—together with Dasein itself as disclosed in it—provides the phenomenal basis for explicitly grasping Dasein's primordial totality of Being. Dasein's Being reveals itself as *care.* If we are to work out this basic existential phenomenon, we must distinguish it from phenomena which might be proximally identified with care, such as will, wish, addiction, and urge.[2] Care cannot be derived from these, since they themselves are founded upon it.

Like every ontological analysis, the ontological Interpretation of Dasein as care, with whatever we may gain from such an Interpretation, lies far from what is accessible to the pre-ontological understanding of Being or even to our ontical acquaintance with entities. It is not surprising that when the common understanding has regard to that with which it has only ontical familiarity, that which is known ontologically seems rather strange to it. In spite of this, even the ontical approach with which we   183 have tried to Interpret Dasein ontologically as care, may appear far-fetched and theoretically contrived, to say nothing of the act of violence one might discern in our setting aside the confirmed traditional definition of "man". Accordingly our existential Interpretation of Dasein as care requires pre-ontological confirmation. This lies in demonstrating that no sooner has Dasein expressed anything about itself to itself, than it has already interpreted itself as *care* (*cura*), even though it has done so only pre-ontologically.

The analytic of Dasein, which is proceeding towards the phenomenon of care, is to prepare the way for the problematic of fundamental ontology— *the question of the meaning of Being in general.* In order that we may turn our glance explicitly upon this in the light of what we have gained, and go beyond the special task of an existentially *a priori* anthropology, we must look back and get a more penetrating grasp of the phenomena which are most intimately connected with our leading question—the question of Being. These phenomena are those very ways of Being which we have been hitherto explaining: readiness-to-hand and presence-at-hand, as attributes

entities Not Dasein (handwritten margin note)

---

[1] 'Angst'. While this word has generally been translated as 'anxiety' in the post-Freudian psychological literature, it appears as 'dread' in the translations of Kierkegaard and in a number of discussions of Heidegger. In some ways 'uneasiness' or '*malaise*' would be more appropriate still.

[2] '. . . Wille, Wunsch, Hang und Drang.' For further discussion see H. 194 ff. below.

Reality (handwritten)

of entities within-the-world whose character is not that of Dasein. Because the ontological problematic of Being has heretofore been understood primarily in the sense of presence-at-hand ('Reality', 'world-actuality'), while the nature of Dasein's Being has remained ontologically undetermined, we need to discuss the ontological interconnections of care, worldhood, readiness-to-hand, and presence-at-hand (Reality). This will lead to a more precise characterization of the concept of *Reality* in the context of a discussion of the epistemological questions oriented by this idea which have been raised in realism and idealism.

Entities *are*, quite independently of the experience by which they are disclosed, the acquaintance in which they are discovered, and the grasping in which their nature is ascertained. But Being 'is' only in the understanding of those entities to whose Being something like an understanding of Being belongs. Hence Being can be something unconceptualized, but it never completely fails to be understood. In ontological problematics *Being and truth* have, from time immemorial, been brought together if not entirely identified. This is evidence that there is a necessary connecton between Being and understanding, even if it may perhaps be hidden in its primordial grounds. If we are to give an adequate. preparation for the question of Being, the phenomenon of *truth* must be ontologically clarified. This will be accomplished in the first instance on the basis of what we have gained in our foregoing Interpretation, in connection with the phenomena of disclosedness and discoveredness, interpretation and assertion.

184   Thus our preparatory fundamental analysis of Dasein will conclude with the following themes: the basic state-of-mind of anxiety as a distinctive way in which Dasein is disclosed (Section 40); Dasein's Being as care (Section 41); the confirmation of the existential Interpretation of Dasein as care in terms of Dasein's pre-ontological way of interpreting itself (Section 42); Dasein, worldhood, and Reality (Section 43); Dasein, disclosedness, and truth (Section 44).

¶ *40. The Basic State-of-mind of Anxiety as a Distinctive Way in which Dasein is Disclosed*

One of Dasein's possibilities of Being is to give us ontical 'information' about Dasein itself as an entity. Such information is possible only in that disclosedness which belongs to Dasein and which is grounded in state-of-mind and understanding. How far is anxiety a state-of-mind which is distinctive? How is it that in anxiety Dasein gets brought before itself through its own Being, so that we can define phenomenologically the character of thé entity disclosed in anxiety, and define it as such in its Being, or make adequate preparations for doing so?

falling

Since our aim is to proceed towards the Being of the totality of the structural whole, we shall take as our point of departure the concrete analyses of falling which we have just carried through. Dasein's absorption in the "they" and its absorption in the 'world' of its concern, make manifest something like a *fleeing* of Dasein in the face of itself—of itself as an authentic potentiality-for-Being-its-Self.[1] This phenomenon of Dasein's fleeing *in the face of itself* and in the face of its authenticity, seems at least a suitable phenomenal basis for the following investigation. But to bring itself face to face with itself, is precisely what Dasein does *not* do when it thus flees. It turns *away from* itself in accordance with its ownmost inertia [Zug] of falling. In investigating such phenomena, however, we must be careful not to confuse ontico-existentiell characterization with ontologico-existential Interpretation nor may we overlook the positive phenomenal bases provided for this Interpretation by such a characterization.

From an existentiell point of view, the authenticity of Being-one's-Self has of course been closed off and thrust aside in falling; but to be thus closed off is merely the *privation* of a disclosedness which manifests itself phenomenally in the fact that Dasein's fleeing is a fleeing *in the face of itself.* That in the face of which Dasein flees, is precisely what Dasein comes up 'behind'.[2] Only to the extent that Dasein has been brought before itself in an ontologically essential manner through whatever disclosedness belongs to it, *can* it flee *in the face of* that in the face of which it flees. To be sure, that in the face of which it flees is *not grasped* in thus turning away [Abkehr] in falling; nor is it experienced even in turning thither [Hinkehr]. Rather, in turning away *from* it, it is disclosed 'there'. This existentiell-ontical turning-away, by reason of its character as a disclosure, makes it phenomenally possible to grasp existential-ontologically that in the face of which Dasein flees, and to grasp it as such. Within the ontical 'away-from' which such turning-away implies, that in the face of which Dasein flees can be understood and conceptualized by 'turning thither' in a way which is phenomenologically Interpretative.

the Wovor of anxiety

185

So in orienting our analysis by the phenomenon of falling, we are not in principle condemned to be without any prospect of learning something ontologically about the Dasein disclosed in that phenomenon. On the contrary, here, least of all, has our Interpretation been surrendered to an artificial way in which Dasein grasps itself; it merely carries out the

---

[1] '. . . offenbart so etwas wie eine *Flucht* des Daseins vor ihm selbst als eigentlichem Selbst-sein-können.' The point of this paragraph is that if we are to study the totality of Dasein, Dasein must be brought '*before* itself' or 'face to face with itself' ('*vor* es selbst'); and the fact that Dasein flees '*from* itself' or 'in the face of itself' ('*vor ihm selbst*'), which may seem at first to lead us off the track, is actually very germane to our inquiry.

[2] 'Im Wovor der Flucht kommt das Dasein gerade "hinter" ihm her.'

explication of what Dasein itself ontically discloses. The possibility of proceeding towards Dasein's Being by going along with it and following it up [Mit- und Nachgehen] Interpretatively with an understanding and the state-of-mind that goes with it, is the greater, the more primordial is that phenomenon which functions methodologically as a disclosive state-of-mind. It might be contended that anxiety performs some such function.

We are not entirely unprepared for the analysis of anxiety. Of course it still remains obscure how this is connected ontologically with fear. Obviously these are kindred phenomena. This is betokened by the fact that for the most part they have not been distinguished from one another: that which is fear, gets designated as "anxiety", while that which has the character of anxiety, gets called "fear". We shall try to proceed towards the phenomenon of anxiety step by step.

Dasein's falling into the "they" and the 'world' of its concern, is what we have called a 'fleeing' in the face of itself. But one is not necessarily fleeing whenever one shrinks back in the face of something or turns away from it. Shrinking back in the face of what fear discloses—in the face of something threatening—is founded upon fear; and this shrinking back has the character of fleeing. Our Interpretation of fear as a state-of-mind has shown that in each case that in the face of which we fear is a detrimental entity within-the-world which comes from some definite region but is close by and is bringing itself close, and yet might stay away. In falling, Dasein turns away from itself. That in the face of which it thus shrinks back must, in any case, be an entity with the character of threatening; yet this entity has the same kind of Being as the one that shrinks back: it is Dasein itself. That in the face of which it thus shrinks back cannot be taken as something 'fearsome', for anything 'fearsome' is always encountered as an entity within-the-world. The only threatening which can be 'fearsome' and which gets discovered in fear, always comes from entities within-the-world.

Thus the turning-away of falling is not a fleeing that is founded upon a fear of entities within-the-world. Fleeing that is so grounded is still less a character of this turning-away, when what this turning-away does is precisely to *turn thither* towards entities within-the-world by absorbing itself in them. *The turning-away of falling is grounded rather in anxiety, which in turn is what first makes fear possible.*

To understand this talk about Dasein's fleeing in the face of itself in falling, we must recall that Being-in-the-world is a basic state of Dasein. *That in the face of which one has anxiety [das Wovor der Angst] is Being-in-the-world as such.* What is the difference phenomenally between that in the face of which anxiety is anxious [sich ängstet] and that in the face of

186

which fear is afraid? That in the face of which one has anxiety is not an entity within-the-world. Thus it is essentially incapable of having an involvement. This threatening does not have the character of a definite detrimentality which reaches what is threatened, and which reaches it with definite regard to a special factical potentiality-for-Being. That in the face of which one is anxious is completely indefinite. Not only does this indefiniteness leave factically undecided which entity within-the-world is threatening us, but it also tells us that entities within-the-world are not 'relevant' at all. Nothing which is ready-to-hand or present-at-hand within the world functions as that in the face of which anxiety is anxious. Here the totality of involvements of the ready-to-hand and the present-at-hand discovered within-the-world, is, as such, of no consequence; it collapses into itself; the world has the character of completely lacking significance. In anxiety one does not encounter this thing or that thing which, as something threatening, must have an involvement.

Accordingly, when something threatening brings itself close, anxiety does not 'see' any definite 'here' or 'yonder' from which it comes. That in the face of which one has anxiety is characterized by the fact that what threatens is *nowhere*. Anxiety 'does not know' what that in the face of which it is anxious is. 'Nowhere', however, does not signify nothing: this is where any region lies, and there too lies any disclosedness of the world for essentially spatial Being-in. Therefore that which threatens cannot bring itself close from a definite direction within what is close by; it is already 'there', and yet nowhere; it is so close that it is oppressive and stifles one's breath, and yet it is nowhere.

In that in the face of which one has anxiety, the 'It is nothing and no-where' becomes manifest. The obstinacy of the "nothing and nowhere within-the-world" means as a phenomenon that *the world as such is that in* 187 *the face of which one has anxiety*. The utter insignificance which makes itself known in the "nothing and nowhere", does not signify that the world is absent, but tells us that entities within-the-world are of so little import-ance in themselves that on the basis of this *insignificance* of what is within-the-world, the world in its worldhood is all that still obtrudes itself.

What oppresses us is not this or that, nor is it the summation of every-thing present-at-hand; it is rather the *possibility* of the ready-to-hand in general; that is to say, it is the world itself. When anxiety has subsided, then in our everyday way of talking we are accustomed to say that 'it was really nothing'. And *what* it was, indeed, does get reached ontically by such a way of talking. Everyday discourse tends towards concerning itself with the ready-to-hand and talking about it. That in the face of which anxiety is anxious is nothing ready-to-hand within-the-world. But this "nothing ready-to-hand", which only our everyday circumspective discourse understands, is not totally nothing.[1] The "nothing" of readiness-to-hand is grounded in the most primordial 'something'—in the *world.* Ontologically, however, the world belongs essentially to Dasein's Being as Being-in-the-world. So if the "nothing"—that is, the world as such—exhibits itself as that in the face of which one has anxiety, this means that *Being-in-the-world itself is that in the face of which anxiety is anxious.*

Being-anxious discloses, primordially and directly, the world as world. It is not the case, say, that the world first gets thought of by deliberating about it, just by itself, without regard for the entities within-the-world, and that, in the face of this world, anxiety then arises; what is rather the case is that the *world as world* is disclosed first and foremost by anxiety, as a mode of state-of-mind. This does not signify, however, that in anxiety the worldhood of the world gets conceptualized.

Anxiety is not only anxiety in the face of something, but, as a state-of-mind, it is also *anxiety about* something. That which anxiety is profoundly anxious [sich abängstet] about is not a *definite* kind of Being for Dasein or a *definite* possibility for it. Indeed the threat itself is indefinite, and therefore cannot penetrate threateningly to this or that factically concrete potentiality-for-Being. That which anxiety is anxious about is Being-in-the-world itself. In anxiety what is environmentally ready-to-hand sinks away, and so, in general, do entities within-the-world. The 'world' can offer nothing more, and neither can the Dasein-with of Others. Anxiety thus takes away from Dasein the possibility of understanding itself, as it falls, in terms of the 'world' and the way things have been publicly interpreted. Anxiety throws Dasein back upon that which it is anxious about —its authentic potentiality-for-Being-in-the-world. Anxiety individualizes Dasein for its ownmost Being-in-the-world, which as something that understands, projects itself essentially upon possibilities. Therefore, with that

188 which it is anxious about, anxiety discloses Dasein *as Being-possible,* and indeed as the only kind of thing which it can be of its own accord as something individualized in individualization [vereinzeltes in der Vereinzelung].

Anxiety makes manifest in Dasein its *Being towards* its ownmost potentiality-for-Being—that is, its *Being-free for* the freedom of choosing itself and taking hold of itself. Anxiety brings Dasein face to face with its *Being-free for* (*propensio in . . .*) the authenticity of its Being, and for this authenticity as a possibility which it always is.[2] But at the same time, this is the

[1] 'Allein dieses Nichts von Zuhandenem, das die alltägliche umsichtige Rede einzig versteht, ist kein totales Nichts.' This sentence is grammatically ambiguous.
[2] 'Die Angst bringt das Dasein vor sein *Freisein für* . . . (*propensio in . . .*) die Eigentlichkeit seines Seins als Möglichkeit, die es immer schon ist.'

Being to which Dasein as Being-in-the-world has been delivered over. That *about which* anxiety is anxious reveals itself as that *in the face of which* it is anxious—namely, Being-in-the-world. The selfsameness of that in the face of which and that about which one has anxiety, extends even to anxiousness [Sichängsten] itself. For, as a state-of-mind, anxiousness is a basic kind of Being-in-the-world. *Here the disclosure and the disclosed are existentially selfsame in such a way that in the latter the world has been disclosed as world, and Being-in has been disclosed as a potentiality-for-Being which is individualized, pure, and thrown; this makes it plain that with the phenomenon of anxiety a distinctive state-of-mind has become a theme for Interpretation.* Anxiety individualizes Dasein and thus discloses it as '*solus ipse*'. But this existential 'solipsism' is so far from the displacement of putting an isolated subject-Thing into the innocuous emptiness of a worldless occurring, that in an extreme sense what it does is precisely to bring Dasein face to face with its world as world, and thus bring it face to face with itself as Being-in-the-world.

Again everyday discourse and the everyday interpretation of Dasein furnish our most unbiased evidence that anxiety as a basic state-of-mind is disclosive in the manner we have shown. As we have said earlier, a state-of-mind makes manifest 'how one is'. In anxiety one feels '*uncanny*'.[1] Here the peculiar indefiniteness of that which Dasein finds itself alongside in anxiety, comes proximally to expression: the "nothing and nowhere". But here "uncanniness" also means "not-being-at-home" [das Nicht-zuhause-sein]. In our first indication of the phenomenal character of Dasein's basic state and in our clarification of the existential meaning of "Being-in" as distinguished from the categorial signification of 'insideness', Being-in was defined as "residing alongside . . .", "Being-familiar with . . .".[ii] This character of Being-in was then brought to view more concretely through the everyday publicness of the "they", which brings tranquillized self-assurance—'Being-at-home', with all its obviousness—into the average everydayness of Dasein.[iii] On the other hand, as Dasein falls, anxiety brings it back from its absorption in the 'world'. Everyday familiarity collapses. Dasein has been individualized, but individualized *as* Being-in-the-world. Being-in enters into the existential 'mode' of the "*not-at-home*". Nothing else is meant by our talk about 'uncanniness'.

By this time we can see phenomenally what falling, as fleeing, flees in the face of. It does not flee *in the face of* entities within-the-world; these are precisely what it flees *towards*—as entities alongside which our concern,

189

---

[1] '*Befindlichkeit, so wurde früher gesagt, macht offenbar, "wie einem ist". In der Angst ist einem "unheimlich".*' The reference is presumably to H. 134 above. While 'unheimlich' is here translated as 'uncanny', it means more literally 'unhomelike', as the author proceeds to point out.

lost in the "they", can dwell in tranquillized familiarity. When in falling we flee *into* the "at-home" of publicness, we flee *in the face of* the "not-at-home"; that is, we flee in the face of the uncanniness which lies in Dasein —in Dasein as thrown Being-in-the-world, which has been delivered over to itself in its Being. This uncanniness pursues Dasein constantly, and is a threat to its everyday lostness in the "they", though not explicitly. This threat can go together factically with complete assurance and self-sufficiency in one's everyday concern. Anxiety can arise in the most innocuous Situations. Nor does it have any need for darkness, in which it is commonly easier for one to feel uncanny. In the dark there is emphatically 'nothing' to see, though the very world itself is *still* 'there', and 'there' *more obtrusively.*

If we Interpret Dasein's uncanniness from an existential-ontological point of view as a threat which reaches Dasein itself and which comes from Dasein itself, we are not contending that in factical anxiety too it has always been understood in this sense. When Dasein "understands" uncanniness in the everyday manner, it does so by turning away from it in falling; in this turning-away, the "not-at-home" gets 'dimmed down'. Yet the everydayness of this fleeing shows phenomenally that anxiety, as a basic state-of-mind, belongs to Dasein's essential state of Being-in-the-world, which, as one that is existential, is never present-at-hand but *is* itself always in a mode of factical Being-there[1]—that is, in the mode of a state-of-mind. That kind of Being-in-the-world which is tranquillized and familiar is a mode of Dasein's uncanniness, not the reverse. *From an existential-ontological point of view, the "not-at-home" must be conceived as the more primordial phenomenon.*

And only because anxiety is always latent in Being-in-the-world, can such Being-in-the-world, as Being which is alongside the 'world' and which is concernful in its state-of-mind, ever be afraid. Fear is anxiety, fallen into the 'world', inauthentic, and, as such, hidden from itself.

After all, the mood of uncanniness remains, factically, something for which we mostly have no existentiell understanding. Moreover, under the ascendancy of falling and publicness, 'real' anxiety is rare. Anxiety is often conditioned by 'physiological' factors. This fact, in its facticity, is a problem *ontologically*, not merely with regard to its ontical causation and course of development. Only because Dasein is anxious in the very depths of its Being, does it become possible for anxiety to be elicited physiologically.

Even rarer than the existentiell Fact of "real" anxiety are attempts to

---

[1] Here we follow the earlier editions in reading 'Da-seins'. In the later editions the hyphen appears ambiguously at the end of a line.

Interpret this phenomenon according to the principles of its existential-ontological Constitution and function. The reasons for this lie partly in the general neglect of the existential analytic of Dasein, but more particularly in a failure to recognize the phenomenon of state-of-mind[iv]. Yet the factical rarity of anxiety as a phenomenon cannot deprive it of its fitness to take over a methodological function *in principle* for the existential analytic. On the contrary, the rarity of the phenomenon is an index that Dasein, which for the most part remains concealed from itself in its authenticity because of the way in which things have been publicly interpreted by the "they", becomes disclosable in a primordial sense in this basic state-of-mind.

Of course it is essential to every state-of-mind that in each case Being-in-the-world should be fully disclosed in all those items which are constitutive for it—world, Being-in, Self. But in anxiety there lies the possibility of a disclosure which is quite distinctive; for anxiety individualizes. 191 This individualization brings Dasein back from its falling, and makes manifest to it that authenticity and inauthenticity are possibilities of its Being. These basic possibilities of Dasein (and Dasein is in each case mine) show themselves in anxiety as they are in themselves—undisguised by entities within-the-world, to which, proximally and for the most part, Dasein clings.

How far has this existential Interpretation of anxiety arrived at a phenomenal basis for answering the guiding question of the Being of the totality of Dasein's structural whole?

¶ *41. Dasein's Being as Care*

Since our aim is to grasp the totality of this structural whole ontologically, we must first ask whether the phenomenon of anxiety and that which is disclosed in it, can give us the whole of Dasein in a way which is phenomenally equiprimordial, and whether they can do so in such a manner that if we look searchingly at this totality, our view of it will be filled in by what has thus been given us. The entire stock of what lies therein may be counted up formally and recorded: anxiousness as a state-of-mind is a way of Being-in-the-world; that in the face of which we have anxiety is thrown Being-in-the-world; that which we have anxiety about is our potentiality-for-Being-in-the-world. Thus the entire phenomenon of anxiety shows Dasein as factically existing Being-in-the-world. The fundamental ontological characteristics of this entity are existentiality, facticity, and Being-fallen. These existential characteristics are not pieces belonging to something composite, one of which might sometimes be missing; but there is woven together in them a primordial context which makes up that totality of the structural whole which we are seeking. In the unity of those characteristics of Dasein's Being which we have mentioned, this Being becomes something which it is possible for us to grasp as such ontologically. How is this unity itself to be characterized?

Dasein is an entity for which, in its Being, that Being is an issue. The phrase 'is an issue' has been made plain in the state-of-Being of understanding—of understanding as self-projective Being towards its ownmost potentiality-for-Being. This potentiality is that for the sake of which any Dasein is as it is. In each case Dasein has already compared itself, in its Being, with a possibility of itself. Being-free *for* one's ownmost potentiality-for-Being, and therewith for the possibility of authenticity and inauthenticity, is shown, with a primordial, elemental concreteness, in anxiety. But ontologically, Being towards one's ownmost potentiality-for-Being means that in each case Dasein is already *ahead* of itself [ihm selbst . . . vorweg] in its Being. Dasein is always 'beyond itself' ["über sich hinaus"], not as a way of behaving towards other entities which it is *not*, but as Being towards the potentiality-for-Being which it is itself. This structure of Being, which belongs to the essential 'is an issue', we shall denote as Dasein's *"Being-ahead-of-itself"*.

But this structure pertains to the whole of Dasein's constitution. "Being-ahead-of-itself" does not signify anything like an isolated tendency in a worldless 'subject', but characterizes Being-in-the-world. To Being-in-the-world, however, belongs the fact that it has been delivered over to itself—that it has in each case already been thrown *into a world*. The abandonment of Dasein to itself is shown with primordial concreteness in anxiety. "Being-ahead-of-itself" means, if we grasp it more fully, *"ahead-of-itself-in-already-being-in-a-world"*. As soon as this essentially unitary structure is seen as a phenomenon, what we have set forth earlier in our analysis of worldhood also becomes plain. The upshot of that analysis was that the referential totality of significance (which as such is constitutive for worldhood) has been 'tied up' with a "for-the-sake-of-which". The fact that this referential totality of the manifold relations of the 'in-order-to' has been bound up with that which is an issue for Dasein, does not signify that a 'world' of Objects which is present-at-hand has been welded together with a subject. It is rather the phenomenal expression of the fact that the constitution of Dasein, whose totality is now brought out explicitly as ahead-of-itself-in-Being-already-in . . ., is primordially a whole. To put it otherwise, existing is always factical. Existentiality is essentially determined by facticity.

Furthermore, Dasein's factical existing is not only generally and without further differentiation a thrown potentiality-for-Being-in-the-world; it is always also absorbed in the world of its concern. In this falling Being-alongside . . ., fleeing in the face of uncanniness (which for the most part remains concealed with latent anxiety, since the publicness of the "they" suppresses everything unfamiliar), announces itself, whether it does so explicitly or not, and whether it is understood or not. Ahead-of-itself-Being-already-in-a-world essentially includes one's falling and one's *Being alongside* those things ready-to-hand within-the-world with which one concerns oneself.

The formally existential totality of Dasein's ontological structural whole must therefore be grasped in the following structure: the Being of Dasein means ahead-of-itself-Being-already-in-(the-world) as Being-alongside (entities encountered within-the-world). This Being fills in the significa-tion of the term *"care"* [*Sorge*], which is used in a purely ontologico-existential manner. From this signification every tendency of Being which one might have in mind ontically, such as worry [Besorgnis] or carefreeness [Sorglosigkeit], is ruled out.

Because Being-in-the-world is essentially care, Being-alongside the ready-to-hand could be taken in our previous analyses as *concern*, and Being with the Dasein-with of Others as we encounter it within-the-world could be taken as *solicitude*.[1] Being-alongside something is concern, because it is defined as a way of Being-in by its basic structure—care. Care does not characterize just existentiality, let us say, as detached from facticity and falling; on the contrary, it embraces the unity of these ways in which Being may be characterized. So neither does "care" stand primarily and exclusively for an isolated attitude of the "I" towards itself. If one were to construct the expression 'care for oneself' ["Selbst-sorge"], following the analogy of "concern" [Besorgen] and "solicitude" [Fürsorge], this would be a tautology. "Care" cannot stand for some special attitude towards the Self; for the Self has already been character-ized ontologically by "Being-ahead-of-itself", a characteristic in which the other two items in the structure of care—Being-already-in . . . and Being-alongside . . .—have been *posited as well* [*mitgesetzt*].

In Being-ahead-of-oneself as Being towards one's ownmost potentiality-for-Being, lies the existential-ontological condition for the possibility of *Being-free* for authentic existentiell possibilities. For the sake of its potenti-ality-for-Being, any Dasein is as it factically is. But to the extent that this Being towards its potentiality-for-Being is itself characterized by freedom, Dasein *can* comport itself towards its possibilities, even *unwillingly*; it *can* be inauthentically; and factically it is inauthentically, proximally and for the most part. The authentic "for-the-sake-of-which" has not been taken

193

[1] Cf. H. 121 and 131 above.

hold of; the projection of one's own potentiality-for-Being has been abandoned to the disposal of the "they". Thus when we speak of "Being-ahead-of-itself", the 'itself' which we have in mind is in each case the Self in the sense of the they-self. Even in inauthenticity Dasein remains essentially ahead of itself, just as Dasein's fleeing in the face of itself as it falls, still shows that it has the state-of-Being of an entity *for which its Being is an issue.*

Care, as a primordial structural totality, lies 'before' ["vor"] every factical 'attitude' and 'situation' of Dasein, and it does so existentially *a priori*; this means that it always lies *in* them. So this phenomenon by no means expresses a priority of the 'practical' attitude over the theoretical. When we ascertain something present-at-hand by merely beholding it, this activity has the character of care just as much as does a 'political action' or taking a rest and enjoying oneself. 'Theory' and 'practice' are possibilities of Being for an entity whose Being must be defined as "care".

The phenomenon of care in its totality is essentially something that cannot be torn asunder; so any attempts to trace it back to special acts or drives like willing and wishing or urge and addiction,[1] or to construct it out of these, will be unsuccessful.

Willing and wishing are rooted with ontological necessity in Dasein as care; they are not just ontologically undifferentiated Experiences occurring in a 'stream' which is completely indefinite with regard to the meaning of its Being. This is no less the case with urge and addiction. These too are grounded in care so far as they can be exhibited in Dasein at all. This does not prevent them from being ontologically constitutive even for entities that merely 'live'. But the basic ontological state of 'living' is a problem in its own right and can be tackled only reductively and privatively in terms of the ontology of Dasein.

Care is ontologically 'earlier' than the phenomena we have just mentioned, which admittedly can, within certain limits, always be 'described' appropriately without our needing to have the full ontological horizon visible, or even to be familiar with it at all. From the standpoint of our present investigation in fundamental ontology, which aspires neither to a thematically complete ontology of Dasein nor even to a concrete anthropology, it must suffice to suggest how these phenomena are grounded existentially in care.

That very potentiality-for-Being for the sake of which Dasein is, has Being-in-the-world as its kind of Being. Thus it implies ontologically a relation to entities within-the-world. Care is always concern and solicitude,

---

[1] '... besondere Akte oder Triebe wie Wollen und Wünschen oder Drang und Hang...' Cf. H. 182.

even if only privatively. In willing, an entity which is understood—that is, one which has been projected upon its possibility—gets seized upon, either as something with which one may concern oneself, or as something which is to be brought into its Being through solicitude. *Hence, to any willing there belongs something willed*, which has already made itself definite in terms of a "for-the-sake-of-which". If willing is to be possible ontologically, the following items are constitutive for it: (1) the prior disclosedness of the "for-the-sake-of-which" in general (Being-ahead-of-itself); (2) the disclosedness of something with which one can concern oneself (the world as the "wherein" of Being-already);[1] (3) Dasein's projection of itself understandingly upon a potentiality-for-Being towards a possibility of the entity 'willed'. In the phenomenon of willing, the underlying totality of care shows through.

As something factical, Dasein's projection of itself understandingly is in each case already alongside a world that has been discovered. From this world it takes its possibilities, and it does so first in accordance with the way things have been interpreted by the "they". This interpretation has already restricted the possible options of choice to what lies within the range of the familiar, the attainable, the respectable—that which is fitting and proper. This levelling off of Dasein's possibilities to what is proximally at its everyday disposal also results in a dimming down of the possible as such. The average everydayness of concern becomes blind to its possibilities, and tranquillizes itself with that which is merely 'actual'. This tranquillizing does not rule out a high degree of diligence in one's concern, but arouses it. In this case no positive new possibilities are willed, but that which is at one's disposal becomes 'tactically' altered in such a way that there is a semblance of something happening.

All the same, this tranquillized 'willing' under the guidance of the "they", does not signify that one's Being towards one's potentiality-for-Being has been extinguished, but only that it has been modified. In such a case, one's Being towards possibilities shows itself for the most part as mere *wishing*. In the wish Dasein projects its Being upon possibilities which not only have not been taken hold of in concern, but whose fulfilment has not even been pondered over and expected. On the contrary, in the mode of mere wishing, the ascendancy of Being-ahead-of-oneself brings with it a lack of understanding for the factical possibilities. When the world has been primarily projected as a wish-world, Being-in-the-world has lost itself inertly in what is at its disposal; but it has done so in such a way that, in the light of what is wished for, that which is at its disposal (and this is all that is ready-to-hand) is never enough. Wishing is an existential

---

[1] '. . . (Welt als das Worin des Schon-seins) . . .'

modification of projecting oneself understandingly, when such self-projection has fallen forfeit to thrownness and just keeps *hankering* after possibilities.[1] Such hankering *closes off* the possibilities; what is 'there' in wishful hankering turns into the 'actual world'. Ontologically, wishing presupposes care.

In hankering, Being-already-alongside . . . takes priority. The "ahead-of-itself-in-Being-already-in . . ." is correspondingly modified. Dasein's hankering as it falls makes manifest its *addiction* to becoming 'lived' by whatever world it is in. This addiction shows the character of Being out for something [Ausseins auf . . .]. Being-ahead-of-oneself has lost itself in a 'just-always-already-alongside'.[2] What one is addicted 'towards' [Das "Hin-zu" des Hanges] is to let oneself be drawn by the sort of thing for which the addiction hankers. If Dasein, as it were, sinks into an addiction then there is not merely an addiction present-at-hand, but the entire structure of care has been modified. Dasein has become blind, and puts all possibilities into the service of the addiction.

On the other hand, the *urge* 'to live' is something 'towards' which one is impelled, and it brings the impulsion along with it of its own accord.[3] It is 'towards this at any price'. The urge seeks to crowd out [verdrängen] other possibilities. Here too the Being-ahead-of-oneself is one that is inauthentic, even if one is assailed by an urge coming from the very thing that is urging one on. The urge can outrun one's current state-of-mind and one's understanding. But then Dasein is not—and never is—a 'mere urge' to which other kinds of controlling or guiding behaviour are added from time to time; rather, as a modification of the entirety of Being-in-the-world, it is always care already.

In pure urge, care has not yet become free, though care first makes it ontologically possible for Dasein to be urged on by itself.[4] In addiction, however, care has always been bound. Addiction and urge are possibilities rooted in the thrownness of Dasein. The urge 'to live' is not to be annihilated; the addiction to becoming 'lived' by the world is not to be rooted out. But because these are both grounded ontologically in care, and only because of this, they are both to be modified in an ontical and existentiell manner by care—by care as something authentic.

With the expression 'care' we have in mind a basic existential-ontological phenomenon, which all the same is *not simple* in its structure. The

---

[1] '. . . das, der Geworfenheit verfallen, den Möglichkeiten lediglich noch *nachhängt*.'

[2] '. . . in ein "Nur-immer-schon-bei . . ."'. Here we follow the reading of the later editions. The earlier editions have ' "Nur-immer-schon-sein-bei . . ." ' ('just-always-Being-already-alongside').

[3] 'Dagegen ist der *Drang* "zu leben" ein "Hin-zu", das von ihm selbst her den Antrieb mitbringt.' The italicization of '*Drang*' appears only in the later editions.

[4] '. . . das Bedrängtsein des Daseins aus ihm selbst her . . .'

ontologically elemental totality of the care-structure cannot be traced back to some ontical 'primal element', just as Being certainly cannot be 'explained' in terms of entities. In the end it will be shown that the idea of Being in general is just as far from being 'simple' as is the Being of Dasein. In defining "care" as "Being-ahead-of-oneself—in-Being-already-in . . .—as Being-alongside . . .", we have made it plain that even this phenomenon is, in itself, still structurally *articulated*. But is this not a phenomenal symptom that we must pursue the ontological question even further until we can exhibit a *still more primordial* phenomenon which provides the ontological support for the unity and the totality of the structural manifoldness of care? Before we follow up this question, we must look back and appropriate with greater precision what we have hitherto Interpreted in aiming at the question of fundamental ontology as to the meaning of Being in general. First, however, we must show that what is ontologically 'new' in this Interpretation is ontically quite old. In explicating Dasein's Being as care, we are not forcing it under an idea of our own contriving, but we are conceptualizing existentially what has already been disclosed in an ontico-existentiell manner.

¶ *42. Confirmation of the Existential Interpretation of Dasein as Care in terms of Dasein's Pre-ontological Way of Interpreting Itself*[1]

In our foregoing Interpretations, which have finally led to exhibiting care as the Being of Dasein, everything depended on our arriving at the right *ontological* foundations for that entity which in each case we ourselves are, and which we call 'man'. To do this it was necessary from the outset to change the direction of our analysis from the approach presented by the traditional definition of "man"—an approach which has not been clarified ontologically and is in principle questionable. In comparison with this definition, the existential-ontological Interpretation may seem strange, especially if 'care' is understood just ontically as 'worry' or 'grief' [als "Besorgnis" und "Bekümmernis"]. Accordingly we shall now cite a document which is pre-ontological in character, even though its demonstrative force is 'merely historical'.

We must bear in mind, however, that in this document Dasein is expressing itself 'primordially', unaffected by any theoretical Interpretation and without aiming to propose any. We must also note that Dasein's Being is characterized by historicality, though this must first be demonstrated ontologically. *If* Dasein is 'historical' in the very depths of its Being, then a deposition [Aussage] which comes from its history and goes back to it,

197

---

[1] '*Die Bewährung der existenzialen Interpretation des Daseins als Sorge aus der vorontologischen Selbstauslegung des Daseins.*'

and which, moreover, is *prior* to any scientific knowledge, will have especial
weight, even though its importance is never purely ontological. That
understanding of Being which lies in Dasein itself, expresses itself pre-
ontologically. The document which we are about to cite should make plain
that our existential Interpretation is not a mere fabrication, but that as
an ontological 'construction' it is well grounded and has been sketched
out beforehand in elemental ways.

There is an ancient fable in which Dasein's interpretation of itself as
'care' has been embedded: v

> *Cura cum fluvium transiret, vidit cretosum lutum*
> *sustulitque cogitabunda atque coepit fingere.*
> *dum deliberat quid iam fecisset, Jovis intervenit.*
> *rogat eum Cura ut det illi spiritum, et facile impetrat.*
> *cui cum vellet Cura nomen ex sese ipsa imponere,*
> *Jovis prohibuit suumque nomen ei dandum esse dictitat.*
> *dum Cura et Jovis disceptant, Tellus surrexit simul*
> *suumque nomen esse volt cui corpus praebuerit suum.*
> *sumpserunt Saturnum iudicem, is sic aecus iudicat:*
> *'tu Jovis quia spiritum dedisti, in morte spiritum,*
> *tuque Tellus, quia dedisti corpus, corpus recipito,*
> *Cura eum quia prima finxit, teneat quamdiu vixerit.*
> *sed quae nunc de nomine eius vobis controversia est,*
> *homo vocetur, quia videtur esse factus ex humo.'*

198

'Once when 'Care' was crossing a river, she saw some clay; she thought-
fully took up a piece and began to shape it. While she was meditating on
what she had made, Jupiter came by. 'Care' asked him to give it spirit,
and this he gladly granted. But when she wanted her name to be bestowed
upon it, he forbade this, and demanded that it be given his name instead.
While 'Care' and Jupiter were disputing, Earth arose and desired that
her own name be conferred on the creature, since she had furnished it
with part of her body. They asked Saturn to be their arbiter, and he made
the following decision, which seemed a just one: 'Since you, Jupiter, have
given its spirit, you shall receive that spirit at its death; and since you,
Earth, have given its body, you shall receive its body. But since 'Care'
first shaped this creature, she shall possess it as long as it lives. And because
there is now a dispute among you as to its name, let it be called '*homo*',
for it is made out of *humus* (earth).'[1]

---

[1] In both the earlier and later editions Heidegger has 'videt' in the first line of the Latin
version of the fable, where Bücheler, from whom the text has been taken, has 'vidit'; in
the 12th line Heidegger has 'enim' where Bücheler has 'eum'. The punctuation of the
Latin version is as Bücheler gives it. The single quotation marks in the English translation

This pre-ontological document becomes especially significant not only in that 'care' is here seen as that to which human Dasein belongs 'for its lifetime', but also because this priority of 'care' emerges in connection with the familiar way of taking man as compounded of body (earth) and spirit. *"Cura prima finxit"* : in care this entity has the 'source' of its Being. *"Cura teneat, quamdiu vixerit"* ; the entity is not released from this source but is held fast, dominated by it through and through as long as this entity 'is in the world'. 'Being-in-the-world' has the stamp of 'care', which accords with its Being. It gets the name *"homo"* not in consideration of its Being but in relation to that of which it consists (*humus*). The decision as to wherein the 'primordial' Being of this creature is to be seen, is left to Saturn, 'Time'.[vi] Thus the pre-ontological characterization of man's essence expressed in this fable, has brought to view in advance the kind of Being which dominates his *temporal sojourn in the world*, and does so through and through.

199

The history of the signification of the ontical concept of 'care' permits us to see still further basic structures of Dasein. Burdach [vii] calls attention to a double meaning of the term *'cura'* according to which it signifies not only 'anxious exertion' but also 'carefulness' and 'devotedness' ["Sorgfalt", "Hingabe"]. Thus Seneca writes in his last epistle (*Ep.* 124): 'Among the four existent Natures (trees, beasts, man, and God), the latter two, which alone are endowed with reason, are distinguished in that God is immortal while man is mortal. Now when it comes to these, the good of the one, namely God, is fulfilled by his Nature; but that of the other, man, is fulfilled by *care* (*cura*): *"unius bonum natura perficit, dei scilicet, alterius cura, hominis."*

Man's *perfectio*—his transformation into that which he can be in Being-free for his ownmost possibilities (projection)—is 'accomplished' by 'care'. But with equal primordiality 'care' determines what is basically specific in this entity, according to which it has been surrendered to the world of its concern (thrownness). In the 'double meaning' of 'care', what we have in view is a *single* basic state in its essentially twofold structure of thrown projection.

As compared with this ontical interpretation, the existential-ontological Interpretation is not, let us say, merely an ontical generalization which is theoretical in character. That would just mean that ontically all man's ways of behaving are 'full of care' and are guided by his 'devotedness' to

correspond strictly to the double quotation marks in Heidegger's version; some of these are not found in Burdach's translation, which, except for two entirely trivial changes, Heidegger has otherwise reproduced very accurately. (On Bücheler and Burdach, see Heidegger's note v, ad loc.) Our translation is a compromise between Burdach and the original Latin.

something. The 'generalization' is rather one that is *ontological and a priori*. What it has in view is not a set of ontical properties which constantly keep emerging, but a state of Being which is already underlying in every case, and which first makes it ontologically possible for this entity to be addressed ontically as "*cura*". The existential condition for the possibility of 'the cares of life' and 'devotedness', must be conceived as care, in a sense which is primordial—that is ontological.

The transcendental 'generality' of the phenomenon of care and of all fundamental *existentialia* is, on the other hand, broad enough to present a basis on which *every* interpretation of Dasein which is ontical and belongs to a world-view must move, whether Dasein is understood as affliction [Not] and the 'cares of life' or in an opposite manner.

The very 'emptiness' and 'generality' which obtrude themselves ontically in existential structures, have an ontological definiteness and fulness of their *own*. Thus Dasein's whole constitution itself is not simple in its unity, but shows a structural articulation; in the existential conception of care, this articulation becomes expressed.

Thus, by our ontological Interpretation of Dasein, we have been brought to the *existential conception* of care from Dasein's pre-ontological interpretation of itself as 'care'. Yet the analytic of Dasein is not aimed at laying an ontological basis for anthropology; its purpose is one of fundamental ontology. This is the purpose that has tacitly determined the course of our considerations hitherto, our selection of phenomena, and the limits to which our analysis may proceed. Now, however, with regard to our leading question of the meaning of Being and our way of working this out, our investigation must give us *explicit* assurance as to what we have so far achieved. But this sort of thing is not to be reached by superficially taking together what we have discussed. Rather, with the help of what we have achieved, that which could be indicated only crudely at the beginning of the existential analytic, must now be concentrated into a more penetrating understanding of the problem.

¶43. *Dasein, Worldhood, and Reality*

The question of the meaning of Being becomes possible at all only if there *is* something like an understanding of Being. Understanding of Being belongs to the kind of Being which the entity called "Dasein" possesses. The more appropriately and primordially we have succeeded in explicating this entity, the surer we are to attain our goal in the further course of working out the problem of fundamental ontology.

In our pursuit of the tasks of a preparatory existential analytic of Dasein,

there emerged an Interpretation of understanding, meaning, and interpretation. Our analysis of Dasein's disclosedness showed further that, with
this disclosedness, Dasein, in its basic state of Being-in-the-world, has been
revealed equiprimordially with regard to the world, Being-in, and the
Self. Furthermore, in the factical disclosedness of the world, entities
within-the-world are discovered too. This implies that the Being of these
entities is always understood in a certain manner, even if it is not conceived
in a way which is appropriately ontological. To be sure, the pre-ontological understanding of Being embraces all entities which are essentially
disclosed in Dasein; but the understanding of Being has not yet Articulated itself in a way which corresponds to the various modes of Being.

At the same time our interpretation of understanding has shown that,
in accordance with its falling kind of Being, it has, proximally and for the
most part, diverted itself [sich . . . verlegt] into an understanding of the
'world'. Even where the issue is not only one of ontical experience but
also one of ontological understanding, the interpretation of Being takes its
orientation in the first instance from the Being of entities within-the-
world. Thereby the Being of what is proximally ready-to-hand gets passed
over, and entities are first conceived as a context of Things (*res*) which are
present-at-hand. *"Being"* acquires the meaning of *"Reality"*.viii Substantiality becomes the basic characteristic of Being. Corresponding to this
way in which the understanding of Being has been diverted, even the
ontological understanding of Dasein moves into the horizon of this conception of Being. Like any other entity, *Dasein* too is *present-at-hand as Real*.
In this way *"Being in general"* acquires the meaning of *"Reality"*. Accordingly the concept of Reality has a peculiar priority in the ontological
problematic. By this priority the route to a genuine existential analytic
of Dasein gets diverted, and so too does our very view of the Being of what
is proximally ready-to-hand within-the-world. It finally forces the general
problematic of Being into a direction that lies off the course. The other
modes of Being become defined negatively and privatively with regard to
Reality.

Thus not only the analytic of Dasein but the working-out of the question
of the meaning of Being in general must be turned away from a one-sided
orientation with regard to Being in the sense of Reality. We must demonstrate that Reality is not only *one* kind of Being *among* others, but that ontologically it has a definite connection in its foundations with Dasein, the
world, and readiness-to-hand. To demonstrate this we must discuss in
principle the *problem of Reality*, its conditions and its limits.

Under the heading 'problem of Reality' various questions are clustered:
(1) whether any entities which supposedly 'transcend our consciousness'

are at all; (2) whether this Reality of the 'external world' can be adequately *proved*; (3) how far this entity, if it is Real, is to be known in its Being-in-itself; (4) what the meaning of this entity, Reality, signifies in general. The following discussion of the problem of Reality will treat three topics with regard to the question of fundamental ontology: (*a*) Reality as a problem of Being, and whether the 'external world' can be proved; (*b*) Reality as an ontological problem; (*c*) Reality and care.

(a) Reality as a problem of Being, and whether the 'External World' can be Proved

Of these questions about Reality, the one which comes first in order is the ontological question of what "Reality" signifies in general. But as long as a pure ontological problematic and methodology was lacking, this question (if it was explicitly formulated at all) was necessarily confounded with a discussion of the 'problem of the external world'; for the analysis of Reality is possible only on the basis of our having appropriate access to the Real. But it has long been held that the way to grasp the Real is by that kind of knowing which is characterized by beholding [das anschauende Erkennen]. Such knowing 'is' as a way in which the soul—or consciousness—behaves. In so far as Reality has the character of something independent and "in itself", the question of the meaning of "Reality" becomes linked with that of whether the Real can be independent 'of consciousness' or whether there can be a transcendence of consciousness into the 'sphere' of the Real. The possibility of an adequate ontological analysis of Reality depends upon how far *that of which* the Real is to be thus independent—how far *that which* is to be transcended[1]—has *itself* been clarified with regard to its *Being*. Only thus can even the kind of Being which belongs to transcendence be ontologically grasped. And finally we must make sure what kind of primary access we have to the Real, by deciding the question of whether knowing can take over this function at all.

These investigations, which *take precedence over* any possible ontological question about Reality, have been carried out in the foregoing existential analytic. According to this analytic, knowing is a *founded* mode of access to the Real. The Real is essentially accessible only as entities within-the-world. All access to such entities is founded ontologically upon the basic state of Dasein, Being-in-the-world; and this in turn has care as its even more primordial state of Being (ahead of itself—Being already in a world —as Being alongside entities within-the-world).

The question of whether there is a world at all and whether its Being

[1] '. . . das, *wovon* Unabhängigkeit bestehen soll, *was* transzendiert werden soll . . .'

can be proved, makes no sense if it is raised by *Dasein* as Being-in-the-world; and who else would raise it? Furthermore, it is encumbered with a double signification. The world as the "wherein" [das Worin] of Being-in, and the 'world' as entities within-the-world (that in which [das Wobei] one is concernfully absorbed) either have been confused or are not distinguished at all. But the world is disclosed essentially *along with the* Being of Dasein; with the disclosedness of the world, the 'world' has in each case been discovered too. Of course entities within-the-world in the sense of the Real as merely present-at-hand, are the very things that can remain concealed. But even the Real can be discovered only on the basis of a world which has already been disclosed. And only on this basis can anything Real still remain *hidden*. The question of the 'Reality' of the 'external world' gets raised without any previous clarification of the *phenomenon of the world* as such. Factically, the 'problem of the external *world*' is constantly oriented with regard to entities within-the-world (Things and Objects). So these discussions drift along into a problematic which it is almost impossible to disentangle ontologically.

Kant's 'Refutation of Idealism'[ix] shows how intricate these questions are and how what one wants to prove gets muddled with what one does prove and with the means whereby the proof is carried out. Kant calls it 'a scandal of philosophy and of human reason in general'[x] that there is still no cogent proof for the 'Dasein of Things outside of us' which will do away with any scepticism. He proposes such a proof himself, and indeed he does so to provide grounds for his 'theorem' that 'The mere consciousness of my own Dasein—a consciousness which, however, is empirical in character—proves the Dasein of objects in the space outside of me.'[xi]

We must in the first instance note explicitly that Kant uses the term 'Dasein' to designate that kind of Being which in the present investigation we have called 'presence-at-hand'. 'Consciousness of my Dasein' means for Kant a consciousness of my Being-present-at-hand in the sense of Descartes. When Kant uses the term 'Dasein' he has in mind the Being-present-at-hand of consciousness just as much as the Being-present-at-hand of Things.

The proof for the 'Dasein of Things outside of me' is supported by the fact that both change and performance belong, with equal primordiality, to the essence of time. My own Being-present-at-hand—that is, the Being-present-at-hand of a multiplicity of representations, which has been given in the inner sense—is a process of change which is present-at-hand. To have a determinate temporal character [Zeitbestimmtheit], however, presupposes something present-at-hand which is permanent. But this cannot be 'in us', 'for only through what is thus permanent can my

203

Dasein in time be determined'.[xii] Thus if changes which are present-at-
204   hand have been posited empirically 'in me', it is necessary that along with
these something permanent which is present-at-hand should be posited
empirically 'outside of me'. What is thus permanent is the condition which
makes it possible for the changes 'in me' to be present-at-hand. The
experience of the Being-in-time of representations posits something
changing 'in me' and something permanent 'outside of me', and it posits
both with equal primordiality.

Of course this proof is not a causal inference and is therefore not
encumbered with the disadvantages which that would imply. Kant gives,
as it were, an 'ontological proof' in terms of the idea of a temporal entity.
It seems at first as if Kant has given up the Cartesian approach of positing
a subject one can come across in isolation. But only in semblance. That
Kant demands any proof at all for the 'Dasein of Things outside of me'
shows already that he takes the subject—the 'in me'—as the starting-
point for this problematic. Moreover, his proof itself is then carried
through by starting with the empirically given changes *'in me'*. For only
'in me' is 'time' experienced, and time carries the burden of the proof.
Time provides the basis for leaping off into what is 'outside of me' in the
course of the proof. Furthermore, Kant emphasizes that "The problematical kind [of idealism], which merely alleges our inability to prove by
immediate experience that there is a Dasein outside of our own, is reasonable and accords with a sound kind of philosophical thinking: namely, to
permit no decisive judgment until an adequate proof has been found."[xiii]

But even if the ontical priority of the isolated subject and inner experience should be given up, Descartes' position would still be retained
ontologically. What Kant proves—if we may suppose that his proof is
correct and correctly based—is that entities which are changing and
entities which are permanent are necessarily present-at-hand together.
But when two things which are present-at-hand are thus put on the same
level, this does not as yet mean that subject and Object are present-at-
hand together. And even if this were proved, what is ontologically decisive
would still be covered up—namely, the basic state of the 'subject', Dasein,
as Being-in-the-world. *The Being-present-at-hand-together of the physical and
the psychical is completely different ontically and ontologically from the phenomenon
of Being-in-the-world.*

Kant presupposes both the distinction between the 'in me' and the
'outside of me', *and also the connection* between these; factically he is correct
in doing so, but he is incorrect from the standpoint of the tendency of his
proof. It has not been demonstrated that the sort of thing which gets
established about the Being-present-at-hand-together of the changing and

the permanent when one takes time as one's clue, will also apply to the 205
connection between the 'in me' and the 'outside of me'. But if one were
to see the whole distinction between the 'inside' and the 'outside' and the
whole connection between them which Kant's proof presupposes, and if
one were to have an ontological conception of what has been presupposed
in this presupposition, then the possibility of holding that a proof of the
'Dasein of Things outside of me' is a necessary one which has yet to be
given [noch ausstehend], would collapse.

The 'scandal of philosophy' is not that this proof has yet to be given, but
that *such proofs are expected and attempted again and again.* Such expectations,
aims, and demands arise from an ontologically inadequate way of starting
with *something* of such a character that independently *of it* and 'outside'
of it a 'world' is to be proved as present-at-hand. It is not that the proofs
are inadequate, but that the kind of Being of the entity which does the
proving and makes requests for proofs has *not been made definite enough.* This
is why a demonstration that two things which are present-at-hand are
necessarily present-at-hand together, can give rise to the illusion that
something has been proved, or even can be proved, about Dasein as
Being-in-the-world. If Dasein is understood correctly, it defies such
proofs, because, in its Being, it already *is* what subsequent proofs deem
necessary to demonstrate for it.

If one were to conclude that since the Being-present-at-hand of Things
outside of us is impossible to prove, it must therefore 'be taken merely on
faith',[xiv] one would still fail to surmount this perversion of the problem.
The assumption would remain that at bottom and ideally it must still be
possible to carry out such a proof. This inappropriate way of approaching
the problem is still endorsed when one restricts oneself to a 'faith in the
Reality of the external world', even if such a faith is explicitly 'acknow-
ledged' as such. Although one is not offering a stringent proof, one is
still in principle demanding a proof and trying to satisfy that demand.

Even if one should invoke the doctrine that the subject must presuppose
and indeed always does unconsciously presuppose the presence-at-hand 206
of the 'external world', one would still be starting with the construct of
an isolated subject. The phenomenon of Being-in-the-world is something
that one would no more meet in this way than one would by demonstrating that the physical and the psychical are present-at-hand together.
With such presuppositions, Dasein always comes 'too late'; for in so far
as it does this presupposing as an entity (and otherwise this would be
impossible), it is, *as an entity*, already in a world. 'Earlier' than any presupposition which Dasein makes, or any of its ways of behaving, is the
'*a priori*' character of its state of Being as one whose kind of Being is care.

To *have faith* in the Reality of the 'external world', whether rightly or wrongly; to *"prove"* this Reality for it, whether adequately or inadequately; to *presuppose* it, whether explicitly or not—attempts such as these which have not mastered their own basis with full transparency, presuppose a subject which is proximally *worldless* or unsure of its world, and which must, at bottom, first assure itself of a world. Thus from the very beginning, Being-in-a-world is disposed to "take things" in some way [Auffassen], to suppose, to be certain, to have faith—a way of behaving which itself is always a founded mode of Being-in-the-world.

The 'problem of Reality' in the sense of the question whether an external world is present-at-hand and whether such a world can be proved, turns out to be an impossible one, not because its consequences lead to inextricable impasses, but because the very entity which serves as its theme, is one which, as it were, repudiates any such formulation of the question. Our task is not to prove that an 'external world' is present-at-hand or to show how it is present-at-hand, but to point out why Dasein, as Being-in-the-world, has the tendency to bury the 'external world' in nullity 'epistemologically' before going on to prove it.[1] The reason for this lies in Dasein's falling and in the way in which the primary understanding of Being has been diverted to Being as presence-at-hand—a diversion which is motivated by that falling itself. If one formulates the question 'critically' with such an ontological orientation, then what one finds present-at-hand as proximally and solely certain, is something merely 'inner'. After the primordial phenomenon of Being-in-the-world has been shattered, the isolated subject is all that remains, and this becomes the basis on which it gets joined together with a 'world'.

In this investigation we cannot discuss at length the many attempts to solve the 'problem of Reality' which have been developed in various kinds of realism and idealism and in positions which mediate between them. Certainly a grain of genuine inquiry is to be found in each of these; but certain as this is, it would be just as perverse if one should want to achieve a tenable solution of the problem by reckoning up how much has been correct in each case. What is needed rather is the basic insight that while the different epistemological directions which have been pursued have not gone so very far off epistemologically, their neglect of any existential analytic of Dasein has kept them from obtaining any basis for a well secured phenomenal problematic. Nor is such a *basis* to be obtained by subsequently making phenomenological corrections on the concepts of subject and consciousness. Such a procedure would give no guarantee

207

[1] '. . . warum das Dasein als In-der-Welt-sein die Tendenz hat, die "Aussenwelt" zunächst "erkenntnistheoretisch" in Nichtigkeit zu begraben um sie dann erst zu beweisen.'

that the inappropriate *formulation of the question* would not continue to stand.

Along with Dasein as Being-in-the-world, entities within-the-world have in each case already been disclosed. This existential-ontological assertion seems to accord with the thesis of *realism* that the external world is Really present-at-hand. In so far as this existential assertion does not deny that entities within-the-world are present-at-hand, it agrees—doxographically, as it were—with the thesis of realism in its results. But it differs in principle from every kind of realism; for realism holds that the Reality of the 'world' not only needs to be proved but also is capable of proof. In the existential assertion both of these positions are directly negated. But what distinguishes this assertion from realism altogether, is the fact that in realism there is a lack of ontological understanding. Indeed realism tries to explain Reality ontically by Real connections of interaction between things that are Real.

As compared with realism, *idealism*, no matter how contrary and untenable it may be in its results, has an advantage in principle, provided that it does not misunderstand itself as 'psychological' idealism. If idealism emphasizes that Being and Reality are only 'in the consciousness', this expresses an understanding of the fact that Being cannot be explained through entities. But as long as idealism fails to clarify what this very understanding of Being means ontologically, or how this understanding is possible, or that it belongs to Dasein's state of Being, the Interpretation of Reality which idealism constructs is an empty one. Yet the fact that Being cannot be explained through entities and that Reality is possible only in the understanding of Being, does not absolve us from inquiring into the Being of consciousness, of the *res cogitans* itself. If the idealist thesis is to be followed consistently, the ontological analysis of consciousness itself is prescribed as an inevitable prior task. Only because Being is 'in the consciousness'—that is to say, only because it is understandable in Dasein—can Dasein also understand and conceptualize such characteristics of Being as independence, the 'in-itself', and Reality in general. Only because of this are 'independent' entities, as encountered within-the-world, accessible to circumspection.   208

If what the term "idealism" says, amounts to the understanding that Being can never be explained by entities but is already that which is 'transcendental' for every entity, then idealism affords the only correct possibility for a philosophical problematic. If so, Aristotle was no less an idealist than Kant. But if "idealism" signifies tracing back every entity to a subject or consciousness whose sole distinguishing features are that it remains *indefinite* in its Being and is best characterized negatively as 'un-Thing-like', then this idealism is no less naïve in its method than the most grossly militant realism.

It is still possible that one may give the problematic of Reality *priority* over any orientation in terms of 'standpoints' by maintaining the thesis that every subject is what it is only for an Object, and *vice versa*. But in this formal approach the terms thus correlated—like the correlation itself —remain ontologically indefinite. At the bottom, however, the whole correlation necessarily gets thought of as 'somehow' *being*, and must therefore be thought of with regard to some definite idea of Being. Of course, if the existential-ontological basis has been made secure beforehand by exhibiting Being-in-the-world, then this correlation is one that we can know later as a formalized relation, ontologically undifferentiated.

Our discussion of the unexpressed presuppositions of attempts to solve the problem of Reality in ways which are just 'epistemological', shows that this problem must be taken back, as an ontological one, into the existential analytic of Dasein.[xvi]

209   *(b) Reality as an Ontological Problem*

If the term "Reality" is meant to stand for the Being of entities present-at-hand within-the-world (*res*) (and nothing else is understood thereby), then when it comes to analysing this mode of Being, this signifies that entities *within-the-world* are ontologically conceivable only if the phenomenon of within-the-world-ness has been clarified. But within-the-world-ness is based upon the phenomenon of the *world*, which, for its part, as an essential item in the structure of Being-in-the-world, belongs to the basic constitution of Dasein. Being-in-the-world, in turn, is bound up ontologically in the structural totality of Dasein's Being, and we have characterized care as such a totality. But in this way we have marked out the foundations and the horizons which must be clarified if an analysis of Reality is to be possible. Only in this connection, moreover, does the character of the "in-itself" become ontologically intelligible. By taking our orientation from this context of problems, we have in our earlier analyses Interpreted the Being of entities within-the-world.[xvii]

To be sure, the Reality of the Real can be characterized phenomenologically within certain limits without any explicit existential-ontological basis. This is what Dilthey has attempted in the article mentioned above. He holds that the Real gets experienced in impulse and will, and that Reality is *resistance*, or, more exactly, the character of resisting.[1] He then works out the phenomenon of resistance analytically. This is the positive contribution of his article, and provides the best concrete substantiation

---

[1] 'Realität ist *Widerstand*, genauer Widerständigkeit.'

for his idea of a 'psychology which both describes and dissects'. But he is kept from working out the analysis of this phenomenon correctly by the epistemological problematic of Reality. The 'principle of phenomenality' does not enable him to come to an ontological Interpretation of the Being of consciousness. 'Within the same consciousness,' he writes, 'the will and its inhibition emerge.'xviii What kind of Being belongs to this 'emerging'? What is the meaning of the Being of the 'within'? What relationship-of-Being does consciousness bear to the Real itself? All this must be determined ontologically. That this has not been done, depends ultimately on the fact that Dilthey has left 'life' standing in such a manner that it is ontologically undifferentiated; and of course 'life' is something which one cannot go back 'behind'. But to Interpret Dasein ontologically does not signify that we must go back ontically to some other entity. The fact that Dilthey has been refuted epistemologically cannot prevent us from making fruitful use of what is positive in his analyses—the very thing that has not been understood in such refutations.

Thus Scheler has recently taken up Dilthey's Interpretation of Reality.xix He stands for a 'voluntative theory of Dasein'. Here "Dasein" is understood in the Kantian sense as Being-present-at-hand. The 'Being of objects is given immediately only in the way it is related to drive and will'. Scheler not only emphasizes, as does Dilthey, that Reality is never primarily given in thinking and apprehending; he also points out particularly that cognition [Erkennen] itself is not judgment, and that knowing [Wissen] is a 'relationship of Being'.

What we have already said about the ontological indefiniteness of Dilthey's foundations holds in principle for this theory too. Nor can the fundamental ontological analysis of 'life' be slipped in afterwards as a substructure. Such a fundamental analysis provides the supporting conditions for the analysis of Reality—for the entire explication of the character of resisting and its phenomenal presuppositions. Resistance is encountered in a not-coming-through, and it is encountered as a hindrance to willing to come through. With such willing, however, something must already have been disclosed which one's drive and one's will *are out for*. But what they are out for is ontically indefinite, and this indefiniteness must not be overlooked ontologically or taken as if it were nothing. When Being-out-for-something comes up against resistance, and can do nothing but 'come up against it', it is itself already *alongside* a totality of involvements. But the fact that this totality has been discovered is grounded in the disclosedness of the referential totality of significance. *The experiencing of resistance—that is, the discovery of what is resistant to one's endeavours—is possible ontologically only by reason of the disclosedness of the world.* The character

210

of resisting is one that belongs to entities with-the-world. Factically, experiences of resistance determine only the extent and the direction in which entities encountered within-the-world are discovered. The summation of such experiences does not introduce the disclosure of the world for the first time, but presupposes it. The 'against' and the 'counter to' as ontological possibilities, are supported by disclosed Being-in-the-world.

211   Nor is resistance experienced in a drive or will which 'emerges' in its own right. These both turn out to be modifications of care. Only entities with this kind of Being can come up against something resistant as something within-the-world. So if "Reality" gets defined as "the character of resisting", we must notice two things: first, that this is only *one* character of Reality among others; second, that the character of resisting presupposes necessarily a world which has already been disclosed. Resistance characterizes the 'external world' in the sense of entities within-the-world, but never in the sense of the world itself. *'Consciousness of Reality' is itself a way of Being-in-the-world*. Every 'problematic of the external world' comes back necessarily to this basic existential phenomenon.

If the *'cogito sum'* is to serve as the point of departure for the existential analytic of Dasein, then it needs to be turned around, and furthermore its content needs new ontologico-phenomenal confirmation. The *'sum'* is then asserted first, and indeed in the sense that "I am in a world". As such an entity, 'I am' in the possibility of Being towards various ways of comporting myself—namely, *cogitationes*—as ways of Being alongside entities within-the-world. Descartes, on the contrary, says that *cogitationes* are present-at-hand, and that in these an *ego* is present-at-hand too as a worldless *res cogitans*.

(c) *Reality and Care*

"Reality", as an ontological term, is one which we have related to entities within-the-world. If it serves to designate this kind of Being in general, then readiness-to-hand and presence-at-hand function as modes of Reality. If, however, one lets this word have its traditional signification, then it stands for Being in the sense of the pure presence-at-hand of Things. But not all presence-at-hand is the presence-at-hand of Things. The 'Nature' by which we are 'surrounded' is, of course, an entity within-the-world; but the kind of Being which it shows belongs neither to the ready-to-hand nor to what is present-at-hand as 'Things of Nature'. No matter how this Being of 'Nature' may be Interpreted, *all* the modes of Being of entities within-the-world are founded ontologically upon the worldhood of the world, and accordingly upon the phenomenon of Being-in-the world. From this there arises the insight that among the modes of

Being of entities within-the-world, Reality has no priority, and that Reality is a kind of Being which cannot even characterize anything like the world or Dasein in a way which is ontologically appropriate.

In the order of the ways in which things are connected in their ontological foundations and in the order of any possible categorial and existential demonstration, *Reality is referred back to the phenomenon of care.* But the fact that Reality is ontologically grounded in the Being of Dasein, 212 does not signify that only when Dasein exists and as long as Dasein exists, can the Real be as that which in itself it is.

Of course only as long as Dasein *is* (that is, only as long as an understanding of Being is ontically possible), 'is there' Being.[1] When Dasein does not exist, 'independence' 'is' not either, nor 'is' the 'in-itself'. In such a case this sort of thing can be neither understood nor not understood. In such a case even entities within-the-world can neither be discovered nor lie hidden. *In such a case* it cannot be said that entities are, nor can it be said that they are not. But *now*, as long as there is an understanding of Being and therefore an understanding of presence-at-hand, it can indeed be said that *in this case* entities will still continue to be.

As we have noted, Being (not entities) is dependent upon the understanding of Being; that is to say, Reality (not the Real) is dependent upon care. By this dependency our further analytic of Dasein is held secure in the face of an uncritical Interpretation which nevertheless keeps urging itself upon us—an Interpretation in which the idea of Reality is taken as the clue to Dasein. Only if we take our orientation from existentiality as Interpreted in an ontologically *positive* manner, can we have any guarantee that in the factical course of the analysis of 'consciousness' or of 'life', some sense of "Reality" does not get made basic, even if it is one which has not been further differentiated.

Entities with Dasein's kind of Being cannot be conceived in terms of Reality and substantiality; we have expressed this by the thesis that *the substance of man is existence.* Yet if we have Interpreted existentiality as care, and distinguished this from Reality, this does not signify that our existential analytic is at an end; we have merely allowed the intricate problems of the question of Being and its possible modes, and the question of the meaning of such modifications, to emerge more sharply: only if the understanding of Being *is*, do entities as entities become accessible; only if

---

[1] '. . . "gibt es" Sein.' In his letter *Über den Humanismus* (Klostermann, Frankfurt A.M., n.d., p. 22, reprinted from *Platons Lehre von der Wahrheit*, Francke A.G., Bern, 1947), Heidegger insists that the expression 'es gibt' is here used deliberately, and should be taken literally as 'it gives'. He writes: 'For the "it" which here "gives" is Being itself. The "gives", however, designates the essence of Being, which gives and which confers its truth.' He adds that the 'es gibt' is used to avoid writing that 'Being is', for the verb 'is' is appropriate to entities but not to Being itself.

entities are of Dasein's kind of Being is the understanding of Being possible as an entity.

¶44. *Dasein, Disclosedness, and Truth*

From time immemorial, philosophy has associated truth and Being. Parmenides was the first to discover the Being of entities, and he 'identified' Being with the perceptive understanding of Being: τὸ γὰρ αὐτὸ νοεῖν ἐστίν τε καὶ εἶναι.[xx] Aristotle, in outlining the history of how the ἀρχαί have been uncovered,[xxi] emphasizes that the philosophers before him, under the guidance of 'the things themselves' have been compelled to inquire further: αὐτὸ τὸ πρᾶγμα ὡδοποίησεν αὐτοῖς καὶ συνηνάγκασε ζητεῖν.[xxii] He is describing the same fact when he says that ἀναγκαζόμενος δ'ἀκολουθεῖν τοῖς φαινομένοις[xxiii]—that he (Parmenides) was compelled to follow that which showed itself in itself. In another passage he remarks that these thinkers carried on their researches ὑπ' αὐτῆς τῆς ἀληθείας ἀναγκαζόμενοι[xxiv]—"compelled by the 'truth' itself". Aristotle describes these researches as φιλοσοφεῖν περὶ τῆς ἀληθείας[xxv]—" 'philosophizing' about the 'truth' "—or even as ἀποφαίνεσθαι περὶ τῆς ἀληθείας[xxvi]—as exhibiting something and letting it be seen with regard to the 'truth' and within the range of the 'truth'. Philosophy itself is defined as ἐπιστήμη τῆς ἀληθείας[xxvii]—"the science of the 'truth' ". But it is also characterized as ἐπιστήμη, ἣ θεωρεῖ τὸ ὂν ᾗ ὄν[xxviii]— as "a science which contemplates entities as entities"—that is, with regard to their Being.

What is signified here by 'carrying on researches into the "truth" ', by "science of the 'truth' " ? In such researches is 'truth' made a theme as it would be in a theory of knowledge or of judgment? Manifestly not, for 'truth' signifies the same as 'thing' ["Sache"], 'something that shows itself'. But what then does the expression 'truth' signify if it can be used as a term for 'entity' and 'Being'?

If, however, *truth* rightfully has a primordial connection with *Being*, then the phenomenon of truth comes within the range of the problematic of fundamental ontology. In that case, must not this phenomenon have been encountered already within our preparatory fundamental analysis, the analytic of Dasein? What ontico-ontological connection does 'truth' have with Dasein and with that ontical characteristic of Dasein which we call the "understanding of Being"? Can the reason why Being necessarily goes together with truth and *vice versa* be pointed out in terms of such understanding?

These questions are not to be evaded. Because Being does indeed 'go together' with truth, the phenomenon of truth has already been one of the themes of our earlier analyses, though not explicitly under this title. In giving precision to the problem of Being, it is now time to delimit the phenomenon of truth explicitly and to fix the problems which it comprises. In doing this, we should not just take together what we have previously 214 taken apart. Our investigation requires a new approach.

Our analysis takes its departure from the *traditional conception of truth*, and attempts to lay bare the ontological foundations of that conception (*a*). In terms of these foundations the *primordial* phenomenon of truth becomes visible. We can then exhibit the way in which the traditional conception of truth has been *derived* from this *phenomenon* (*b*). Our investigation will make it plain that to the question of the 'essence' of truth, there belongs necessarily the question of the *kind of Being* which truth possesses. Together with this we must clarify the ontological meaning of the kind of talk in which we say that 'there is truth', and we must also clarify the kind of necessity with which 'we must presuppose' that 'there is' truth (*c*).

(*a*) The Traditional Conception of Truth, and its Ontological Foundations

There are three theses which characterize the way in which the essence of truth has been traditionally taken and the way it is supposed to have been first defined: (1) that the 'locus' of truth is assertion (judgment); (2) that the essence of truth lies in the 'agreement' of the judgment with its object; (3) that Aristotle, the father of logic, not only has assigned truth to the judgment as its primordial locus but has set going the definition of "truth" as 'agreement'.[1]

Here it is not our aim to provide a history of the concept of truth, which could be presented only on the basis of a history of ontology. We shall introduce our analytical discussions by alluding to some familiar matters.

Aristotle says that the παθήματα τῆς ψυχῆς are τῶν πραγμάτων ὁμοιώματα[xxix]—that the soul's 'Experiences', its νοήματα ('representations'), are likenings of Things. This assertion, which is by no means proposed as an explicit definition of the essence of truth, has also given occasion for developing the later formulation of the essence of truth as *adaequatio intellectus et rei*.[2] Thomas Aquinas,[xxx] who refers this definition to Avicenna (who, in turn, has taken it over from Isaac Israeli's tenth-century '*Book of Definitions*') also uses for "*adaequatio*" (likening) the terms "*correspondentia*" ("correspondence") and "*convenientia*" (" coming together").

---

[1] Here we follow the older editions in reading '. . . hat sowohl die Wahrheit dem Urteil als ihrem ursprünglichen Ort zugewiesen als auch die Definition der Wahrheit als "Ubereinstimmung" in Gang gebracht.' The newer editions read '. . . hat sowohl . . . zugewiesen, er hat auch . . .'

[2] This is usually translated as 'adequation of the intellect and the thing'. Heidegger makes the connection seem closer by translating both the Latin *adaequatio* and the Greek ὁμοίωμα by the word 'Angleichung', which we have somewhat arbitrarily translated as 'likening'.

215   The neo-Kantian epistemology of the nineteenth century often characterized this definition of "truth" as an expression of a methodologically
retarded naïve realism, and declared it to be irreconcilable with any
formulation of this question which has undergone Kant's 'Copernican
revolution'. But Kant too adhered to this conception of truth, so much so
that he did not even bring it up for discussion; this has been overlooked,
though Brentano has already called our attention to it. 'The old and
celebrated question with which it was supposed that one might drive the
logicians into a corner is this: "*what is truth?*" The explanation of the
name of truth—namely, that it is the agreement of knowledge with its
object—will here be granted and presupposed . . .'[xxxi].

'If truth consists in the agreement of knowledge with its object, then this
object must thus be distinguished from others; for knowledge is false if it
does not agree with the object to which it is related, even if it should
contain something which might well be valid for other objects.'[xxxii] And
in the introduction to the "Transcendental Dialectic" Kant states: 'Truth
and illusion are not in the object so far as it is intuited, but in the judgment about it so far as it is thought.'[xxxiii]

Of course this characterization of truth as 'agreement', *adaequatio*,
ὁμοίωσις, is very general and empty. Yet it will still have some justification if it can hold its own without prejudice to any of the most various
Interpretations which that distinctive predicate "knowledge" will support.
We are now inquiring into the foundations of this 'relation'. *What else is
tacitly posited in this relational totality of the adaequatio intellectus et rei?
And what ontological character does that which is thus posited have itself?*

What in general does one have in view when one uses the term 'agreement'? The agreement of something with something has the formal
character of a relation of something to something. Every agreement, and
therefore 'truth' as well, is a relation. But not every relation is an agreement. A sign points *at* what is indicated.[1] Such indicating is a relation,
but not an agreement of the sign with what is indicated. Yet manifestly
not every agreement is a *convenientia* of the kind that is fixed upon in the
definition of "truth". The number "6" agrees with "16 minus 10". These
216   numbers agree; they are equal with regard to the question of "how
much?" Equality is *one* way of agreeing. Its structure is such that something
like a 'with-regard-to' belongs to it. In the *adaequatio* something gets
related; what is that with regard to which it agrees? In clarifying the
'truth-relation' we must notice also what is peculiar to the terms of this
relation. With regard to what do *intellectus* and *res* agree? In their kind of
Being and their essential content do they give us anything at all with

---

[1] 'Ein Zeichen zeigt *auf* das Gezeigte.'

regard to which they can agree? If it is impossible for *intellectus* and *res* to be equal because they are not of the same species, are they then perhaps similar? But knowledge is still supposed to 'give' the thing *just as* it is. This 'agreement' has the Relational character of the 'just as' ["So— Wie"]. In what way is this relation possible as a relation between *intellectus* and *res*? From these questions it becomes plain that to clarify the structure of truth it is not enough simply to presuppose this relational totality, but we must go back and inquire into the context of Being which provides the support for this totality as such.

Must we, however, bring up here the 'epistemological' problematic as regards the subject-Object relation, or can our analysis restrict itself to Interpreting the 'immanent consciousness of truth', and thus remain 'within the sphere' of the subject? According to the general opinion, what is true is knowledge. But knowledge is judging. In judgment one must distinguish between the judging as a *Real* psychical process, and that which is judged, as an *ideal* content. It will be said of the latter that it is 'true'. The Real psychical process, however, is either present-at-hand or not. According to this opinion, the ideal content of judgment stands in a relationship of agreement. This relationship thus pertains to a connection between an ideal content of judgment and the Real Thing as that which is judged *about*. Is this agreement Real or ideal in its kind of Being, or neither of these? *How are we to take ontologically the relation between an ideal entity and something that is Real and present-at-hand*? Such a relation indeed subsists [besteht]; and in factical judgments it subsists not only as a relation between the content of judgment and the Real Object, but likewise as a relation between the ideal content and the Real act of judgment. And does it manifestly subsist 'more inwardly' in this latter case?

Or is the ontological meaning of the relation between Real and ideal (μέθεξις) something about which we must not inquire? Yet the relation is to be one which *subsists*. What does such "subsisting" [Bestand] mean ontologically?

Why should this not be a legitimate question? Is it accidental that no headway has been made with this problem in over two thousand years? Has 217 the question already been perverted in the very way it has been approached —in the ontologically unclarified separation of the Real and the ideal?

And with regard to the 'actual' judging of what is judged, is the separation of the Real act of judgment from the ideal content altogether unjustified? Does not the actuality of knowing and judging get broken asunder into two ways of Being—two 'levels' which can never be pieced together in such a manner as to reach the kind of Being that belongs to knowing? Is not psychologism correct in holding out against this separation, even if it neither clarifies ontologically the kind of Being which belongs to the thinking of that which is thought, nor is even so much as acquainted with it as a problem?

If we go back to the distinction between the act of judgment and its content, we shall not advance our discussion of the question of the kind of Being which belongs to the *adaequatio*; we shall only make plain the indispensability of clarifying the kind of Being which belongs to knowledge itself. In the analysis which this necessitates we must at the same time try to bring into view a phenomenon which is characteristic of knowledge—the phenomenon of truth. When does truth become phenomenally explicit in knowledge itself? It does so when such knowing demonstrates itself *as true*. By demonstrating itself it is assured of its truth. Thus in the phenomenal context of demonstration, the relationship of agreement must become visible.

Let us suppose that someone with his back turned to the wall makes the true assertion that 'the picture on the wall is hanging askew.' This assertion demonstrates itself when the man who makes it, turns round and perceives the picture hanging askew on the wall. What gets demonstrated in this demonstration? What is the meaning of "confirming" [Bewährung] such an assertion? Do we, let us say, ascertain some agreement between our 'knowledge' or 'what is known' and the Thing on the wall? Yes and no, depending upon whether our Interpretation of the expression 'what is known' is phenomenally appropriate. If he who makes the assertion judges without perceiving the picture, but 'merely represents' it to himself, to what is he related? To 'representations', shall we say? Certainly not, if "representation" is here supposed to signify representing, as a psychical process. Nor is he related to "representations" in the sense of what is thus "represented," if what we have in mind here is a 'picture' of that Real Thing which is on the wall.[1] The asserting which 'merely represents' is related rather, in that sense which is most its own, to the Real picture on the wall. What one has in mind is the Real picture, and nothing else. Any Interpretation in which something else is here slipped in as what one supposedly has in mind in an assertion that merely represents, belies the phenomenal facts of the case as to that about which the assertion gets made. Asserting is a way of Being towards the Thing itself that is.[2] And what does one's perceiving of it demonstrate? Nothing

---

[1] 'Er ist auch nicht auf Vorstellungen bezogen im Sinne des Vorgestellten, sofern damit gemeint wird ein "Bild" von dem realen Ding an der Wand.' While we follow tradition in translating 'Vorstellung' as 'representation', the literal meaning is somewhat closer to 'putting before us': In this sense our 'picture' or 'image' ('Bild') of the actual picture ('Bild') on the wall, is itself something which we have 'put before us' and which is thus 'vorgestellt', though in English we would hardly call it 'that which we represent'.

[2] 'Das Aussagen ist ein Sein zum seienden Ding selbst.'

else than *that* this Thing *is* the very entity which one has in mind in one's assertion. What comes up for confirmation is that this entity is pointed out by the Being in which the assertion is made—which is Being towards what is put forward in the assertion; thus what is to be confirmed is *that* such Being *uncovers* the entity towards which it is. What gets demonstrated is the Being-uncovering of the assertion.[1] In carrying out such a demonstration, the knowing remains related solely to the entity itself. In this entity the confirmation, as it were, gets enacted. The entity itself which one has in mind shows itself *just as* it is in itself; that is to say, it shows that it, in its selfsameness, is just as *it* gets pointed out in the assertion as being—just as *it* gets uncovered as being. Representations do not get compared, either among themselves or in *relation* to the Real Thing. What is to be demonstrated is not an agreement of knowing with its object, still less of the psychical with the physical; but neither is it an agreement between 'contents of consciousness' among themselves. What is to be demonstrated is solely the Being-uncovered [Entdeckt-sein] of the entity itself—*that entity* in the "how" of its uncoveredness. This uncoveredness is confirmed when that which is put forward in the assertion (namely the entity itself) shows itself *as that very same thing*. "*Confirmation*" signifies *the entity's showing itself in its selfsameness*.[xxxiv] The confirmation is accomplished on the basis of the entity's showing itself. This is possible only in such a way that the knowing which asserts and which gets confirmed is, in its ontological meaning, itself a *Being towards* Real entities, and a Being that *uncovers*.

To say that an assertion "*is true*" signifies that it uncovers the entity as it is in itself. Such an assertion asserts, points out, 'lets' the entity 'be seen' (ἀπόφανσις) in its uncoveredness. The *Being-true* (*truth*) of the assertion must be understood as *Being-uncovering**. Thus truth has by no means the structure of an agreement between knowing and the object in the sense 219 of a likening of one entity (the subject) to another (the Object).

Being-true as Being-uncovering*, is in turn ontologically possible only on the basis of Being-in-the-world. This latter phenomenon, which we have known as a basic state of Dasein, is the *foundation* for the primordial phenomenon of truth. We shall now follow this up more penetratingly.

---

1 'Ausgewiesen wird das Entdeckend-sein der Aussage.' Here and in the following pages we find the expression 'Entdeckend-sein' consistently printed with a hyphen in the more recent editions. In the older editions it is written sometimes as one word, sometimes as two, and it is hyphenated only at the ends of lines. In both editions we sometimes find this word printed with a lower-case initial. We have marked such cases with an asterisk; for while we prefer the translation 'Being-uncovering' in such cases, the lower-case initia suggests that 'to-be-uncovering' may be a better reading.

(b) The Primordial Phenomenon of Truth and the Derivative Character of the Traditional Conception of Truth

"Being-true" ("truth") means Being-uncovering*. But is not this a highly arbitrary way to define "truth"? By such drastic ways of defining this concept we may succeed in eliminating the idea of agreement from the conception of truth. Must we not pay for this dubious gain by plunging the 'good' old tradition into nullity? But while our definition is seemingly *arbitrary*, it contains only the *necessary* Interpretation of what was primordially surmised in the *oldest* tradition of ancient philosophy and even understood in a pre-phenomenological manner. If a λόγος as ἀπόφανσις is to be true, its Being-true is ἀληθεύειν in the manner of ἀποφαίνεσθαι —of taking entities out of their hiddenness and letting them be seen in their unhiddenness (their uncoveredness). The ἀλήθεια which Aristotle equates with πρᾶγμα and φαινόμενα in the passages cited above, signifies the 'things themselves'; it signifies what shows itself—*entities in the "how" of their uncoveredness*. And is it accidental that in one of the fragments of Heracleitus[xxxv]—the oldest fragments of philosophical doctrine in which the λόγος is *explicitly* handled—the phenomenon of truth in the sense of uncoveredness (unhiddenness), as we have set it forth, shows through? Those who are lacking in understanding are contrasted with the λόγος, and also with him who speaks that λόγος, and understands it. The λόγος is φράζων ὅπως ἔχει: it tells how entities comport themselves. But to those who are lacking in understanding, what they do remains hidden —λανθάνει. They forget it (ἐπιλανθάνονται); that is, for them it sinks back into hiddenness. Thus to the λόγος belongs unhiddenness— ἀ-λήθεια. To translate this word as 'truth', and, above all, to define this expression conceptually in theoretical ways, is to cover up the meaning of what the Greeks made 'self-evidently' basic for the terminological use of ἀλήθεια as a pre-philosophical way of understanding it.

220   In citing such evidence we must avoid uninhibited word-mysticism. Nevertheless, the ultimate business of philosophy is to preserve the *force of the most elemental words* in which Dasein expresses itself, and to keep the common understanding from levelling them off to that unintelligibility which functions in turn as a source of pseudo-problems.

We have now given a phenomenal demonstration of what we set forth earlier[xxxvi] as to λόγος and ἀλήθεια in, so to speak, a dogmatic Interpretation. In proposing our 'definition' of "truth" we have not *shaken off* the tradition, but we have *appropriated* it primordially; and we shall have done so all the more if we succeed in demonstrating that the idea of agreement is one to which theory had to come on the basis of the primordial phenomenon of truth, and if we can show how this came about.

Moreover, the 'definition' of "truth" as "uncoveredness" and as "Being-uncovering", it not a mere explanation of a word. Among those ways in which Dasein comports itself there are some which we are accustomed in the first instance to call 'true'; from the analysis of these our definition emerges.

Being-true as Being-uncovering*, is a way of Being for Dasein. What makes this very uncovering possible must necessarily be called 'true' in a still more primordial sense. *The most primordial phenomenon of truth is first shown by the existential-ontological foundations of uncovering.*

Uncovering is a way of Being for Being-in-the-world. Circumspective concern, or even that concern in which we tarry and look at something, uncovers entities within-the-world. These entities become that which has been uncovered. They are 'true' in a second sense. What is primarily 'true'—that is, uncovering—is Dasein. "Truth" in the second sense does not mean Being-uncovering* (uncovering), but Being-uncovered (uncoveredness).

Our earlier analysis of the worldhood of the world and of entities within-the-world has shown, however, that the uncoveredness of entities within-the-world is *grounded* in the world's disclosedness. But disclosedness is that basic character of Dasein according to which it *is* its "there". Disclosedness is constituted by state-of-mind, understanding, and discourse, and pertains equiprimordially to the world, to Being-in, and to the Self. In its very structure, care is *ahead of itself*—Being already in a world—as Being alongside entities within-the-world; and in this structure the disclosedness of Dasein lies hidden. *With* and *through* it is uncoveredness;[1] hence only with Dasein's *disclosedness* is the *most primordial* phenomenon of truth attained. What we have pointed out earlier with regard to the existential Constitution of the "there"[xxxvii] and in relation to the everyday Being of the "there",[xxxviii] pertains to the most primordial phenomenon of truth, nothing less. In so far as Dasein *is* its disclosedness essentially, and discloses and uncovers as something disclosed to this extent it is essentially 'true'. *Dasein is 'in the truth'.* This assertion has meaning ontologically. It does not purport to say that ontically Dasein is introduced 'to all the truth' either always or just in every case, but rather that the disclosedness of its ownmost Being belongs to its existential constitution.

221

If we accept the results we have obtained earlier, the full existential meaning of the principle that 'Dasein is in the truth' can be restored by the following considerations:

[1] '*Mit* und *durch* sie ist Entdecktheit . . .' Our version reflects the ambiguity of the German, which leaves the grammatical function of the pronoun 'sie' obscure and permits it to refer either to 'the disclosedness of Dasein', to 'care', or—perhaps most likely—to 'the structure of care'.

(1) To Dasein's state of Being, *disclosedness in general* essentially belongs. It embraces the whole of that structure-of-Being which has become explicit through the phenomenon of care. To care belongs not only Being-in-the-world but also Being alongside entities within-the-world. The uncoveredness of such entities is equiprimordial with the Being of Dasein and its disclosedness.

(2) To Dasein's state of Being belongs *thrownness*; indeed it is constitutive for Dasein's disclosedness. In thrownness is revealed that in each case Dasein, as my Dasein and this Dasein, is already in a definite world and alongside a definite range of definite entities within-the-world.[1] Disclosedness is essentially factical.

(3) To Dasein's state of Being belongs *projection*—disclosive Being towards its potentiality-for-Being. As something that understands, Dasein *can* understand *itself* in terms of the 'world' and Others or in terms of its ownmost potentiality-for-Being.[2] The possibility just mentioned means that Dasein discloses itself to itself in and as its ownmost potentiality-for Being. This *authentic* disclosedness shows the phenomenon of the most primordial truth in the mode of authenticity. The most primordial, and indeed the most authentic, disclosedness in which Dasein, as a potentiality-for-Being, can be, is the *truth of existence*. This becomes existentially and ontologically definite only in connection with the analysis of Dasein's authenticity.

(4) To Dasein's state of Being belongs *falling*. Proximally and for the most part Dasein is lost in its 'world'. Its understanding, as a projection upon possibilities of Being, has diverted itself thither. Its absorption in the "they" signifies that it is dominated by the way things are publicly interpreted. That which has been uncovered and disclosed stands in a mode in which it has been disguised and closed off by idle talk, curiosity, and ambiguity. Being towards entities has not been extinguished, but it has been uprooted. Entities have not been completely hidden; they are precisely the sort of thing that has been uncovered, but at the same time they have been disguised. They show themselves, but in the mode of semblance. Likewise what has formerly been uncovered sinks back again, hidden and disguised. *Because Dasein is essentially falling, its state of Being is such that it is in 'untruth'*. This term, like the expression 'falling', is here used ontologically. If we are to use it in existential analysis, we must

---

[1] 'In ihr enthüllt sich, dass Dasein je schon als meines und dieses in einer bestimmten Welt und bei einem bestimmten Umkreis von bestimmten innerweltlichen Seienden ist.'

[2] '. . . der Entwurf: das erschliessende Sein zu seinem Seinkönnen. Dasein *kann sich* als verstehendes aus der "Welt" und den Anderen her verstehen oder aus seinem eigensten Seinkönnen.' The earlier editions have a full stop after '*Entwurf*' rather than a colon, and introduce 'das' with a capital. The grammatical function of 'als verstehendes' seems ambiguous.

222

avoid giving it any ontically negative 'evaluation'. To be closed off and covered up belongs to Dasein's *facticity*. In its full existential-ontological meaning, the proposition that 'Dasein is in the truth' states equiprimordially that 'Dasein is in untruth'. But only in so far as Dasein has been disclosed has it also been closed off; and only in so far as entities within-the-world have been uncovered along with Dasein, have such entities, as possibly encounterable within-the-world, been covered up (hidden) or disguised.

It is therefore essential that Dasein should explicitly appropriate what has already been uncovered, defend it *against* semblance and disguise, and assure itself of its uncoveredness again and again. The uncovering of anything new is never done on the basis of having something completely hidden, but takes its departure rather from uncoveredness in the mode of semblance. Entities look as if . . . That is, they have, in a certain way, been uncovered already, and yet they are still disguised.

Truth (uncoveredness) is something that must always first be wrested from entities. Entities get snatched out of their hiddenness. The factical uncoveredness of anything is always, as it were, a kind of *robbery*. Is it accidental that when the Greeks express themselves as to the essence of truth, they use a *privative* expression—ά-λήθεια? When Dasein so expresses itself, does not a primordial understanding of its own Being thus make itself known—the understanding (even if it is only pre-ontological) that Being-in-untruth makes up an essential characteristic of Being-in-the-world?

The goddess of Truth who guides Parmenides, puts two pathways before him, one of uncovering, one of hiding; but this signifies nothing else than that Dasein is already both in the truth and in untruth. The way of uncovering is achieved only in κρίνειν λόγῳ—in distinguishing between   223
these understandingly, and making one's decision for the one rather than the other.xxxix

The existential-ontological condition for the fact that Being-in-the-world is characterized by 'truth' and 'untruth', lies in that state of Dasein's Being which we have designated as *thrown projection*. This is something that is constitutive for the structure of care.

The upshot of our existential-ontological Interpretation of the phenomenon of truth is (1) that truth, in the most primordial sense, is Dasein's disclosedness, to which the uncoveredness of entities within-the-world belongs; and (2) that Dasein is equiprimordially both in the truth and in untruth.

Within the horizon of the traditional Interpretation of the phenomenon of truth, our insight into these principles will not be complete until it can be shown: (1) that truth, understood as agreement, originates from disclosedness by way of definite modification; (2) that the kind of Being which belongs to disclosedness itself is such that its derivative modification first comes into view and leads the way for the theoretical explication of the structure of truth.

Assertion and its structure (namely, the apophantical "as") are founded upon interpretation and its structure (viz, the hermeneutical "as") and also upon understanding—upon Dasein's disclosedness. Truth, however, is regarded as a distinctive character of assertion as so derived. Thus the roots of the truth of assertion reach back to the disclosedness of the understanding.[xl] But over and above these indications of how the truth of assertion has originated, the phenomenon of *agreement* must now be exhibited *explicitly* in its derivative character.

Our Being alongside entities within-the-world is concern, and this is Being which uncovers. To Dasein's disclosedness, however, discourse belongs essentially.[xlii] Dasein expresses itself [spricht sich aus]: it expresses *itself* as a Being-towards entities—a Being-towards which uncovers. And in assertion it expresses itself as such about entities which have been uncovered. Assertion communicates entities in the "how" of their uncoveredness. When Dasein is aware of the communication, it brings itself in its awareness into an uncovering Being-towards the entities discussed. The assertion which is expressed is about something, and in what it is about [in ihrem Worüber] it contains the uncoveredness of these entities. This uncoveredness is preserved in what is expressed. What is expressed becomes, as it were, something ready-to-hand within-the-world which can be taken up and spoken again.[1] Because the uncoveredness has been preserved, that which is expressed (which thus is ready-to-hand) has in itself a relation to any entities about which it is an assertion. Any uncoveredness is an uncoveredness of something. Even when Dasein speaks over again what someone else has said, it comes into a Being-towards the very entities which have been discussed.[3] But it has been exempted from having to uncover them again, primordially, and it holds that it has been thus exempted.

Dasein need not bring itself face to face with entities themselves in an 'original' experience; but it nevertheless remains in a Being-towards these entities. In a large measure uncoveredness gets appropriated not by one's own uncovering, but rather by hearsay of something that has been said.

---

[1] 'Das Ausgesprochene wird gleichsam zu einem innerweltlich Zuhandenen, das aufgenommen und weitergesprochen werden kann.' While we have followed our usual policy in translating 'das Ausgesprochene' as 'what is expressed', it might perhaps be translated as 'that which is spoken out', 'the utterance', or even 'the pronouncement'.

[2] "Auch im Nachsprechen kommt das nachsprechende Dasein in ein Sein zum besprochenen Seienden selbst.'

Absorption in something that has been said belongs to the kind of Being which the "they" possesses. That which has been expressed as such takes over Being-towards those entities which have been uncovered in the assertion. If, however, these entities are to be appropriated explicitly with regard to their uncoveredness, this amounts to saying that the assertion is to be demonstrated as one that uncovers. But the assertion expressed is something ready-to-hand, and indeed in such a way that, as something by which uncoveredness is preserved, it has in itself a relation to the entities uncovered. Now to demonstrate that it is something which uncovers [ihres Entdeckend-seins] means to demonstrate how the assertion by which the uncoveredness is preserved is related *to* these entities. The assertion is something ready-to-hand. The entities to which it is related as something that uncovers, are either ready-to-hand or present-at-hand within-the-world. The relation itself presents itself thus, as one that is present-at-hand. But this relation lies in the fact that the uncoveredness preserved in the assertion is in each case an uncoveredness o f something. The judgment 'contains something which holds for the objects' (Kant). But the relation itself now acquires the character of presence-at-hand by getting switched over to a relationship between things which are present-at-hand. The uncoveredness of something becomes the present-at-hand conformity of one thing which is present-at-hand—the assertion expressed—*to* something else which is present-at-hand—the entity under discussion. And if this conformity is seen only as a relationship between things which are present-at-hand—that is, if the kind of Being which belongs to the terms of this relationship has not been discriminated and is understood as something merely present-at-hand—then the relation shows itself as an agreement of two things which are present-at-hand, an agreement which is present-at-hand itself.

When the assertion has been expressed, the uncoveredness of the entity moves into 225 *the kind of Being of that which is ready-to-hand within-the-world.*[1] *But now to the extent that in this uncoveredness, as an uncoveredness o f something, a relationship to something present-at-hand persists, the uncoveredness (truth) becomes, for its part, a relationship between things which are present-at-hand(intellectus and res)—a relationship that is present-at-hand itself.*

Though it is founded upon Dasein's disclosedness, the existential phenomenon of uncoveredness becomes a property which is present-at-hand but in which there still lurks a relational character; and as such a property, it gets broken asunder into a relationship which is present-at-hand. Truth as disclosedness and as a Being-towards uncovered entities—a

---

[1] *'Die Entdecktheit des Seienden rückt mit der Ausgesprochenheit der Aussage in die Seinsart des innerweltlich Zuhandenen.'*

Being which itself uncovers—has become truth as agreement between
things which are present-at-hand within-the-world. And thus we have
pointed out the ontologically derivative character of the traditional conception of truth.

Yet that which is last in the order of the way things are connected in
their foundations existentially and ontologically, is regarded ontically
and factically as that which is first and closest to us. The necessity of this
Fact, however, is based in turn upon the kind of Being which Dasein itself
possesses. Dasein, in its concernful absorption, understands itself in terms
of what it encounters within-the-world. The uncoveredness which belongs
to uncovering, is something that we come across proximally within-the-
world in that which has been *ex*pressed [im *Aus*gesprochenen]. Not only
truth, however, is encountered as present-at-hand: in general our understanding of Being is such that every entity is understood in the first
instance as present-at-hand. If the 'truth' which we encounter proximally
in an ontical manner is considered ontologically in the way that is closest
to us, then the λόγος (the assertion) gets understood as λόγος τινός—
as an assertion about something, an uncoveredness of something; but
the phenomenon gets Interpreted as something present-at-hand with
regard to its possible presence-at-hand.[1] Yet because presence-at-hand
has been equated with the meaning of Being in general, the question of
whether this kind of Being of truth is a primordial one, and whether there
is anything primordial in that structure of it which we encounter as
closest to us, *can* not come alive at all. *The primordial phenomenon of truth has
been covered up by Dasein's very understanding of Being—that understanding which
is proximally the one that prevails, and which even today has not been surmounted*
explicitly *and* in principle.

At the same time, however, we must not overlook the fact that while this
way of understanding Being (the way which is closest to us) is one which the
Greeks were the first to develop as a branch of knowledge and to master,
the primordial understanding of truth was simultaneously alive among
them, even if pre-ontologically, and it even held its own against the con-
cealment implicit in their ontology—at least in Aristotle.[xlii]

226   Aristotle never defends the thesis that the primordial 'locus' of truth
is in the judgment. He says rather that the λόγος is that way of Being in
which Dasein can *either* uncover *or* cover up. This *double possibility* is what
is distinctive in the Being-true of the λόγος: the λόγος is that way of
comporting oneself which can *also cover things up*. And because Aristotle
never upheld the thesis we have mentioned, he was also never in a

---

[1] '. . . interpretiert aber das Phänomen als Vorhandenes auf seine mögliche Vorhandenheit.'

situation to 'broaden' the conception of truth in the λόγος to include pure νοεῖν. The truth of αἴσθησις and of the seeing of 'ideas' is the primordial kind of uncovering. And only because νόησις primarily uncovers, can the λόγος as διανοεῖν also have uncovering as its function.

Not only is it wrong to invoke Aristotle for the thesis that the genuine 'locus' of truth lies in the judgment; even in its content this thesis fails to recognize the structure of truth. Assertion is not the primary 'locus' of truth. *On the contrary*, whether as a mode in which uncoveredness is appropriated or as a way of Being-in-the-world, assertion is grounded in Dasein's uncovering, or rather in its *disclosedness*. The most primordial 'truth' is the 'locus' of assertion; it is the ontological condition for the possibility that assertions can be either true or false—that they may uncover or cover things up.

Truth, understood in the most primordial sense, belongs to the basic constitution of Dasein. The term signifies an *existentiale*. But herewith we have already sketched out our answers to the question of what kind of Being truth possesses, and to the question of in what sense it is necessary to presuppose that 'there is truth'.

(c) The Kind of Being which Truth Possesses, and the Presupposition of Truth

Dasein, as constituted by disclosedness, is essentially in the truth. Disclosedness is a kind of Being which is essential to Dasein. *'There is'* *truth only in so far as Dasein i s and so long as Dasein i s*. Entities are uncovered only *when* Dasein *is*; and only as long as Dasein *is*, are they disclosed. Newton's laws, the principle of contradiction, any truth whatever —these are true only as long as Dasein *is*. Before there was any Dasein, there was no truth; nor will there be any after Dasein is no more. For in such a case truth as disclosedness, uncovering, and uncoveredness, *cannot* be. Before Newton's laws were discovered, they were not 'true'; it does not follow that they were false, or even that they would become false if ontically no discoveredness were any longer possible. Just as little does this 'restriction' imply that the Being-true of 'truths' has in any way been diminished. 227

To say that before Newton his laws were neither true nor false, cannot signify that before him there were no such entities as have been uncovered and pointed out by those laws. Through Newton the laws became true; and with them, entities became accessible in themselves to Dasein. Once entities have been uncovered, they show themselves precisely as entities which beforehand already were. Such uncovering is the kind of Being which belongs to 'truth'.

That there are 'eternal truths' will not be adequately proved until someone has succeeded in demonstrating that Dasein has been and will be for all eternity. As long as such a proof is still outstanding, this principle remains a fanciful contention which does not gain in legitimacy from having philosophers commonly 'believe' it.

Because the kind of Being that is essential to truth is of the character of Dasein, all truth is relative to Dasein's Being. Does this relativity signify that all truth is 'subjective'? If one Interprets 'subjective' as 'left to the subject's discretion', then it certainly does not. For uncovering, in the sense which is most its own, takes asserting out of the province of 'subjective' discretion, and brings the uncovering Dasein face to face with the entities themselves. And only *because* 'truth', as uncovering, *is a kind of Being which belongs to Dasein*, can it be taken out of the province of *Dasein's* discretion. Even the 'universal validity' of truth is rooted solely in the fact that Dasein can uncover entities in themselves and free them. Only so can these entities in themselves be binding for every possible assertion—that is, for every way of pointing them out.[1] If truth has been correctly understood, is it in the least impaired by the fact that it is ontically possible only in the 'subject' and that it stands and falls with the Being of that 'subject'?

Now that we have an existential conception of the kind of Being that belongs to truth, the meaning of "presupposing the truth" also becomes intelligible. *Why must we presuppose that there is truth?* What is 'presupposing'? What do we have in mind with the 'must' and the 'we'? What does it mean to say 'there is truth'? 'We' presuppose truth because 'we', being in the kind of Being which Dasein possesses, *are* 'in the truth'. We do not presuppose it as something 'outside' us and 'above' us, towards which, along with other 'values', we comport ourselves. It is not we who presuppose 'truth'; but it is *'truth'* that makes it at all possible ontologically for us to be able to *be* such that we 'presuppose' anything at all. Truth is what first *makes possible* anything like presupposing.

What does it mean to 'presuppose'? It is to understand something as the ground for the Being of some other entity. Such understanding of an entity in its interconnections of Being, is possible only on the ground of disclosedness—that is, on the ground of Dasein's Being something which uncovers. Thus to presuppose 'truth' means to understand it as something for the sake of which Dasein i s. But Dasein is already ahead of itself in each case; this is implied in its state-of-Being as care. It is an entity for which, in its Being, its ownmost potentiality-for-Being is an issue. To Dasein's Being and its potentiality-for-Being as Being-in-the-world,

228

[1] 'Auch die "Allgemeingültigkeit" der Wahrheit ist lediglich verwurzelt, dass das Dasein Seiendes an ihm selbst entdecken und freigeben kann. Nur so vermag dieses Seiende an ihm selbst jede mögliche Aussage, das heisst Aufzeigung seiner, zu binden.'

disclosedness and uncovering belong essentially. To Dasein its potentiality-for-Being-in-the-world is an issue, and this includes[1] concerning itself with entities within-the-world and uncovering them circumspectively. In Dasein's state-of-Being as care, in Being-ahead-of-itself, lies the most primordial 'presupposing'. *Because this presupposing of itself belongs to Dasein's Being, 'we' must also presuppose 'ourselves' as having the attribute of disclosedness.* There are also entities with a character other than that of Dasein, but the 'presupposing' which lies in Dasein's Being does not relate itself to these; it relates itself solely to Dasein itself. The truth which has been pre-supposed, or the 'there is' by which its Being is to be defined, has that kind of Being—or meaning of Being—which belongs to Dasein itself. We must 'make' the presupposition of truth because it *is* one that has been 'made' already with the Being of the 'we'.

We *must* presuppose truth. Dasein itself, as in each case m y Dasein and this Dasein, *must* be; and in the same way the truth, as Dasein's dis-closedness, *must be*. This belongs to Dasein's essential thrownness into the world. *Has Dasein as itself ever decided freely whether it wants to come into 'Dasein' or not, and will it ever be able to make such a decision?* 'In itself' it is quite incomprehensible why entities are to be *uncovered*, why *truth* and *Dasein* must be. The usual refutation of that scepticism which denies either the Being of 'truth' or its cognizability, stops half way. What it shows, as a formal argument, is simply that if anything gets judged, truth has been presupposed. This suggests that 'truth' belongs to assertion—that pointing something out is, by its very meaning, an uncovering. But when one says this, *one has to clarify why* that in which there lies the onto-logical ground for this necessary connection between assertion and truth as regards their Being, must be as it is. The kind of Being which belongs to truth is likewise left completely obscure, and so is the meaning of presupposing, and that of its ontological foundation in Dasein itself. Moreover, one here fails to recognize that even when nobody *judges*, truth already gets presupposed in so far as Dasein i s at all.   229

A sceptic can no more be refuted than the Being of truth can be 'proved'. And if any sceptic of the kind who denies the truth, factically *is*, he does *not* even *need* to be refuted. In so far as he *is*, and has understood himself in this Being, he has obliterated Dasein in the desperation of suicide; and in doing so, he has also obliterated truth. Because Dasein, for its own part, cannot first be subjected to proof, the necessity of truth cannot be proved either. It has no more been demonstrated that there ever has 'been' an 'actual' sceptic[2] (though this is what has at bottom

---

[1] Reading 'und darin' with the newer editions. The older editions have 'd.h. u.a.'

[2] '. . . dass es je . . . einen "wirklichen" Skeptiker "gegeben" hat.' The older editions have 'nie' ('never') instead of 'je' ('ever').

been believed in the refutations of scepticism, in spite of what these under-take to do) than it has been demonstrated that there are any 'eternal truths'. But perhaps such sceptics have been more frequent than one would innocently like to have true when one tries to bowl over 'scepticism' by formal dialectics.

Thus with the question of the Being of truth and the necessity of pre-supposing it, just as with the question of the essence of knowledge, an 'ideal subject' has generally been posited. The motive for this, whether explicit or tacit, lies in the requirement that philosophy should have the '*a priori*' as its theme, rather than 'empirical facts' as such. There is some justification for this requirement, though it still needs to be grounded ontologically. Yet is this requirement satisfied by positing an 'ideal subject'? Is not such a subject *a fanciful idealization*? With such a concep-tion have we not missed precisely the *a priori* character of that merely 'factual' subject, Dasein? Is it not an attribute of the *a priori* character of the factical subject (that is, an attribute of Dasein's facticity) that it is in the truth and in untruth equiprimordially?

The ideas of a 'pure "I"' and of a 'consciousness in general' are so far from including the *a priori* character of 'actual' subjectivity that the onto-logical characters of Dasein's facticity and its state of Being are either passed over or not seen at all. Rejection of a 'consciousness in general' does not signify that the *a priori* is negated, any more than the positing of an idealized subject guarantees that Dasein has an *a priori* character grounded upon fact.

Both the contention that there are 'eternal truths' and the jumbling together of Dasein's phenomenally grounded 'ideality' with an idealized absolute subject, belong to those residues of Christian theology within philosophical problematics which have not as yet been radically extruded.

230   The Being of truth is connected primordially with Dasein. And only because Dasein i s as constituted by disclosedness (that is, by under-standing), can anything like Being be understood; only so is it possible to understand Being.

Being (not entities) is something which 'there is' only in so far as truth is. And truth *is* only in so far as and as long as Dasein is. Being and truth 'are' equiprimordially. What does it signify that Being 'is', where Being is to be distinguished from every entity? One can ask this concretely only if the meaning of Being and the full scope of the understanding of Being have in general been clarified. Only then can one also analyse primordially what belongs to the concept of a science *of Being as such*, and to its pos-sibilities and its variations. And in demarcating this research and its truth, the kind of research in which *entities* are uncovered, and its accompanying truth, must be defined ontologically.

The answer to the question of the meaning of Being has yet to be given [steht . . . aus]. What has our fundamental analysis of Dasein, as we have carried it out so far, contributed to working out this question? By laying bare the phenomenon of care, we have clarified the state of Being of that entity to whose Being something like an understanding of Being belongs. At the same time the Being of Dasein has thus been distinguished from modes of Being (readiness-to-hand, presence-at-hand, Reality) which characterize entities with a character other than that of Dasein. Understanding has itself been elucidated; and at the same time the methodological transparency of the procedure of Interpreting Being by understanding it and interpreting it, has thus been guaranteed.

If in care we have arrived at Dasein's primordial state of Being, then this must also be the basis for conceptualizing that understanding of Being which lies in care; that is to say, it must be possible to define the meaning of Being. But *is* the phenomenon of care one in which the most primordial existential-ontological state of Dasein is disclosed? And has the structural manifoldness which lies in this phenomenon, presented us with the most primordial totality of factical Dasein's Being? Has our investigation up to this point ever brought Dasein into view *as a whole*?

DERIVED f. analysis of
the there

(1) Being-in (Existentiality)
(a) disposition
(b) understanding
(c) discourse

WORLDHOOD

(2) Thrownness → no "whence"; no "whither"

(3) Falling
- into dispersal in the they-self

The who of D.
THEY-SELF

DIVISION TWO

DASEIN AND TEMPORALITY[1]

¶ 45. *The Outcome of the Preparatory Fundamental Analysis of Dasein, and the Task of a Primordial Existential Interpretation of this Entity*

WHAT have we gained by our preparatory analysis of Dasein, and what are we seeking? In Being-in-the-world, whose essential structures centre in disclosedness, we have *found* the basic state of the entity we have taken as our theme. The totality of Being-in-the-world as a structural whole has revealed itself as care. In care the Being of Dasein is included. When we came to analyse this Being, we took as our clue existence[1], which, in anticipation, we had designated as the essence of Dasein. This term "existence" formally indicates that Dasein *is* as an understanding potentiality-for-Being, which, in its Being, makes an issue of that Being itself. In every case, I myself am the entity which is in such a manner [dergestalt seiend]. By working out the phenomenon of care, we have given ourselves an insight into the concrete constitution of existence—that is, an insight into its equiprimordial connection with Dasein's facticity and its falling.

What we are *seeking* is the answer to the question about the meaning of Being in general, and, prior to that, the possibility of working out in a radical manner this basic question of all ontology. But to lay bare the horizon within which something like Being in general becomes intelligible, is tantamount to clarifying the possibility of having any understanding of Being at all—an understanding which itself belongs to the constitution of the entity called Dasein.[ii] The understanding of Being, however, cannot be *radically* clarified as an essential element in Dasein's Being, unless the entity to whose Being it belongs, has been Interpreted *primordially* in itself with regard to its Being.

Are we entitled to the claim that in characterizing Dasein ontologically *qua* care we have given a *primordial* Interpretation of this entity? By what criterion is the existential analytic of Dasein to be assessed as regards its

[1] 'Dasein und Zeitlichkeit'. In this heading and in others which follow in this Division, we have capitalized such words as 'temporal' and 'constitution' in accordance with normal practice in titles, even when this violates the orthographic conventions of our translation.

primordiality, or the lack of it? What, indeed, do we mean by the *"primordiality"* of an ontological Interpretation?

Ontological investigation is a possible kind of interpreting, which we have described as the working-out and appropriation of an under- standing.[iii] Every interpretation has its fore-having, its fore-sight, and its fore-conception. If such an interpretation, as Interpretation, becomes an explicit task for research, then the totality of these 'presuppositions' (which we call the *"hermeneutical Situation"*) needs to be clarified and made secure beforehand, both in a basic experience of the 'object' to be dis- closed, and in terms of such an experience. In ontological Interpretation an entity is to be laid bare with regard to its own state of Being; such an Interpretation obliges us first to give a phenomenal characterization of the entity we have taken as our theme, and thus to bring it into the scope of our fore-having, with which all the subsequent steps of our analysis are to conform. But at the same time these steps need to be guided by what- ever fore-sight is possible as to the kind of Being which the entity may possess. Our fore-having and our fore-sight will then give us at the same time a sketch of that way of conceiving (or fore-conception) to the level of which all structures of Being are to be raised.

232

If, however, the ontological Interpretation is to be a *primordial* one, this not only demands that in general the hermeneutical Situation shall be one which has been made secure in conformity with the phenomena; it also requires explicit assurance that the *whole* of the entity which it has taken as its theme has been brought into the fore-having. Similarly, it is not enough just to make a first sketch of the Being of this entity, even if our sketch is grounded in the phenomena. If we are to have a fore-sight of Being, we must see it in such a way as not to miss the *unity* of those struc- tural items which belong to it and are possible. Only then can the question of the meaning of the unity which belongs to the whole entity's totality of Being, be formulated and answered with any phenomenal assurance.

Has the existential analysis of Dasein which we have carried out, arisen from such a hermeneutical Situation as will guarantee the primordiality which fundamental ontology demands? Can we progress from the result we have obtained—that the being of Dasein is care—to the question of the primordial unity of this structural whole?

What is the status of the fore-sight by which our ontological procedure has hitherto been guided? We have defined the idea of existence as a potentiality-for-Being—a potentiality which understands, and for which its own Being is an issue. But this *potentiality-for-Being*, as one which is in each case *mine*, is free either for authenticity or for inauthenticity or for a mode in which neither of these has been differentiated.[iv] In starting with average everydayness, our Interpretation has heretofore been confined to the analysis of such existing as is either undifferentiated or inauthentic. Of course even along this path, it was possible and indeed necessary to reach a concrete determination of the existentiality of existence. Nevertheless, our ontological characterization of the constitution of existence still lacked something essential. "Existence" means a potentiality-for-Being —but also one which is authentic. As long as the existential structure of an authentic potentiality-for-Being has not been brought into the idea of existence, the fore-sight by which an *existential* Interpretation is guided will lack primordiality.

And how about what we have had in advance in our hermeneutical Situation hitherto? How about its fore-having? When and how has our existential analysis received any assurance that by starting with everydayness, it has forced the *whole* of Dasein—this entity from its 'beginning' to its 'end'—into the phenomenological view which gives us our theme? We have indeed contended that care is the totality of the structural whole of Dasein's constitution.ᵛ But have we not at the very outset of our Interpretation renounced the possibility of bringing Dasein into view as a whole? Everydayness is precisely that Being which is 'between' birth and death. And if existence is definitive for Dasein's Being and if its essence is constituted in part by potentiality-for-Being, then, as long as Dasein exists, it must in each case, as such a potentiality, *not yet be* something. Any entity whose Essence is made up of existence, is essentially opposed to the possibility of our getting it in our grasp as an entity which is a whole. Not only has the hermeneutical Situation hitherto given us no assurance of 'having' the whole entity: one may even question whether "having" the whole entity is attainable at all, and whether a primordial ontological Interpretation of Dasein will not founder on the kind of Being which belongs to the very entity we have taken as our theme.

One thing has become unmistakable: *our existential analysis of Dasein up till now cannot lay claim to primordiality*. Its fore-having never included more than the *inauthentic* Being of Dasein, and of Dasein as *less* than a *whole* [*als unganzes*]. If the Interpretation of Dasein's Being is to become primordial, as a foundation for working out the basic question of ontology, then it must first have brought to light existentially the Being of Dasein in its possibilities of *authenticity* and *totality*.

Thus arises the task of putting Dasein as a whole into our fore-having. This signifies, however, that we must first of all raise the question of this entity's potentiality-for-Being-a-whole. As long as Dasein is, there is in every case something still outstanding, which Dasein can be and will be. But to that which is thus outstanding, the 'end' itself belongs. The 'end'

of Being-in-the-world is death. This end, which belongs to the potentiality-for-Being—that is to say, to existence—limits and determines in
every case whatever totality is possible for Dasein. If, however, Dasein's
Being-at-an-end[1] in death, and therewith its Being-a-whole, are to be
included in the discussion of its possibly *Being-a-whole*, and if this is to be
done in a way which is appropriate to the phenomena, then we must have
obtained an ontologically adequate conception of death—that is to say
an *existential* conception of it. But as something of the character of Dasein,
death *is* only in an existentiell *Being towards death* [*Sein zum Tode*]. The
existential structure of such Being proves to be the ontologically constitutive state of Dasein's potentiality-for-Being-a-whole. Thus the whole
existing Dasein allows itself to be brought into our existential fore-having.
But can Dasein also exist *authentically* as a whole? How is the authenticity
of existence to be determined at all, if not with regard to authentic
existing? Where do we get our criterion for this? Manifestly, Dasein
itself must, in its Being, present us with the possibility and the manner of
its authentic existence, unless such existence is something that can be
imposed upon it ontically, or ontologically fabricated. But an authentic
potentiality-for-Being is attested by the conscience. And conscience, as a
phenomenon of Dasein, demands, like death, a genuinely existential
Interpretation. Such an Interpretation leads to the insight that Dasein has
an authentic potentiality-for-Being in that it *wants to have a conscience*. But
this is an existentiell possibility which tends, from the very meaning of its
Being, to be made definite in an existentiell way by Being-towards-death.

By pointing out that Dasein has an *authentic potentiality-for-Being-a-whole*,
the existential analytic acquires assurance as to the constitution of Dasein's
primordial Being. But at the same time the authentic potentiality-for-Being-
a-whole becomes visible as a mode of care. And therewith the phenomenally adequate ground for a primordial Interpretation of the meaning
of Dasein's Being has also been assured.

But the primordial ontological basis for·Dasein's existentiality is *temporality*. In terms of temporality, the articulated structural totality of
Dasein's Being as care first becomes existentially intelligible. The Interpretation of the meaning of Dasein's Being cannot stop with this demonstration. The existential-temporal analysis of this entity needs to be
confirmed concretely. We must go back and lay bare in their temporal
meaning the ontological structures of Dasein which we have previously
obtained. Everydayness reveals itself as a mode of temporality. But by
thus recapitulating our preparatory fundamental analysis of Dasein, we

---

[1] 'Zu-Ende-sein'. This expression is to be distinguished from 'Sein-zum-Ende', which
we shall translate as 'Being-towards-the-end'.

235 will at the same time make the phenomenon of temporality itself more transparent. In terms of temporality, it then becomes intelligible why Dasein is, and can be, historical in the basis of its Being, and why, *as historical*, it can develop historiology.

If temporality makes up the primordial meaning of Dasein's Being, and if moreover this entity is one for which, in its Being, *this very Being* is an *issue*, then care must use 'time' and therefore must reckon with 'time'. 'Time-reckoning' is developed by Dasein's temporality. The 'time' which is experienced in such reckoning is that phenomenal aspect of temporality which is closest to us. Out of it arises the ordinary everyday understanding of time. And this understanding evolves into the traditional conception of time.

By casting light on the source of the 'time' 'in which' entities within-the-world are encountered—time as "within-time-ness"—we shall make manifest an essential possibility of the temporalizing of temporality.[1] Therewith the understanding prepares itself for an even more primordial temporalizing of temporality. In this[2] is grounded that understanding of Being which is constitutive for the Being of Dasein. Within the horizon of time the projection of a meaning of Being in general can be accomplished.

Thus the investigation comprised in the division which lies before us will now traverse the following stages: Dasein's possibility of Being-a-whole, and Being-towards-death (Chapter 1); Dasein's attestation of an authentic potentiality-for-Being, and resoluteness (Chapter 2); Dasein's authentic potentiality-for-Being-a-whole, and temporality as the ontological meaning of care (Chapter 3); temporality and everydayness (Chapter 4); temporality and historicality (Chapter 5); temporality and within-time-ness as the source of the ordinary conception of time (Chapter 6).[vi]

---

[1] 'Die Aufhellung des Ursprungs der "Zeit", "in der" innerweltliches Seiendes begegnet, der Zeit als Innerzeitigkeit, offenbart eine wesenhafte Zeitigungsmöglichkeit der Zeitlichkeit.' On 'zeitigen' see H. 304 below.

[2] 'In ihr . . .' It is not clear whether the pronoun 'ihr' refers to 'Zeitigung' ('temporalizing') or 'Zeitlichkeit' ('temporality').

I

DASEIN'S POSSIBILITY OF BEING-A-WHOLE, AND BEING-TOWARDS-DEATH

¶ *46. The Seeming Impossibility of Getting Dasein's Being-a-whole into our Grasp Ontologically and Determining its Character*

THE inadequacy of the hermeneutical Situation from which the preceding analysis of Dasein has arisen, must be surmounted. It is necessary for us to bring the whole Dasein into our fore-having. We must accordingly ask whether this entity, as something existing, can ever become accessible in its Being-a-whole. In Dasein's very state of Being, there are important reasons which seem to speak against the possibility of having it presented [Vorgabe] in the manner required.

The possibility of this entity's Being-a-whole is manifestly inconsistent with the ontological meaning of care, and care is that which forms the totality of Dasein's structural whole. Yet the primary item in care is the 'ahead-of-itself', and this means that in every case Dasein exists for the sake of itself. 'As long as it is', right to its end, it comports itself towards its potentiality-for-Being. Even when it still exists but has nothing more 'before it' and has 'settled [abgeschlossen] its account', its Being is still determined by the 'ahead-of-itself'. Hopelessness, for instance, does not tear Dasein away from its possibilities, but is only one of its own modes of *Being towards* these possibilities. Even when one is without Illusions and 'is ready *for* anything' ["Gefasstsein *auf* Alles"], here too the 'ahead-of-itself' lies hidden. The 'ahead-of-itself', as an item in the structure of care, tells us unambiguously that in Dasein there is always something *still outstanding*,[1] which, as a potentiality-for-Being for Dasein itself, has not yet become 'actual'. It is essential to the basic constitution of Dasein that there is *constantly something still to be settled* [*eine ständige Unabgeschlossenheit*]. Such a lack of totality signifies that there is something still outstanding in one's potentiality-for-Being.

[1] '. . . im Dasein immer noch etwas *aussteht* . . .' The verb 'ausstehen' and the noun 'Ausstand' (which we usually translate as 'something still outstanding', etc.), are ordinarily used in German to apply to a debt or a bank deposit which, from the point of view of the lender or depositor, has yet to be repaid to him, liquidated, or withdrawn.

But as soon as Dasein 'exists' in such a way that absolutely nothing more is still outstanding in it, then it has already for this very reason become "no-longer-Being-there" [Nicht-mehr-da-sein]. Its Being is annihilated when what is still outstanding in its Being has been liquidated. As long as Dasein *is* as an entity, it has never reached its 'wholeness'.[1] But if it gains such 'wholeness', this gain becomes the utter loss of Being-in-the-world. In such a case, it can never again be experienced *as an entity*.

The reason for the impossibility of experiencing Dasein ontically as a whole which is [als seiendes Ganzes], and therefore of determining its character ontologically in its Being-a-whole, does not lie in any imperfection of our *cognitive powers*. The hindrance lies rather in the *Being* of this entity. That which cannot ever *be such as* any experience which pretends to get Dasein in its grasp would claim, eludes in principle any possibility of getting experienced at all.[2] But in that case is it not a hopeless undertaking to try to discern in Dasein its ontological totality of Being?

We cannot cross out the 'ahead-of-itself' as an essential item in the structure of care. But how sound are the conclusions which we have drawn from this? Has not the impossibility of getting the whole of Dasein into our grasp been inferred by an argument which is merely formal? Or have we not at bottom inadvertently posited that Dasein is something present-at-hand, ahead of which something that is not yet present-at-hand is constantly shoving itself? Have we, in our argument, taken "Being-not-yet" and the 'ahead' in a sense that is genuinely *existential*? Has our talk of the 'end' and 'totality' been phenomenally appropriate to Dasein? Has the expression 'death' had a biological signification or one that is existential-ontological, or indeed any signification that has been adequately and surely delimited? Have we indeed exhausted all the possibilities for making Dasein accessible in its wholeness?

We must answer these questions before the problem of Dasein's totality can be dismissed as nugatory [nichtiges]. This question—both the existentiell question of whether a potentiality-for-Being-a-whole is possible, and the existential question of the state-of-Being of 'end' and 'totality'—is one in which there lurks the task of giving a positive analysis for some phenomena of existence which up till now have been left aside. In the centre of these considerations we have the task of characterizing ontologically Dasein's Being-at-an-end and of achieving an existential conception

[1] 'Die Behebung des Seinsausstandes besagt Vernichtung seines Seins. Solange das Dasein als Seiendes *ist*, hat es seine "Gänze" nie erreicht.' The verb 'beheben' is used in the sense of closing one's account or liquidating it by withdrawing money from the bank. The noun 'Gänze', which we shall translate as 'wholeness', is to be distinguished from 'Ganze' ('whole', or occasionally 'totality') and 'Ganzheit' ('totality').

[2] 'Was *so* gar nicht erst *sein* kann, *wie* ein Erfahren das Dasein zu erfassen prätendiert, entzieht sich grundsätzlich einer Erfahrbarkeit.'

of death. The investigations relating to these topics are divided up as follows: the possibility of experiencing the death of Others, and the possibility of getting a whole Dasein into our grasp (Section 47); that which is still outstanding, the end, and totality (Section 48); how the existential analysis of death is distinguished from other possible Interpretations of this phenomenon (Section 49); a preliminary sketch of the existential-ontological structure of death (Section 50); Being-towards-death and the everydayness of Dasein (Section 51); everyday Being-towards-death, and the full existential conception of death (Section 52); an existential projection of an authentic Being-towards-death (Section 53).

¶ *47. The Possibility of Experiencing the Death of Others, and the Possibility of Getting a Whole Dasein into our Grasp*

When Dasein reaches its wholeness in death, it simultaneously loses the Being of its "there". By its transition to no-longer-Dasein [Nichtmehr-dasein], it gets lifted right out of the possibility of experiencing this transition and of understanding it as something experienced. Surely this sort of thing is denied to any particular Dasein in relation to itself. But this makes the death of Others more impressive. In this way a termination [Beendigung] of Dasein becomes 'Objectively' accessible. Dasein can thus gain an experience of death, all the more so because Dasein is essentially Being with Others. In that case, the fact that death has been thus 'Objectively' given must make possible an ontological delimitation of Dasein's totality.

Thus from the kind of Being which Dasein possesses as Being with one another, we might draw the fairly obvious information that when the Dasein of Others has come to an end, it might be chosen as a substitute theme for our analysis of Dasein's totality. But does this lead us to our appointed goal?

Even the Dasein of Others, when it has reached its wholeness in death, is no-longer-Dasein, in the sense of Being-no-longer-in-the-world. Does not dying mean going-out-of-the-world, and losing one's Being-in-the-world? Yet when someone has died, his Being-no-longer-in-the-world (if we understand it in an extreme way) is still a Being, but in the sense of the Being-just-present-at-hand-and-no-more of a corporeal Thing which we encounter. In the dying of the Other we can experience that remarkable phenomenon of Being which may be defined as the change-over of an entity from Dasein's kind of Being (or life) to no-longer-Dasein. The *end* of the entity *qua* Dasein is the *beginning* of the same entity *qua* something present-at-hand.

However, in this way of Interpreting the change-over from Dasein to

238

Being-just-present-at-hand-and-no-more, the phenomenal content is missed, inasmuch as in the entity which still remains we are not presented with a mere corporeal Thing. From a theoretical point of view, even the corpse which is present-at-hand is still a possible object for the student of pathological anatomy, whose understanding tends to be oriented to the idea of life. This something which is just-present-at-hand-and-no-more is 'more' than a *lifeless* material Thing. In it we encounter something *unalive*, which has lost its life.[1]

But even this way of characterizing that which still remains [des Noch-verbleibenden] does not exhaust the full phenomenal findings with regard to Dasein.

The 'deceased' [Der "Verstorbene"] as distinct from the dead person [dem Gestorbenen], has been torn away from those who have 'remained behind' [den "Hinterbliebenen"], and is an object of 'concern' in the ways of funeral rites, interment, and the cult of graves. And that is so because the deceased, in his kind of Being, is 'still more' than just an item of equipment, environmentally ready-to-hand, about which one can be concerned. In tarrying alongside him in their mourning and commemoration, those who have remained behind *are with him*, in a mode of respectful solicitude. Thus the relationship-of-Being which one has towards the dead is not to be taken as a *concernful* Being-alongside something ready-to-hand.

In such Being-with the dead [dem Toten], the deceased *himself* is no longer factically 'there'. However, when we speak of "Being-with", we always have in view Being with one another in the same world. The deceased has abandoned our '*world*' and left it behind. But *in terms of that world [Aus ihr her]* those who remain can still *be with him*.

The greater the phenomenal appropriateness with which we take the no-longer-Dasein of the deceased, the more plainly is it shown that in such Being-with the dead, the authentic Being-come-to-an-end [Zuen-degekommensein] of the deceased is precisely the sort of thing which we do *not* experience. Death does indeed reveal itself as a loss, but a loss such as is experienced by those who remain. In suffering this loss, however, we have no way of access to the loss-of-Being as such which the dying man 'suffers'. The dying of Others is not something which we experience in a genuine sense; at most we are always just 'there alongside'.[2]

And even if, by thus Being there alongside, it were possible and feasible

239

---

[1] 'Das Nur-noch-Vorhandene ist "mehr" als ein *lebloses* materielles Ding. Mit ihm begegnet ein des Lebens verlustig gegangenes *Unlebendiges*.'

[2] '. . . sind . . . "dabei".' Literally the verb 'dabeisein' means simply 'to be at that place', 'to be there alongside'; but it also has other connotations which give an ironical touch to this passage, for it may also mean, 'to be engaged in' some activity, 'to be at it', 'to be in the swim', 'to be ready to be "counted in"'.

for us to make plain to ourselves 'psychologically' the dying of Others, this would by no means let us grasp the way-to-be which we would then have in mind—namely, coming-to-an-end. We are asking about the ontological meaning of the dying of the person who dies, as a possibility-of-Being which belongs to *his* Being. We are not asking about the way in which the deceased has Dasein-with or is still-a-Dasein [Nochdaseins] with those who are left behind. If death as experienced in Others is what we are enjoined to take as the theme for our analysis of Dasein's end and totality, this cannot give us, either ontically or ontologically, what it presumes to give.

But above all, the suggestion that the dying of Others is a substitute theme for the ontological analysis of Dasein's totality and the settling of its account, rests on a presupposition which demonstrably fails altogether[1] to recognize Dasein's kind of Being. This is what one presupposes when one is of the opinion that any Dasein may be substituted for another at random, so that what cannot be experienced in one's own Dasein is accessible in that of a stranger. But is this presupposition actually so baseless?

Indisputably, the fact that one Dasein *can be represented*[2] by another belongs to its possibilities of Being in Being-with-one-another in the world. In everyday concern, constant and manifold use is made of such representability. Whenever we go anywhere or have anything to contribute, we can be represented by someone within the range of that 'environment' with which we are most closely concerned. The great multiplicity of ways of Being-in-the-world in which one person can be represented by another, not only extends to the more refined modes of publicly being with one another, but is likewise germane to those possibilities of concern which are restricted within definite ranges, and which are cut to the measure of one's occupation, one's social status, or one's age. But the very meaning of such representation is such that it is always a representation 'in' ["in" und "bei"] something—that is to say, in concerning oneself with something. But proximally and for the most part everyday Dasein understands itself in terms of that with *which* it is customarily concerned. 'One *is*' what one does. In relation to this sort of Being (the everyday manner in which we join with one another in absorption in the 'world' of our concern) representability is not only quite possible but is even constitutive for our

[1] '. . . eine völlige Verkennung . . .' The older editions have 'totale' rather than 'völlige'.

[2] 'Vertretbarkeit'. The verb 'vertreten' means 'to represent' in the sense of 'deputizing' for someone. It should be noted that the verb 'vorstellen' is also sometimes translated as 'to represent', but in the quite different sense of 'affording a "representation" or "idea" of something'.

240   being with one another. *Here* one Dasein can and must, within certain
limits, '*be*' another Dasein.

However, this possibility of representing breaks down completely if the
issue is one of representing that possibility-of-Being which makes up
Dasein's coming to an end, and which, as such, gives to it its wholeness.
No one can take the Other's dying away from him. Of course someone can 'go to
his death for another'. But that always means to sacrifice oneself for the
Other '*in some definite affair*'. Such "dying for" can never signify that the
Other has thus had his death taken away in even the slightest degree.
Dying is something that every Dasein itself must take upon itself at the
time. By its very essence, death is in every case mine, in so far as it 'is' at
all. And indeed death signifies a peculiar possibility-of-Being in which
the very Being of one's own Dasein is an issue. In dying, it is shown that
mineness and existence are ontologically constitutive for death.[1] Dying is
not an event; it is a phenomenon to be understood existentially; and it is
to be understood in a distinctive sense which must be still more closely
delimited.

But if 'ending', as dying, is constitutive for Dasein's totality, then the
Being of this wholeness itself must be conceived as an existential phenomenon of a Dasein which is in each case one's own. In 'ending', and in
Dasein's Being-a-whole, for which such ending is constitutive, there is,
by its very essence, no representing. These are the facts of the case existentially; one fails to recognize this when one interposes the expedient of
making the dying of Others a substitute theme for the analysis of totality.

So once again the attempt to make Dasein's Being-a-whole accessible
in a way that is appropriate to the phenomena, has broken down. But our
deliberations have not been negative in their outcome; they have been
oriented by the phenomena, even if only rather roughly. We have
indicated that death is an existential phenomenon. Our investigation is
thus forced into a purely existential orientation to the Dasein which is in
every case one's own. The only remaining possibility for the analysis of
death as dying, is either to form a purely *existential* conception of this
phenomenon, or else to forgo any ontological understanding of it.

When we characterized the transition from Dasein to no-longer-
Dasein as Being-no-longer-in-the-world, we showed further that *Dasein's*
going-out-of-the-world in the sense of dying must be distinguished from
the going-out-of-the-world of that which merely has life [des Nur-leben-
den]. In our terminology the ending of anything that is alive, is denoted
241   as "perishing" [Verenden]. We can see the difference only if the kind
of ending which Dasein can have is distinguished from the end of a life.[ii]
Of course "dying" may also be taken physiologically and biologically.

But the medical concept of the '*exitus*' does not coincide with that of "perishing".

From the foregoing discussion of the ontological possibility of getting death into our grasp, it becomes clear at the same time that substructures of entities with another kind of Being (presence-at-hand or life) thrust themselves to the fore unnoticed, and threaten to bring confusion to the Interpretation of this phenomenon—even to the *first* suitable *way of presenting* it. We can encounter this phenomenon only by seeking, for our further analysis, an ontologically adequate way of defining the phenomena which are constitutive for it, such as "end" and "totality".

¶ 48. *That which is Still Outstanding; the End; Totality*

Within the framework of this investigation, our ontological character-ization of the end and totality can be only provisional. To perform this task adequately, we must not only set forth the *formal* structure of end in general and of totality in general; we must likewise disentangle the struc-tural variations which are possible for them in different realms—that is to say, deformalized variations which have been put into relationship respec-tively with definite kinds of entities as 'subject-matter', and which have had their character Determined in terms of the Being of these entities. This task, in turn, presupposes that a sufficiently unequivocal and positive Interpretation shall have been given for the kinds of Being which require that the aggregate of entities be divided into such realms. But if we are to understand these ways of Being, we need a clarified idea of Being in general. The task of carrying out in an appropriate way the ontological analysis of end and totality breaks down not only because the theme is so far-reaching, but because there is a difficulty in principle: to master this task successfully, we must presuppose that precisely what we are seeking in this investigation—the meaning of Being in general—is something which we have found already and with which we are quite familiar.

In the following considerations, the 'variations' in which we are chiefly interested are those of end and totality; these are ways in which Dasein gets a definite character ontologically, and as such they should lead to a primordial Interpretation of this entity. Keeping constantly in view the existential constitution of Dasein already set forth, we must try to decide how inappropriate to Dasein ontologically are those conceptions of end and totality which first thrust themselves to the fore, no matter how 242 categorially indefinite they may remain. The rejection [Zurückweisung] of such concepts must be developed into a positive *assignment* [*Zuweisung*] of them to their specific realms. In this way our understanding of end and totality in their variant forms as *existentialia* will be strengthened, and this will guarantee the possibility of an ontological Interpretation of death.

But even if the analysis of Dasein's end and totality takes on so broad an orientation, this cannot mean that the existential concepts of end and totality are to be obtained by way of a deduction. On the contrary, the existential meaning of Dasein's coming-to-an-end must be taken from Dasein itself, and we must show how such 'ending' can constitute *Being-a-whole* for the entity which *exists*.

We may formulate in three theses the discussion of death up to this point: 1. there belongs to Dasein, as long as it is, a "not-yet" which it will be—that which is constantly still outstanding; 2. the coming-to-its-end of what-is-not-yet-at-an-end (in which what is still outstanding is liquidated as regards its Being) has the character of no-longer-Dasein; 3. coming-to-an-end implies a mode of Being in which the particular Dasein simply cannot be represented by someone else.

In Dasein there is undeniably a constant 'lack of totality' which finds an end with death. This "not-yet" 'belongs' to Dasein as long as it is; this is how things stand phenomenally. Is this to be Interpreted as *still outstanding*?[1] With relation to what entities do we talk about that which is still outstanding? When we use this expression we have in view that which indeed 'belongs' to an entity, but is still missing. Outstanding, as a way of being missing, is grounded upon a belonging-to.[2] For instance, the remainder yet to be received when a debt is to be balanced off, is still outstanding. That which is still outstanding is not yet at one's disposal. When the 'debt' gets paid off, that which is still outstanding gets liquidated; this signifies that the money 'comes in', or, in other words, that the remainder comes successively along. By this procedure the "not-yet" gets filled up, as it were, until the sum that is owed is "all together".[3] Therefore, to be still outstanding means that what belongs together is not yet all together. Ontologically, this implies the un-readiness-to-hand of those portions which have yet to be contributed. These portions have the same kind of Being as those which are ready-to-hand already; and the latter, for their part, do not have their kind of Being modified by having the remainder come in. Whatever "lack-of-togetherness" remains [Das bestehende Unzusammen] gets "paid off" by a cumulative piecing-together. *Entities for which anything is still outstanding have the kind of Being of something*

---

[1] 'Aber darf der phänomenale Tatbestand, dass zum Dasein, solange es ist, dieses Noch-nicht "gehört", als *Ausstand* interpretiert werden?' The contrast between 'Tatbestand' and 'Ausstand' is perhaps intentional.

[2] 'Ausstehen als Fehlen gründet in einer Zugehörigkeit.'

[3] 'Tilgung der "Schuld" als Behebung des Ausstandes bedeutet das "Eingehen", das ist Nacheinanderankommen des Restes, wodurch das Noch-nicht gleichsam aufgefüllt wird, bis die geschuldete Summe "beisammen" ist.' On 'Schuld' see note 1, p. 325, H. 280.

ready-to-hand. The togetherness [Das Zusammen] is characterized as a "*sum*", and so is that lack-of-togetherness which is founded upon it.

But this lack-of-togetherness which belongs to such a mode of together-   243
ness—this being-missing as still-outstanding—cannot by any means define ontologically that "not-yet" which belongs to Dasein as its possible death. Dasein does not have at all the kind of Being of something ready-to-hand-within-the-world. The togetherness of an entity of the kind which Dasein is 'in running its course' until that 'course' has been completed, is not constituted by a 'continuing' piecing-on of entities which, somehow and somewhere, are ready-to-hand already in their own right.[1]

That Dasein should *be* together only when its "not-yet" has been filled up is so far from the case that it is precisely then that Dasein is no longer. Any Dasein always exists in just such a manner that its "not-yet" *belongs* to it. But are there not entities which are as they are and to which a "not-yet" can belong, but which do not necessarily have Dasein's kind of Being?

For instance, we can say, "The last quarter is still outstanding until the moon gets full". The "not-yet" diminishes as the concealing shadow disappears. But here the moon is always present-at-hand as a whole already. Leaving aside the fact that we can never get the moon *wholly* in our grasp even when it is full, this "not-yet" does not in any way signify a not-yet-*Being*-together of the parts which belongs to the moon, but pertains only to the way we *get it in our grasp* perceptually. The "not-yet" which belongs to Dasein, however, is not just something which is provisionally and occasionally inaccessible to one's own experience or even to that of a stranger; it 'is' not yet 'actual' at all. Our problem does not pertain to *getting into our grasp* the "not-yet' which is of the character of Dasein; it pertains to the possible *Being* or *not-Being* of this "not-yet". Dasein must, as itself, *become*—that is to say, *be*—what it is not yet. Thus if we are to be able, by comparison, to define that *Being of the "not-yet" which is of the character of Dasein,* we must take into consideration entities to whose kind of Being becoming belongs.

When, for instance, a fruit is unripe, it "goes towards" its ripeness. In this process of ripening, that which the fruit is not yet, is by no means pieced on as something not yet present-at-hand. The fruit brings itself to ripeness, and such a bringing of itself is a characteristic of its Being as a fruit. Nothing imaginable which one might contribute to it, would eliminate the unripeness of the fruit, if this entity did not come to ripeness *of its*

---

[1] Throughout this sentence Heidegger uses words derived from the verb 'laufen', 'to run'. Thus, 'in running its course' represents 'in seinem Verlauf', ' "its course" has been completed' represents 'es "seinem Lauf" vollendet hat'; 'continuing' represents 'fortlaufende'.

own accord. When we speak of the "not-yet" of the unripeness, we do not have in view something else which stands outside [aussenstehendes], and which—with utter indifference to the fruit—might be present-at-hand in it and with it. What we have in view is the fruit itself in its specific kind of Being. The sum which is not yet complete is, as something ready-to-hand, 'a matter of indifference' as regards the remainder which is lacking and un-ready-to-hand, though, taken strictly, it can neither be indifferent to that remainder nor not be indifferent to it.[1] The ripening fruit, however, not only is not indifferent to its unripeness as something other than itself, but it is that unripeness as it ripens. The "not-yet" has already been included in the very Being of the fruit, not as some random characteristic, but as something constitutive. Correspondingly, as long as any Dasein is, it too *is already its "not-yet"*.[iii]

244

That which makes up the 'lack of totality' in Dasein, the constant "ahead-of-itself", is neither something still outstanding in a summative togetherness, nor something which has not yet become accessible. It is a "not-yet" which any Dasein, as the entity which it is, has to be. Nevertheless, the comparison with the unripeness of the fruit shows essential differences, although there is a certain agreement. If we take note of these differences, we shall recognize how indefinite our talk about the end and ending has hitherto been.

Ripening is the specific Being of the fruit. It is also a kind of Being of the "not-yet" (of unripeness); and, as such a kind of Being, it is formally analogous to Dasein, in that the latter, like the former, *is* in every case already its "not-yet" in a sense still to be defined. But even then, this does not signify that ripeness as an 'end' and death as an 'end' coincide with regard to their ontological structure as ends. With ripeness, the fruit *fulfils* itself.[2] But is the death at which Dasein arrives, a fulfilment in this sense? With its death, Dasein has indeed 'fulfilled its course'. But in doing so, has it necessarily exhausted its specific possibilities? Rather, are not these precisely what gets taken away from Dasein? Even 'unfulfilled' Dasein ends. On the other hand, so little is it the case that Dasein comes to its ripeness only with death, that Dasein may well have passed its ripeness before the end.[3] For the most part, Dasein ends in unfulfilment, or else by having disintegrated and been used up.

[1] 'Die noch nicht volle Summe ist als Zuhandenes gegen den fehlenden unzuhandenen Rest "gleichgültig". Streng genommen kann sie weder ungleichgültig, noch gleichgültig dagegen sein.'

[2] 'Mit der Reife *vollendet* sich die Frucht.' Notice that the verb 'vollenden', which we here translate as 'fulfil', involves the verb 'enden' ('to end'). While 'vollenden' may mean 'to bring fully to an end' or 'to terminate', it may also mean 'to complete' or 'to perfect'.

[3] While we have translated 'Reife' by its cognate 'ripeness', this word applies generally to almost any kind of maturity, even that of Dasein—not merely the maturity of fruits and vegetables.

Ending does not necessarily mean fulfilling oneself. It thus becomes more urgent to ask *in what sense, if any, death must be conceived as the ending of Dasein.*

In the first instance, "ending" signifies "*stopping*", and it signifies this in senses which are ontologically different. The rain stops. It is no longer present-at-hand. The road stops. Such an ending does not make the road disappear, but such a stopping is determinative for the road as this one, which is present-at-hand. Hence ending, as stopping, can signify either 245 "passing over into non-presence-at-hand" or else "Being-present-at-hand only when the end comes". The latter kind of ending, in turn, may either be determinative for something which is present-at-hand *in an unfinished way*, as a road breaks off when one finds it under construction; or it may rather constitute the 'finishedness" of something present-at-hand, as the painting is finished with the last stroke of the brush.

But ending as "getting finished" does not include fulfilling. On the other hand, whatever has got to be fulfilled must indeed reach the finishedness that is possible for it. Fulfilling is a mode of 'finishedness', and is founded upon it. Finishedness is itself possible only as a determinate form of something present-at-hand or ready-to-hand.

Even ending in the sense of "disappearing" can still have its modifications according to the kind of Being which an entity may have. The rain is at an end—that is to say it has disappeared. The bread is at an end— that is to say, it has been used up and is no longer available as something ready-to-hand.

By none of these modes of ending can death be suitably characterized as the "end" of Dasein. If dying, as Being-at-an-end, were understood in the sense of an ending of the kind we have discussed, then Dasein would thereby be treated as something present-at-hand or ready-to-hand. In death, Dasein has not been fulfilled nor has it simply disappeared; it has not become finished nor is it wholly at one's disposal as something ready-to-hand.

On the contrary, just as Dasein *is* already its "not-yet", and is its "not-yet" constantly as long as it is, it *is* already its end too. The "ending" which we have in view when we speak of death, does not signify Dasein's Being-at-an-end [Zu-Ende-sein], but a *Being-towards-the-end* [*Sein zum Ende*] of this entity. Death is a way to be, which Dasein takes over as soon as it is. "As soon as man comes to life, he is at once old enough to die.'[iv]

Ending, as Being-towards-the-end, must be clarified ontologically in terms of Dasein's kind of Being. And presumably the possibility of an existent Being of that "not-yet" which lies 'before' the 'end',[1] will become

---

[1] '... die Möglichkeit eines existierenden Seins des Noch-nicht, das "vor" dem "Ende" liegt ...' The earlier editions have '... das ja "vor" dem "Ende" ∴ ...'

intelligible only if the character of ending has been determined existentially. The existential clarification of Being-towards-the-end will also give us for the first time an adequate basis for defining what can possibly be the meaning of our talk about a totality of Dasein, if indeed this totality is to be constituted by death as the 'end'.

Our attempt to understand Dasein's totality by taking as our point of departure a clarification of the "not-yet" and going on to a characterization of "ending", has not led us to our goal. It has shown only *in a negative way* that the "not-yet" which Dasein in every case *is*, resists Interpretation as something still outstanding. The end *towards* which Dasein *is* as existing, remains inappropriately defined by the notion of a "Being-at-an-end". These considerations, however, should at the same time make it plain that they must be turned back in their course. A positive characterization of the phenomena in question (Being-not-yet, ending, totality) succeeds only when it is unequivocally oriented to Dasein's state of Being. But if we have any insight into the realms where those end-structures and totality-structures which are to be construed ontologically with Dasein belong, this will, in a negative way, make this unequivocal character secure against wrong turnings.

If we are to carry out a positive Interpretation of death and its character as an end, by way of existential analysis, we must take as our clue the basic state of Dasein at which we have already arrived—the phenomenon of care.

¶ 49. How the Existential Analysis of Death is Distinguished from Other Possible Interpretations of this Phenomenon

The unequivocal character of our ontological Interpretation of death must first be strengthened by our bringing explicitly to mind what such an Interpretation can *not* inquire about, and what it would be vain to expect it to give us any information or instructions about.[1]

Death, in the widest sense, is a phenomenon of life. Life must be understood as a kind of Being to which there belongs a Being-in-the-world. Only if this kind of Being is oriented in a privative way to Dasein, can we fix its character ontologically. Even Dasein may be considered purely as life. When the question is formulated from the viewpoint of biology and physiology, Dasein moves into that domain of Being which we know as the world of animals and plants. In this field, we can obtain data and statistics about the longevity of plants, animals and men, and we do this by ascertaining them ontically. Connections between longevity, propagation, and

[1] '. . . wonach diese *nicht* fragen, und worüber eine Auskunft und Anweisung von ihr vergeblich erwartet werden kann.' The older editions have 'kann' after 'fragen', and 'muss' where the newer editions have 'kann'.